Fighting the Foreclosure Machine

FIGHTING THE FORECLOSURE MACHINE

MACHINE

The Homeowner's Hammer

Robert M. Janes, B.B.A., M.P.A., J.D.

eSprouts, LLC

Fighting the Foreclosure Machine

First edition

Printed in the United States of America

ISBN-13: 978-0-985128609
ISBN-10: 0-985128607

eSprouts, LLC
PO Box 4458
Santa Fe, NM 87502

Important Notice

The information in this book is not intended as legal advice. It contains the author's thoughts, understandings, and assessments about public matters, which, of course, include laws. Each person's situation is different and only you can determine the usefulness, if any, of this information to you. Please consult an attorney regarding your circumstances as you deal with matters involving foreclosure and your rights and legal options.

For more information, visit:
www.FightingTheForeclosureMachine.com

To those people made foreclosure victims by the mortgage finance industry which so aggressively and irresponsibly induced them to become borrowers.

Contents

Acknowledgements

Most of the hours and years spent working on this book were mine, but not all. My family and friends also endured and lost their time to my stream of comments and speculations as I tried to understand what was happening, why and what might be done about unfair and wrongful foreclosures. To them I extend my apologies and appreciation for their patience and willingness to act as sounding boards.

When I first began investigating the state of foreclosures back in 2009, I never imagined that path would lead to this book or to my need to help borrowers targeted for foreclosure. I guess I should not be surprised, however, because so much of my life has been unexpected result rather than product of a well-designed plan. I researched many legal issues over my career, and most did not demand or warrant prolonged study or interest. Borrowers whose plight was partially recorded in decisions of our courts and media releases proved to be a class of people unfairly drawn into real estate loans, unfairly placed at risk without advance warning, unfairly labeled the architect of their own misfortune and unfairly pitted against slick foreclosure shops acting under the pretext of legal and moral justification. Their need for understanding and support in light of the wrongs laid at their doorsteps was too loud to be ignored. We all must acknowledge the past contributions made in courts across our land by borrowers who fought back against the foreclosure machine. Their efforts, whether successful or not, lit the path that others needed to see.

My piles of work papers, notes and drafts did not miraculously jell into a book. Writing is simply not that easy. Substantial credit is owed to my editor, Margaret Lucke. She contributed skill and critical advice, along with generous portions of patience and support. *Fighting The Foreclosure Machine* is more readable and its contents more easily absorbed because of her invaluable services.

Finally, my parents deserve credit for having imbedded in me the idea that people's rights should be protected regardless of the size or strength of their opponent. Fairness and respect for others were evident in the daily lives of my parents. I think they would be pleased to know their examples were not wasted.

Fighting the Foreclosure Machine: The Short Version

Fighting The Foreclosure Machine gives information that can help you assess whether fighting the foreclosure machine makes sense for you. This information is about the machine's weaknesses, your strengths and how to get the most out of your situation.

You will learn about the foreclosure fundamentals which include the basic legal principles and concepts that define your rights by law—rights that are frequently violated in foreclosures. You will see that borrowers under attack have a lot more rights and control than they realize.

Fighting The Foreclosure Machine is also a litigation resource if you decide to defend your rights and your home in a court of law. It can assist you in laying the foundation for your fight and provide you with specific strategies that, if properly applied, will help you prevail. This information is explained in plain language with examples and suggestions you can use to lead your judge to the correct ruling. Substantial references to legal authorities are provided so you and your advisor can avoid time consuming and costly duplication of legal research and analysis.

The foreclosure machine often has no right to demand payments from you and no right to take your home. Whether or not you have made all of your mortgage payments is not even relevant unless the machine first proves that you actually owe it something, and, then, that it has not already been paid by insurance or other resources about which you know nothing.

The most fundamental foreclosure law addresses the same question that you should be asking before accepting defeat: can the machine actually prove by law that you have any obligation to it?

Don't make the mistake of assuming they win just because you're behind on your mortgage payments. When put to the test, the foreclosure machine often falls on its face. You have the power to make it take that test in a court of law.

This book is also a public acknowledgement that you and other borrowers targeted for foreclosure did not cause our depressed real estate markets or the weakened economy in which we all now live. You are instead a victim of the tragedy brought upon our country by the mortgage finance industry.

It harvested borrowers so it would have a bigger inventory of saleable mortgage loans. Its agenda was to generate profits through sales and exchanges of mortgage-backed securities. To accomplish that aim, the industry nurtured predatory lending practices, neutralized long-standing consumer protection laws, and generated an artificially high real estate market that was destined to fall. Adding insult to injury, the industry created the foreclosure machine, which is commissioned to take homes away from the very people made victims by the industry's excesses and poor judgment. You are not the cause of our depressed real estate markets or the distressed construction industries, contrary to the reports made by the misleading, misinformed and distracting media, which are churned and left uncorrected by the industry and its foreclosure machine.

Unfortunately, your losses and stress are not important enough to warrant meaningful government intervention on your behalf. You must fix your problems or walk away from your home with no compensation for the injury caused you by the industry's folly. Protecting your home is an opportunity to make them accountable, an opportunity to make them pay a fairer share of the damages they have caused, and a chance for a better result than what they offer.

PART ONE

Facing Foreclosure?
You Have an Ally

CHAPTER 1

An Introduction to the Foreclosure Machine

HOW THIS BOOK CAME TO BE WRITTEN

In 2009 a friend of mine—I'll call him John—came home from work to find a registered letter in his mailbox. It was a letter he had dreaded. It informed him that he was behind on his mortgage payments and a Notice of Default had been recorded. The foreclosure process had begun.

John's first reaction was to get angry. He wadded the letter into a ball and threw it away. Then he had second thoughts and fished the paper out of the trash can. He spread it out on the kitchen table and read it again. His outrage was joined by feelings of fear, depression, and hopelessness.

John knew he'd gotten behind in the monthly mortgage payments he'd been making for years. The economy had turned so bad that he just did not have enough money on which to live and to also pay mortgage bills. He had tried for many months to sell his house in hopes of paying off the debt, but no one was buying in his neighborhood.

Four years earlier, when he refinanced the original purchase loan, the house had appraised for substantially more than the amount of the modified loan. But real estate values had dropped. At this point, the amount he owed was greater than the value of the house.

Now he had run out of time.

He was threatened with a routine nonjudicial foreclosure in California, the kind that was and still is happening thousands of times every month across that state. By nonjudicial, I mean that no court was involved. The company demanding payment and threatening foreclosure was not subject to supervision by any court or government agency. That company just said it had a right to demand payment from him and to sell or take his house if the money was not paid.

John was in a bind. He had pretty much accepted that he would lose the house, lose all the money he had put down to buy it, and lose the many thousands of dollars he had spent improving and making it a much nicer home. He conceded that he would have to move and leave the neighborhood he liked so much. His house was scheduled to be sold at a public foreclosure sale in mid-October 2009.

A couple of weeks before the sale was to take place, John found a handwritten note on his front door. The writer was a neighbor. She had seen a foreclosure notice about John's house in the local newspaper, and she noticed that it mentioned the name Mortgage Electronic Registration Systems, Inc., or MERS. She suggested that John might want to look at a recent Kansas Supreme Court decision that talked about MERS, and she wished him, "All the best."

John sent the note to me to find out if I knew what his neighbor was talking about. I had retired from the practice of law a few years earlier, but John, like other past clients, had stayed in touch.

Most of my clients, including John, were owners of small businesses. Their enterprises might involve real estate, ranching, or a start-up venture of some kind, but each situation called for services of an attorney who understood business. I had been a certified public accountant before commencing my legal career. That background and the fact that I liked working with entrepreneurial people helped me do a better job for my clients.

In the early 1980s our country had widespread economic problems related to massive financial losses within the U.S. oil and gas industry. Then came the demise of the savings and loan industry in the late 1980s through mid-1990s. While not as serious as America's current economic crisis, those earlier downturns also caused widespread unemployment, business closures, and depressed real estate markets. The ripple effect of those national problems increasingly placed me in bankruptcy court representing a client's complicated reorganization efforts. My client and I were frequently pitted against well-financed banks, large creditors, and government agencies. I would often be in court by myself while the opposition had two, three, or more attorneys at their table.

John had resorted to bankruptcy protection in order to keep his business alive. He, like other small business owners, didn't have the luxury of separating the financial health of his business from his family's well-being. When someone's business is threatened, the risk is perceived as, and actually is, extremely personal.

I had represented John during his good and bad times over about fifteen years, and had become part of his extended family. I knew he was asking others about the note he got from his neighbor, but I was pleased to hear from him and pleased he still valued my thoughts.

I had not previously heard of MERS. In fact, I hadn't been involved with any real estate foreclosure for many years. I had no idea why John's neighbor thought a Kansas Supreme Court decision might be related to the foreclosure he faced in California. So often the laws of one state simply don't apply in another state. But John was my friend, so I went online to learn what I could, just in case there was even the slightest chance that his neighbor was pointing to something that might help him. What I discovered set me on the path of the research that led to this book.

The Case in the Neighbor's Note

I found that the Supreme Court of Kansas had issued a decision on August 28, 2009, in a case titled *Landmark National Bank v. Kesler.*[1] It involved a mortgage foreclosure that had already happened and a resulting legal fight between two creditors who held mortgages on the same house. The borrower, Kesler, had taken out two loans, each secured by his house. The senior lien holder, Landmark National Bank, conducted the foreclosure. Kesler didn't contest the foreclosure, so the house was sold and Kesler was out of the picture.

After the house was sold, but before that sale was finalized by judicial approval, the holder of the second and junior mortgage stepped forward to protest the sale. Sovereign Bank claimed the foreclosure was invalid because all of the required statutory notices had not been given. Ultimately the court ruled that Landmark National Bank had done everything correctly under Kansas law and that the foreclosure sale had been valid. Sovereign Bank lost.

Landmark was not about a borrower's fight to defend his home. The case did not address whether Kesler actually owed any money to either of the banks, nor did it discuss which, if either, bank actually had a right to take Kesler's home through foreclosure. Kesler never raised those questions in 2006 when his home was foreclosed. *Landmark* looked solely at the technical fight that came later between the creditors.

The result in *Landmark* was based on Kansas law, not California law. Furthermore, Kesler's house was taken in a judicial foreclosure that was supervised by a Kansas court, whereas John was threatened by a nonjudicial foreclosure in which no court was involved. Regarding these several factors, at least, *Landmark* didn't appear helpful for John's situation.

The Involvement of MERS

What made the case noteworthy was what it had to say about MERS, the company John's neighbor had mentioned in her note. *Landmark* was my introduction to Mortgage Electronic Registration Systems, Inc. Its name appeared on the mortgage being asserted by Sovereign Bank. MERS was identified in that mortgage "solely as nominee for Lender, as hereinafter defined, and Lender's successors and assigns." If you aren't sure what all those words mean, you're in good company. Many courts have labored when trying to understand MERS's role in such documents. But MERS was involved in John's California deed of trust, and similarly described. Could *Landmark*'s comments about MERS help John?

In the *Landmark* case, Sovereign Bank claimed that Kesler's mortgage had first belonged to MERS and that MERS had transferred it to Sovereign years later. MERS was still listed in the Kansas land records as the holder of the mortgage because Sovereign had never filed anything in the land records to let people know that it was the new owner of the mortgage. All parties agreed that Kansas law did not require Landmark National Bank to give notice of the foreclosure to Sovereign Bank because Sovereign was not listed in the public records as the owner of that junior, second-position mortgage. Sovereign's challenge to the validity of the foreclosure was based on the fact that MERS did not get notice of the foreclosure lawsuit either. Sovereign argued that because MERS was identified in the land records, the law required that MERS be notified. If MERS had been properly notified, Sovereign Bank argued, then Sovereign would have learned about the foreclosure and could have protected its legal rights in court before the house was foreclosed.

Ultimately the Kansas Supreme Court ruled that no notice had to be given to MERS, because even though its name was listed in the public records as being involved with that mortgage, MERS in fact had no ownership interest in it. Under Kansas law, the notices only had to be sent out to an actual owner of the mortgage, based on information in the public land records. Thus, MERS was not entitled to notice of the foreclosure suit, so Sovereign Bank's objection to the validity of the foreclosure was overruled.

Landmark was interesting because of the Kansas Supreme Court's struggle to try to figure out what MERS was and what its legal relationship was to the mortgage it claimed to have given to Sovereign Bank. The court basically asked: did MERS talk, walk, and act like an owner of the subject mortgage? You know: the old duck test. If yes, MERS should have received notice of the foreclosure, but if no, the foreclosure was valid without notice going to MERS. The Kansas Supreme Court concluded that MERS did not have the right talk or walk, and that its noises and its hopping and skipping about were not evidence of ownership rights, but merely its effort to confuse people and to appear to be what it was not.

In order to finalize the legal dispute between Landmark National Bank and Sovereign Bank, the court did not have to decide what MERS really was. The fact that it had never been the owner of the subject mortgage, and therefore could not have transferred ownership to Sovereign Bank, was enough for Sovereign Bank to lose.

Landmark was a good and academically entertaining decision, one that showed sound legal reasoning as the Kansas justices delved into the substance of MERS. They looked past the MERS charade to the legal substance that was important, at least to the issue in *Landmark*.

What This Case Meant for John—and for You

John's neighbor had indeed pointed to a case that shed some light on the workings of MERS, but for John that was too little and too late.

Landmark did not address whether MERS had a right to conduct a foreclosure in California. The case simply did not go that far. Even if MERS was not the owner of John's mortgage, as it had not been the owner in *Landmark*, maybe MERS would have the right in California to conduct a foreclosure on behalf of the real owner. California courts had not yet tackled the ownership question addressed by *Landmark,* or the question of whether MERS might be authorized to foreclose as an agent or servant of the real owner. The MERS described by *Landmark* was indeed an odd duck of a business, but not necessarily an illegal one, based on what *Landmark* said. *Landmark*, in and of itself, did not appear to be very important for John.

I suggested that John speak with attorneys he knew close to his home. Perhaps they would see something I might have missed, or would have more information that could help him defeat the threatened foreclosure.

They also gave him little hope. They just didn't have enough information. The foreclosure sale was only a few days away, and John needed to make a "go" or "no go" decision quickly. Those attorneys would have done more research if John wanted to pay for it, but they could not assure him that the cost would produce something helpful. John decided to save his money. He let his house be foreclosed without a fight. Nothing else made much sense for him at the time.

That was 2009, not today. John would have most likely beaten the foreclosure if his attorneys knew then what is known now. The *Landmark* decision highlighted one weakness of the MERS charade— that is, its pretense of being an owner of the mortgage and related promissory note. More about its weaknesses and deceptions have surfaced in lawsuits across America since *Landmark*. We now know that the mere presence of MERS in the chain of title for a mortgage or deed of trust makes legal foreclosure extremely difficult. That is important, because MERS is involved in about one-half of all foreclosures. More important, however, is the information we now have about certain fundamental legal principles that can be used to defeat foreclosure when MERS is involved, and also when it is not.

Landmark did not address whether Kesler actually owed anything to either Landmark National Bank or Sovereign Bank. Each bank had sent letters telling him he was behind on his mortgage payments, but Kesler did not have enough money to bring them current. He assumed the banks had a right to foreclose if he didn't pay what they demanded. The same was true for John. He knew he had missed some payments and so he assumed foreclosure was imminent. His attorneys and I made that same mistake. As you may have already guessed, the operative word is *assumed.* Kesler, John, their attorneys, and I were wrong back then.

Many borrowers will incorrectly assume that when they have missed some monthly payments, somebody has a right to take their house. Before this century, that was typically how things worked. But in recent years the mortgage finance industry changed the way it used mortgage loans to make money. It abandoned the historical role of lender in order to become traders of loans.

The selling and buying of residential loans triggered application of the law of negotiable instruments as found in the Uniform Commercial Code (UCC). The UCC is law in every state, and it is available to homeowners regardless of whether or not MERS is involved in their mortgage.

Kesler and John would likely have their homes today had all of us known more about the growing importance of the UCC in the foreclosure arena. We now have seen many examples of its application in federal and state courts.

Let me emphasize this important point: *Whether or not MERS is involved in a foreclosure, the starting point in the defense of the homeowner's rights has to be the most basic question: does the borrower actually owe anything to the company threatening to foreclose. You should never assume that the company threatening you has a legal right to do so. When you face threats of a judicial or nonjudicial foreclosure, the first thing you should do is make your attacker prove it has a legal right to demand money from you under a threat of foreclosure. You may have several promising legal theories that offer hope of defeating the threatened foreclosure, but you never want to concede that your attacker has any right under the note or mortgage you executed. If you are going to make assumptions, assume your opponent has no right to make demands for payment and no right to take your home via foreclosure.*

The proof of what I say hasn't been easy to gather. Like the *Landmark* case, most published court decisions only address a small part of the bigger picture, which is about the vulnerability of the foreclosure machine. You, however, need the complete story. You need to know how to best avoid the foreclosure machine's well-rehearsed tactics and how to position yourself to have the strongest possible legal case upon which to defend your home and your rights.

Over the past couple of years I've studied hundreds of published and unpublished state and federal court decisions and reams of related articles and papers, pulling out the relevant information, a little something here and a little more there. The lessons of that work are here for you. You and your attorney won't have the time or the money to put that much work into formulating your case, but you don't have to. The information is already summarized for you in this book. *Fighting the Foreclosure Machine* makes your work easier and your prospects for success substantially better.

I have tried to explain the legal concepts in plain language but with enough added legal authorities to help you and your attorney avoid repetitive legal research and analysis. This information was not available for Kesler in 2006 when he lost his home nor for John in 2009. You, however, now have it.

I will do my best to keep the information updated with my ongoing studies. Check my website for new developments involving foreclosure litigation: www.FightingTheForeclosureMachine.com

As discussed more in the following chapters, you were unknowingly placed in harm's way by the mortgage finance industry. You were encouraged to be a borrower with easy money sales pitches and artificially pumped-up real estate market values. Your legal rights under consumer protection laws were terribly impaired because of how the industry harvested borrowers in its quest for more money—money that was available only by generating more loans that could be sold and resold. The industry knew your protections were being eroded but did not let you know. Your ability to repay the inflated mortgage debt that the industry placed on your back was stripped from you as the economy grew sick because of the excesses and bad judgment of the mortgage finance industry. You are a victim, but not without legal rights.

You can use the foreclosure fundamentals summarized in this book to your advantage and to the disadvantage of the foreclosure machine. These fundamentals can only complement and strengthen other legal defenses or claims that may be available to you.

I hope that the results of my research will help balance your fight against the foreclosure machine, and that ultimately the voice of foreclosure victims will be loud enough for those in places of power to hear. Maybe the day will come when people in authority will help correct a sad wrong that is afflicting so many good people. I can't predict how this book will play in the bigger drama involving wrongful foreclosures, but maybe, just maybe, it will help a little.

YOU—BECAUSE THIS IS PERSONAL

I will write this directly to you rather than use a less personal style of narrative. Being a foreclosure victim is personal and there is no way to avoid that reality. Whether you have already been foreclosed or are under threat of losing your home, foreclosure is embarrassing, frustrating, and extremely stressful. This is not a sterile life event that you can treat like your next cup of coffee. Unfortunately, foreclosure is what follows on the heels of serious financial problems that have already begun to drain your energy and optimism.

The mortgage finance industry caused our economy's problems and yours. It now sends its foreclosure representatives to your state, your town, your neighborhood, and your home. You can't dismiss their notices and threats like the junk mail you so easily toss in the trash. Unlike the employees of the foreclosure shops, the industry isn't going to pay you to be in a foreclosure lawsuit. You may feel like you are pretty much on your own.

The mortgage finance industry and its foreclosure troops want you to bow to the pressures. They want you despondent and ignorant. They want you to give up.

You don't, however, have to let them hurt you more. You can fight back with tools they know but keep from you.

Fighting the Foreclosure Machine was written to help you understand your opponent's weaknesses, the history and fundamental laws that balance a foreclosure fight in your favor, and reasons to expect something good to come from fighting back. My work focuses on a powerful body of foreclosure law that is yours to use if you decide to fight back through a court of law.

You actually have more control than you might realize. You definitely have more power and rights than they want you to know.

The rights of which I speak are your legal rights. The foreclosure machine can't take them from you nor stop you from using them in a court of law—that is your power.

Writing this book to you makes sense because it is about your legal rights, your ways to leverage those rights against the foreclosure machine, and the very personal decision that only you can make regarding what response the machine will get from you. I write this book for you as my way of lending a hand in these trying times.

Fighting the Foreclosure Machine is directed to the substantive matters that can let you, as a borrower threatened with foreclosure, have a chance to win once you get to court. I hope it will motivate you to think seriously about what you can do to protect your rights. The purposes of this book are to:

- Help you understand your opponent, the mortgage finance industry and its foreclosure machine

- Tell you about the foreclosure fundamentals—the basic legal principles and concepts that define your rights in your fight against the foreclosure machine

- Give you the information that can help you assess whether fighting the machine makes sense for you, given your personal circumstances

- Assist you in laying the foundation for your battle

- Provide you with specific strategies that, if properly applied, can help you prevail

Here is a brief guide to the book, letting you know what you'll find as you proceed through it.

Part One. Facing Foreclosure? You Have an Ally

My intent in the opening part of the book is to let you know that I'm on your side should you choose to fight back against the foreclosure machine that is trying to take your house. Chapter 1, *An Introduction to the Foreclosure Machine,* introduces you to the book and tells the story of how I came to write it, while Chapter 2, *What This Book Is and Is Not,* lets you know what kind of help you can expect to get. Chapter 2 also briefly acquaints you with the fundamental aspects of foreclosure law that provide the foundation on which this book is built.

Part Two. Hurt by the Mortgage Finance Industry

How did our country get into the economic mess that has come to be called the Great Recession? Read this part of the book to find out. Chapter 3, *The Foreclosure Disaster in America,* provides a history of the rise and ultimate fall of the mortgage financial industry over the past two decades. In its effort to generate more and more profits, the industry induced borrowers into signing on for ever-increasing numbers of mortgage loans, and this practice led directly to the current economic collapse. Knowing how the industry caused this economic crisis should reassure you that the financial troubles you may be having are not your fault, and may inspire you to fight back.

Part Three. Getting Ready to Fight the Foreclosure Machine

A successful fight against the foreclosure machine requires careful thought and planning. This part of the book is designed to help you with that process.

Start with Chapter 4, *Key Concepts You Should Know*. It defines and discusses some of the basic ideas, principles, and entities that have been part of the typical mortgage transaction in recent years. You're likely to encounter these terms many times in the course of your fight. Therefore, it will be to your advantage to have a good understanding of them.

Everyone's circumstances are different. While I believe that most borrowers facing the foreclosure machine will gain from fighting back, this is not true in every case. Chapter 5, *Making the Decision to Fight Back*, sets out the options, the factors to consider, and the potential benefits. It will help you figure out whether fighting back is the right choice for you.

In Chapter 6, *Laying the Groundwork for Your Fight*, you'll find information on what you can expect when you confront the foreclosure machine in court. This chapter also discusses resources and approaches for obtaining legal help and suggestions that may assist you in handling the financial aspects of your fight.

While it is impossible to guarantee what will happen in any legal proceeding, the chances are good that when a lawsuit pits a borrower against the foreclosure machine, the outcome will be in the borrower's favor if the borrower is prepared. Chapter 7, *What Winning Could Mean to You*, outlines some of the possible results and what they might mean to you.

Part Four. Recipe for the Foreclosure Fight

This section is the heart of *Fighting the Foreclosure Machine*. Here you'll find the details, including how-to suggestions and related legal authorities, about what I refer to as the foreclosure fundamentals:

- The fundamental questions that must be answered in order for the court to determine which of the parties in the conflict—you or your opponent—is in the right

- The fundamental principles of fairness that are embodied in the law in order to protect your rights

- The fundamental strategies, or rules, that I believe are most likely to enable you to wage a successful fight

I refer to these foreclosure fundamentals frequently throughout this book. In Chapter 8, *The Fundamentals of Foreclosure,* you'll find them collected and defined. You may find it helpful to refer to this chapter from time to time as your lawsuit proceeds.

The subsequent chapters spell out in detail the specific strategies. They give you the rules that, if you follow them, will make it easier for the judge in your case to arrive at the decision that is right for you.

Rule 1: Don't Accept the Machine's Word—Demand Strict Proof— Chapter 9 cautions you not to assume that the claims of the foreclosure machine are valid. Often they are not. Your goal is to refuse to fall for your opponent's intimidation tactics and make it prove that it legitimately has the rights it is asserting against you. It is your opponent, not you, who bears the burden of proof. Since the foreclosure machine tends to resist providing the proof it is required to give, you'll find tactics you can use to make it do so throughout the chapters in Part Four.

*Rule 2: Gather and Use Facts to Beat the Machine—*Chapter 10 explains why fact-finding is essential and how to go about collecting the facts that are at the core of your case.

*Rule 3: Make the Machine Prove Its Right to Foreclose —*Chapter 11 goes in depth into the important concept of the "Boss of the Note." This is the only person, whether an indivual or a company, that has the right to collect money from you in payment of your obligation under the Note you signed when you bought your home. It is also the only person that has the right to conduct a foreclosure if you don't meet that obligation. The concept of the Boss is defined in an important body of law known as the Uniform Commercial Code. This code and its key provisions are described for you in this chapter.

*Rule 4: Don't Give the Machine an Easy Win—*Chapter 12 sets out various matters of procedures and protocols that can be important to a lawsuit involving a foreclosure, and it recommends ways to best handle them. It describes some of the ploys that the foreclosure machine uses in court and describes ways to defend against them.

Part Five. Parting Thoughts

If you are facing foreclosure, you are not alone. Many other homeowners have been and continue to be subjected to the same kind of unfortunate experience. Your decision to fight back can help not only you, but others who find themselves in a similar situation. Your voice will be added to the growing chorus of people calling for the mortgage finance industry to release its grip on the economy, and your experience can provide encouragement and help for others. Chapter 13, *Help Others Fight Back,* explains why you are an important part of the solution to the foreclosure crisis.

Exhibits and References

At the back of the book, you'll find additional help and resources. Several exhibits are provided, giving you checklists and examples of documents that you may want to adapt for your use. The Table of Authorities and Endnotes contain citations and references that support the information provided throughout the book.

CHAPTER 2

What This Book Is and Is Not

THIS BOOK IS … NOT LEGAL ADVICE

Attorneys like me, who are retired and no longer engaged in the practice of law, have to be careful that a person (or a person's enemy) doesn't mistakenly think we are practicing law when we are not. My thoughts and analysis about foreclosure topics are information for you to use or disregard as you choose.

Many people are appalled at the problems created for our country by the mortgage finance industry. Each has his or her way of trying to help foreclosure victims. I have chosen the pen rather than the practice of law as my way to contribute. *Fighting the Foreclosure Machine* reflects years of research, analysis, and thought. It is intended to supplement other resources available to you. Legal authorities underlying my work are included so you might more easily evaluate and ascertain the accuracy of my results and their usefulness to you. I am a writer, however, and that is my only role in creating and presenting this book. *I am not your attorney and you are not my client.*

A legal treatise at a library, an article in a law journal, or a discussion of public law in a newspaper or magazine may all contain information. It is up to the reader to decide how, if at all, to apply that information to his or her specific circumstances. Similarly, only you and your attorney can know if the information I share in this book has value regarding your particular situation. How you use the content of this book is strictly and solely up to you and the people you select to represent or guide you as you deal with the foreclosure machine.

I hope you'll come to view *Fighting the Foreclosure Machine* as a valuable resource, and I wish you all the best as you handle your predicament. I do this as a person commenting on public matters by sharing information, ideas, and opinions. But let me repeat this important point: *I am not your attorney and you are not my client.*

The mortgage finance industry has created too many classes of victims to list. Look around—you can easily see that people, businesses, and government agencies are struggling financially. All too frequently, businesses are closing, employees are being laid off, pension benefits are being decreased or postponed, and public services are being reduced. Heated disputes about budgets are disrupting government at the national, state, and local levels. If you're like me, you may hear your friends, neighbors, or colleagues comment about being thankful that they have a job or that their family and friends are getting by. Everyone is experiencing uncomfortable uncertainty about our tomorrows.

Meanwhile, the mortgage finance industry smugly pretends to be unaware of the horrific burden its incompetence and greed have caused. It feigns ignorance of the dishonest and deceptive practices used by its foreclosure machine, which pits coordinated and well-funded resources against those people least able to defend themselves. To the industry, foreclosures are little more than a sterile business activity that it pursues aggressively in order to improve its own bottom line. By taking your home, some members of the mortgage finance industry are trying to make money. Others are hoping to minimize their exposure to lawsuits that may be filed by unhappy investor groups or insurers.[2] The industry doesn't care about the impact on you or other victims personally.

Many persons and groups are working to assist the victims of this weak and uncertain economy and to advocate change and improvement. No one, however, can be actively involved with all of the needs born of the economic mess. While I hope my work will contribute to helping our nation find ways to avoid a repeat of this economic catastrophe, this book is intended for the people most directly injured by wrongful foreclosures—namely, you and the millions of other homeowners under attack.

... ABOUT BROADLY APPLICABLE BASICS OF FORECLOSURE LAW

Fighting the Foreclosure Machine focuses on a few basic principles of law and litigation guidelines that have broad application when protecting a borrower's legal rights. Federal and state courts have many rules, statutes, procedures, and terms of art and legalese that are comfortably known to those who regularly work in those places, but which are too numerous to discuss in this book. I will try to put the legalese into plain language as much as I can, while including enough citations of legal and other authorities so you and your legal adviser can assess the merit of my work. Hopefully, my summarized results can help you avoid the long hours of research and analysis I've already done.

My research and assessments suggest that if you concentrate on certain foreclosure fundamentals, you'll be positioned to better navigate and manage the details of a foreclosure lawsuit. Foreclosure victims have had success in courts arguing such legal concepts as standing, real party in interest, lack of agency authority, invalid assignments of Notes or mortgages, and law of negotiable instruments. Some borrowers, unfortunately, toss out labels like these without understanding their significance or knowing how to help judges reach the legal substance of those words. In those instances, the machine is likely to prevail unless the judge, without help from the borrower, pushes the case to its legal significance.

The foreclosure fundamentals stressed in *Fighting the Foreclosure Machine* offer the broadest promise of maximum relief for the largest number of foreclosure victims. These concepts and principles are at the core of our legal systems across America. They are there to protect people against claims that have no legal merit and lead to unnecessary litigation and uncertainty rather than finality, which is a desired result in the administration of law.

These fundamentals reflect the common threads of law and procedural do's and don'ts that have created problems for your opponent. Creating more problems for the foreclosure machine puts you on the best path to the most fair and just result. Incorporating the foreclosure fundamentals into your case can aid the judge's efforts to deliver the most correct and legal ruling.

The Basic Questions to Be Decided

In a nutshell, this book is a guide on how to make your opponent, not you, prove two things: (1) the identity of the person or company that has the legal right to enforce the Note you signed (what I call the Boss of the Note), and (2) that the foreclosure was initiated by the Boss of the Note. (The word *Note,* with a capital N, is used in this book to indicate the promissory note or loan document that, by whatever title, contains your promise to repay the real estate loan which has become involved in the foreclosure machine's effort to take your home or property.)

The Boss of your Note, whether it is an individual or a company, is the only person or entity who has the right to demand payment from you; the only one to whom you can make payments and have them result in reduction of your debt; the only one who has the right to declare a default; the only one with the right to initiate a foreclosure; and the only one with the authority to settle disputes regarding how much, if anything, you might owe respecting your obligation under the Note. The foreclosure machine's Achilles heel is the machine's difficulty proving that it knows or represents that Boss. Chapters 4 and 11, therefore, provide in-depth information about what the machine must prove regarding the Boss of your Note.

The Importance of the Uniform Commercial Code

When it comes to your fight, the single most important body of law, in my opinion, is the law of negotiable instruments found in the Uniform Commercial Code (UCC). Accordingly, *Fighting the Foreclosure Machine* is primarily the story of how and why the UCC puts you at an advantage and your opponent at a disadvantage. Chapter 11 contains a discussion of the UCC that will help you understand this crucial body of law and its application in foreclosure lawsuits.

The Uniform Commercial Code defines the Boss of the Note. Any person or company who can't satisfy the UCC tests has no right to enforce the Note and no right to foreclose. In many instances, because of how the mortgage finance industry has conducted its business since the late 1990s, your opponent won't be able to identify the Boss of the Note, and its claims will be exposed as meritless. If this happens in your situation, the case should be yours and the foreclosure stopped.

Chapter 11 demonstrates how the UCC requires the machine, not you, to identify the Boss of your Note. This chapter discusses the heavy burden on your opponent to prove its rights against you with solid evidence, and ways to keep the weight of that burden on the machine's back.

But suppose your opponent can identify the actual Boss of the Note. That may still be to your advantage, because many wrongs that borrowers suffer at the hands of predatory lenders can be asserted against a Boss of the Note who is not what is called a holder in due course. The UCC also defines what is meant by holder in due course and the proof the machine must provide if it claims that status. Furthermore, even if your opponent can identify the Boss of your Note, a foreclosure may nevertheless not be proper under your state law.

The Importance of Fact-Finding

Facts are crucial when addressing the question of who has a right to enforce the Note, or who has a right to commence or conclude a foreclosure. This book stresses the aggressive use of fact-finding. It gives considerable attention to the kind of facts your opponent needs to prove and suggests how you can help the judge see that your opponent can't prove it has the rights it asserts against you. (See Chapter 10.)

The foreclosure machine routinely tries to use various summary procedures in court in its effort to avoid having a case decided on the real facts. This book offers basic techniques for drafting claims and responses that can take away your opponent's ability to get an easy win. (See Chapter 12.)

The Importance of Fairness

The fundamental legal principles I stress are rooted in fairness. They are incorporated into our laws in order to protect people and are available for you to use in fighting the foreclosure machine. For example, fairness dictates that you are required to pay only debts that are legally recognized. You have no duty to give your hard-earned money to someone not legally entitled to it. Your opponent may say you are required to pay it. It may have a copy of the Note you signed, or even have possession of the original Note. Nevertheless, your opponent may have no right by law to demand payment from you and no right to foreclose.

Fairness also recognizes that you pledged your home as collateral but only for the benefit of the Boss of the Note, not for anyone else. No foreclosure, therefore, is valid unless the Boss actually has the right to trigger a foreclosure pursuant to your agreements with your lender. Even then, it isn't valid unless it is conducted in strict compliance with your state's foreclosure laws.

As discussed in Part Four, our legal system upholds these principles of fairness. Courts, however, can get bogged down in the sheer numbers of lawsuits they handle, and in all of the words and details that are part of the formal dispute resolution process. Judges need help keeping sight of the fairness principles and important legal issues amidst all of the papers, practices, and protocols that litigation entails. *Fighting the Foreclosure Machine* is written to help you help the court stay focused on these extremely important foreclosure fundamentals.

The Importance of Not Admitting
You Owe Anything to the Machine

The foreclosure fundamentals concentrate on determining whether your opponent has the legal right to enforce your Note under the UCC. If it doesn't have that right, it loses. You may have other grounds for challenging the foreclosure, but the starting point for a strong foreclosure fight must address whether you owe anything to those demanding your money and trying to foreclose. If you start your case by admitting that you actually owe anything to your opponent, you are most likely wrong and will have cut off your right to later raise that question should your other legal theories collapse under the court's legal analysis.

I think it a mistake to concede that your opponent is owed anything under your Note or that it has any right to foreclose. You can't possibly know that you owe it anything without first forcing your opponent to disclose all of its facts to you. As you'll learn in Chapters 4 and 11, just being behind on your house payment doesn't mean that you are in default of your obligations or that the company threatening foreclosure has any legal right to do that. Thinking otherwise is a costly assumption that has frequently gotten borrowers in trouble.

What This Book Does Not Address

Borrowers fighting back against foreclosure sometimes have legal defenses and rights that are based on facts and legal arguments unrelated to the core matters discussed here. For example, it could be that the loan documents were not properly notarized, that a loan originator lied or was deceitful, that all of the owners of the home who should have signed the documents did not sign, that all assignments of the mortgage were not recorded properly or in a timely manner in the public records, that a loan modification agreement was breached, or that notices required under the nonjudicial process were not issued.

There are too many laws and too many fact patterns to discuss them all in this book. One type of consumer protection or fair business practice law may be available in Michigan, but not in Missouri, and vice versa. Federal consumer protection laws often provide little relief for foreclosure victims. For example, to use the Real Estate Procedure Act (12 U.S.C. § 2601, et seq.) or the Truth In Lending Act (15 U.S.C. § 1601, et seq.), the borrower's claim for relief must be formally filed in a court of law within a relatively short time after the loan was made. Those laws are useless if invoked after the specified time frames have passed. Another law may offer a solution that has no practical use for most borrowers. For example, the Truth in Lending Act sometimes can be used to totally undo a loan transaction, but only if the original loan amount gets paid back by the borrower at the end of that lawsuit. This, of course, is not possible for most borrowers who can't even make the monthly house payments.

If your facts indicate you may be entitled to relief under laws not discussed in *Fighting the Foreclosure Machine,* by all means add those to your quiver so all of your good arrows can be used in the fight. The scope of this book, however, must necessarily concentrate on the core fundamentals that have the broadest application for most people facing the foreclosure machine. You'll probably find that when you assert the foreclosure fundamentals, you can strengthen your overall case and improve your odds of beating the machine.

The UCC burden you can place on your opponent is important. This body of protective law can be used in every state, and it creates a hole that is often too deep for the foreclosure machine to escape. I see no reason to stand out in the open against an oncoming tank when you can start the fight with the tank being stuck in a deep mud pit.

Your odds of success should be substantially better if the foreclosure fundamentals are part of your case against your attacker. You have the opportunity to defeat it with the foreclosure fundamentals while simultaneously obtaining more time and complete information upon which to help prove whatever other defenses or claims you might have against your opponent.

Do yourself a favor and go into the foreclosure lawsuit with both fists swinging. Don't tie one hand behind your back by making the erroneous assumption that you must owe your opponent something just because it says so or because you know you missed a few house payments.

… NOT FOR BAD GUYS, LIARS, OR LOW-LIFE OPPORTUNISTS

One day as I was getting a haircut I happened to mention to my barber that I was writing this book. She was puzzled. "Foreclosure victims?" she asked. "But they're the ones who falsified their loan applications or foolishly bought more house than they could afford. Then they created problems for the rest of us by not paying their bills. Why are you interested in helping those people?"

Like many others, she had heard the insinuations and read the accusations in the media that blame delinquent borrowers for causing their own problems and ours as well. I explained to her that pointing the finger at the borrowers was wrong.

The mortgage finance industry's public relations groups have spun those untruths, and they have not attempted to correct the negative images of delinquent borrowers put forth by people who don't understand what caused our economic pickle. In Chapter 3, you'll see that the mortgage finance industry, not the borrowers, is responsible for our financial difficulties. The major factor in mortgage delinquencies today is what the bad economy has done to borrowers, not what their financial situations were when they took out their loans. If I believed that borrowers who are being foreclosed deserve to lose their homes, I would not have had the motivation or energy to spend more than two years working on this book.

Yes, some individuals falsified their loan documents, often acting in complicity with loan brokers, mortgage bankers, and appraisers. But the evidence indicates that borrowers as a group did not participate in loan fraud. The Financial Crisis Inquiry Commission of the U.S. Congress, following $10 million in costs of research and analysis over a two-year period, found no appreciable evidence that borrowers caused or even made worse the economic tragedy America is enduring. In its *Financial Crisis Inquiry Report,* issued in January 2011, borrower fraud was not identified as a cause or even a quantifiable factor in the crisis.[3]

Thieves are in our midst (at all economic levels) but most Americans are honest people. That is what I was raised to believe, and it is consistent with my experiences in life.

Please understand that this book is not an attempt to help liars, crooks, or con artists get free housing. If you are one of the few who lied about something important in order to get a new loan, whether you did that on your own or in collusion with someone else, this book is not written for your benefit. If your opponent's counsel can muster any evidence about a false loan application, they will inject it into the foreclosure proceedings. If your judge comes to believe that you participated in defrauding the lender, either on your own or in complicity with a real estate agent, appraiser, loan officer, or anyone else, the judge will likely find and apply law to make sure you cannot now benefit from wrongs you committed. I suggest that if you took part in such a fraud, you should not waste your time and money asking a judge to help you when you face foreclosure. True foreclosure victims don't need their plight tainted by people who don't warrant the compassion or assistance of our legal system.

But if you are like most people facing foreclosure, you were unknowingly placed in harm's way by the mortgage finance industry as it did its very best to get you to sign up for another loan. *Fighting the Foreclosure Machine* is for you. This book is intended to help you have more options when you are facing the ugliness of the mortgage finance industry's foreclosure machine. Ignorant or malicious media and public sentiment that suggests delinquent borrowers are bad people who deserve what they get belongs in the trash can. Enough said on that point.

... DEFINITELY NOT PERFECT

I truly hope that the information in this book is correct and that my research and thoughts are useful. My goal has been to provide accurate information and reasonable interpretation and analysis. I've spent extensive effort and time studying judicial trends, looking for threads that might be woven together to create a better protective blanket for foreclosure victims. Typos and mistakes happen, however. My moments of perfection are fewer every year.

My pride of authorship is boosted by those who take my work seriously enough to help me make it as good as possible. Please feel free, therefore, to provide editorial or corrective assistance. I welcome and encourage your input. I will update *Fighting the Foreclosure Machine* as law evolves in response to the escalating numbers of foreclosures or as corrections or clarifications are warranted. You will find my contact information at www.FightingTheForeclosureMachine.com.

PART TWO

Hurt by the Mortgage

Finance Industry

CHAPTER 3

The Foreclosure Disaster in America

YOU ARE NOT ALONE

If you are struggling financially in the current economy, you are not alone.

We Americans are enduring one of the weakest economies since the Great Depression. We are all feeling the pinch, but for far too many people the pain and distress go way beyond a mere need to tighten their belts. They are suffering the pain and distress that comes from losing their homes, or being threatened with that loss. If you're reading this book, then you or someone you know—a friend, a neighbor, or a family member—may be among the millions who are in this difficult situation.

In May 2009, Congress established the Financial Crisis Inquiry Commission to look into the causes of the economic crisis that had hit the United States. The independent, ten-member panel issued its *Financial Crisis Inquiry Report* in January 2011. This report and similar studies by others include some grim statistics.

The Commission estimated that roughly 4 million homes have been foreclosed since 2006 and that the total might be 13 million before the economy recovers.[4] In other words, another 9 million homes could be foreclosed in the next few years if the U.S. economy doesn't improve enough. As of October 2011 the economy had not seen much recovery, so the Commission's estimate may have been substantially understated. Houses, of course, are occupied by individuals, couples, families, and extended families. The number of people displaced by these foreclosures, therefore, is substantially larger than 13 million.

In October 2010 the inventory of bank-owned foreclosed housing (that is, homes not yet sold by whichever company did the foreclosure) was about one million homes. Another 5.2 million homes were then in a foreclosure process or had owners who were at least two months behind on mortgage payments and were being targeted for foreclosure in the near term.[5]

The projected number of foreclosures did not happen in 2011. As one news article noted: "Foreclosures were in full delay in 2011."[6] The mortgage finance industry and its foreclosure machine got sidetracked by having to deal with embarrassing media coverage of fraudulent foreclosure practices involving what have come to be called robo-signers. That label is applied to the industry's people and service providers who falsified foreclosure documents in legal proceedings in order to take people's homes. The news reports indicated wrongful foreclosures of over a million homes at the hands of those robo-signers. As a result, I think the machine was instructed to back off temporarily until the media frenzy had cooled down.

We are now in 2012, and foreclosures are in fact expected to resume in full force. For example, on December 28, 2011, *USA Today* reported that 6 million homes were targeted for foreclosure as of the end of September 2011 and 22% of all homeowners owed more than the value of their homes.[7]

In November 2007 one out of 617 homes were being foreclosed.[8] By October 2010 the foreclosures had increased to one out of 371[9]—a 66% increase over three years. The rate of foreclosures fluctuates monthly. At times when the mortgage finance industry is negotiating to improve its political or bargaining posture, it is likely to show fewer new foreclosures.[10] The rate of foreclosures, at any level, is far too high.

Foreclosures of large numbers of commercial properties are also a fact of life. You can see evidence of this in virtually all communities, although numbers and projections regarding the injured economy's impact on commercial real estate aren't as readily available as statistics about foreclosed homes.

New home construction in America is at one of the worst levels experienced in half a century.[11] Accounts vary as to whether national real estate values are, on average, 30% or 40% lower now than they were in 2006, but values have clearly taken a big hit.

The dreadful economic news isn't limited to real estate. The Financial Crisis Inquiry Commission estimates that American households lost $17 trillion—that's trillion with a T—in their net household assets between late 2007 and the end of the first quarter of 2009. This is several trillions more than the entire gross domestic product (GDP) of the United States for 2008.[12]

Unemployment continues in the 8-10% range. The published statistic doesn't, of course, reflect the numbers of full-time workers whose pay or benefits have been reduced, full-time workers who have been relegated to part-time work but are still employed, those who have given up looking for work because they have been unable to locate new employment for such a long time, or those who are scraping by with multiple part-time jobs because no full-time employment is available. If you no longer have enough money to pay all of your bills due to the economic downturn, then the national employment statistics, whether higher or lower, are not very important.

We can't pick up a newspaper or visit an online news site without seeing more news of federal, state, and local government budget cuts and financial difficulties. The federal government's spending and temporary fiscal measures may be helping to keep things afloat—time will tell. Congress, however, has no long-term unified solution for how best to deal with the current economic woes.

Bottom line: the economy has been hurting for several years and is expected to continue that way for many to come.

Our terrible financial situation, however, isn't "just one of those things that happens" or "an act of God." We are victims of an irresponsible mortgage finance industry that has managed to drag all of us into this current mess.

As stated by the Commission's *Financial Crisis Inquiry Report* and other sources,[13] the single most identifiable factor underlying the economic tragedy with which we now have to live is the irresponsible conduct of the mortgage finance industry over the past fifteen years. The industry induced borrowers to take out record levels of new loans secured by American real estate, seduced private funds into investing record amounts of money in these loans, and flooded the real estate market with easily accessible funds, causing inflated and unsustainable real estate market values.

Now, following the rupture of the real estate market bubble it created, the mortgage finance industry has the arrogance and gall to soothe its self-made financial difficulties by aggressively taking homes and properties from borrowers who are unable to make mortgage payments because of the soured economy.[14] The industry's discomfort with the financial pain that has grown from its own avarice and poor judgment is hardly justification for visiting further injury and insult upon the borrowers it seduced and misled.

THE RISE OF THE MORTGAGE FINANCE INDUSTRY

Mortgage finance industry, as used in this book, means the network of businesses and governmental organizations that, since the mid-1990s, has engaged in the creation, packaging, marketing, and selling of investment products called mortgage-backed securities. Real estate loans backed by mortgages are packaged together and then bought and sold in various markets. Investment law defines those products as securities. Hence—mortgage-backed securities.

Until about two decades ago, taking out a real estate loan was usually a transaction between you and a local bank or mortgage company. You knew the company that you were dealing with, and you made your payments to it for the life of the loan.

Then things changed and became more complicated. In the 1990s, banks and financial institutions decided to pursue a different way of doing business, one that could make them a lot more money. They took a business practice that had been a small part of how banks and lenders made money and made it the primary objective. These profit-driven companies were supported in this endeavor by certain government agencies, which apparently believed that the private sector's moneymaking schemes were consistent with the American dream that anyone who wants one can own a home.

Combining their resources and reputations, these businesses and governmental organizations concentrated on designing, building, and marketing mortgage-backed securities. These investment products proved to be attractive to investors who controlled literally trillions of dollars.

You may be familiar with securities like stocks. An investor who buys a share of a company's stock is purchasing a small piece of that company and becomes, in essence, one of its owners. A mortgage-backed security is similar, except that what the investor owns is a right to a share of the proceeds from the Note and the mortgage if the house is foreclosed.

Of course, no single mortgage loan is sufficient to draw investor attention, so the industry puts together packages of thousands of real estate loans to sell to investors. Some of the loans are made to borrowers by banks and some by mortgage companies. The loans are typically put into investment trusts, and investors then purchase shares of the money expected to be made by the trust.

In other words, investors buy the right to share in the cash flow generated for the investment trust by the entire package of loans. The cash comes from mortgage payments received and sales of homes foreclosed if borrowers have defaulted on their Note obligations. One investor group might own a 10% share while another investor group might own a .5% share.

Over the past two decades, the investor trusts used the investors' money to buy existing real estate loans, to fund new real estate loans, and to pay hefty fees to the many people and businesses who put together the trust and its inventory of loans. Because investors' money, not money belonging to a lender, was being used to make loans, more loans could be made and more fees could be earned by those making, packaging, and selling the mortgage-backed securities. A huge cycle of moneymaking was created for the industry.

At some point you may have received a letter instructing you to send your mortgage payments to a company that was not your lender. In fact you may have received several such letters over the years. There are other reasons these notices could have been sent to you, but receiving one was often a signal that the securitization process was at work—that your Note and mortgage had been sold and sold again as investor groups were buying investment securities backed by mortgages, and, in particular, backed by your mortgage.

The leaders of this movement were the most powerful financial institutions of the world. (I'm not in a position to know which individuals within the industry were most instrumental, but my suspicion is that those standing to make the biggest bucks were probably the best organizers and promoters of the securitization business.) When they said, "Take our word for it … you'll love our new investment product," investors' dollars were there for the taking. Investors were attracted to the promises of high profits and safe investments because mortgage-backed securities represented promises to repay loans by borrowers backed by mortgages against American homes.

What I call the mortgage finance industry includes banks, Wall Street corporations, title insurance companies, and government agencies whose names you would recognize and an even larger cadre of support businesses, professional associations, and governmental agencies that have participated in and supported the growth of the mortgage-backed security business since the late 1990s. The short list includes many high-profile names, such as Bank of America, JPMorgan Chase Bank, CitiMortgage, Stewart Title Guaranty Company, Fannie Mae (a/k/a Federal National Mortgage Association), Goldman Sachs, Standard & Poor's, Freddie Mac (the Federal Home Loan Mortgage Corporation), Wells Fargo Bank, Mortgage Bankers Association, AIG, PMI Mortgage Insurance Company, Ginnie Mae (a/k/a Government National Mortgage Association), Commercial Mortgage Securities Association, Moody's, GE Capital Mortgage Services, GMAC Residential Funding Corporation, First American Title Insurance Corporation, Fitch Ratings, HSBC Finance Corporation, Washington Mutual Bank, Bank One, Sterling Savings Bank, Deutsche Bank, and Merrill Lynch. A long list would include thousands more.

The mortgage finance industry created MERS—that is, MERSCORP, Inc., and its wholly owned subsidiary, Mortgage Electronic Registration Systems, Inc., the entity I call ShellGame-MERS—to speed the creation and sales of mortgage-backed securities. ShellGame-MERS went from being a start-up, empty shell of a company in 1995 to having some 63 million American residential loans recorded in its name by May 2009.[15] This helps demonstrate that the mortgage finance industry's access to private investor money was not just good from the late 1990s to mid-2009, it was phenomenal.[16]

Most, maybe all, of the companies and agencies of the mortgage finance industry are or were members of MERS. I tried to count the number of members listed in the ShellGame-MERS membership directory,[17] but I lost track after reaching 6,000. Whatever the exact number, a lot of businesses and government agencies are and have been involved in the mortgage finance industry.

The whole world got suckered into the industry's sales pitch of "invest safely in American real estate." Real estate loans, secured by the borrower's promise to repay the debt and a pledge of the borrower's home, were promoted and rigged by the mortgage finance industry to be the hottest investment products here at home and around the world.

Pension, retirement, and other private[18] investor funds loved the sales pitch. They put their dollars on the table for the taking. To get its hands on the money, all the mortgage finance industry had to do was generate more real estate loans and then sell them, via either public sales registered with the U.S. Securities Exchange Commission or private placements by Wall Street and large banks. Whether public or private, the sale of real estate loans is said to take place in the secondary market, which refers to the system through which those who create real estate loans sell them to others. Sales of real estate loans to investors in the secondary market were not new in the mid to late 1990s, but the mortgage finance industry took that small part of its business to a whole new level.

Before the 1990s, investment products based on mortgage-backed securities were less plentiful because various oversight controls were in place to protect the borrowers and lenders. In those days, lenders who funded mortgages routinely stayed involved with the borrowers over the life of the loans.[19] Both the borrower and the lender knew more about the person sitting across the table when the loan was made, and each had more personal and legal motivation to make sure the transaction was successful for both.

In order to make the really big bucks, the industry elevated its development of secondary market activities to all-time highs. To maximize sales to investors, residential loans had to be gathered, packaged, and marketed to look more like stocks and bonds, because those were the types of investments that made investors most comfortable when letting go of their money. Making mortgage-backed securities a more comfortable investment product for investors had its challenges, however.

Real estate loans involved old industry practices that would cause delays and difficulties in packaging investment products. They also presented many legal issues not normally associated with securities investments, such as the great variation in real estate laws among the fifty states plus the need to comply with laws of the Uniform Commercial Code that apply to negotiable instruments like a real estate–related promissory note. The mortgage finance industry, however, decided the difficulties could be managed, especially when such huge profits were at stake.

One notable change from the old lender-borrower relationship was the shift of loan origination and foreclosure activities from lenders to non-lender businesses that focused on just their little part of the entire life of the loan.[20] Many sub-businesses emerged that made their money by harvesting borrowers, providing loan payment collection and reporting services, or initiating and conducting foreclosures. Subjected to less supervision and oversight, these companies helped the industry move more toward private, unregulated ways of doing business. Because those who put up the money for the loans—the investors—were not technically the lenders, they were afforded a measure of legal shielding from federal and state consumer protection laws that were supposed to protect borrowers. As noted in one study of the industry: "[O]ne of the principal characteristics of securitization [i.e., making a mortgage-backed loan into a securities product tradable like stocks and bonds] is that it tends to erect many barriers that prevent consumers from complaining effectively about unethical, unfair, or illegal treatment by loan brokers, originators, or servicers."[21]

The industry was able to attract investor dollars more easily and in larger amounts because it made mortgage-backed securities appear to be an investment in which people could reasonably place their money without needing to know anything about the business in which they were investing. Investor groups bought shares of mortgage-backed securities packages that came with loans already made, with companies already lined up to collect the borrowers' payments, and with foreclosure management services ready to take care of that aspect of the business. An investor was offered shares in turn-key packages that contained not only real estate loans but all of the services necessary to manage the business of owning and making money with those loans. The investor appeared to be buying into a complete business that owned the loans and also had the ability to collect and account for the mortgage payments made by borrowers, distribute profits to the investors, handle whatever legal matters might arise, take care of tax compliance and reporting, deal with borrower communications, and conduct home foreclosures when necessary to protect the investor's investment. The industry even arranged for investment managers who supposedly knew what they were doing and who would manage all of those business details on behalf of the investors. Thus the industry created investment products that appealed to the huge population of investors who had no meaningful understanding of the real estate loan business.

Of course, to get its hands on the trillions of dollars of private investment funds, the mortgage finance industry had to have inventory to sell—that is, it had to produce a lot more real estate loans. Unfortunately for borrowers and our country, the industry was too successful in pursuing that aim.

The amount of money at stake was astonishing. ShellGame-MERS claims that the 63 million loans registered with it by 2009 represented about 50% of the total residential mortgages in the U.S.[22] As best I have been able to learn, ShellGame-MERS has not disclosed the exact dollar amount of those mortgages, but some reasonable estimates can be made. Given that MERS didn't exist until the mid-1990s, the vast majority of MERS-registered loans reflect new money used to make new real estate loans from then to 2009. If the average amount of the mortgage loans in the ShellGame-MERS registry is $200,000, which is less than the $227,100 average home price in 2006,[23] the value of the real estate held under the MERS umbrella would be $12 trillion (yes, $12,000,000,000,000, with twelve 0's). If MERS loans account for 50% of total residential mortgages, then 100% of the mortgage money flow during those years was about $24 trillion. Add in the loans made for office buildings, multifamily housing units, and other commercial properties, and you can see that the infusion of new money into the real estate markets during those ten to fifteen years was massive.

LOANS AND MORE LOANS

With so much money in play, the message from the top down was "Get more real estate loans," "Get more real estate loans," and "We have buyers for whatever number and whatever quality can be put together." The mortgage finance industry created and promoted investor demand for real estate–backed investment products—the mortgage-backed securities. Then, in response to that demand, it became a master of getting Americans to take out real estate loans.

The industry created tiers of loan originators and mortgage brokers who were quite gifted at convincing people to borrow money. The industry had a loan package with interest rates and repayment terms for virtually everyone. It convinced millions and millions of people that they could afford to buy a house, speculate on real estate value growth, or use their real estate to finance some business or personal thing they wanted.

Potential borrowers were sold the idea that real estate values could only go up. If they had a hard time making mortgage payments, they became convinced they could sell the real estate to pay off the debt and make a profit. They were persuaded that easy refinancing would be available in the future, so keeping mortgage payments low would always be an option, even if the terms of their loan included increasingly higher monthly payments or a balloon payment in the near future. The industry set appraisal standards and selected the appraisers, who obligingly came up with attractive values for the properties, which further convinced borrowers they could afford whatever loan the lender wanted them to take out.

Adjustable rate mortgages, or ARMs, grew in popularity. ARMs let the industry induce borrowers to take out a loan with the promise of low monthly payments early on. After a few years the interest rate would increase, leading to much higher monthly payments; in some cases the entire loan would come due. But this would pose no problem, the borrowers were told. With the appreciation in real estate values that was sure to occur, they could easily refinance their loans.

The "no doc" loan also was used to help speed the making of a new residential loan. A loan of this type required no documentation of income, but was approved by the lender based on nothing more than a high credit rating for the borrower and a favorable appraisal for the real estate being purchased. The lender made no independent investigation to verify the borrower's ability to repay the loan.

A "good loan" came to be defined by marketing and salesmanship, rather than by responsible and transparent loan underwriting standards. Virtually any loan secured by an American home,[24] under any repayment terms, could be sold to some investment group somewhere—and they were.

Loan creation was no longer driven by sound economic reason or full compliance with the legal rights of borrowers. Sadly, the mortgage finance industry's master plan did not include full disclosure of the risks to which it was subjecting you and the rest of us.

Loan originators quickly adapted to the situation. Banks, mortgage companies, and mortgage brokers learned how to make huge profits by farming real estate loans for sale in the secondary market. As long as they delivered loans, they were successful, and they made money. Their payments and commissions were driven by the number of residential loans delivered and the amount of money borrowed.[25] The more loans they created for the investment world, the more money they made, and the less oversight or supervision was imposed as to how they went about gathering those real estate borrowers.

If the number of borrowers was not high enough, the loan originators designed new and more attractive loan repayment terms and sales pitches. From the late 1990s through 2006 they proved themselves extremely good at their borrower-gathering skills. Their profits were so high that more and more people wanted to get in on the game. The number of loan originators and mortgage brokers in the U.S. rose from 7,000 in 1987 to 53,000 by 2006.[26]

Wall Street segments of the mortgage finance industry also found ways to make money from real estate loans. They profited from packaging, selling, and managing large numbers of mortgage-backed securities for investor groups, whom history has now disclosed had more money than good sense. Big banks took their share of profits from their own loan originations, from loans originated by smaller companies which the bigger bank helped sell in the secondary market, and from fees tied to allegedly helping service the investment products after they were acquired by investors.

A vicious circle was created. As real estate values rose, more investors saw opportunities to make profits by pumping money into loans. As money for real estate transactions became more available, the need for a larger inventory of home loans grew, which resulted in more loans being made. That pushed home prices even higher. Congress's *Financial Crisis Inquiry Report* estimates that the average value of a home increased 67% in an eight-year period.[27]

On Wall Street and the streets of our cities, the mortgage finance industry spun the ridiculous story that real estate values always go up.[28] That story was used to convince potential borrowers that they had little risk in taking out a real estate loan. The story was also used to obtain high investment ratings for the packaged loans the industry sold to investors.

Investor communities, even those that are often thought to have smart and careful management, jumped on board. They rushed to buy more and more mortgage-backed securities. Maybe their investment managers and advisors actually believed the industry's sales pitch. Some may simply have been too naive. Or maybe they ignored reality in order to make more money for themselves.

It turns out that there is truth in the old saying, "What goes up must come down."

THE BUBBLE BURSTS

Exactly when the first leak in the bubble was noticed is not clear. The rupture became too big to ignore, however, late in 2008 when one of the industry's preeminent members, Lehman Brothers, collapsed.

I'm old enough to have experienced real estate market downturns, first in the early 1980s when the oil industry was struggling and again in the late 1980s and early 1990s as the savings and loan industry died. Only ignorance, foolishness, or corruption would lead people to build business models and investment-rating protocols based on the broad premise that real estate values will perpetually increase, but that's what the mortgage finance industry did in the mid-1990s through about 2008.

That flawed premise helped churn Wall Street's mortgage-backed securities business and the borrower-gathering antics on Main Street USA. During the years when the mortgage finance industry was driving so much money into real estate markets, it was simultaneously driving us to disaster in its sparkling everyone-should-be-a-borrower bus.

The sheer number of residential loans in existence in May 2009 points to the craziness underlying the industry's borrower-gathering frenzy. The industry's activities had not been based on a sustainable long-term business model.

If the 63 million loans registered with MERS were 50% of the total, then the mortgage finance industry generated some 126 million residential real estate loans as of May 2009. The total U.S. population was only about 308 million in July 2010.[29] For most of the period between the late 1990s through sometime in 2008, when the industry generated the great bulk of these loans, the total U.S. population was less than 300 million.

That means the borrower-gatherers of the industry were able to get something like 40 to 42% of the entire U.S. population—including women, men, children, teenagers, homeless individuals, institutionalized persons, college students, etc.—to take out new real estate loans for the purchase or refinancing of American homes. How impressive!

I'm not a statistician, but my guess is that the industry ran into a saturation difficulty. It needed to generate more and more borrowers in order to keep new money flowing into real estate, but there simply were not enough borrowers to keep that train on the track. The leaders of the mortgage finance industry apparently overlooked or ignored that little detail in their business planning.

The private-sector portions of the industry, which to my mind include the profit-motivated and government-supported enterprises Freddie Mac and Fannie Mae,[30] were bedazzled by all the money they were making. The government agencies that are part of the industry, such as the Department of Veteran Affairs, the Federal Home Authority, and Ginnie Mae, the federal insurer of repayments for certain types of residential loans, may have let the dream of home ownership for all Americans cloud their judgment about the industry's poor business model and the faulty planning associated with its desire to drive so much capital to the real estate markets in such a short time.

I'm not in a position to know which individual leaders within the mortgage finance industry or the government were corrupt, naïve, or merely incompetent, but the industry, with the support of our government, drove these huge amounts of money into our economy in a way that created inflated and unsustainable increases in home prices. Simultaneously the industry threw borrowers to the wolves at both the loan origination and foreclosure ends of the real estate loan chain. Because people in the private sector stood to make more money than those in the public sector, I'm inclined to think the private-sector bosses led the parade. The result is that America got shafted, whether or not any particular businessperson, legislator, or company can ever be proven culpable.

Our so-called captains of industry should have seen it coming, and they should not have permitted it to happen. We can only hope that brighter and more competent people are today guiding the power of the mortgage finance industry so a similar catastrophe might be avoided in the future. I hope those in charge of moving our country forward will remember that the large players of the mortgage finance industry may be "too big to fail," but they are also too big not to be controlled for the protection of the public.

Understanding market fundamentals doesn't require a Ph.D. in economics. If there is only one potential buyer for a house, its market value is not very good. However, if ten buyers compete for the same house, the competition drives the market value much higher. By injecting trillions of dollars into our economy through increasing numbers of real estate loans, the mortgage finance industry effectively drove the housing market higher and higher and higher. Borrowers were induced to buy more homes and take on more debt predicated upon an artificial and unsustainable real estate market. Then the fantasy cloak fell off, leaving borrowers with loans exceeding the value of their homes, no friendly creditors to help them refinance, and a sick economy that took away the income they needed to make their mortgage payments.

Now it is the foreclosure businesses that are making money as they target people for foreclosure and strip away their homes. In the process, they often act in ways that ignore the interests and rights of the homeowners. Published court decisions, testimony, and other evidence increasingly paint a picture of routine violation of borrowers' rights by those hired to initiate and carry out foreclosures.

Industry leaders consistently deny knowing about such practices, but that's hard to accept. Foreclosures of millions of homes translate into billions to trillions of dollars, depending on the value of the repossessed houses. I have difficulty believing that the investment groups or mortgage insurers who own the right to the sales proceeds of foreclosed properties are unaware of how their hired companies are handling those valuable assets. But I may just be too skeptical.

The mortgage finance industry as a whole is expected to lose 20 to 40% of its assets as our crippled economy struggles back to health. The final tally must await future accounting, but there can be no doubt that the industry has itself been injured. Lower profits, reduced asset portfolios, business closures and consolidations, and downsizing of office space and personnel are all signs that the mortgage finance industry is suffering. Of course, the industry caused the problem, so condolences are not easily tossed its way.

Some of the largest members of the mortgage finance industry have been helped with government stimulus funds and government-directed settlements of legal battles. Foreclosure victims, of course, don't fare as well.

Persons who go through foreclosure lose almost everything they own, not just 20 to 40% like the industry. The down payment they used to buy the house is gone. The years of mortgage payments have returned nothing to them in the way of investment value or savings. Their meager savings, if they have any, get consumed with moving and relocation expenses. Sometimes they're exposed to the embarrassment, stigma, and cost of bankruptcy. They suffer the strain of having to leave friends and neighborhoods they love. They further suffer the degradation and insults of the mortgage finance industry as it spins a false story that says the sick economy is largely the responsibility of people who bought more house than they could afford and those debtors who are not responsible enough citizens to make their mortgage payments.

Shamefully, the same mortgage finance industry that led all of us, without our knowledge, into this economic pit, has the gall to point an accusatory finger at the people it placed in jeopardy. Fairness dictates that foreclosed victims should receive more respect, more honesty, and more tools, like this book, with which to withstand wrongful foreclosures.

SUBPRIME MORTGAGE CRISIS: A RESULT, NOT THE CAUSE

The expression *subprime mortgage* has been tossed about frequently since our economy's instability started to appear in 2005-2006. The phrase captured the media's attention when everyone was first trying to understand emerging signs of serious financial difficulties.

Naturally the mortgage finance industry did not stand up and say, "Oh, it was our fault!" So journalists and economists, seeing a sharp increase in delinquent mortgages and a decline in real estate values, adopted the phrases *subprime mortgages* and *subprime mortgage crisis* in their effort to understand and report on what was happening.

A subprime mortgage is a loan made to a borrower whose credit rating suggests that he or she might have trouble meeting the repayment schedule. In its eagerness to generate more and more loans, the industry issued a larger number of subprime loans than had been the case in the past. They were bundled with other loans into the mortgage-backed security packages that were sold to investors.

As the industry's ability to generate ever-increasing real estate values and growing ranks of new borrowers began to wane, mortgage defaults were one of the earlier symptoms of a larger illness.

All too often, the media has directly or indirectly blamed delinquent borrowers for America's economic woes, including depressed real estate values and a stifled construction industry. Unfortunately, the subprime label has been used to insinuate that irresponsible people had sought loans they could not possibly repay. The word implied that the borrower was at fault for having accepted the loan in the first place or for committing some other wrong at the time when the loan was made.

Such views are inconsistent with the facts and the reality of delinquent loans. In most cases, when people become unable to make their mortgage payments it is because of circumstances present when the loan goes bad, not when it was first made.

An infected economy is responsible for the rash of foreclosures. Our current troubles were served to us by the mortgage finance industry, not by delinquent borrowers, Consider these comments from journalists and economists who have studied the mortgage meltdown:

> "The distinction between prime and subprime borrowers is not clear. For example, individuals can be considered either prime or subprime borrowers with FICO scores [i.e., credit ratings] below 620, and the same is true for those with scores above 620. Indeed, the distinction is artificial insofar as risk-based pricing is used ... Most importantly, the factors that cause individuals to enter foreclosure are generally not based on the type of [loan] they receive, but rather the financial circumstances they find themselves in after they obtain mortgage loans. These factors include unemployment, divorce, health problems, and especially declines in housing prices that leave homes worth less than their outstanding mortgage balances."[31]

> "Most often, homeowners fall behind on their mortgages because their income has dropped due to unemployment or other causes."[32]

> "Those sliding into foreclosure today are more likely to be modest borrowers whose loans fit their income than the consumers of exotically lenient mortgages that formerly typified the crisis. Economy.com said in 2009 that it expected that 60 percent of the mortgage defaults that year would be set off primarily by unemployment, up from 29 percent in 2008."[33]

"Now most foreclosures occur with prime loans."[34]

It would be better to apply the subprime label to a review of the trauma caused by bad judgment and excesses of our so-called leaders, so that similar problems can be avoided in the future. The term has little to do with the class of people who became borrowers and are now foreclosure victims.

The mortgage finance industry, not borrowers, set lending standards, borrower qualifications, and appraisal guidelines. It is the industry that controls access to money available for real estate loans, and it is the one with the power and resources to monitor and police both loan origination and foreclosure practices. People were talked into becoming borrowers with sales pitches that included themes of ever-increasing home values and loan repayment options that could always be affordable. Borrowers did not create those stories or marketing ploys. The people who became borrowers in response to the industry's actions are not responsible for the widespread economic upheaval this country has experienced.

Individual leaders of the mortgage finance industry, whether in its private or government sectors, don't openly accept responsibility for the injury to which their industry has subjected our country. They want the public to be upset with borrowers rather than to look more deeply at the real roots of the problem.

But the industry's mistakes, poor judgment, and avarice cannot be ignored. The evidence is clear that the mortgage finance industry, not borrowers, led and caused the economic strife, as these comments attest:

"Three important catalysts of the subprime crisis were the influx of moneys from the private sector, the banks entering into the mortgage bond market and the predatory lending practices of the mortgage lenders, specifically the adjustable-rate mortgage that mortgage lenders sold directly or indirectly via mortgage brokers."[35]

"During a period of strong global growth, growing capital flows, and prolonged stability earlier this decade, market participants sought higher yields without an adequate appreciation of the risks and failed to exercise proper due diligence. At the same time, weak underwriting standards, unsound risk management practices, increasingly complex and opaque financial products, and consequent excessive leverage combined to create vulnerabilities in the system. Policy-makers, regulators and supervisors, in some advanced countries, did not adequately appreciate and address the risks building up in financial markets, keep pace with financial innovation, or take into account the systemic ramifications of domestic regulatory actions."[36]

"The crisis was the result of human action and inaction, not of Mother Nature or computer models gone haywire. The captains of finance and the public stewards of our financial system ignored warnings and failed to question, understand, and manage evolving risks within a system essential to the well-being of the American public. Theirs was a big miss, not a stumble. While the business cycle cannot be repealed, a crisis of this magnitude need not have occurred. To paraphrase Shakespeare, the fault lies not in the stars, but in us."[37]

In 2008, according to *The Financial Crisis Inquiry Report*, "the International Monetary Fund estimated subprime losses at nearly a trillion dollars, about $143 for every person on the planet."[38] The 2010 documentary film *Inside Job* mentions worldwide losses of $20 trillion, almost $3,000 per person in the world.[39] The magnitude of the problem is monstrous. History will have to calculate the final loss suffered here and abroad once the crisis is over. Whatever the ultimate loss to be borne by the U.S. taxpayers, we know it will be paid by us, our children, and their children.

Historians will undoubtedly use the subprime label some way when describing these times. If they use it to describe a result of the mortgage finance industry's folly, it will have been used correctly.

THIS IS NOT YOUR FAULT

I hope that you receive my message loud and clear—in the situation you are facing, you are not the one who is at fault.

BORROWER, NOT DEBTOR, IS THE CORRECT WORD

You'll note my use of the word "borrower" rather than "debtor" throughout this book when I speak about foreclosure victims. Virtually all Americans who support themselves or others are debtors, having financial obligations to someone or some business. Credit cards, student loans, automobile loans, home loans, lease obligations—these are all part of the American way.

However, if you are a foreclosure victim, you are not in that situation because you became a debtor. You now face the foreclosure machine because the mortgage finance industry had you borrow against artificially inflated real estate and under terms that set you up for a fall once the economy turned sour.

I think it best to preserve and use the title of borrower when speaking of those who are fighting back against the industry's foreclosure machine, lest the mortgage finance industry and its leaders be allowed to redefine or whitewash their own role in the creation of our economic mess and your financial headaches.

You are a borrower, not a debtor, regarding your mortgage loan. That is the correct word to describe the sad situation in which you now find yourself.

The subsequent chapters of this book are intended to help you discover and assess your rights and options, and to give you tools for fighting back if you choose to do so.

PART THREE

Getting Ready to Fight the

Foreclosure Machine

CHAPTER 4

KEY CONCEPTS YOU SHOULD KNOW

NOTE, MORTGAGE, AND MORTGAGE LOAN

For most of us, purchasing a house involves borrowing money. Once the deal has been negotiated and the loan has been approved, we go to the closing or settlement (the name of that final step varies), where we sign a stack of papers and are given the keys to our new home. This is the time when the house becomes titled in our name. It is also when the loan is finally and formally made and the money provided.

Among the documents we sign are two that will become especially important if a foreclosure should ever occur. These are the *Note,* or the promise to repay the loan, and the *mortgage,* a document that subjects your home to being sold at a foreclosure sale if your debt to the lender isn't fully paid per the terms of the Note. In some situations you may have a deed of trust rather than a mortgage. They both serve the same purpose, and in this book I use the word mortgage for both. Notes and mortgages can vary greatly in their verbiage, length, and appearance, but they are both documents intended to set out the rights and obligations of you and your lender.

A Note exists whether or not it has a corresponding mortgage. In other words, a borrower can have a debt obligation that isn't secured by a mortgage against his or her home or any other type of collateral. In that case, the Note is known as an unsecured debt.

A mortgage, however, has no existence independent of the Note. The mortgage is merely incidental to the Note.[40] If a debt exists but steps are not taken to create a valid mortgage or to maintain a mortgage as a legal claim against the real estate, the debt may still be there but the mortgage and the right to foreclose can legally evaporate. The mortgage doesn't define or create the debt, but the Note does define the limitations of the mortgage.

The foreclosure machine will frequently mention the Note and mortgage. It sometimes refers to both together as the *mortgage loan*. This is simply a collective term meaning the Note and mortgage. A mortgage loan isn't a separate document.

Of these two common real estate documents, remember that your Note, not the mortgage, is the more important and is the one that should receive your undivided attention. It defines what you owe and to whom.

THE BOSS OF THE NOTE

Boss of the Note isn't an official term, but it's a very important concept to understand. I coined this phrase to have a consistent way to refer to the person or entity that has control of your Note—in other words, who has the right to receive your payments and to initiate foreclosure proceedings if you should fail to make those payments. Various contracts and laws may use different words to describe what I call the Boss—beneficiary, creditor, lender, and mortgagee are among the possibilities—but no matter what term is used, the principle remains the same.

Only one person or entity can be the Boss of your Note at any given time. The original Boss was the party with whom you initiated your loan agreement. In all likelihood, that person later sold the Note, and the rights that go along with it, to someone else. The purchaser could have become the new Boss. Your Note may have been bought and sold several times, and each transaction created a possibility of a new Boss if all of the legal requirements were met.

The Boss of your Note is the only person who has the right to foreclose your Note. The Boss may appoint another party to act as an agent or servant on its behalf, but in that case the line of authority connecting the Boss and the agent must be clear. If anyone besides the Boss or the Boss's agent tries to initiate a foreclosure proceeding against you, that threat of legal action isn't valid.

Therefore, the focus of your fight against the foreclosure machine is to force your opponent to prove that it is the Boss of your Note or else that it is acting on the Boss's authority. It is quite likely that such proof won't come forth. If it doesn't, you should win your battle. Even if your opponent produces the required proof, then you have information that may strengthen other legal claims you can make.

FORECLOSURE

Since foreclosure is the subject of this entire book, it would seem that what a foreclosure is ought to be clear. Yet I'm aware that many people find this term a bit confusing. Therefore, a brief comment is in order.

A foreclosure occurs as a means to satisfy a debt or financial obligation that has been secured by a home. It comes about when the person who has borrowed money to purchase the house, or who has otherwise pledged it as security for repayment of a loan, fails to make payments in accordance with the terms of his or her agreement with the lender.

Foreclosure is the formal process by which a homeowner's rights to his or her home can be terminated. If by law the borrower actually has an unsatisfied obligation to the lender or its successor, the real estate can be sold and the sales proceeds applied to satisfy the balance then due. The person making the highest bid at the foreclosure sale becomes the new owner of the house. That owner could be the person to whom the obligation was owed and who conducted the foreclosure, or it could be a person with no relationship whatsoever to the borrower or the person who directs the foreclosure. Some states, but not all, permit the foreclosed owner to redeem the house by reimbursing the foreclosure buyer.

If the foreclosure comes about through a court order, then it is known as a judicial foreclosure. A nonjudicial foreclosure is one in which the court isn't involved, although the proceeding must conform to state laws. Some states require foreclosures to be handled by the court, some use nonjudicial foreclosures, and some permit both judicial and nonjudicial foreclosures.

Regardless of the method of foreclosure, no state permits or condones foreclosure of a person's home by a person who isn't owed anything by that homeowner. The one person with the legal right to enforce your Note must have initiated the foreclosure or else the foreclosure violates law. This fact directs our attention to the Uniform Commercial Code (UCC), because it is the law that defines what a person must prove in order to establish a legal right to enforce the Note. (See the introductory remarks about the UCC later in this chapter and the discussion in Chapter 11.)

Conceptually, a foreclosure is proper only if the Boss of your Note decides a default exists and then decides to foreclose. The Boss can use a servant or agent to help collect the debt claimed due, but the Boss must initiate the collection effort and the servant's conduct must be in response to instructions from the Boss.

The identity of that Boss is crucial to the question of whether your opponent has any right to make demands regarding your Note or to foreclose. Your leverage against your opponent is that it must prove it is the Boss or the Boss's servant. It must also prove that you actually owe it something. If it can't, it has no right to foreclose. It is that simple.

If your opponent isn't the Boss or the Boss's servant regarding the enforcement of your Note, the lawsuit should be decided in your favor. The UCC describes what your opponent must prove to carry its burden. (See Chapters 11 and 12.) If it fails to prove it has the right to enforce your Note, your judge should rule that the foreclosure is improper. The Note and the rules regarding what person can enforce it according to the UCC are therefore central to protecting your rights and your home.

DEFAULT—WHAT IT MEANS IN FORECLOSURE

A lot more than missed mortgage payments is required for your Note to be in default or for someone to take your home in a legal foreclosure!

Default is a word you want to understand and use correctly. Misuse of this word can have more serious and adverse results than misuse of other words. Admitting that you're in default under your Note when you can't possibly know if that's true is a bad mistake. It gives your opponent an undeserved and possibly irreversible appearance of legal authority and right.

Like many words, default has different meanings depending on the context in which it's used. In the world of home foreclosures, the meaning that is most important is whether or not the Boss of the Note has declared a default by commencing enforcement of your Note. A default exists if, and only if, that Boss has initiated efforts to collect what the Boss thinks is due regarding your obligation under the Note you executed and gave to your lender when you took out the real estate loan. Collection efforts could involve demands by the Boss for alleged past-due payments. They could also involve foreclosure of your home if the money demanded by that Boss isn't paid on time. The Boss, however, and no one else, is the only person with the right to start the collection process.

Whether or not you think you're in default of your obligations under the Note isn't relevant when you face a company threatening to take your home. If the Boss of the Note has not contacted you and told you the Note is in default, it isn't.

Your Note may state conditions of default—the occurrences and circumstances that could permit the Boss to initiate legal steps to collect money it thinks is past due or to foreclose. The text of your Note may even say that a default occurs if you don't make a payment every month.

However, until the Boss decides that a default actually exists and it begins collection activities, there has been no default. This is law pursuant to the Uniform Commercial Code (UCC), as explained in more depth in Chapter 11.

Your opponent can talk until it's blue in the face about your alleged default, insisting you owe this or that. None of those words means anything when said by a person who doesn't have Boss status. Mere talk doesn't heighten or improve your opponent's right to enforce the Note. Nor does having a copy of the Note you gave your lender. Lots of people can get copies of the Note. Someone's having a copy of your Note or talking about it doesn't create a legal debt that you must satisfy. It's the same as if you wanted to have a million dollars in the bank—just talking about how much money Wells Fargo Bank has won't make your bank account bigger. That's not how the real world works. That's not how legal rights are created.

First, your opponent must prove either that it is the Boss or else that it is the duly appointed servant of that one true Boss and is acting under the Boss's instructions to enforce your Note. Until then, if that day ever comes, your opponent has no right to discuss your relationship with the Boss, including whether or not a default exists regarding your Note.

Until your opponent proves its Boss-derived status, it is a mere interloper and a stranger to your Note and mortgage. Its questions and comments about your Note have no legal significance unless that Boss status is proven.

Your opponent hopes its comments about your payment history and the customary relationships between a lender and a borrower facing foreclosure will let it imply itself into Boss status with your judge. You need to make sure your judge isn't allowed to assume your opponent has Boss status just because it talks as if it is the Boss of your Note or the servant of that person.

Your opponent will try to get you to admit you're in default, hoping the judge will interpret your words to mean that you're granting Boss status to your opponent. Don't do that. Don't make the mistake of saying that you owe anything to your opponent, or that your Note is in default when you don't know whether the Boss has actually told you that your Note is in default. Remember, default in a foreclosure means what the one true Boss thinks, not what you or anyone else talks about or guesses.

Even if you've missed one or more mortgage payments, that doesn't mean the Boss of your Note has decided to start collection activities or is even owed anything anymore. Only the Boss actually knows how much is still due and whether others have already paid all or part of the remaining amount you thought was due under the terms of your Note. For example, your Note may have been paid off by insurance proceeds. Or a company involved with a sale of your Note may have created an indorsement warranty per the UCC that later resulted in that company having to pay off the obligation per your Note. Or the Boss may have received a settlement payment from a company it sued for having duped it into buying your Note. That settlement payment may have reduced or eliminated your obligation to the Boss of your Note. The UCC also creates what's called a statute of limitations, which means the Boss of your Note may no longer be allowed to enforce your obligation by law. The facts and circumstances related to how much is still owed under your Note are not information about which you're likely to have any knowledge. Unless a person who proves Boss status appears, you can't possibly know how much is still owed under your Note. Your obligation may no longer exist, or it may be substantially less than what you or the foreclosure machine thinks.

Therefore, if you're asked to state whether you're in default, the accurate answer is: "No. I haven't been approached by anyone proving the right to enforce my Note pursuant to the provisions of the UCC. I'm unaware of a default having been declared by such a person and I also haven't received information from that person regarding the balance due, if any, under my Note."

Tell the truth if you're asked questions about any payments that may have been missed under a payment schedule of which you're aware. Make that answer knowing that neither your answer nor your opponent's question have any bearing on the essential legal issue of whether your opponent can prove that it has the enforcement rights of the Boss. The matter of how much is still due per your Note can't even be logically addressed before your opponent proves the identity of the Boss of your Note, because only the Boss has information regarding whether a default has been declared and how much is actually still owed.

Until the Boss is identified and says otherwise, you're not in default and nothing is currently owed under your Note. Until the Boss is identified and communicates with you, you don't know the current balance remaining due under your Note. Your obligation may no longer exist, and that may be why the Boss has not yet come forward demanding payment from you.

Defeating your opponent in court requires only that you help the judge see that your opponent can't prove it is the Boss. You have no duty to identify the Boss yourself. Don't let the judge think your opponent has Boss status by mistakenly admitting you owe anything to your opponent or that your Note is in default. Be accurate when you use the word default. That will help lead your judge to the correct issues of fact and law.

MORTGAGE-BACKED SECURITIES

A *mortgage-backed security* is an investment product similar to stocks or bonds. It is sold to investors wanting to make a profit, by persons who also want to make a profit.

Mortgage-backed securities are created by gathering a large group of mortgage loans—that is, Notes and their associated mortgages—from banks or other lenders and bundling or pooling them together. Investors are then sold shares of the pool. An investment firm may, for example, put 10,000 mortgage loans into a pool, and an investor can then buy a percentage of the profits expected to flow from that pool. The investor essentially buys a portion of the payment stream to be received as borrowers pay off their Notes and as homes are sold after foreclosure in the event the borrower doesn't pay the full obligation under the Note.

The term mortgage-backed security sounds complicated, and the documents used in the creation and sale of such securities are typically long and wordy. When you hear that expression, however, just think about an investment product that involves real estate loans backed by mortgages. Your Note and mortgage were probably packaged and sold to an investment fund along with thousands of other mortgage-backed securities.

If you face an opponent that claims to be an investment fund that acquired your mortgage loan or to be the servant of that type of business, the fight is no different than if your opponent is a bank or a mortgage company. The foreclosure fundaments emphasized by *Fighting the Foreclosure Machine* apply equally well to any type of opponent.

As you read in Chapter 3, the desire of the mortgage finance industry to make bigger profits led to the harvesting of borrowers, artificially high real estate values, and our economy's serious problems. Accounts of that history involve frequent references to mortgage-backed securities. An early symptom of the economy's illness was a pattern of profits that were below expectations for those who invested in mortgage-backed securities.

To help stabilize markets for mortgage-backed securities, in 2009 the United States even guaranteed that the investors would not lose money, at least on $1.2 trillion of mortgage-backed securities.[41] Sadly, foreclosed homeowners and those now being targeted for foreclosure haven't received any financial guarantees that their losses will ever be recovered.

CHAIN OF OWNERSHIP AND
CONTROL OF THE NOTE

As Notes and mortgages change hands and become pooled with other mortgage loans to create mortgage-backed securities, the legal rights of ownership and control of a Note may become fuzzy. This has proved to be a big problem for the foreclosure machine.

In order for your attacker to prove it has the right to enforce your Note and to foreclose, it must provide documentary evidence of its rights respecting your Note. That is, it must have trustworthy records that document the Note's chain of ownership and control. This means verifying each transaction that involved a change in the ownership or control of the Note—the date of the transaction, who sold it, who bought it, the rights given and those retained respecting the Note, and the agreements defining the transaction. If that chain of ownership and control involves five transactions, your opponent must prove that each transaction resulted in its current claim to Boss status pursuant to the UCC. (See Chapters 11 and 12.) If there are gaps in the chain, your opponent will have considerable difficulty in meeting its burden of proof.

The chain is described as involving ownership and control. Boss status per the UCC isn't defined by either of those terms, but together they hint at factors that could be important in whether or not your opponent can prove it is the Boss or the Boss's servant respecting your Note.

Real estate transactions often involve matters of title. Most rights in real estate, including ownership of the property and mortgage rights, must be recorded in public land records to be legally effective. The person or entity that, according to those records, possesses those rights is said to hold title to the property in question. A chain of title regarding a house would include all documents recorded in the appropriate public land office which indicate any legal claim on the house. A recorded mortgage, however, won't contain information sufficient to define who has the right to foreclose that mortgage. That issue requires a determination of the person entitled to enforce the Note for which the mortgage was given as extra security.

The UCC considers Notes to be negotiable instruments. As negotiable instruments, they can change hands and be impacted by agreements without any requirement that those transactions be recorded in public records. Therefore, an investigation of public land records rarely discloses the ownership or control of the Note for which a related mortgage has been filed in those records. This is one reason why the UCC requires the person claiming the right to enforce the Note to prove, with facts, that it holds that status by law. That person must produce and prove the details involving changes in the ownership and control of the Note, or else that person holds no such legal right. The UCC requirements look beyond simply who has possession of your Note or who might have a piece of paper saying they are in charge of it. (See Chapter 11.)

If you engage in a lawsuit against the foreclosure machine, you need to place your attention primarily on the Note's chain of ownership and control, and less so on recorded documents within the public records. Your opponent should lose if it can't or won't produce evidence sufficient to prove Boss status per the UCC. A person can't prove Boss status without demonstrating all the facts regarding the ownership and control of your Note.

UNIFORM COMMERCIAL CODE

This legal code is described in detail in Chapter 11, but I want to draw your attention to it here because you'll find references to it throughout this book.

The Uniform Commercial Code (UCC) is a comprehensive body of law that addresses various aspects of commercial law. It was crafted about sixty years ago to create clarity, stability, and consistency among the laws of all fifty states, as well as the District of Columbia, Puerto Rico, and the Virgin Islands, and it continues to be reviewed and updated. Having this type of code is important to business stability and predictability because so many kinds of commercial transactions extend across state boundaries.

The UCC isn't law in itself. Its purpose is to set standards to which the laws of individual states should adhere. It was created by a nonpartisan body called the Uniform Law Commission, which comprises more than 300 experts — attorneys, judges, legislators and law professors — who volunteer their time and knowledge. All Commissioners must be members of the bar, and they come from all over the country. The Commission's role is to review the laws of the states, research the relevant issues, and propose and draft specific statutes in the many areas of the law where uniformity is desirable.[42]

It is up to the states to adopt legislation that incorporates the principles of uniformity while addressing their local experience and needs. Every state has ensured that the relevant laws on its books conform to the UCC. That is, each state has adopted the UCC, even though the numbering and labeling of the various parts differ amongst states.

Mortgage loans come under the purview of the UCC because the typical real estate Note is a negotiable instrument and therefore covered by commercial law. The UCC incorporates principles of fairness and is concerned with protecting the rights of all parties in a transaction involving a negotiable instrument.

When your opponent claims to be the Boss of the Note or an agent of the Boss, your state's UCC provides tests that can help you and your judge assess whether your opponent has proven that it qualifies to assert that status. Mounting evidence indicates that the foreclosure machine has difficulty proving Boss status under the UCC when challenged to do so. For that reason, the UCC is a strong framework on which to build your case against the foreclosure machine.

SHELLGAME-MERS:
CONTRIVED CONFUSION

"Oh, what a tangled web we weave,
when first we practice to deceive."

If the Scottish author Sir Walter Scott were penning these famous words today instead of in 1808, he probably would have been talking about the contrived confusion called MERS.

A corporation named Mortgage Electronic Registration Systems, Inc., claimed to have its name on some 63 million home mortgages in the United States in 2009. Its name is abbreviated as MERS in those documents. In other words, 50 to 60% of the residential mortgages involved MERS at that time.

Your's may be one of them. If so, the first few pages will identify MERS as beneficiary or mortgagee and also as nominee. If your mortgage doesn't mention MERS, the material that follows won't be important to your fight against the foreclosure machine and you may want to skip the remainder of this section.

Whether or not MERS is involved in your mortgage, the discussion, suggestions, and foreclosure fundamentals in *Fighting the Foreclosure Machine* apply equally well for you. The rules of the fight, set out in Chapters 9 through 12, are just as important to you as to those borrowers whose mortgages don't mention MERS. I think, however, you will find that the inclusion of MERS offers additional defensive and offensive legal weapons not available to the other borrowers.

The title of this section is also the title of my next book, which is scheduled to be released shortly. *ShellGame-MERS: Contrived Confusion* is the result of work that has spanned almost two years. A judge or jury presented with the evidence I've compiled will likely think the title appropriate. I think the evidence, most of which should be admissible in a court of law, establishes that Mortgage Electronic Registration Systems, Inc., is an entity of no substance, and is used as part of a contrived scam to help the industry's foreclosure machine more easily take homes from borrowers. The MERS name is invoked in foreclosure processes in ways that confuse both judges and borrowers. The uses of its name imply proper and legal circumstances when the facts strongly suggest that the industry and its machine know otherwise.

The mortgage finance industry, its foreclosure machine, and people unfamiliar with the circumstances surrounding what they refer to as MERS paint the wrong picture for judges in foreclosure cases, and they don't correct the record when an incorrect description of MERS is before the judge. A typical misleading statement about MERS might be "Mortgage Electronic Registration Systems, Inc., is a private company that operates an electronic registry which tracks servicing rights and ownership of mortgage loans as it performs its responsibilities for lenders and their successors." The descriptions suggest that MERS is actually an active entity, involved with the mortgages registered in its name and engaged in being a good servant to the Bosses of the Notes secured by those mortgages.

The growing body of evidence suggests a totally different reality. *ShellGame-MERS: Contrived Confusion* will set out the evidence in detail. The essential facts, however, are summarized below.

To begin with, the acronym MERS refers to two entities— MERSCORP, Inc., and its subsidiary, Mortgage Electronic Registration Systems, Inc. The use of MERS for both entities means that an unwary person who sees the name MERS in a document can think the information is about Mortgage Electronic Registration Systems, Inc., when the comments and testimony are actually about MERSCORP, Inc.

The wealth of the mortgage finance industry and the vast resources available to it lead one to think that the resulting confusion is intentional. You may want to give the benefit of the doubt to the industry and its foreclosure machine, but I'm not so inclined.

Some of the confusion to which I refer relates to the fact that the parent corporation has a copyright on the acronym MERS. The parent's business members are regularly identified as MERS Members, and the rules by which that membership operates have historically been called MERS Rules of Membership. MERSCORP's website address is www.mersinc.org, which looks like it belongs to the subsidiary rather than the parent company. MERSCORP also owns and operates an electronic database it calls the MERS System, which is filled with information owned and provided by parent's business members. Yet in foreclosure lawsuits the four letters "MERS" are supposed to be about Mortgage Electronic Registration Systems, Inc., because that name is on the mortgage document. The information provided to the courts, however, is usually about MERSCORP rather than its subsidiary.

The term MERS can't be used in court or even here in this discussion without risk of confusion. That has been happening for too many years and it is time to get things straight. I have elected, therefore, to assign the name ShellGame-MERS to Mortgage Electronic Registration Systems, Inc.

Facts about ShellGame-MERS conflict with the typical descriptions of that entity that judges see. The evidence, for example, appears to support the following:

- ShellGame-MERS has no employees.

- It has no operating revenue.

- It has no tangible assets.

- It owns no mortgage and has no ownership or financial stake in any mortgage, meaning it is never a beneficiary or mortgagee under any normal use of those terms.

- It doesn't own or operate an electronic registry involving mortgage loans.

- It doesn't track information as to mortgage loan ownership or control.

- It did not compile the information included on the electronic database its parent company makes available to the industry, nor does it own any rights to that information.

- It conducts no audit regarding the accuracy of the information placed by the industry on the parent company's electronic data system, nor does it have any legal right to audit any of that information.

- Its parent company, MERSCORP, Inc., authorizes other companies to appoint people to execute formal documents in the name of ShellGame-MERS. The so-called certifying officers sign legal documents as if they are a Vice President or Assistant Secretary of ShellGame-MERS.

- The certifying officers who execute documents in the name of ShellGame-MERS receive their instructions from, and report to, the companies they work for, rather than ShellGame-MERS.

- Assignments and transfers or affidavits issued in the name of ShellGame-MERS during foreclosure lawsuits are issued by a company helping take a borrower's home, and not by ShellGame-MERS.

- ShellGame-MERS doesn't know about all of the documents that are executed in its name, and it has no right to demand that the certifying officers provide such information, or that their employers do so.

- It doesn't know the identity of the Boss of a particular Note and doesn't maintain information that would permit it to do so. That is, it doesn't track the ownership and control of Notes or mortgages.

- ShellGame-MERS doesn't communicate with Bosses of Notes during foreclosure processes. That is, it doesn't act as a servant in those cases and isn't carrying out instructions from a Boss respecting the subject Note and mortgage. That lack of communication with a Boss regarding a foreclosure also means that ShellGame-MERS isn't directing any company or certifying officer to carry out the wishes of a Boss regarding the subject Note and mortgage.

These are the kinds of conclusions that a judge or jury could possibly reach based on evidence that is compiled, cited, and referenced in *ShellGame-MERS: Contrived Confusion.* This type of information could help educate your judge about things important to your lawsuit.

Having ShellGame-MERS involved in your foreclosure might turn out to be a plus for you. Here are a few reasons why:

Reason One: The law in your state may require a mortgage to identify a bona fide beneficiary, mortgagee, or servant holding title for the true owner of the mortgage. In such states, the mere presence of ShellGame-MERS in the mortgage's chain of title may create legal issues as to the validity of the mortgage. ShellGame-MERS doesn't appear to satisfy any of those requirements, yet it is identified as the title holder in millions of mortgages. If your mortgage can be invalidated, or there is even the risk to your opponent of that happening, this might improve settlement opportunities for you. (See Chapter 7.)

Reason Two: The presence of ShellGame-MERS tends to negate, or at least make questionable, each and every assignment or transfer of the Note or mortgage to any company the machine says obtained interests in either from ShellGame-MERS. If it doesn't own the Note or mortgage, and it isn't acting as a servant for the Boss of the Note, it can't transfer them. So, if your opponent says its right to foreclose traces back to ShellGame-MERS or something received from ShellGame-MERS, your opponent's claims would be invalid under this scenario.

You, therefore, want to make your opponent prove the detailed circumstances of each transfer, assignment or affidavit allegedly made by ShellGame-MERS. Failure to provide that information will show that your opponent can't prove Boss status for itself or the company for which it works.

Reason Three: The name of ShellGame-MERS shows up when the mortgage is first made. After that, it rarely surfaces in the documents about your Note until a foreclosure is in progress or anticipated. If a purported transfer of a Note or mortgage is made in anticipation of a foreclosure, that fact may undermine the recipient's right to status as a holder in due course. (See Chapter 11.) Accordingly, if ShellGame-MERS is involved in your lawsuit, there is a strong likelihood your opponent is not a holder in due course in accordance with the UCC. Even if it can prove Boss status, without holder in due course status, it would be subject to legal claims and defenses you might have related to predatory or deceptive lending practices of your lender.

Reason Four: The foreclosure machine generally manages the foreclosure process and also gives directions regarding the use of ShellGame-MERS's name. That means your opponent also probably knows that ShellGame-MERS isn't actually involved as an owner, or servant of the Boss, of your Note. If the judge or jury understands this, your opponent may be liable for trying to foreclose when it knows it has no right to do so. That would be a form of deception or bad faith. If your state recognizes deceptive or bad faith business or foreclosure practice claims in lawsuits, the presence of ShellGame-MERS, along with admissible evidence about its true colors, might be enough for you to launch an even stronger case against it when protecting your rights and home.

Reason Five: You may be able to put more pressure on your opponent if your judge becomes aware of how the name of ShellGame-MERS is used and that it has no genuine substance. Your cause and your case are stronger the more your judge is suspicious of your opponent's methods, motivation, and connections with ShellGame-MERS.

You may find that you have more ammunition with which to take on your opponent if ShellGame-MERS is named in your mortgage. Diligently applying the rules and strategies in *Recipe For The Foreclosure Fight* (see Chapters 9 through 12) is a strong approach to take when you're challenging an opponent that is tied in any way to ShellGame-MERS.

THE FORECLOSURE MACHINE

Many companies make up what I refer to as the foreclosure machine. They don't refer to themselves this way and I doubt they have badges or secret handshakes that proclaim their membership in what I think is clearly an organized foreclosure network. This network, whether united by common business practices or contractual arrangement does the bidding of the mortgage finance industry. Some members of the industry make extra money by providing foreclosure services for the machine. A particular foreclosure shop may be a bank, loan servicer, foreclosure trustee or law office. My experience and research convince me they are cut from the same cloth, use the same tactics, and have the same vulnerabilities. I coined this descriptive phrase for their group, and think it appropriate as an educational tool.

CHAPTER 5

MAKING THE DECISION TO FIGHT BACK

WHY FIGHTING BACK MIGHT MAKE SENSE FOR YOU

The mortgage finance industry and its mortgage machine are well-financed, experienced, and powerful. Why would you want to undertake a battle against such formidable foes?

First, and foremost, you should know that the mortgage finance industry fraternity does, in fact, lose in court. Its members have experienced more adverse decisions in recent times.[43] As an article in *The Washington Post* noted in October 2010, "Now, as many of these loans have fallen into default and banks have sought to seize homes, judges around the country have increasingly ruled that lenders had no right to foreclose...."[44]

The law, the infrastructure of the mortgage finance industry, and its recent foreclosure record support optimism that the mortgage finance industry will lose by escalating numbers as more borrowers assert their fundamental legal rights. Many reasons for this hopefulness are mentioned in this book.

When you enter a lawsuit, you and your legal advisor, if you have one, can only estimate the outcome. Certainty of result is rarely part of the litigation process. That is just how it is. The uncertainty can be uncomfortable, but people go to court about civil matters like foreclosure because they think litigation is the best of their alternatives.

You have been targeted and made a foreclosure victim by the mortgage finance industry. Your debt and the condition of the real estate market in your area reflect the artificial appraisal values created by the industry when you took out the loan. Your inability to make payments reflects an economy weakened by the mortgage finance industry. You were put at risk without your knowledge, and your reward, if the industry has its way, is to make you pay more than a fair share of the national recovery costs now being borne across these United States. At the most rudimentary level, your choices are to let the industry do what it wants, or else to fight back. *Fighting the Foreclosure Machine* is written so you and your advisers might be better informed as you decide which course of action is best for you.

You may have no choice about the path you now take, but if you choose to fight back to protect your home, I believe you'll discover that it will be worth the effort and that you'll find more rewards than disadvantages. A foreclosure lawsuit is your opportunity to reduce or eliminate the debt on your home, to live there for an extended time without making mortgage payments or owing rent, to reinstate or at least improve your credit report, and to get some relief from the wrongs caused by the mortgage finance industry that won't otherwise be there for you. Not fighting eliminates those possibilities.

Your chances of beating the machine are high. You will gain the satisfaction of having your legal rights upheld against the system that put you and our country in this economic mess.

Right now, I can almost hear you saying, "There's no way I can afford to fight my foreclosure." You may be surprised to learn that the cost of your fight should be less than the amount of money you'll save by not paying for a place to live while the litigation is ongoing, or, if you rent your home to a tenant during the fight, less than the rental income you can generate while your judge is deciding the questions about your legal rights.

I recognize that deciding whether or not to fight back is not easy. It's a matter to which you will want to give careful and thoughtful consideration. This chapter and the two that follow go into more detail about some of the points that you'll want to take into account.

LITIGATION MAY BE YOUR ONLY HOPE

As a foreclosure victim, you won't likely find much relief outside a courtroom. Consumer advocates, the media, and the government are not going to be of real help.

Advocates for foreclosure victims have been pushing for years for investigations and change, without notable success.

Reports of fraud or deceptive predatory lending and foreclosure practices make the news when high-profile corporate or governmental entities and individuals are involved. Stories about down-on-their-luck people who are being foreclosed rarely get attention, and certainly not in a way that provides them with real assistance.

Government officials face complex problems as they try to undo the widespread hurt that the mortgage finance industry has caused. They must grapple with equally difficult issues as they seek to devise ways to protect America from more of the same in future years. Whatever may come from the complicated process of democratic give-and-take, it will likely come too late to help most people reading this book.

If you have been foreclosed, or if you can see that possibility looming, you can't reasonably anticipate that legislative or regulatory change will happen before your dealings with the foreclosure machine are finished. When change comes, it will probably be prospective—in other words, it will make a difference only to people who may face such problems in the future. It will be of little help to those who, by then, will have already been foreclosed and moved on with their lives.

So, if you join the ranks of those who have been foreclosed, don't anticipate help from any future national disaster relief fund or consumer protection law. Hope for it, yes; expect it, no.

If you're reading this book, your alternatives have probably been reduced to one of two actions: do what the foreclosure machine tells you to do, or fight it in court. You can let them ruin your credit, take your home, and continue the industry's pretense that delinquent borrowers have caused the current economic mess, or you can force their hand.

LITIGATION MAY NOT BE A GOOD OPTION

You may have been dealt a hand that gives you no room for litigation. It could be that the economy has left you with barely enough money to cover basic necessities, or that you must move to find employment, or that you're working multiple jobs to get by and have no time to devote to protecting your credit and home through formal litigation. The high cost and many demands involved in earning a living and taking care of yourself and your loved ones may have you stretched too thin to take on other endeavors.

Keep in mind that you're but one person within ranks of millions of foreclosure victims, and don't feel guilty if going to court isn't the best option for you and your family. If you can't make a formal fight, you can't do it.

Something you can do is look for opportunities to vote for legislators interested in a cure that is more than just a Band-Aid or lip service with little genuine merit. Your voice, whether in or out of court, can help other foreclosure victims and America find a way to avoid a similar catastrophe in the future. (See Chapter 13.) Regardless of the path you have to take, be OK with yourself and with others who are also foreclosure victims.

THE PRESENCE OF SHELLGAME-MERS MAY BE A PLUS

About half of all foreclosures today involve a mortgage or a deed of trust that includes Mortgage Electronic Registration Systems, Inc., as a beneficiary, mortgagee, or nominee (meaning agent or servant). That is the company I refer to as ShellGame-MERS. Some people who don't know the facts behind this company or who choose to ignore them still refer to it as MERS. I believe my label is more accurate.

If your mortgage mentions ShellGame-MERS, you're in luck. You have better odds and more opportunities to defeat the industry's foreclosure machine. While you should stick to the foreclosure fundamentals mentioned in this book, you have an additional weapon. Whether ShellGame-MERS is listed as a party to your foreclosure or in the chain of title for the mortgage, its involvement improves your chances that the mortgage will be unenforceable. Its presence helps keep the burden of proof on the foreclosure machine and taints the machine's credibility, which makes stopping your foreclosure more doable. If your foreclosure involves ShellGame-MERS, look at the section titled *ShellGame-MERS: Contrived Confusion* in Chapter 4.

JUDICIAL VERSUS NONJUDICIAL FORECLOSURE

The decision you make about fighting the foreclosure machine may be affected by whether yours is a judicial or nonjudicial foreclosure. That distinction affects the nature of your options and the timeframe you have available for taking action.

Judicial Foreclosure

If your home is taken in an uncontested judicial foreclosure, you should not anticipate ever receiving any compensation or relief. In the judicial foreclosure arena, if you decline to put up a fight when you're first given an opportunity to contest the foreclosure machine's claims, you won't likely get another chance. When you're served a summons and complaint by the foreclosure machine, you have to fight back right then or else just walk away.

Some courts permit you to reopen a case when extreme circumstances caused you to miss a response deadline. Your failure to respond may be excused if, for example, you were never actually served the summons, or if serious illness or injury prevented your response, or if deception by your opponent caused you not to respond, or if your opponent has no jurisdiction to have initiated the legal action in the first place.

However, a court isn't required to let you reopen a case just because you ask it to. The only certain way to have your day in court is to respond to the lawsuit in accordance with the court's rules and its time schedule.

Nonjudicial Foreclosure

If your home is taken in an uncontested nonjudicial foreclosure, most states permit you to sue the machine later with a primary goal of getting paid for the wrongful taking of your home. If the machine still owns the house when you start that suit, you may be able to get it back if that is your choice. However, if the house has been already foreclosed and sold to a company or person unrelated to your opponent, it is probably gone forever.

If you don't contest the nonjudicial foreclosure before the foreclosure takes place, you may or may not be able to stay in the house while you sue the machine. After the house is sold, your opponent will want to evict whoever is living there.

Some states won't stop an eviction when the complaining person is challenging the validity of the foreclosure. For example, Texas and Oregon don't let the person facing eviction challenge the foreclosure as part of the eviction case. After the house has been sold, the person being evicted can bring a separate lawsuit challenging the foreclosure and seeking money damages. But he or she must vacate the premises after the sale unless the legal argument is based on something more than the claim that the nonjudicial foreclosure was invalid.

California, on the other hand, requires the person challenging eviction to raise the question about the validity of the foreclosure during the eviction trial. If the issue isn't raised then, the person loses the right to bring up that legal question later.

Therefore, if you want to stay in the house while you fight back, you need to make certain that your state permits you to challenge the validity of the nonjudicial foreclosure process during the eviction case. If it doesn't, you must sue to stop the foreclosure before it happens.

Once the foreclosure has taken place, you may still be able to recover monetary damages by suing whoever caused the foreclosure. Most states will permit you to do this. Usually the very fact that the foreclosure was not supervised or monitored by a court means you can still have your day in court later if you so desire. As discussed in Chapter 6, suing for money rather than home ownership also gives you more opportunities to access legal services on a contingency-fee basis.

SOME BENEFITS OF FIGHTING BACK

The Benefits of More Time

Time may be your friend. If you sue to stop a foreclosure, or if you respond in opposition to a foreclosure lawsuit filed against you, the machine will have to put more time and money into the fight, and no foreclosure can take place during the litigation.

In 2010, the foreclosure machine experienced delays of about 16 months from the time the borrower ceased making mortgage payments to the time when he or she was evicted.[45] This was true even though the vast majority of borrowers targeted for foreclosure never put up a fight. The average amount of time for a foreclosure case to run its course will most likely increase, and substantially so, as more homeowners resist wrongful foreclosures. A lawsuit that seriously engages the foreclosure machine in the fundamental legal issues and procedures stressed by this book will most likely last for one-and-a-half to two-and-a-half years. Your case might be shorter or it might be longer, but that is a reasonable estimate. Your house remains yours during this period.

Having this extra time offers you a number of options and benefits, as outlined below. Some of them will be more important to you than others, so focus on those that seem the most relevant to your situation.

➤ No Mortgage Payments During the Lawsuit

If you elect to fight to hold onto your home, you won't need to make mortgage payments during the litigation, even if you continue to live there. It is your home until the machine proves otherwise. If the lawsuit goes the way you hope, no mortgage payments may be required after the lawsuit ends either. But at least during the fight you won't need to pay mortgage costs or rent if you stay in your home. That savings may be enough to pay for the lawsuit, and perhaps with some left over to help you get by.

➤ More Time for Your Home's Value to Rise

The longer you hold on to your home, the more chance its value may increase. Keeping another foreclosed home out of your neighborhood market will help improve property values for you and your neighbors. You will have a better chance of settling with the machine if your home has a higher market value. An increase in value is also to your benefit if you manage to keep the house with reduced debt or no debt against it at all.

➤ *More Time to Sell Your Home*

The real estate market is terrible in most places, but if you're able to hold onto your home longer, a buyer may show up. A serious offer from a purchaser at a reasonable price may enable you to settle the lawsuit on favorable terms.

If what you would like to have is a restored credit rating (the machine can do that as part of a settlement), some cash in your pocket, and freedom from continued litigation, a ready and willing buyer may be just what's needed to structure a settlement that works for both you and the machine. The machine knows that the results of litigation are uncertain, and the sale will give it the opportunity for some measure of recovery under the Note. This may be the right combination upon which you and your opponent can strike a reasonable bargain.

➤ *The Potential for Rental Income*

If you decide that your best course is to leave your home while you fight the foreclosure, you might rent the house as a way to gain some income. It is your home unless and until it is actually taken in a foreclosure. While it's yours, you have the right to rent it to others and use the proceeds in any way you see fit. The rental income could help defray your litigation costs or contribute to your living expenses. As much as possible, you'll want to find responsible tenants who will take care of your home, because you may still be the owner when the fight is over.

If you have a tenant, and a foreclosure actually happens, the tenant will have a minimum of 90 days notice to vacate the premises under the federal Protecting Tenants at Foreclosure Act of 2009 (PTFA), which is in force through 2014. Under this law, a reasonable lease made prior to a notice of foreclosure or a foreclosure lawsuit must be honored by the party that does the foreclosure. Any person or business that buys the house from the foreclosing party must also respect the terms of your tenant's lease unless the buyer wants the home as his or her residence. A purchaser who buys the house to live in also has to give the tenant at least 90 days to move out. If the PTFA is of interest to you, it can be viewed online.[46]

➤ *More Pain for the Industry*

Gaining revenge and teaching the bad guys a lesson are part of American tradition. This is especially so when the retribution and punishment are dispensed through our courts. The mortgage finance industry has hurt you, your neighbors, and our country. Your lawsuit is an opportunity to inflict financial pain on the industry. (See "More Voices Are Easier To Hear" in Chapter 13 for more information about the magnitude of the money pain that can be inflicted by borrowers who fight back.) The longer your litigation lasts, the more pain the industry will experience. The more defeats the industry suffers, the more pain it will feel. Fighting back against the industry that caused our problems and that now sends its lackeys to take your house may feel good regardless of the ultimate outcome of the lawsuit. That may be of value also, in and of itself.

➤ *More Time for Leaders to Find a Fair Solution*

If the nationwide fight against the foreclosure machine grows longer and more massive, the more likely it becomes that people in power will find solutions that may help you and others in your predicament. A legal fight gives you a chance to best the foreclosure machine by yourself. It also adds your voice to the voices of other foreclosure victims. The chorus of Americans demanding help and change could potentially lead to a fairness and wisdom not currently present in our system.

The Possibility of Judicial Appeal

After a ruling is made in your lawsuit, either you or your opponent can ask a higher court to review and change the lower court's judgment. An appeal could stretch out the suit for another year or two or three.

If you stopped the foreclosure and your opponent appeals the decision, the house is yours during the appeal. But suppose the lower court rules in favor of your opponent. You probably can continue to live there pending the appeal. The conceptual ground for postponement of the foreclosure is this: the house must still be there for you should you win on appeal, and the only way to make sure this happens is to suspend the foreclosure until the whole legal dispute is fully resolved.

What if the house is rented during the appeal? If the lower court's order was in your favor, the rental income should be available to you. If you're appealing an unfavorable court decision, then the rent income may not be available to you during the appeal. Treatment of rental income under that circumstance will depend on the law of your state. If the rental income is not available to you during the appeal, you will most likely get it, less the costs of maintaining the house, when a favorable decision is issued by the appellate court.

The Possibility of Improving Your Credit

If you need this book, your credit rating is already a mess, or soon will be. A foreclosure won't make it worse. Fighting the foreclosure machine might, however, do a lot to clean up your credit report.

Beat the machine in court and you will have the right proof to demonstrate that past mortgage payment glitches were a mistake and should be expunged from your credit history. If the machine offers to settle with you, cleaning up the black marks it put on your credit history could be made part of the settlement.

There's no guarantee that fighting back will improve your credit score, but your score definitely won't get better if you let your house go without a fight.

Improved Settlement Options

If your opponent sees that you're serious and are raising good legal arguments, it may at some point offer to settle the lawsuit under terms you find acceptable. A settlement could entail reduction of the principal of your loan, waiver of past interest or penalty charges, improvement of your credit history, or affordable loan repayment terms.

Not fighting back cuts off these possibilities, however. If a borrower doesn't fight back, the foreclosure machine has no incentive to modify the loan to something that is fairer and more just. As with a bike, only the squeaky wheel gets special attention. Making noise is good, if your circumstances let you get into the fight.

It isn't advisable to enter a lawsuit with a hope of settling. In fact, my suggestion would be to not waste time thinking about settlement unless and until your opponent opens that door. You need to believe in the merit of your case and commit to the fight. That is, I think, the most comfortable and effective way to be in a lawsuit.

You have a chance to beat the machine using laws designed to protect you from such bullies, and that's where your focus should lie. If the machine doesn't like the fact that you're identifying and picking on its weaknesses, settlement may become a viable possibility.

CUT YOUR LOSSES WHEN POSSIBLE

The foreclosure machine will be able to foreclose in some instances. Statistical probability alone suggests that the mammoth mortgage finance industry has to get things right now and then.

If your opponent comes forward with legally sufficient proof of its right to demand payments under the Note and its right to foreclose, you should again weigh your options. That may be a good time for you to initiate settlement. Your leverage would be that, unless the machine settles, you could tie it up in court for a long time. Once the first suit finishes, you could appeal, adding months to the process. Then you might stretch things out even more with a bankruptcy. Until the machine has your rights limited and defined by a written and court-approved settlement agreement, the possibility exists that new evidence might appear that will weaken its case or that our leaders may require a fairer and better-reasoned treatment of people in your situation.

If a decent settlement isn't likely, cutting your losses may be the right move. Being prepared to stop spending time and money when the facts are against you is a good way to remain comfortable with the legal process. Engaging in litigation doesn't mean you have to continue the formalities after you no longer believe you can prevail.

Information is the key to your decision about when to stop the fight, should that day come. This book stresses aggressive fact-finding pursuant to your court's rules. (See Chapter 10.) One purpose of your fact-finding work is to enable you to assess the merit or lack thereof of your opponent's case, and sooner rather than later. The more you learn about your opponent's facts, the better positioned you will be to estimate the weakness or strength of your opponent's case and your own.

If your opponent has a strong case, it should be able to produce its proof early on in response to your informal or formal discovery. If the machine makes a lot of excuses about why it should not be required to provide the information you demand, or if you see a lack of the information necessary for it to prove its case, those are signs that should inspire confidence.

Pushing to see your opponent's proof for its claims early in the case will help you avoid wasting time or money. If you're one of the unlucky borrowers who can't beat the machine, at least not by using the foreclosure fundamentals discussed in this book, you will learn that fairly quickly. The time, energy, and money you spend to reach that decision point should not be unbearable. You have already been placed in the uncomfortable spot of being targeted for foreclosure. A little more discomfort may not be so bad, especially since you will have the satisfaction of knowing that you have done everything you could.

Foreclosure victims are tough and are made tougher by the role forced on them by the mortgage finance industry. Unless you have circumstances that strongly point you away from a legal fight with the machine, don't be too concerned about the money and effort you're spending. You control when you stop the fight. Be diligent and relentless in demanding and getting whatever facts your opponent can muster. Use the methods of informal and formal discovery as a way to maintain focus and control. If the day comes when you think you should stop the fight, you will have that power. The result won't likely be worse than losing your home.

JUDGMENT PROOF?

Will litigation expose you to more risks than the foreclosure itself? Probably not. Sure, there will be extra costs and more time committed to defending your home, but if tackling the machine in court doesn't actually make your financial situation a lot worse, then why not give yourself the chance to beat the machine?

If the amount of the debt your opponent claims is due is more than the price your house would bring if it were sold at a foreclosure sale (which is the usual result these days), your attacker may have a right to collect the difference after the house is sold. That is called a deficiency judgment.

Your state law dictates whether you risk being saddled with a deficiency judgment against you even if the house is taken by foreclosure. If that is your situation, then fighting back is your opportunity to avoid a deficiency judgment. If your finances are upside down, one more unpaid creditor claim is probably not very important. Go into your court battle knowing that, if you lose, your opponent won't be scarier just because it claims you still owe it something. A deficiency judgment is unsecured, and it can be virtually eliminated in bankruptcy if your creditors get to be too much of a bother.

When a creditor must spend more to collect money from someone than it can expect to recover, that debtor is said to be judgment proof. Creditors often have little interest in a debt owed by someone who can't pay or who can easily dismiss the debt in bankruptcy. If you're judgment proof, fighting back to defend your house is a chance to salvage something for you and your family, and without much, if any, risk that your situation can get any worse.

BANKRUPTCY PROTECTION

The foreclosure fundamentals highlighted by *Fighting the Foreclosure Machine* work equally well in state and federal courts, including the federal bankruptcy court. If you're having trouble with bill collectors, even though you've stopped or will have to stop paying the mortgage, bankruptcy may be right for you.

Most people who choose bankruptcy are embarrassed and hate doing it. Nevertheless, the ranks of bankrupt citizens have expanded as a result of the bad economy we've been experiencing. Seeking protection in bankruptcy doesn't bear the societal taint that it had before the oil industry downturn in the early 1980s, the demise of the savings and loan industry in the late 1980s and early 1990s, and now the lingering recession caused by the mortgage finance industry, which has been with us since 2007.

Bankruptcy is actually a highly regarded financial planning tool within the business community and among people seeking stability when creditor pressures become overwhelming. Bankruptcy protection is available by law because it forces a fair balance of the rights of the debtor and all of the creditors. Otherwise the biggest, wealthiest, most aggressive, or loudest companies would bully the debtor and the other creditors and ignore their legitimate interests. Placing yourself before the bankruptcy court may be the best action to take as you fight back against the foreclosure machine.

A bankruptcy court is comfortable denying claims of companies that assert creditor status but cannot prove their claims when challenged. Many bankruptcy judges have demonstrated skill at uncovering and not being swayed by the hot air of the foreclosure machine.[47] The machine often does a poor job when filing the required proof of claim against the bankrupt person. That sloppiness plus the difficulty the machine has in simply identifying the Boss of the Note can give the bankrupt borrower improved odds of success.

Bankruptcy court is a federal court that applies state law under an umbrella of federal bankruptcy law. Your rights regarding your home and the protections to which you are entitled will be mostly determined by the bankruptcy judge's application of your state law or by the judge's sending your case against the foreclosure machine to a state court for determination of those state law issues. The lessons of *Fighting the Foreclosure Machine* are important in a bankruptcy setting, just as in any other court. That's another reason why, when I talk about key topics addressed in this book—the Boss of your Note, the UCC, aggressive informal and formal fact-finding, the burden of proof being your opponent's problem, and the necessity of being accurate in how formal statements are presented to your judge—I label them as foreclosure fundamentals.

When you elect bankruptcy protection, that step halts all creditor threats and pressures against you until and unless the bankruptcy judge rules otherwise. The people and companies trying to take your money have to stop doing that as soon as the bankruptcy is filed. Protection under the Bankruptcy Code may be what you need so you can better manage all of your debts and minimize creditor distractions while you focus on your fight with the foreclosure machine.

An individual may qualify for more than one type of bankruptcy. You get to pick the type that's best for you before the bankruptcy starts. The types of bankruptcy cases are typically labeled with the number of the related chapter of the Bankruptcy Code (11 U.S.C. §§ 101, et seq.). The qualification standards, what the bankrupt debtor can and cannot do, the level of control over the debtor's property, and the expected results vary depending on the type of bankruptcy selected. Depending on your circumstances, you might be allowed to choose treatment under the Code's Chapter 7 (liquidation), Chapter 11 (reorganization), Chapter 12 (family farmer or fisherman), or Chapter 13 (individual adjustment of debt). The facts of your situation and what you want to accomplish will determine which type of bankruptcy would be best for you.

Bankruptcies under Chapters 11, 12, and 13 give you the most control and management of your assets during and after the bankruptcy. The Chapter 7 bankruptcy gives you the least control.

You do not have to be totally broke or destitute before you initiate a bankruptcy and have its protection available. In fact, you can file a bankruptcy even if the value of all of your assets is higher than the total debt from all of your legitimate creditors. If that court can help you better manage and reasonably take care of your debts, you'll usually have that choice. I mention this in case you live in a state where the bankruptcy court has been more actively addressing the foreclosure fundamentals addressed by this book. If you think bankruptcy court is the best judicial forum for your fight, then you might want to look more into that possibility. You can use bankruptcy even when your plan is to pay 100% of the debt to all of your legitimate creditors while achieving a stronger litigation posture against the foreclosure machine or others who do not have legitimate claims against you.

Whether you fight back in a state court, the federal district court, or the bankruptcy court, the act of challenging the machine keeps open the potential for a settlement or some kind of relief that you will not get if you let the foreclosure machine take your home without a fight.

If the machine causes you to use bankruptcy protection, don't feel bad. A bankruptcy undertaken for the purpose of fighting back against the foreclosure machine should not be that difficult to explain to friends and family who care about you.

If you need breathing room because of too many bills and bill collectors, think about bankruptcy. If you think the bankruptcy judge is more experienced with the laws designed to protect you, think about bankruptcy. Learn more about your options, costs, and likely results by consulting with a bankruptcy attorney who represents debtors. The initial session with the attorney will be more useful if you take a summary of your assets and debts with you. That information will help the attorney give you better guidance.

CHAPTER 6

LAYING THE GROUNDWORK FOR YOUR FIGHT

MAYBE, JUST MAYBE, YOU NEED TO FIGHT BACK

Your financial worries have been on your back too long. You know your house will be taken, your credit will be ruined, and you will have to find somewhere else to live unless something changes. You have more than enough problems and uncertainty in your life. Deciding to fight back may bring a little comfort and certainty you didn't have before. Fighting back through your court offers you a possibility—not a guarantee—of getting something better than what you'll have if you don't challenge the foreclosure machine.

The money side of the possibility is an incentive, but you may also gain refreshing stability that won't be yours if all you do is take instructions from the foreclosure machine. The fight will let you stay at home longer, and the "how long" will no longer be dictated solely by those who want to kick you out. Extra time may be just what you need so you can get a little breathing room.

Many borrowers who elect to fight back will find a higher level of comfort and purpose. Just engaging in the fight may make you feel better about yourself. Your fight may also help your neighbors. They don't need their home values depressed further by having another foreclosed home dumped on the market at a below-market price by the same industry that created our economic mess.

You have a lot to think about. *Fighting the Foreclosure Machine* is an information resource that can help you make a well-reasoned and balanced decision. If you decide to assert your legal rights, the foreclosure fundamentals this book discusses should serve you well during your lawsuit against the foreclosure machine.

YOUR LITIGATION ADVERSARIES

The mortgage finance industry has nurtured and grown a foreclosure network that appears to coordinate its overall effort in order to get the maximum number of foreclosures. Most often, it uses businesses that specialize in foreclosures to do the dirty work. Foreclosure shops handle foreclosures for the industry members, whether or not ShellGame-MERS is involved.

You will be up against people who pretty much use the same procedures and methods nationwide, regardless who they say they are working for when attacking you. What these foreclosure shops do for Deutsche Bank is basically the same as what they do for Wells Fargo, U.S. Bank, Bank of America, and other companies whose names may be less familiar to you.

They use local attorneys when a foreclosure actually goes to court. In those cases the directions to the attorney come from the management team working for the industry's foreclosure machine.

In court your opponents will be nicely dressed, and they will generally be pleasant, friendly people. They are often in a good mood. Of course, they are being paid to be there and they don't have much at stake whether the case is won or lost. Don't you wish you were so fortunate?

The days of people "duking it out" on the courthouse steps are in the past. Most courts have no patience with rudeness or uncivil behavior. If you decide to put up a fight, you should anticipate a polite and respectful courtroom environment, and you should do your part to keep it that way. Even if your opponent makes provoking or vexatious statements, do yourself a favor by ignoring them. Concentrate on helping your judge and yourself stick to the controlling facts and law.

DON'T ACCEPT FORECLOSURE VICTIM PROFILING

For all of their politeness, don't expect that your adversaries will be kind or understanding. Their intention is to fit you into their carefully cultivated profile of foreclosure victims—people who are under so much pressure that they don't defend themselves. The foreclosure machine has enjoyed substantial success by simply telling the borrowers that the foreclosure process has started. Millions of people, when faced with the machine's threats, have walked away from a sad situation that did not look like it could get better. Who could blame them? They had too little money, too much grief and embarrassment, and not enough understanding of their legal rights—and they were being threatened by what appeared to be a well-funded and knowledgeable adversary.

The mortgage finance industry knows the profile of the typical borrower it targets for foreclosure. It will approach you assuming you're cut of that same old cloth.

As an example, look at the situation of a typical borrower—we'll call her Mary—who misses a few mortgage payments. Aware that she's falling behind, she begins to worry. When she gets a notice of default tied to a threat of foreclosure, she assumes that the notice has legal merit. She believes it is coming from someone who has a legal right to demand payment from her and to foreclose if she doesn't pay what that person demands.

Mary knows her financial situation is terrible. Her mortgage debt is higher than the value of her house, so she has little chance of selling the house to pay off the debt. She knows she can't bring the mortgage current. She can't even make the monthly payments required by her contract, according to her understanding of what that contract entails. Mary has a lot less money now that the economy has turned so sour. She sees no upside and no future that includes keeping her home.

She tries to engage the threatening company in dialogue with a hope of finding a solution with which she can live. But she gets no response, or else a response that is little more than a repeat of the default notice— "Pay up or lose your house."

Mary is embarrassed at the prospect of being kicked out of her home and neighborhood. She is concerned about what her friends and family will think when she's forced to disclose that she can't pay her bills. Her energies are expended on guilt, coping with a tough day-to-day existence, and trying to deal with a foreclosure shop that can only repeat, "Our way or the highway."

Mary has all the symptoms of a foreclosure victim, and that is exactly what the industry's machine wants. The machine knows, based on millions of uncontested foreclosures, that treating the borrower as a loser usually leads to an easy taking of the victim's home. The machine wants Mary to remain ignorant of her legal rights and the cause of her predicament. It wants her to stay immersed in debilitating emotions.

What Mary doesn't know is that notices threatening foreclosure are often sent by companies that have no legal right to demand payment and no right to start a foreclosure. Her attacker, of course, won't disclose this flaw. It definitely doesn't want to relieve her stress. The machine will do what it can to keep her in the dark and maintain pressures designed to wear her down. It will give no hint of weakness and will act as if it is right in everything it says and does.

The machine's objective is to do the same to you.

Contrary to the industry's master plan, you and other borrowers targeted for foreclosure do have options and bargaining power. You no longer have to take your opponent's word for anything. The legal system gives you the power to make the foreclosure machine leave you alone unless it can prove each of its claims with hard facts. Coming up with that proof is something the machine is struggling with these days, and there is a good chance it will be unable to do so in your case.

The foreclosure machine will treat you like the other borrowers who walked away once they knew they had been targeted for foreclosure. It wants you to wear a coat fashioned from its preferences about how you should respond to their advance. It wants to include you in the historical profile of foreclosure victims.

You, however, have more information and more options than Mary and other borrowers had in past years. That fact alone excludes you from the profile of foreclosure victims that has been constructed by the industry's foreclosure machine.

LEGAL HELP AND RESOURCES

You need to go to court if you want to protect your rights and defend your home. Being represented by an attorney is your wisest course because the courtroom can be a confusing place. The body of law consists of procedures and legal guides which are defined by statutes, court rules, and judicial interpretations. Each is a source of legal authority which has a measure of importance to the final outcome of a lawsuit.

You can lose a case by not following proper procedures even if your underlying legal theory has merit. Legal documents are an interactive maze that is best navigated by people familiar with that exercise. I therefore hope you will have an attorney helping you at some level. I say "at some level" because, as discussed below, there are various ways that an attorney can be involved in assisting you.

Yes, you're allowed to represent yourself in our courts. However, the foreclosure machine has attorneys who are comfortable with the legal system. Your independent study and diligence can definitely help, but combining your efforts with the services of an attorney would put you in a stronger and more competitive position.

Prepare to Help Your Attorney Help You

Your first step in your fight is to collect all of the documents and paperwork you have that might pertain to your case. Your attorney will want to review these documents.

At the top of the list, of course, is your Note and your mortgage or deed of trust. In addition, you will want to assemble, to the extent that you have them, all communications you sent to any company or received from anyone in regard to your mortgage loan. It doesn't matter if they are originals or copies, or if they are signed or unsigned. Exhibit A, *Items to Be Organized for Your Attorney,* offers a checklist, along with suggestions for how you can organize and use your documents.

From this point forward, take care to maintain a complete file of such information and records. Keep all of the relevant documents, including emails. For phone calls, write down the date, the time, the name of the person with whom you spoke, and notes about what was discussed. If anyone, including your attorney, asks for the documentation, provide copies, so that you will still have the complete file in your possession.

Finding an Attorney

You're looking for an attorney who represents borrowers who are being foreclosed or who have already had their home taken in a foreclosure. Some attorneys do that type of legal work and others don't.

How do you find one who can help? You can do an online search of attorneys in your area, gather suggestions from friends or acquaintances, consult the phonebook Yellow Pages, call the office in your state that licenses attorneys, and look at newspaper or online classified ads published by attorneys offering services.

Check out newspaper classified ads or websites like www.craigslist.org or www.backpage.com for advertisements by attorneys offering legal services, or consider posting your own "legal services wanted" ad. I know a person who hired a retired attorney to help as a legal coach after seeing the attorney's legal services ad posted on www.craigslist.org. You may get lucky and locate a good attorney who for some reason needs some cash but who doesn't have an office or want to be in the full-time practice of law.

A little homework will generate names of several attorneys or law firms that might be of help.

The Attorney Interview

Once you've collected some names, you need to interview the potential candidates. A personal interview, whether face-to-face or via phone or email, is important. If you don't like or trust the attorney, don't hire him or her. Litigation can span years. You need to be working with a person you respect and with whom you're comfortable.

Questions to ask the attorney you're interviewing might include the following:

1. *Do you represent borrowers in residential foreclosure cases in my area?*

   Ask this question to be certain that the attorney is, in fact, a possibility. You don't want to waste time if your lead to that attorney was in error. If the attorney says, "No," ask him or her to name an attorney or firm that might be able to help you—get something out of the interview even if you must take that attorney off your list of candidates. Then go to the next name on your list.

2. *Can you represent me if I will be in a lawsuit against X, Y or Z companies?*

   You need to compile a list of the companies that may be in some way connected with your Note. The work you did to organize your documents per Exhibit A will provide these names. Any of them could possibly be a party to your lawsuit. Share the entire list with the attorney you're interviewing. This information is necessary because the attorney must make sure he or she has not previously represented any person or company you will be suing. If the attorney doesn't want to be involved with a lawsuit against those companies, the interview is over. Again, ask for names of others who might be able to help you.

3. *Are you familiar with the application of the Uniform Commercial Code in residential foreclosures as discussed by* Fighting the Foreclosure Machine?

   This question is important because not all attorneys who assist with foreclosure defenses are aware of or experienced with the UCC. If that is true of your attorney, ask if he or she would be willing to learn about it. I think that accepting legal advice from an attorney who has no experience with the UCC, and who is unwilling to investigate how it might help you, is a mistake.

If the answers to these questions leave you interested in working with the attorney you're interviewing, let him or her know that you want to fight back. Also, tell the attorney that you want your legal arsenal to include use of the UCC protections. Of course, you would like to use any other legal defenses or claims that can help you, but you definitely don't want to admit that you owe anything to the company attacking you or that your Note is in default. Never make admissions like that unless and until you see genuine proof of Boss status in full compliance with the UCC.

If you live in a small community, you may have to engage an attorney from a nearby city or work with one who offers services online. Only a small portion of the entire lawsuit will involve hearings in front of the judge, so the added costs of travel or lodging for an attorney who lives outside your community may not necessarily be a big factor.

Interviewing several attorneys is a good idea. The interviews can be educational. You may hear some good ideas about how to approach the lawsuit from one or more attorneys whom you ultimately decide not to hire. So take notes as you interview the prospective attorneys.

Of those who are acceptable, pick the one who represents the best balance of experience, attitude, competence, and affordability. Look around and you will find an attorney who can help you protect your rights and home.

Talking about Fees

During your interview, you should speak with the attorney about his or her charges and billing practices. Legal services are available at a range of prices, which reflect the customary charges where you live, the scope of legal assistance you want, the attorney's interest in your type of lawsuit, and the usual billing practices of the attorney you select. Interviewing attorneys is how you learn what you can expect to pay for what you want the attorney to provide.

Talk with the attorney and learn what financial arrangement might work for the two of you. Attorneys are businesspeople. Most are comfortable discussing money matters, so don't hesitate to broach the subject so you can learn your options. Some attorneys are more flexible than others.

There are various ways that you and your attorney can set up the fee and payment arrangements. Here are some of the possibilities:

- A one-time upfront fee, either for full service or with an agreement that you will help with document review and organization

- A retainer (that is, an advance payment) plus an hourly fee you will pay each month for the number of hours that the attorney has put in on your lawsuit during the previous month

- A fixed monthly payment, which may last however long it takes you to pay the attorney's charges during the litigation, if that is necessary to accommodate your cash flow situation

If your home has already been taken, you may sue to get money reimbursing you for the value of your home rather than trying to get the house back. If that is your direction, the attorney might be willing to take the case on a contingency fee basis. In that situation, the attorney is paid a percentage of the amount you receive if and when the case generates money for you. Or he or she may want a small hourly fee, or a fixed amount up front, plus a reasonable percentage of whatever you get as a result of the lawsuit. This, too, may be a possible way for you to afford to fight back.

Alternatives to Full Representation

If you can work out an acceptable fee arrangement, your attorney can take care of all the legal documents, research, procedural matters, and discovery, as well as the trial. That way you don't have to learn how to do all of those things during your lawsuit.

However, if your finances are too strained to afford full legal services, you may still be able to get an attorney's help. Some attorneys will consider providing limited services such as coaching, drafting of specific documents, helping with responses to complicated motions, legal research, or trial work—in other words, handling only pieces of the overall litigation process. If you find an attorney with whom you're comfortable but you can't afford full services, ask if he or she could be called upon for little projects when you think you need more assistance. If that attorney doesn't provide limited services, ask for a referral to an attorney who might be able to help you.

Also, watch for signs that an attorney you can't afford by yourself might be available to assist an entire group. If you know other individuals or families who are also in your situation, you might engage an attorney to present a lecture or offer a workshop on the basics of filing or conducting a foreclosure case. This approach could give all of you some benefit from the attorney's advice and expertise while keeping the cost reasonable for each participant.

For example, you may not be able to afford $200 per hour for the attorney's time on your own, but if five people each pay $80 to attend a two-hour session, then the cost becomes more affordable. The attorney would be acting more like a professor.

Another alternative is to find out if a legal aid office in your area might be able to assist you. Some legal aid offices can provide limited litigation services, although most do not when the case involves a foreclosure. Call around and find out if any such office or agency is available in your community. You can learn about such service organizations by asking a court clerk, attorneys you meet, or your state or county's bar association. Even if the legal aid office can't help in court, maybe it can provide guidance or research if you're representing yourself.

If you decide to represent yourself and think you can handle the lawsuit on your own, you probably should nevertheless find an attorney who could be available to help with some piece of the case should you get in a bind. Having an attorney you can call to chat with about this or that can be comforting and highly beneficial. If something happens during your lawsuit that makes you want backup, you may not have enough time to locate the right attorney. An ounce of prevention is worth a little added effort.

Other Sources of Legal Help and Information

CAUTION: *People who have never been attorneys have written books and set up websites that sell services and information to borrowers facing foreclosure. If the information comes from a person who has not practiced as an attorney, be wary. If the item or service being sold comes from a person who has not actually represented others in a court of law, be wary. Relevant credentials necessarily require a lot more than the ability to publish a book, build a website, or show empathy for foreclosure victims.*

Even attorneys can make mistakes or be uninformed on specific legal issues, but, when litigation is pending or expected, their advice is more trustworthy than that of a person who has not practiced as an attorney before our courts. A proactive attitude is healthy in dealing with attorneys. It is even more important when you're being asked to accept technical legal advice from a person not experienced in the practice of law or legal analysis.

The sources of law most important to the foreclosure fundamentals I discuss are readily available to you. They are the content of your Note and mortgage, and your state's foreclosure law, which necessarily looks to the UCC for guidance regarding who is legally owed anything related to your Note or the mortgage that supports it. You should already have a copy of your Note and mortgage. Your state's foreclosure laws and UCC statutes are probably available online. They are also accessible in law school and court libraries, and you may be able to find them in a public library with a legal section.

You can find your court's procedural rules online or with the help of your court's clerk. Your judge will expect you to comply with those rules, and that is what you should do. The rules are in place to help your judge manage the lawsuit and to ensure that all of the parties have the same opportunities.

Your attorney, whether fully handling your case or providing limited legal services, can also be a good resource person. Attorneys usually have easy access to all of the important case law, statutes, and rules.

A paralegal can be a valuable resource person, also. Paralegals are legal professionals who help attorneys with research and preparation of forms and documents used in courts. They typically have a special degree and education that prepare them for that work. Some paralegals provide research or drafting services outside of their main place of employment. You can locate a paralegal through referrals from people you know, classified ads in your newspaper or on the Internet, and local schools that train paralegals. Your state also may have a paralegal membership organization that can provide leads in your area.

Attorneys and paralegals usually have good access to online legal search engines that let them research and find judicial decisions, statutes, and procedural rules. Those legal search tools, however, can be very expensive. If you want to do your own research, or if you want to make that type of search engine available to the person helping you, companies such as www.loislaw.com, www.caseclerk.com, or www.versuslaw.com provide powerful and affordable services that let the user search federal and state court decisions, federal and state statutes, and administrative rules. They are not all alike, but with a little effort you can match your needs with a reasonable service product.

Books like *Fighting the Foreclosure Machine* can be a good lead to legally significant cases, treatises, other authoritative and persuasive documents, and suggestions that may help with your situation. The more helpful books support the author's statements with verifiable and relevant references and legal citations.

If your opponent claims to be, or to represent, an investment fund that allegedly acquired the rights to your Note and mortgage, you may find a lot of information about it by searching the online files of the Securities Exchange Commission (SEC). I include this information not because the SEC provides legal information, but because the information it makes available is so trustworthy that many judges will accept information from that source as admissible evidence regarding factual matters. Companies that raise investor dollars often file statements under oath about their history and operations. Public records of the SEC can be searched at www.sec.gov/edgar/searchedgar/companysearch.html.

For example, you may be told that Mortgage Investment Trust VI (the Trust) is the Boss and that it acquired all of the rights to your Note in 2003 from Company X. The SEC filing may, however, state that every Note placed in the Trust was acquired from Company Y in 2002. These discrepancies of fact demonstrate possible confusion or fraud on the part of the Trust. The Trust's books may be wrong and it may never have actually acquired any Boss type interest in your Note. The Trust may have paid for your Note, but failed to become the Boss because it did not purchase the Note from the real Boss. And, as discussed in Chapter 11, if your opponent can't prove its status as Boss or servant of the Boss, it loses.

The Need for Citations and References

Many things we read or hear are not recognized sources of law or fact that a judge can consider when deciding the outcome of a lawsuit. A judge typically can't treat as admissible evidence newspaper articles, statements made on websites by supporters of foreclosure victims, or statements made by anyone not involved in the lawsuit. A lot of information may be evidence of this or that, but only certain trustworthy and verifiable sources of information can be considered by the judge who has to rule on your case.

Therefore, when you tell your judge, "This is a fact," you need to reference where that fact is found in the evidence before the court. Anything that one of the parties to a lawsuit alleges to be fact must be contained in the formal papers filed with the court. An exception involves documents or information that is deemed so trustworthy that a judge will also consider or take judicial notice of it if you direct his or her attention to it. Likewise, your statements to the judge about the law must be supported by verifiable references to statutes, judicial decisions, court rules, or authoritative books or legal treatises.

Your judge wants to resolve the dispute between you and your opponent in a way that follows the law which he or she has sworn to uphold. Be sure to present your case with verifiable legal citations and references. In that way, you will help your judge focus on the important legal issues and see that authoritative sources of law support the conclusion you're asking the judge to make.

THOUGHTS ABOUT MONEY

I'm not aware of any federal stimulus money or state funds that are currently available to help foreclosure victims protect their rights or homes. Until you have an attorney who is paid by the government to challenge the foreclosure machine on your behalf, don't expect the government to protect your rights or your home. Whether your home has already been taken or you're concerned that the foreclosure machine may target you in the future, you're pretty much on your own.

There are, however, ways to make things work. The previous section of this chapter discusses how to obtain legal assistance and how to pay for the help you get. If none of those ideas work for you and you're tempted to let the foreclosure machine take your home, here are a few other alternatives to consider.

Chapter 7 Bankruptcy Benefits

I'll make a few comments about the Chapter 7 bankruptcy that may be helpful if you think you can't afford to fight back, at least not at this time. At a minimum, if you're living in your house when the bankruptcy is filed, you'll be able to continue living there for many months.

All of your earnings after the Chapter 7 bankruptcy is filed belong to you. Creditors can't take that money. Get a job or a raise or make profits after the bankruptcy is filed, and that money is yours to do with as you wish.

You will be allowed to keep some, maybe even all, of your possessions, because bankruptcy law permits the debtor to keep some things. The bankruptcy system doesn't take the shirt off your back. What you can keep as "exempt" property varies from state to state.

In a Chapter 7 bankruptcy the court will appoint a trustee. The trustee can sell your non-exempt property, which may include your home if the trustee thinks that will generate enough money to pay his or her fees and costs and something towards your old bills.

The trustee could elect to fight the foreclosure machine with a goal of eliminating your mortgage debt, thus freeing up more money when the house is sold. If the trustee wins that fight, which could span many months or years, and then sells the house, you will probably receive some of that money as part or all of the homestead exemption which the related state law makes available to you as the bankrupt homeowner. Therefore, if your circumstances don't permit you to fight the machine yourself, you may want to buy a copy of *Fighting the Foreclosure Machine* for the trustee to motivate him or her to take on the machine. The relatively small cost of the book may lead to many thousands of dollars for you if the trustee wins that fight. In addition, you will most likely be allowed to live in the house during the trustee's fight with the machine.

But the trustee does not have to fight the foreclosure machine. He or she could choose not to fight the foreclosure machine and instead give up or abandon all control and interests in your house. The reasons why that choice might be made are too numerous to cover in detail, but it could happen in your case. In that event you would again be in charge of your home, and you could then decide if you might want to challenge the machine in a court of law. By then you will likely have been discharged from all of your old debts, so if you chose to fight back, you would no longer be exposed to any personal liability should you be unsuccessful.

In addition, you can live in the house longer during your fight with the machine.

Your financial situation may have improved by the time the trustee would abandon the house back to you. By then you might have more freedom and ability to get into a good fight with the foreclosure machine. Your fight, of course, might lead to your ownership of your home without the debt or to a favorable settlement that could also make money for you.

Therefore, even if everything seems hopeless, and your only realistic recourse is to seek Chapter 7 bankruptcy protection, don't give up hope. The results of that decision might prove more beneficial than you realized when you first considered it.

Ask the Foreclosure Machine for Money

At this point you're saying to yourself, "Oh, sure. These people are trying to take away my house, and I'm supposed to ask them for money." The idea is not as farfetched as it seems.

If you're not certain you want to fight back, it may be helpful to know whether the machine will pay you to go away. If your opponent doesn't approach you with an offer, ask it how much it would pay you if you decide to not contest the foreclosure. Its answer may surprise you.

The machine would lose, at a minimum, a lot of legal fees and a lot of time if you were to challenge it in court. There is also the strong possibility that it could be defeated if a serious courtroom fight took place. To be free of those risks, some foreclosure shops are willing to offer a settlement if that stops the litigation threat.

The machine might pay you cash and even give you extra time to live in the house. Typically the amount of money isn't much and the extra time you gain is a lot less than you would have if you actually filed a lawsuit. But if that is the kind of deal you need under your circumstances, something may be available if you just ask. The machine may even do a little to improve your credit history as part of the settlement deal. If the machine makes an offer without your asking, an even better offer may be available if you negotiate a bit.

Find One or More Investors

Remember the stories of the Gold Rush days? A prospector would get a grubstake to help pay for his living expenses and prospecting equipment while he looked for the Mother Lode. Most often a grubstake was not a loan. Rather, it was money that someone paid in advance to buy a portion of whatever riches the prospector might find.

You might be able to set up a similar arrangement, where the "gold" being sought is money. Someone you know may be willing to put up the money for the fight in anticipation that the foreclosure machine may have to pay you money for having improperly taken payments from you or for having taken your home through a wrongful foreclosure that can still be contested in the courts.

There are various ways you and your investor could define the terms of your agreement. If, for example, the court orders the machine to pay you money, that money could be shared with your investor in a prearranged amount. If you use the grubstake to keep the house, the return to your investor might be a monthly payment that you make for as long as you continue to live in the house, plus a specified percentage of the net sale proceeds, if any, that you receive when the house is sold.

Reasonable people can make reasonable business arrangements.

Sell Your Right to Sue

Another option is to sell your right to sue the machine to someone who wants that right. If you go with that option, the person buying your right could pay you a lump sum right away or give you some percentage of the money he or she receives if the lawsuit is successful.

Sell Your Right of Redemption

Some states permit the person whose home was sold through a foreclosure to redeem or buy back the house from the foreclosure buyer. This is usually a right that exists when the foreclosure was conducted pursuant to a court order, as contrasted with a nonjudicial foreclosure, which doesn't involve court supervision of that process. Some states, however, permit a right of redemption after the foreclosure sale whether the machine uses a nonjudicial or judicial foreclosure process. Do you have a right of redemption in your state? If you do, the right of redemption is usually a property right you can sell or give away as you wish.

If your house is sold and you have a right to redeem it under your state's statutes, you will have a period of time during which to buy it back at a price defined by that law. Typically, the redemption price is the amount paid by the foreclosure buyer plus interest for the time the buyer's money was tied up.

If your house gets sold at a bargain price and you have a saleable right of redemption, maybe someone will want to buy your redemption right. There are usually two potential buyers under those circumstances. The foreclosure buyer may be willing to pay you for it in order to make sure no one else gets the house by using your right of redemption. Or someone else wanting your house may be willing to pay to use your right of redemption so they can get the bargain price.

Therefore, if your home gets foreclosed and your state grants you a right to redeem the house after the foreclosure, keep in mind the possibility that your right of redemption may be worth money to you.

Don't Borrow the Money

Observe that I don't suggest borrowing money to mount your fight, because borrowed funds have to be repaid. You're already under enough pressure without taking on the additional stress of another loan.

Since the grubstake arrangement isn't a loan, it doesn't have to be repaid, regardless of the result that comes from your using your legal rights. Let the potential investor or grubstake partner take the risk associated with the uncertain outcome. Businesspeople pay money to take such chances when they think the upside potential is worth the risk. Debt is unfriendly in good times, and downright mean in bad times. My suggestion is to avoid more debt if you can.

HELP THE LEGAL SYSTEM HELP YOU

Americans are fortunate. Our legal system aspires to do the right thing. Our laws and our adjudication process are designed to reach a technically correct legal result. When justice is also done, the judges, their staff, and the people they know feel good. Our courts aspire to make decisions that are both fair and legally right under the circumstances.

I say "aspire" because in the courts, as in other institutions created by man, the desired goal isn't always evident in each result. Courts are swamped with too much work and too few resources. Judges work long hours and are inundated with too many words and papers, too many legal maneuverings, and too many disputes that need judicial resolution. Courts also have to pay their bills. When the economy is down, courts also have to make adjustments which sometimes leave less time and energy to address the cases before their judges.

We're a country of laws that can be harsh and unyielding, but most judges prefer to see legal outcomes that feel good in addition to being correct under the law. The "feel good" message of the fundamental fairness principles is the part that most often gets lost in a foreclosure lawsuit, and, therefore, the part of the story that deserves extra attention.

You will be helping your judge keep everything in balance if you show how the law and facts of your situation are aligned with the message of your fundamental rights. Exhibit B, *Example—Foreclosure*

Fundamentals Woven into the Story, is a good example of how the more complete story can be presented to the judge. Helping your judge is the best assurance that the decision he or she renders will succeed in following both the intent and the letter of the law.

DON'T FEEL BAD DOING WHAT'S RIGHT

The mortgage finance industry's foreclosure machine is an ugly force. Make no mistake, it will take your home if you don't resist. It has already taken millions of homes in the past few years. It hopes to take millions more in the next couple of years, and it will unless people start saying, "Enough is enough."

Our legal system gives you weapons with which to fight back. Your rights, recognized by law, were created to protect you against abuse. Fairness principles are incorporated into our laws to stop those who would illegally take your money or home. These legal tools give you leverage that you would not otherwise have. A courtroom victory against the machine is, of course, the clearest form of vindication. As discussed in Chapter 7, even if you ultimately lose your house in a foreclosure, you may nevertheless be a winner.

A wrongful foreclosure occurs each time the machine takes a home when it actually isn't the Boss of the Note or the Boss's servant. Another occurs when it conducts the foreclosure without fully complying with the law. The foreclosure is not raised to a higher moral plane just because the machine was able to take a home from a person too weak and uninformed to put up a good fight. The machine might make excuses like, "Well, the borrower did not object to how we did it," or "We were able to talk the judge into an order in our favor," but wrong is wrong. A technical win doesn't make it right. The end doesn't justify the means, at least not in America.

The machine's work is tainted by the industry's past, which has created so many victims. In a purely legal fight, the machine is also handicapped because when it is tested, it frequently can't prove that it has either a right to payments under the Note or the right to foreclose. Only a judge can answer the question of whether the rights claimed by the machine are correct under the law. But unless you ask that question, the judge won't answer it.

Don't treat the foreclosure process as if anyone you know or want to know is doing the foreclosure. You have no personal relationship with the foreclosure shop that is attacking you. You don't know those people, and they definitely don't know you. To them, you represent only a regular paycheck and a challenge to money their company gets with each home it takes through foreclosure.

The mortgage finance industry opted to use its power, resources, and prestige to snare the biggest bucks it could. At the same time, it intentionally or negligently overlooked the need and responsibility to protect borrowers from predatory lending and wrongful foreclosure practices.

The easy credit and higher real estate values that we enjoyed for more than a decade turned out to be the artificial and temporary results of the industry's high-risk profit-taking. But we didn't understand this at the time, because the industry chose not to disclose what was happening. It still keeps quiet about its role in causing our financial problems and its own need for a serious management overhaul.

The mortgage finance industry won't acknowledge that your real estate debt is high because of the inflated and unsustainable real estate values it generated across America. It won't fess up to having subjected you to predatory lending practices. It doesn't admit that it effectively defanged many of your consumer protection laws or that it discouraged classic lender-borrower relationships so that it could make more money by selling mortgage-backed securities. It won't concede that your inability to sell your home for more than the debt is a result of the artificial real estate market it built without letting you know the risk you took on as a borrower. And it definitely will not own up to its unchecked folly having been the primary cause of the economic upheaval that now makes it difficult for you to pay your bills.

The industry, instead, suggests that borrowers who no longer make mortgage payments have caused our country's real estate market problems. It remains mute when the public, the media, or government officials make comments that support this erroneous viewpoint. Unfortunately, the industry is big and wealthy, and it includes a lot of people of so-called high esteem. When that industry speaks, the whole world listens. When it keeps silent about its responsibility for our economic woes, others in high places take the cue and keep their mouths shut too.

Most people who have stopped making mortgage payments feel so bad that they don't fight back. They are typically good, hard-working Americans who pride themselves on sticking to their promises and being responsible citizens and good neighbors. The stigma of not being able to pay the mortgage is terribly hard for them to bear. Family financial difficulties are emotionally devastating, just like divorce or the death of a loved one. These are facts with which you and other borrowers have to deal.

The same industry that coaxed you into being a borrower now counts on you to have low self-esteem. It wants delinquent borrowers to give up and not ask questions. It definitely doesn't want you to ask whether your attacker has a legal right to demand payments from you under a threat of foreclosure. The industry wants you to wallow in shame and guilt, because those emotions drain a person's energy for much except self-degradation and introspection. The yoke of guilt works to the industry's advantage. The more quickly you toss that yoke aside, the better.

The practices of the industry and its foreclosure machine are designed to make it difficult to get to the truth about their alleged foreclosure rights. The only way to learn whether your attacker has any genuine rights regarding your Note and mortgage is to exercise your legal rights through litigation. Unless you engage in a formal lawsuit, you can never know whether the company threatening to take your home actually has the legal right to do that.

The legal system will support a foreclosure that appears on the surface to be legal. It will let the foreclosure machine have its way unless you help the judge see that the machine is wrong. Direct your judge's attention to the right laws and the right facts, and he or she will make correct rulings.

America is a unique country built upon a legal system designed to address wrongs and to protect rights for people in all economic and social strata. That is why the laws have been written. Don't feel guilty using your legal rights to challenge the bully.

The mere fact that you're resisting the machine's advances may make you feel better. Your effort and experience can also help other borrowers who find themselves in a similar situation. Greater numbers of challenges to the foreclosure machine will, at a minimum, drive a negative cash-flow message to the industry. The growing voices of wronged borrowers will, I predict, lead to fiscal controls of those who have too much monetary power and too little social conscience. Fighting back through the use of your legal rights should help motivate our country to find ways to avoid letting history repeat itself.

How you and your family deal with foreclosure is an extremely personal and private matter. Your circumstances may not let you actively engage in litigation. That is perfectly understandable. If you can't fight back in court, you can still help by voting for politicians who are unwilling to accept the status quo when doing so leaves our economy at risk of another massive catastrophe at the hands of irresponsible people and systems. You can also help by letting others know that the problems our economy is enduring were caused by the mortgage finance industry. These problems are not the fault of the borrowers who, like most of us, are victims, in varying degrees, of the mortgage finance industry's excesses and shortsightedness.

Feel as good as possible doing what you can. You did not create the real estate bubble or make it burst. Nor are you responsible for the economy's downturn or the depressed real estate and credit markets in which we now find ourselves. Among all of the other pressures you endure, please don't feel bad if you decide to challenge the march of the mortgage finance industry's foreclosure machine.

CHAPTER 7

WHAT WINNING COULD MEAN FOR YOU

WHAT DEFINES WINNING AND LOSING

The outcome of any lawsuit is impossible to predict. It depends on many factors that are too numerous and complicated to support an accurate forecast. Your ability to anticipate the judge's final order may increase as the case develops, but a lawsuit by its nature is uncertainty being molded to a final result. Yet, while no one can know what the outcome of your foreclosure lawsuit will be, the odds are in your favor that you will come out ahead.

I try not to speak in terms of winning or losing, because the results of litigation are not always that easily classified. At the end of the formalities, each side will determine for itself whether it realized a net gain or a net loss.

The case titled *SEC v. Goldman Sachs* is an example of a win-win result.[48] The Securities Exchange Commission sued the global investment banking and securities firm Goldman Sachs in 2010, alleging dishonesty, deception, and misleading business practices regarding Goldman's dealings in mortgage-backed securities. The case was settled a few months later with Goldman Sachs paying $550 million. So did Goldman Sachs lose? The company might well have put several results of the case into its "win" column. Not only did the government cease delving into Goldman's affairs, but, when news of the settlement became public, its stock value increased by multiples of the amount it paid to stop the SEC investigations. The SEC and its attorneys could claim a win for their side as well, as they picked up more than one-half billion dollars as well as favorable publicity. Questions continue about whether the public achieved any genuine benefit,[49] but this legal dispute shows that a lawsuit doesn't always end with a winner and a loser.

In the foreclosure arena, I estimate the win–loss tally sheet kept by borrowers will substantially be in their favor. Some will keep their homes free of debt. Some will negotiate settlements that put them in a much better position than the one they held when the foreclosure machine first made its demands and threats. Others will lose their homes, but only after having another year or two, or even more time, to live there without having to make mortgage payments. Few if any borrowers are expected to be worse off financially than if they did not fight back, but even those few are likely to feel better for having made the effort.

Only time will tell if you will be one of the most fortunate—that is, if you will be able to keep your house and be freed of the mortgage debt—or if you will gain more modest financial relief. You might also find your good effort will bring you little more than the comfort of knowing that you made a reasonable stand against the foreclosure machine, and that you, too, can be counted as a borrower who fought back. The end result of your case is uncertain, but the fight warrants your effort. There is a substantial body of law and fact on which to base your work to save your home and get some relief from the industry that placed you in harm's way.

Many things can happen in a lawsuit. It can run its full course of fact-finding, intermediate motions, and trial, and end when the judge issues a final order. The judge's order might then be appealed to a higher court, which has several options: it could affirm the lower court's ruling, or it could send the case back to the lower court for more determinations of factual and legal issues, or it might issue its own order, which could produce a different result from that of the lower court.

Another possibility is that the case could be settled and ended if the two sides are able to come to a mutually acceptable arrangement.

The case can even lay dormant with no trial or ruling from a judge, except a possible dismissal if the case is too inactive too long.

If the case isn't in a bankruptcy court to start with, it can be converted to a bankruptcy case if you later choose to protect your rights with bankruptcy law.

You won't know the outcome of your litigation until the dust settles and something final has happened. The many possibilities, however, offer you a lot more control and benefit than you might think.

Mounting evidence suggests that, because of the flawed mortgage-banking process since the late 1990s, millions of foreclosures would have been unsuccessful if contested. This likelihood was acknowledged by the chairman of the Federal Deposit Insurance Corporation in testimony before a Senate committee in May 2011.[50]

Reason suggests that, more times than not, borrowers who fight back will realize positive results. The foreclosure machine appears to be more huff and puff than legal substance. The mortgage finance industry, in its rush to sell more loans to investors, engaged in shoddy business practices that helped increase its saleable inventory of mortgage-backed securities, but which often made that inventory worthless or of highly questionable value.[51] Mortgage-backed securities are only as valuable as the legal rights to demand and receive mortgage payments from borrowers and the rights to foreclose real estate that have been pledged as security backing up those Notes. We see more and more that the foreclosure shops have a hard time proving that they have bona fide rights to take your money or home.

The industry's difficulty is much deeper than just needing to have another piece of paper or using different words to make a prettier argument to a judge. Law defines who is entitled to payments under a Note, and who has a right to foreclose. The legal result is dictated by facts. Hard facts, not conjecture or self-serving unsupported statements, have to be put forward by your foreclosure opponent, or else it will lose. As noted in *The New York Times* in October 2010, "If this were a mere procedural problem, the banks could foreclose once they marshaled their evidence. But banks who are challenged in many cases don't resume these foreclosures, indicating that their lapses go well beyond minor paperwork."[52]

Foreclosure isn't proper if your opponent has no legal right to demand payment under the Note you executed, but you must direct the judge's attention to that reality. You have an opportunity, and I think a reasonable and affordable opportunity for most, to make the machine either put up or shut up. In most instances the foreclosure shops are going to fall short when challenged as to the core principles stressed in this book.

Recent county audits of foreclosures also indicate that the machine frequently obtains foreclosures in violation of law. San Francisco County, California, conducted a limited audit of foreclosures from January 2009 to November 2011 and reported that 84% violated the law.[53] The Southern Essex Registry of Deeds, Essex County, Massachusetts, revealed that 75% of the 2010 foreclosures involving JPMorgan Chase Bank, Wells Fargo Bank, and Bank of America were also invalid.[54] These audits are further reason to expect good results for those who challenge the foreclosure legalities claimed by the industry's foreclosure machine.

Whether or not you elect to engage in formal legal action is up to you. You have been bashed by the terrible economy created by the mortgage finance industry. Your circumstances may have tied your hands so thoroughly that you can't participate in a court battle. We all have to live with what life has dealt us.

Don't assume, however, that foreclosure litigation isn't for you or that you have no way to fight back. First, do your homework and learn more about your options. The odds favor most targeted borrowers. You, too, may decide the fight that the industry has pushed on you deserves more of your attention.

The Mortgage May Be Eliminated

Your lawsuit might result in your mortgage or deed of trust being declared invalid or unenforceable. In that case, your opponent can't sell your home at a foreclosure sale. Courts don't frequently deny the validity of the mortgage, but that happens when the law and the facts make invalidation the correct result.

Mortgages are bound by state law and are subject to challenge.[55] The rules about mortgages vary quite a bit. For example, one state may define the mortgage as being owned by the Boss of the Note regardless in whose name the mortgage is recorded.[56] Another state may say the mortgage has to be recorded in the Boss's name for a foreclosure to be permitted.[57] Your state may have rules that are not the focus of this book but which work nicely to your advantage. If your state has one that can help you, by all means you should use it.

Fighting the Foreclosure Machine emphasizes the principle that only the Boss of the Note has the right to trigger a foreclosure. That rule should serve you well wherever your case is fought and regardless of other defensive or offensive legal strategies you chose to use.

There are a number of circumstances in which a mortgage can be invalid. Some possibilities could be:

- If the mortgage isn't properly notarized

- If it isn't properly recorded in public records

- If all the required signatures are not included (for instance, in cases where the property is owned by a husband and wife or other joint owners, and not all of them have signed the document)

- If the identity of the person or company intended to benefit from the mortgage is unclear, whether the label for such person or company is grantor, beneficiary, or mortgagee

- If the mortgage is held by a company that isn't the Boss of the Note[58]

- If the mortgage doesn't correctly identify the location of the home

A mortgage might also become invalid when one company transfers or assigns it to a different company if the transfer is not executed by the then Boss of the Note[59] or it is executed by a company that doesn't own the mortgage according to the public land records. Some states require, without exception, every change in ownership of a mortgage to be recorded.[60]

A mortgage can also be invalid if it no longer secures a legally enforceable debt. If the debt can't be enforced, it stands to reason that any mortgage that secures that debt has no legal meaning.

Attacking the validity or enforceability of the mortgage is not an attack on the Note. This distinction can be important.

If, for example, you're considering a legal defense that involves rescinding or undoing the entire loan transaction (in other words, undoing both the Note and the mortgage), you may want to think instead about challenging the mortgage but not the Note. Unwinding or rescinding the whole loan might require you to quickly pay back whatever funds you received from the lender when the loan was made. Sure, that could get you off the hook for interest, penalties, and other fees, but most borrowers facing foreclosure don't have enough money or credit to make that kind of repayment.

Defeating the mortgage may, in a practical sense, be just as powerful for you as rescinding the entire transaction, especially if you're not required to pay anything to your opponent to beat its mortgage. Making the mortgage invalid or unenforceable would mean that the Note is no longer secured by your house. That would definitely be a good thing, even if the Note is still in existence.

You may say, "So what if the mortgage isn't valid. There is still the possibility that the Note has to be paid." Good point. If the Note is legally enforceable but isn't collateralized by a valid mortgage, then it is an unsecured obligation. An unsecured debt is difficult to collect and can even be discharged in a bankruptcy. If you're able to eliminate the mortgage, the owner of the Note could get nothing or only pennies on the dollar.

A similar result is possible if the court grants an equitable mortgage. This may occur if a party can't directly enforce the existing mortgage because the mortgage recorded in the public records is, for some reason, not valid or enforceable. An equitable mortgage is basically a court-ordered judgment that can be recorded as a new lien against the house. The fact that it's new means it can be released from your home in a bankruptcy, making the Note unsecured.

From the viewpoint of the foreclosure machine, having an unsecured Note or a Note secured only by a court-created equitable mortgage is almost like having no Note at all. Your opportunity to achieve a favorable settlement of your lawsuit will go up dramatically if your mortgage is invalid or unenforceable, or if your opponent winds up with only a new equitable mortgage against your house. Your ability to declare bankruptcy and not pay an unsecured Note can be a great card to play in the negotiation game. You don't need to actually file bankruptcy first. You might as well, therefore, look closely at your options under your state law to challenge the validity of the mortgage itself.

The Mortgage Debt of Your Note May Be Eliminated

Just as it can with a mortgage, a court can decide that the Note is invalid or unenforceable. Judges have that power.

Such a ruling pretty much negates foreclosure, because a mortgage is only valid to the extent that the related debt is still owed.

The reasons why Notes may be declared invalid stem from facts and law that apply to a particular borrower's situation. No common thread has been identified that permits borrowers in all states to expect success when challenging the validity of a Note. Congratulations, if you're one of the people who can do so. Most people, however, won't be that fortunate. Neither their specific facts nor available law will ensure that they can prove their Note isn't legally binding.

Fighting the Foreclosure Machine isn't about challenging the validity of the Note. It is about challenging the right of your opponent to enforce your Note. This is a challenge that people can make in any state and with extremely promising results.

Only one person, the Boss, has the legal right to enforce the Note you signed. If your opponent doesn't have that right, you win that battle, whether or not the Note is a legally enforceable obligation. Moreover, a court order issued against your opponent won't likely be binding on the one true Boss because the Boss won't likely be a party to your lawsuit.

Your strategy and objective when fighting foreclosure is to show the judge that your opponent has no right to enforce your Note—that is, no right to demand payments from you and no right to foreclose. Your focus is to defeat that particular opponent and the immediate threat it poses. At the same time you'll be making a loud statement that anyone else who tries to take your money or home is also going to face stiff opposition.

Your Note may not even have a Boss anymore. It could be that no person is now able to qualify as the Boss per the requirements of the Uniform Commercial Code. If your opponent can't prove it has the right to enforce the Note, and can't identify the person who does have that right, the foreclosure sought by that company should be denied.[61] Don't let a concern about winning the entire war put you at risk of losing the battle already raging in your front yard.

The foreclosure machine has often demonstrated an inability to prove the identity of the Boss of the Note. The machine is very good at alleging and insinuating that it has the right to take your money or home. But when it's required to prove what it says, it starts mumbling. Hot claims and high-sounding words are no substitute for the facts that the machine, not you, must prove in a court of law. If your opponent can't produce the legally essential facts, it can't enforce the Note.

A California homeowner named Rickie Walker was attacked by Citibank N.A. and BAC Home Loan Servicing, L.P. Those two companies said Mr. Walker owed more than $1.4 million under the two involved Notes and mortgages against his home. In the bankruptcy proceeding, neither Citibank nor BAC was able to prove it was the Boss of the Note, so the judge denied their claims against Mr. Walker. The judge acknowledged in his orders, however, that his ruling against those companies meant only that they lacked the right to enforce the Notes and mortgages; he was not making any ruling regarding the real Bosses of the Notes should they appear someday.[62] Thus Mr. Walker defeated those two companies, each of which was then acting as nothing more than a foreclosure shop against him, but the ultimate result was not decided in that bankruptcy case. The machine lost the battle, but the outcome of the war wasn't fully determined by that loss. Mr. Walker had been fighting with those two companies for years. At the time of this writing, I don't know whether Mr. Walker later had to face the real Boss or Bosses or if those mortgages may have lost their power by the passage of time or other legal proceedings. He did, however, meet and defeat the immediate threat, and that is the primary objective of the foreclosure fundamentals stressed in this book.

If the correct identity of the Boss can't be proven, there's a good chance the Note will never be enforced, though that isn't guaranteed. The court's ruling against your opponent doesn't bind the real Boss. Theoretically, you could stop your opponent's foreclosure and later find the real Boss knocking at your door. However, that isn't likely. If your opponent failed to locate proof that it or the person it serves has the rights of the Boss, that's a strong indication that no such proof exists and the trail to such proof is too cold for anyone to follow. Defeating the first foreclosure action, therefore, will be good evidence—but, again, not a certainty—that your Note is no longer enforceable by law.[63]

It may turn out that the actual Boss is present in your case. If so, the Boss nevertheless may be denied the right to enforce the Note. For example, the Boss may be suing you but may have already been paid in full by insurance or by settlement of a lawsuit with some other company. If the Note is ruled unenforceable or already paid off, you will no longer be obligated to pay the debt that it represents.

The main reason to defend yourself and your home against the machine is to stop the immediate threat. Take care of that problem first and worry about other problems when and if they arise someday. Don't be like a college football team that becomes so convinced it will win the national championship that it forgets to win the game at hand.

Statutes of Limitations May Apply

Some debts can't be enforced or collected if they are too old. Our laws block the enforcement of obligations when a lawsuit to enforce the debt isn't filed soon enough after the debt goes unpaid. These laws—frequently referred to as statutes of limitations—vary from state to state in many ways, such as how they are labeled, how much time can pass without formal collection or enforcement efforts, when and how the obligation might get reinstated, under what circumstances the collection period can be lengthened, and whether the debt is evidenced by a written or oral agreement. What's common among all of the states, however, is the Uniform Commercial Code. It defines the statute of limitations regarding enforcement of negotiable instruments, and a Note is one such instrument. This statute of limitations applies in foreclosures because the essence of foreclosure is the enforcement of the Note.[64]

UCC § 3-118(a)—the symbol § stands for the word *section*— permits the Boss of the Note six years within which to initiate formal collection actions.[65] An enforcement lawsuit doesn't have to be concluded within the six years, but the case must start within that six-year period. Otherwise the court can stop collection of the overdue amounts. The six-year period basically runs from the first day the Boss has a right to demand payment of a past-due amount, whether or not such a demand is made. For example, if the Note requires monthly installment payments, the six-year period usually starts the day after the payment is due for that unpaid installment and each later installment that is not made.[66] If the text of the Note makes the entire debt due in the event of a delinquent monthly payment, the six year period for the entire debt starts when the entire obligation is accelerated or made immediately due because of the missed payment. During that six year time, the Boss or its servant must either start a lawsuit to collect the money or commence a formal nonjudicial foreclosure if permitted in the respective state.

If the Boss demands payment of a past due amount, and the appropriate amount is paid, that resets the clock to zero. However, if the Note isn't brought current in response to the Boss's demand, and the Boss neither sues to enforce the Note nor initiates a nonjudicial foreclosure during those six years, this real estate Note by law may be uncollectible in total or to the extent of six years of installment payments, including interest, administrative fees and penalties related to unpaid and unenforceable amounts.

State law answers questions about whether or not a debt otherwise barred for being too old can be reinstated. Those laws may increase the time within which a person can enforce an old debt because of circumstances like an intervening bankruptcy or some other event recognized by that state's law as giving the creditor more time to collect.[67] The UCC provides, however, the starting point regarding how much time is permitted to collect an obligation due by the terms of a real estate Note.

The basic six-year statute of limitations can be extended in some states by written agreement between the borrower and the Boss. An agreement you make with a company that isn't the Boss or the Boss's servant wouldn't likely extend the statute of limitations applicable to your Note.

In the foreclosure arena, how might this statute of limitations rule become important?

During your fight with the foreclosure machine you may learn that you sent your mortgage payments to the wrong company for more than six years. Given the way mortgages have been bought and sold in the past two decades, this would not be surprising. But it could mean that the Boss, whoever it is, wasn't paid what was due during those years. The statute of limitations began to run at the moment the payments became late and overdue. If, therefore, you think more than six years have passed since the Boss, even if unknown to you, received payments, you should investigate how your state deals with the UCC's statute of limitations regarding negotiable instruments. All or a substantial part of your obligation might no longer be due.

The statute of limitations creates a legal defense, but it doesn't, in and of itself, automatically void or terminate the obligations of your Note. If, after those six years, someone shows up claiming the right to payments under the Note, you would use your state's equivalent of UCC § 3-118(a) to shield you against the new claim. Your argument would be that the new opponent, whether or not the Boss of your Note, is too late to start enforcement action.

If collection of the obligation is barred by the statute of limitations, the mortgage is also unenforceable because it is valid only so long as something is still due under the Note. Thus, you should think about having a court release the mortgage from your home if the obligation of the Note is no longer collectible.

Quieting of Title May Be Possible

Every state has a judicial mechanism that can be used to remove mortgages that are filed against real estate.[68] A quieting-of-title lawsuit asks the judge to issue an order that releases the mortgage so it is no longer an encumbrance or lien against the house. If you use this procedure, you would let the judge know that you're unaware of the identity of the Boss of the Note that is secured by the mortgage against your house and that you don't believe anyone has the right to enforce the mortgage. Your quiet-title suit would, in essence, give notice to the whole world that you believe the mortgage should be released, and that anyone who disagrees had better step forward to prove otherwise within the time permitted by the court's rules or forever lose the right to do so.

Quiet-title procedures typically require you to send formal notice to everyone you think might claim the right to enforce the mortgage and also give public notice to those you may not know. If, for example, your lender was Company A, and Company B is now claiming the right to foreclose, you would want to specifically sue both companies in addition to making the public notice required by your state's quiet-title rules. The public notice usually involves placing a classified ad or using other media specified by the court's rules. The public notice is intended to give people and companies not known to you the opportunity to contest the release of the mortgage. If, as is almost always the case, you don't know the identity of the Boss of the Note, the public notice procedure gives that unknown Boss the opportunity to step forward to protect whatever interest it might claim in the mortgage.

If someone objects to eliminating the mortgage, that person must formally become a party in your quiet-title lawsuit. Then it must prove it has a right to enforce the mortgage—in other words, that it is the Boss of the Note—or else you should prevail. If no one files an objection within the time permitted by the court, you should get a court order directing the release of the mortgage. The mortgage gets formally released when the judge's order is filed in the public land records. At that point, it is no longer a lien or encumbrance on your home.

When might filing a quiet-title lawsuit be a good idea?

A good time to file a quiet-title action is when the statute of limitations regarding your Note has expired. At that point you would know that no one has a right to foreclose the mortgage and any objection that is raised would have no merit. You can file a quiet-title action, however, whether or not the statute of limitations has run regarding your Note.

Another good time is when you feel comfortable that the Boss of the Note won't appear to challenge your quiet-title suit. If, for example, the foreclosure machine has not been able to identify the Boss during its lawsuit with you, the Boss probably doesn't exist or can't be found.

You may also want to consider filing a quiet-title action if your state permits nonjudicial foreclosure and you doubt that the court will let you address the Boss-status legal issues if you challenge the threatened foreclosure. If you have those concerns, you could begin the quiet-title action either before or after your opponent has formally commenced the nonjudicial foreclosure process. I would think filing the quiet-title action before the foreclosure has begun would place you in the strongest possible position and give you the best leverage for getting the foreclosure postponed until your quiet-title case has been fully decided.

You may also elect to use the quiet-title suit if you want the fastest and most certain result, as contrasted with the possibility of enduring multiple lawsuits that could span more years. If your funds and patience are limited, you might want to pre-empt an inevitable foreclosure fight by forcing the UCC issues through a quiet-title action.

If your opponent lacks the requisite Boss status, your win of the quiet-title suit will bar that opponent from bothering you again. It will also eliminate the mortgage so others can't later threaten your house. The Note may continue as a valid debt, at least until the statute of limitations expires, but without the mortgage it would be only an unsecured debt that is more easily discounted or eliminated.

You May Get Back Past Mortgage Payments

Perhaps your opponent received mortgage payments from you prior to the lawsuit and it can't prove it had a right to receive those payments pursuant to the strict requirements of the UCC. If this is your situation, your opponent owes that money back to you, and suing for its return is a natural consideration. While you're challenging your opponent's right to receive payments from you, you may also want to demand that it reimburse you for what it took from you in the past.

Your opponent's only defense will rest with whether it can prove not only the identity of the Boss of the Note, but also that all mortgage payments it obtained from you actually went to the person who was the Boss when those payments were made. If that proof isn't forthcoming, you might have an opportunity to get back money you paid to the wrong person while simultaneously defending your home against foreclosure by someone who can't prove it has the right to take it from you.

Other Possibilities for Judgments in Your Favor May Be Enhanced

UCC § 3-302 defines what's meant by "holder in due course." If the Boss is identified in your lawsuit but it doesn't qualify as a holder in due course, you have an opportunity to raise extra claims and defenses against it.

For example, it may be that your lender or its agent engaged in deception, fraud, misrepresentation, or unfair business practices when your loan was taken out. Those wrongs would give rise to legal claims you could make against those who perpetrated the wrongs. But those people and companies are probably not the ones now trying to take your home, because your Note was most likely sold over and over again to others. If Company A has hurt you, you can't sue Company B for those wrongs unless the law and facts specifically authorize such a suit. You may be able to use such claims or defenses against the Boss pursuant to UCC § 3-305, *Defenses and Claims in Recoupment.* The company that actually hurt you may not exist anymore, but, with the right circumstances, you can sue the Boss so it has to cover your damages or reduce your obligation under your Note.

If the Boss is a holder in due course, it will have protection against most claims of that type, the ones related to injury you suffered at the hands of the actual lender or its agent. The Boss must prove with hard facts that it indeed has the status of a holder in due course. Otherwise, it took the Note subject to the claims and defenses you could have used against the original lender. The burden of proving this status falls on your opponent pursuant to UCC § 3-308. (For more information see the *Holder in Due Course* discussion of Chapter 11.)

Many consumer protection laws are worthless in a foreclosure fight. They don't permit you to assert your claims against anyone other than the predatory lender that caused your problems, and your foreclosure opponent is rarely that lender. So you generally get little benefit from threatening your opponent with claims based on those laws.

When you apply the UCC, however, you may open avenues for litigation against the Boss that might be blocked under the provisions of the other laws. Therefore, if you were wronged during the loan process, it may be beneficial to assert those wrongs against your opponent pursuant to the UCC. If your opponent can prove it is entitled to payment from you, the amount due may be reduced or even eliminated if it isn't a holder in due course. However, if your opponent isn't the Boss or the Boss's servant, it won't be subject to the claims you may have that are related to predatory lending practices, but it also will have no right to take your money or home.

The involvement of ShellGame-MERS could make it easier to break down a holder-in-due-course defense by your opponent. I say this because the foreclosure machine's use of the name of ShellGame-MERS (i.e., Mortgage Electronic Registration Systems, Inc.) usually happens after the machine thinks the Note is in default. A company cannot enjoy status as a holder in due course if it acquires its interests in the related debt after there is a collection problem.

Suing your opponent for wrongs committed by your lender requires what is called pleading in the alternative or alternative pleading. You would simultaneously claim your opponent lacks Boss status and also that it is liable for the wrongs you suffered at the hands of the lender, if the judge decides your opponent is the actual Boss of your Note. This is a way to raise legal claims that are mutually exclusive. Your opponent either has Boss status or it doesn't. This form of stating claims that cannot both be true is common and familiar to judges. With an alternative type of pleading, you can easily state the result you want from the judge if the opponent is not the Boss and, alternatively, the result you want if it does have Boss status.

PART FOUR

Recipe for the Foreclosure Fight

CHAPTER 8

THE FUNDAMENTALS OF THE FORECLOSURE FIGHT

THE FUNDAMENTAL QUESTIONS

If you are like most people in your situation, you will find that success against the foreclosure machine will involve application of certain fundamentals. *Whether the foreclosure you face is valid can hinge on many legal issues, but the most basic to any attempted foreclosure is the primary and fundamental foreclosure question:Does your opponent have a legal right to demand payment from you because of your Note?*

A foreclosure might be illegal due to procedural violations or rare occurrences that apply only to a handful of people being foreclosed, but foreclosure is always invalid if you don't owe anything to your opponent. If your opponent is owed nothing under your Note, it has no right by law to foreclose.

Your objective in this battle is to force your opponent to demonstrate that it has a right by law to make demands based on your Note. The foreclosure machine often can't produce the kind of proof required in a foreclosure lawsuit, at least when challenged to do so.

If there is one key idea to take away from *Fighting the Foreclosure Machine,* it is that only the Boss of the Note has the right to receive your payments and the right to foreclose. I emphasize that point throughout this book. When challenged to prove the right to demand payments from a borrower, the machine typically has great difficulty. You, therefore, always want to force your opponent to prove that it has those Boss powers, and nothing less. The Boss may authorize a servant to act on its behalf when it comes to enforcing your Note, but, in that instance, the link that connects the Boss and the company claiming to be its servant must be equally clear and proven.

The foreclosure machine will do its best to confuse you into thinking it should win regardless of what you say or do. If you buy into its story and don't challenge the machine in court, it will most likely get a quick win. If you raise only a hollow objection in court, spouting words about which you have no understanding, you will not likely win. If you don't make your opponent prove that it has a legal right to win, you may have wasted your time. Sometimes judges will help, but you can't plan on their fighting your battle for you.[69] They're too busy and not sufficiently informed about the facts of your specific case, so do not expect them to act like an attorney for you. It is up to you to ensure that your judge fully understands the facts and legal issues present in your case.

THE FUNDAMENTAL PRINCIPLES OF FAIRNESS AND TELLING THE STORY

The laws that govern the foreclosure process are rooted in principles of fairness. Fairness dictates that you should not lose your home to anyone to whom you do not legally owe anything. Fairness dictates that the house you gave your lender as collateral securing payment of your debt should be available to protect the interests of the Boss, if any, consistent with the agreement you made when you took out the loan. You didn't pledge your house so someone who is owed nothing under your Note could take it in a foreclosure.

Three sources of legal authority support these fairness principles: the Note, the mortgage, and your state's foreclosure laws. Each state's foreclosure laws necessarily invoke the state's version of the Uniform Commercial Code (UCC), because that is the body of law by which we learn who is owed the obligation under your Note and, accordingly, who has the right to foreclose to help satisfy the debt evidenced by that Note.

The Note

The text of the Note defines the rights of the borrower and the lender. It sets forth the terms and conditions under which the debt is to be repaid. The Note will state that the lender—the bank, mortgage company, or however the lender is identified—is the one that is owed payments under the Note. In the event that the borrower falls behind on the payments, the Note typically will provide a "cure period," which gives the borrower added time, after receiving notice from the Boss of the Note, to bring the debt current. If the borrower fails to do so, then the Note permits the Boss—and only the Boss—to declare that the Note is in default.

Default is the event that triggers the enforcement rights. At that point, the Boss—and only the Boss—is entitled to pursue the remedies permitted under the Note and applicable law. Enforcement of those rights is not automatic. The Boss must actually do something to start collection efforts or foreclosure.

Default is not a concept that looks at your payment history. In foreclosure litigation, the legal meaning of *default* is whether the one true Boss has appeared and elected to exercise its enforcement rights. Again, I recommend that you not assume that your Note is in default, and that you maintain that no default exists unless and until you face the one and only Boss who says otherwise. Until that time, you can't possibly know whether your Note is in default as that term is used in the legal foreclosure arena. Don't help your opponent beat you by saying otherwise. (See the discussion of "default" in Chapter 4.)

Your Note does *not* state that just anyone may arbitrarily declare a default and start legal proceedings against you even if you owe nothing to that person or company. The Note does *not* mention the UCC, but that is the law that controls who has a right to enforce your Note, because it is the law of your state and your Note, except in rare instances, is a type of document (a negotiable instrument) covered by the law of the UCC. (See Chapter 11.)

The Note also does *not* state that you can stop making payments once the debt has been paid, whether by you or some other person. That, however, is implied in the agreements you made with your lender, and it is required by the UCC—the Boss was intended to get paid the amount due under the Note at the time it became the Boss, but no more. Only the Boss knows how much money is still due regarding your Note. Until the Boss shows up, you have no way of knowing what, if anything, is still owed. So don't make guesses about something that important. Do not assume that the company demanding your money is the Boss of your Note or that Boss's servant.

The Mortgage

The mortgage document is different from the Note. The Note creates your debt obligation, while the mortgage document creates collateral to give the lender extra assurance that the debt will get paid. In other words, the mortgage is your pledge that, if you fail to make payments on your loan in the agreed-upon manner, the lender may foreclose and take your house.

The mortgage instrument, whether called a mortgage or deed of trust or something similar, typically includes language stating that the document is created to secure benefits for the lender. The mortgage does *not* state that you agreed to let someone foreclose and take your house if you do not owe them anything.

A mortgage further states that the lender—by whatever name is used in that document—is in charge of what happens under the mortgage. The lender is the only one authorized to commence a foreclosure, either by direct action or via instructions to a trustee or some other servant. Yes, a servant can sometimes start or conduct a foreclosure for the Boss, but that is legal only when the facts make it unequivocally clear that the servant actually is doing the current Boss's bidding. This applies to any servant, even to ShellGame-MERS, if it is involved with your mortgage.

Your Note and mortgage granted rights to your lender. Those documents don't grant those rights to any person other than the original lender or its successor by law. What those documents do not say is that, after the Note and mortgage get transferred and passed around in the mortgage finance industry, the UCC takes over and supplies the definition of who can be the successor to the lender, but that's what happens. After the first time your lender sold, transferred, pledged or exchanged your Note and mortgage to someone else, each use of "lender" or "successor to the lender" in your Note and mortgage then became a reference to the Boss as defined by the UCC. It defines the one and only person entitled to enforce the provisions of the Note, and, therefore, the provisions of the mortgage—that is, the UCC, not the Note or mortgage, answers the question of who is the Boss of the Note. If your opponent cannot satisfy the UCC test, it is not the Boss or the Boss's servant, and does not own the rights that previously belonged to your lender. (See Chapter 11.)

Now read your Note and mortgage. Identify the power that is exclusively available to your lender through those agreements. For example, what notices, communications, and payments are supposed to go to the lender? What instructions must the lender issue to make this or that happen? With whom are you supposed to communicate about things involving your Note or mortgage? As you read, keep in mind that the lender's rights are now held by the Boss of your Note and only the Boss can exercise them. These two documents may be wordy and strange, because their language is full of legalese. But they most likely contain information that will help you protect your home. That prospect should be enough to keep you from falling asleep as you study them.

The Laws of Your State

Each state's legal fabric includes laws, legislative history, and case law that define the person for whom the right to foreclose exists. That entitlement belongs to the person to whom the obligation under the Note is owed. Different labels are used to identify that person, but the intended result is the same whether your state refers to that person as a beneficiary, creditor, mortgagee, or lender, or by another label with a similar meaning.

States that permit nonjudicial foreclosures include trustees as persons who can start and conduct a foreclosure. If you live in one of those states, look closely at the nonjudicial foreclosure statutes. You'll see that the trustee's right is subject to the authority granted it by the deed of trust. The trustee is required to do what is best for the person to whom the obligation of the Note is owed. The deed of trust (or trust deed, or whatever your state might call it) will say that the trustee has no authority to start a foreclosure without instruction from the Boss or its servant.

To my knowledge, no state has ever intentionally or knowingly permitted a mortgage or deed of trust to be foreclosed for the benefit of anyone other than the Boss at the time of foreclosure. If the Boss has not declared the Note to be in default and commenced collection efforts, then the foreclosure is wrong,

A foreclosure not for the benefit of the Boss is either a mistake or theft. A wrongful foreclosure deprives you of your home, which was pledged to help you take care of your obligation under the Note—an obligation you owe only to the Boss of the Note. A wrongful foreclosure also deprives the Boss, if one still exists, of the asset that was supposed to serve as security to help make sure the debt gets paid.

A foreclosure by a person owed nothing under your Note is wrongful because it is contrary to the agreements you made with the original lender, agreements that are now under the control of the Boss. It is also wrongful because it is contrary to the fairness principles incorporated in the laws of your state, including the protections within your state's version of the UCC.

Telling Your Story

During your fight with the foreclosure machine, try to help your judge understand how these many principles and facts define your rights against your opponent. Make your story clear, persuasive, and accurate. Your opportunity to tell it will come as you file motions in court, respond to motions filed by your opponent, and make your arguments during the trial.

Because you're in a court of law, your story needs to include references to legal authorities and facts. Show how your Note and mortgage and the state's foreclosure laws, including the UCC, define your rights. Show how the UCC and your state laws require your opponent, not you, to prove it is the Boss of your Note or the Boss's servant.

Your description should make clear that you are not in default (again, see the discussion of "default" in Chapter 4), that you owe nothing to your opponent, and that the status of your relationship with the one true Boss is not relevant to whether your opponent can prove that it is the Boss or the Boss's servant. Demonstrate how the fairness principles built into the foreclosure laws apply to protect your rights and also the rights of the Boss of your Note.

Exhibit B, *Example—Foreclosure Fundamentals Woven into the Story,* demonstrates how this story of borrower rights and protections under the law was recently presented in a case before a court in Nevada. In that case, the borrower (we will call him Steve) tried to stop a nonjudicial foreclosure of his home, but he was unsuccessful. The house was sold and someone else became its new owner. Because the house was gone, Steve sued the banks and companies involved in the foreclosure, asking that they repay him for the house they took from him. Steve's suit is still in court with unknown results at this time.

Steve did a noteworthy job of weaving the foreclosure fundamentals into a formal document that he filed with the court. His hope was that the information would help his judge make the correct decision. Exhibit B contains excerpts from this document, taken from an answer he filed objecting to a motion filed jointly by the defendants who took his home. In asking the court to dismiss Steve's lawsuit, they asserted that his complaint had not stated any legal claims recognized under Nevada law. A motion to dismiss is typically filed before the defendants answer the complaint and before a borrower has the opportunity to engage in formal discovery. That's what happened to Steve. He wanted to make sure his judge understood how his Note and mortgage (in this instance, a deed of trust) related to Nevada's nonjudicial foreclosure law and UCC. He hoped to strengthen his case by showing how the foreclosure fundamentals interact to protect borrowers like him.

Steve's work is a good example of how the story can be told and how it needs to be supported with legal and factual citations. It may help you craft the statements of fact and law you want to put before your judge.

Make sure your judge is aware of the connection between your Note and mortgage and your state's foreclosure law, which necessarily incorporates the UCC. The more the judge understands this, the better position he or she will be in to help achieve the fairness intended by the legislators who passed the laws.

THE FUNDAMENTAL STRATEGIES

Unfortunately, the foreclosure machine is not interested in the principles of fairness, so you'll have to work hard to protect your home and your own best interests. How do you avoid letting the machine take advantage of you? How do you keep your opponent from confusing you to the point where you give up? How can you persuade your judge that your arguments, not your opponent's, are the ones with legal merit?

The answer is to keep focused on certain fundamental strategies that can help you win your case. When you apply them properly, they are both defensive and offensive weapons.

My list of these strategies includes the following. Together they are the recipe for the foreclosure fight:

Rule 1:   Don't Accept the Machine's Word (Chapter 9)

Rule 2:   Gather and Use Facts to Beat the Machine (Chapter 10)

Rule 3:   Make the Machine Prove Its Right to Foreclose (Chapter 11)

Rule 4:   Don't Give the Machine an Easy Win
            (Chapter 12)

Each of these basic strategies is discussed at length in its respective chapter. You will find helpful background information, detailed explanations, and guidance, along with citations of cases that will help you present your own case to the judge. Later in the book, you will find exhibits that are intended to help you see how the strategies can be applied and used:

Exhibit A.   Items to Be Organized for Your Attorney

Exhibit B.   Example—Foreclosure Fundamentals Woven into the Story

Exhibit C.   Examples—Responses and Claims

Exhibit D.   Checklist—Investigation of Boss Status

Exhibit E.   Example—Informal Discovery

Exhibit F.   Examples—Formal Discovery

Litigation will not seem so daunting if you stick to these strategies and let them guide you. By "you," I am referring collectively to you personally and whomever you choose to assist you. This list of basics can help you define your lawsuit and avoid being distracted by your opponent's maneuvers and antics.

The strategies presented in this book give you a good chance of winning at the trial level and also on appeal if you're unsuccessful with the lower-level court. By adhering to them, you'll improve your chances of actually having your case decided on essential facts and relevant law rather than on incomplete information or procedural technicalities.

The more you focus on the foreclosure fundamentals, the more you'll reduce your own stress and the more you'll put the judge in a better position to help you. In addition, sticking with the fundamentals can be a strong complement to the total package of defensive and offensive legal theories you decide to put before your judge.

CHAPTER 9

RULE 1:
DON'T ACCEPT THE MACHINE'S WORD —
DEMAND STRICT PROOF

DON'T ASSUME THE MACHINE'S CLAIMS ARE VALID

Borrowers who assumed that they actually owed money to the entity trying to take their house, or that it had some legal right to foreclose, were doing exactly what the mortgage finance industry intended. The industry's foreclosure machine wants you to assume it has a legal right to demand mortgage payments. It wants you to assume that it has a legal right to foreclose. It wants you to assume that you have no rights and can't possibly win in a legal fight. It wants you to assume that the machine must be right because you know you missed some mortgage payments. It has taken homes from millions of people who mistakenly made those very assumptions.

The industry doesn't have to say that it wants you to assume this or assume that. Assumptions are of our own making. Human nature compels us to try to guess a result when we do not have all the facts. The foreclosure machine knows this, and it hopes you will be like millions of other borrowers who "assumed" themselves into losing their homes.

The best way to approach your opponents from the mortgage finance industry is to assume that what they say is false and that their arguments are little more than smoke screens. If they say, "The sun came up this morning," you had better go outside and look for yourself.

The foreclosure machine's history over the past several years does not warrant your taking its word or letting the judge simply assume that what your opponent says is true. Evidence is too plentiful that the machine's tactics are designed to confuse and intimidate, rather than to demonstrate, through the presentation of meaningful fact and law, that it has a right to demand payments from you or to foreclose.

I'm not saying all of the people working for the foreclosure machine are outright liars, but their schooled approach to taking your property is more driven by their determination to win than by accuracy of fact or law. I think it wise to give your opponent the freedom to prove its honesty and integrity, but that is a status that must be earned. Be polite. Be cautious. Forewarned is forearmed.

THE INDUSTRY'S USE OF FORECLOSURE SHOPS

Early in my research I thought foreclosure shops involved in any way with ShellGame-MERS deserved more distrust than those trying to take someone's property using a mortgage that did not involve ShellGame-MERS. I was wrong.

The architecture of the mortgage-backed securities industry of the late 1990s included the creation of specialty foreclosure shops to take care of foreclosures so investor money could be gathered even from those with no or little knowledge of real estate law or foreclosures.

Most investors and their investment managers were ignorant about the complexities of business and law involving mortgage-backed securities. They didn't know about the intricacies of dealing with thousands of borrowers, monitoring and supervising loan contract compliance, collecting and accounting for payments, or dealing with loan renegotiations, dispute settlements, or payoffs. They were ignorant of the federal laws and the laws of the fifty states that related to an investment product that involves consumers, real estate, contracts, mortgages, deeds of trust, loan collections, foreclosure, creditor-debtor relationships, and bankruptcy.

There were some private investor groups knowledgeable enough to make an informed decision about investing in mortgage-backed securities, but the industry wanted to tap the money available to the thousands of investor groups that were ignorant and inexperienced with that type of investment. So, it put together packages that included masses of loans, mortgages and prearranged services, and appeared to take care of all the business and legal matters involved in the management of a residential loan portfolio. This approach made the investment fund manager look more knowledgeable and competent to the investors entrusting their money to the manager's care. Investors began to view mortgage-backed securities as a no-brainer investment that offered good and safe returns with no need to understand how the investment actually worked.

In addition to being a way to sell residential loan portfolios, this packaging gave the industry the opportunity to create long-term service fees for those in charge of the packaging and sales. A bank like Wells Fargo, for example, might make money gathering and selling 10,000 loans, whether generated by Wells Fargo or other banks or mortgage companies. At the same time, it could lock itself into a lucrative long-term contract that paid it fees to allegedly supervise sub-servicers—businesses that got paid in turn to take care of details such as borrower relations, collections, dispute resolution, and foreclosure. This packaging and sales structure was used with residential loans, whether or not ShellGame-MERS was involved.

The result was that investment funds bought loan packages that used the same tiers of servicers, including the same companies to handle foreclosures. The evidence indicates that the foreclosure squads have received similar training, employ similar tactics, and coordinate their nationwide pillage, under a common and single-minded goal of taking more homes through foreclosure.

You would be wise, therefore, to use caution in dealing with any entity or person that represents the foreclosure fraternity. Court decisions over the past few years show too many instances in which foreclosure businesses have made inaccurate, untrue, and fabricated claims that they can't prove when challenged.[70] Sometimes the foreclosure machine claims ownership of a note or mortgage but can't prove that assertion when put to the test. Or it uses affidavits provided under oath that turn out to be false or highly suspicious, or that don't actually rise to the level of admissible evidence. Or it changes its claims when challenged and argues that some other company has the right to do the foreclosure, leaving open the question of whether it is conspiring with that other company, especially when neither puts forward verifiable evidence of having those rights.

The foreclosure shops' poor record for accuracy or honesty can put them at a disadvantage when they face a borrower who forces them to use legally admissible evidence. Push them to prove with facts what they claim or insinuate, and your case and resulting benefits should be much better. *Fighting the Foreclosure Machine* emphasizes the legal defenses and claims that appear to have the broadest and most successful promise for the class of Americans targeted for foreclosure.

Use of foreclosure shops allows the big-name players of the industry to play innocent. When faced with public complaints about deceptive, illegal, or immoral conduct by the businesses they hire to conduct foreclosures, they typically claim, directly or through public statements by their "friends," that small mistakes were made, or that a few documents were flawed, or that some nominal technical oversight occurred.

However, if you Google "robo-signing," you'll locate numerous news articles describing questionable practices by the industry that have been uncovered by the media and government agencies. Robo-signing originally referred to the industry's practice of having foreclosure processors sign thousands of documents that they didn't even bother to read, let alone verify to be accurate. The term has come to be a shorthand expression for a variety of illegal and deceptive activities perpetrated by the foreclosure machine. Robo-signers were first discovered in contested court cases. We have no reason to doubt that those same corrupt practices also occur in nonjudicial foreclosures that involve no court management at all.

Mortgage finance industry leaders respond to accusations with statements that imply, "Oh, goodness. We didn't know." Some even sever ties with a foreclosure shop they've used for years when too much public scrutiny comes to rest at that shop's doorstep.

Notably, no member of the mortgage finance industry has said, "We are investigating the situation and will do everything in our power to help people who had their homes taken in violation of law or by companies not legally permitted to enforce the related Notes." No apologies. No offers to right the wrongs that have been done.

Yet, do we really think the industry is uniformed about the tactics and procedures used by its foreclosure machine? Do we think the industry entrusts the fate of literally billions of dollars of assets—the homes targeted for foreclosure—to its hired foreclosure offices without knowing how those offices do their work? Do we think the mortgage finance industry lacks attorneys who can monitor the foreclosure shop procedures and legal tactics? Ask yourself these questions each time you hear the representative of a bank, Wall Street finance house, investment fund, Freddie Mac, Ginnie Mae, or title insurance company allege ignorance about improper or deceitful foreclosure practices. Use this exercise to remind yourself that the foreclosure machine's tactics may (perhaps probably?) reflect the ethics and attitudes of the companies it serves.

THE INSINUATION TACTIC

Rest assured that the industry uses misdirected words, insinuations, implications, and formal-looking papers to create the appearance that it has legal rights. Often, without making an outright lie, it will suggest or imply things in hopes you and the judge will assume that what is implied is true and can be proven.

A recent case, for example, involved a foreclosure shop alleging to represent U.S. Bank and claiming U.S. Bank had a right to payment under the Note. Who has the right to enforce a Note is extremely important in foreclosure lawsuits, as it was in this particular case. Commenting on that crucial legal issue, the court said:

"Although the Motion does not explicitly state that U.S. Bank is the holder of the Note, it is implicit in the Motion and the arguments presented by the Movant at the hearing. However, the record demonstrates that the Movant has produced no evidence, documentary or otherwise, that U.S. Bank is the rightful holder of the Note."[71]

You will face the machine's routine effort to suggest, imply, and insinuate that they have all the things they need to beat you in a court battle. It will direct its effort at you and the judge, who, it hopes, will simply take its word for each thing important in the foreclosure suit. You don't want the judge to assume your opponent has supportive facts when it does not, and you don't want to make that mistake either.

If you're going to fight for your rights, then set your mind on distrusting the machine. Distrust what it claims in its letters to you before a lawsuit happens. Distrust the fine-sounding words in the formal documents it files with the court. If your opponent says it represents someone else, ask for proof from that someone else. If it says an assignment or declaration came from some other company, require proof from the other company. If it argues that the company it represents has the right to enforce the Note and to foreclose, ask both your opponent and that other company for proof about those rights.

If that other company is not a party in your lawsuit, you may get what you need from it by sending an informal letter pursuant to the authority of the UCC (See Chapter 10.), which means that the other company will either answer with genuine evidence or else be deemed to have no rights regarding your Note. If an informal approach does not work for some reason, you can ask your judge to make that other company become a party to your lawsuit so you can engage in formal discovery against it. Regardless of how you go about it, be constant in making them prove full compliance with the UCC and the foreclosure policies of your state. Questioning, bothersome questioning, will serve you well.

Winning against this arrogant force is possible, but not if you follow your assumptions. Prepare for a good legal fight by getting rid of your willingness to assume facts that are not in evidence. (Sound like something you may have heard in a TV courtroom drama?) Each day remind yourself by reciting, "I am not going to assume they got it right, I am not going to assume they got it right, I am not going to assume they got it right."

THE MACHINE, NOT YOU, BEARS THE BURDEN OF PROOF

The foreclosure machine is often beaten in court when it has to address what I call the foreclosure fundamentals—whether the borrower's opponent has a legal right to demand payment under the Note, and whether it has a right to start or finish a foreclosure.

When a case comes to court, the machine's pleadings before the court summarily allege that it is legally entitled to payments under the Note and to foreclose when not paid. However, in cases where the court has actually evaluated the facts underlying these alleged rights, what often has been demonstrated is that the machine's threats are an empty façade rather than anything of legal merit. More and more, the courts are seeing valid challenges of substance, and they are responding with thoughtfully reasoned decisions that protect the borrower's rights consistent with well-established law.

The mortgage finance industry's response to its courtroom losses is typically to argue that the problem involves mere technicalities or sloppy paperwork that only involved the particular case in which the loss was recorded. But the truth seems to be substantially different.[72]

A big difficulty for the mortgage finance industry is that the law requires it to prove a right to make demands under the Note. *This is an important point that bears repeating: when you fight back against the foreclosure machine, you do not have to prove who actually has the right to enforce the Note.* Your opponent claims to have that right, so the burden is on its shoulders to prove that it is the Boss of the Note or the legally appointed servant of the Boss. Winning your case is about using the machine's lack of proof to your advantage.

The mortgage is inextricably tied to the Note. If your opponent has no right to demand or receive payment under the Note, it also has no right to take your home. Your home was pledged as assurance of payment for the person legally entitled to payment under the Note, not for the benefit of any other person or company. Only one company, if any,[73] has the right to enforce the Note—that is, to demand payments under the Note or to carry out a foreclosure if those payments are not made. A servant or agent company may have the right to administer that enforcement process, but its authority exists only to the extent empowered by the Boss of your Note. The company that initiates a foreclosure must, by law, prove that it has the right to do so if you demand that.

It's a sad fact that most borrowers facing foreclosure, whether judicial or nonjudicial, do not contest their opponent's rights and actions in court. Millions of uncontested foreclosures have happened in the past few years. When no one makes a formal objection, the industry's machine can say or claim whatever it wants, and it usually wins. An uncontested foreclosure, however, does not mean the foreclosure was proper. Many of the affected borrowers would have prevailed had they put up a fight.

If you do not challenge the machine's claims, your opponent will most likely win. Most judges will assume that your silence affirms what the opponent alleges. If, however, you demand that your opponent show actual facts to support its claimed rights, then it had better put on a really good case, or else accept defeat. Your best strategy is to keep your case focused on the machine's burden of proof under basic foreclosure law. The rules discussed in Part Four, *Recipe for the Foreclosure Fight*, demonstrate what you can do to keep the weight of that burden on its back and how you can help the judge understand when the foreclosure machine has not proven its case.

The burden of proof imposed by law on your opponent is a powerful tool available for you to use as you defend your home. Law imposes the burden on your opponent so you will not be exposed to the possible loss of money or your home to someone who is not entitled to either. As you will learn in the next chapter, your Note is a negotiable instrument, and the strict requirements of the UCC are there to help you make sure the wrong person does not try to extort money from you under a false or mistaken claim that you owe it money pursuant to your Note. Your opponent's burden of proof is your ally. It is a big thorn in the side of the industry's machine. The prick of this thorn can lead to the only relief you will ever get from the mortgage finance industry.

CHAPTER 10

RULE 2:
GATHER AND USE FACTS TO BEAT THE MACHINE

FACTS ARE CRUCIAL TO SUCCESS

Facts are crucial. Facts, hard, cold facts, dictate the winner of most legal fights, not guesses, insinuations, self-serving conclusions, or emotional pleas. Laws are created to be applied to the facts of the dispute before the court. A correct legal result means that the right law was properly applied to those facts.

The foreclosure machine likes to obfuscate and suggest, rather than prove, that the facts which are legally necessary to establish their case actually exist. Your opponent may provide piles of paper in hopes the heap will discourage you, but stay your course. When you actually look at the papers, often you'll find they do not support the claims made by the machine.

Every court has access to law that can help assure that you aren't facing demands for payment or foreclosure by a company that has no right by law to make those demands. You need to help the court arrive at the right decision by making sure genuine facts are before the court for analysis, not merely the words and insinuations presented by your opponent. If your opponent says, "I am the owner of the Note," or "I possess the Note," or "I am the duly appointed agent representing the true owner of the Note," or "I am communicating with you on behalf of your creditor," your response should be, "So what?" and "I deny that you have any legal rights regarding my Note or property unless and until you prove your claims with relevant facts."

I want to emphasize the importance of gathering and using facts. The mortgage finance industry, in its haste to grab more investor money, often ignored the law as the volume of loans it sold escalated. It frequently failed to do what is necessary to establish who, if any, has a legitimate right to demand payment of a mortgage loan, or who, if any, has a right to conduct a foreclosure.

The industry's massive success in foreclosing millions of homes is founded, more than anything else, on its having faced people so weakened, embarrassed, and discouraged by the economy that they did not put up a fight. The foreclosure machine has typically won with little more than statements that sounded convincing but which were not supported by fact. The machine may say, "I have a right to demand payment," or "I have a right to foreclose and sell your house for my own benefit," but seldom has it been forced to demonstrate the genuine facts that would support its self-serving contentions. You have an opportunity to change that pattern and help the legal system protect your rights and those of other foreclosure victims.

The foreclosure machine is big, well-funded, and pretty good at beating up on people who can't defend themselves. But it makes mistakes—and those mistakes can often be proven when the machine is forced to show true facts. Its shortcomings can be the strength of your case when you are being foreclosed or facing that threat.

Court cases that have been decided in favor of the borrower over the past few years have always involved a serious look at the underlying facts, a look that goes beyond the unproven conclusions and incomplete picture the machine had hoped would give it another victory. The machine does not own or control our judges and courts. They can be your ally in this war, but you need to help them do their job.

Your mortgage may involve ShellGame-MERS, or it may not. Regardless, making your opponent show facts is the best way to defend yourself. The foreclosure shops use the same music and dance steps from East Coast to West Coast as they try to dazzle borrowers and the courts with their choreographed footwork. Your opponent, however, has the burden in court to prove its claims with facts. You can unplug the jukebox by not letting them off the hook.

As I explained in the previous chapter, one of your objectives in your litigation should be to avoid assumptions. Look instead to facts, or the lack thereof, to prove that your opponent should lose. When suing or being sued by the foreclosure machine, always state the facts correctly. Be truthful and as accurate as possible throughout the litigation process. You don't want misstatements, errors, or inaccuracies on your part to backfire against you.

Exhibit C, *Examples—Responses and Claims*, provides examples of ways to word responses and state claims that highlight the foreclosure fundamentals while making accurate statements. You have the final responsibility for whatever you draft and submit in court. You will make the determination as to whether your documents are accurate to the best of your knowledge. The examples may, however, let you more quickly and accurately formulate the text you need. They are included to help you emphasize the differences between fact and assumption, and to help you formulate statements designed to minimize the likelihood that the judge will become confused and erroneously assume too much. Yes, judges can fall victim to assumptions just as you and I can. An example of this technique follows:

Opponent claims:

Borrower has not made all mortgage payments required under the Note and is therefore in breach of his obligations under the Note.

Sample response:

First, I deny that the payment status regarding my Note has any bearing on the controlling issue of whether my opponent has any right by law to enforce the Note. Second, I deny that my opponent has proven that it has a right to enforce the Note I executed. Third, I have not received an accounting of the balance owed, if any, under the Note from a person who has the right to enforce it. I may have, in fact, overpaid. Accordingly, I don't have information sufficient to admit the claims and implications of my opponent's statement, and, therefore, I deny them.

Exhibit C is about how to write responses more clearly and accurately. It is not part of a cutesy game designed for purposes of delay or distraction. In order to win, you need to be certain the foreclosure fundamentals are issues clearly before the judge. Your case needs to present accurate information to the judge, meaning as few assumptions as possible. Stating that your opponent has not proved it is entitled to make demands under the Note is not an assumption, but a fact. It is a fact until and unless your opponent comes forward with hard facts proving a right to actually enforce the Note.

HOW TO GET THE FACTS YOU NEED

Informal and formal ways to gather the important facts are available to you. These methods have different benefits and procedures, and I think it wise to use both whenever possible. Each can be used to help develop your case against the machine, even if your claims or defenses are broader than the foreclosure fundamentals featured in this book.

I speak interchangeably of discovery and fact-finding. Both labels describe the effort to learn things that can help you win a legal dispute. When you are not engaged in litigation with the machine, you can use whatever methods you think will help you prepare for the fight. Once litigation begins, however, you will be bound by rules of the court regarding permitted scope and methods of gathering facts.

Discovery can involve different purposes, but for a targeted borrower who wants to argue the foreclosure fundamentals, I think the most important goals of your fact-finding are (1) to learn what you don't know and (2) to gather proof that will help you convince the judge to rule in your favor.

You have no choice but to enter the fight without knowing everything necessary to resolve the legal issues in your case. Regardless of how many pieces of paper you've received from collection companies or the foreclosure shop now attacking you, you cannot possibly know with legal certainty if any more payments are due under your Note, if you have actually overpaid, if your adversary has a legal right to demand payments under the Note, or if the threatened foreclosure would be legal. What I just wrote is fact. Prepare yourself to enter litigation with more questions than answers about what your opponent may or may not be able to prove.

Informal and formal discovery are the keys to helping get past the uncertainty. Knowledge is power. Your right to look into your opponent's information and files lets you take control of the litigation process.

I anticipate that most people who challenge the foreclosure machine will move more and more toward the certainty that their attacker has no rights against them. If, however, you discover that your opponent has all the facts necessary to win in court, then your common sense will tell you not to spend more time or money in a losing battle, at least regarding the foreclosure fundamentals I stress. Uncertainty is part of litigation experience, but it need not be terribly uncomfortable so long as you expect it and keep your energies bent toward doing what is necessary to beat your opponent.

Your opponent has the burden to prove with genuine fact that it is right. It has to prove with legally sufficient evidence that it has a right to enforce the Note and a right to foreclose. Your fact-finding, therefore, should be aimed at gathering information that demonstrates that your opponent can't prove its case. Exhibit D, *Checklist—Investigation of Boss Status,* shows the relationship of the foreclosure fundamentals and the kind of factual evidence the machine will need to have if it is to beat you.

For example, to prove its right to enforce the Note, your opponent needs to present a complete evidentiary history of all transfers or sales of your Note. Your discovery will involve asking your attacker to show that it has that necessary proof. A break in the chain of ownership and control of your Note can be a serious problem for your opponent. It has to be able to prove strict UCC compliance of every sale or transfer of the Note that led to its claimed Boss rights.

Your opponent can only become the Boss by having acquired the full rights of the previous Boss of your Note. Missing proof about the circumstances and results of a previous sale or transaction means your opponent can't prove it acquired Boss rights that can be traced all the way back to your original lender. For example, if a gap appears between Owner #1 and Owner #3, your opponent will have difficulty proving that its rights can be traced all the way back to Owner #1. Maybe your opponent has good evidence about how it got the Note and mortgage from Owner #3, but under this example, it wouldn't be able to prove that Owner #3 was actually the Boss of your Note because there wouldn't be proof about what Owner #3 got from Owner #2.

You, on the other hand, do not have to explain why the gap occurred. Nor do you have to prove who, if not your opponent, is legally entitled to enforce your Note. Your opponent has to prove its right to enforce your Note, or else it should go away and leave you alone.

Be wary if your lender is your opponent or the alleged master being served by your opponent. The industry practice, a tactic used to win suits against borrowers, has sometimes involved having the lender feign being the Boss even though side deals made it clear that the lender was not actually an owner or Boss of the Note at that time. Use the same fact-finding and suspicions when dealing with your lender as you would with a total stranger trying to take your home. Keep reminding yourself that all of them are members of the same club.

Because the burden of proof is on your opponent, the facts you need are going to come, for the most part, from your opponent. You will ask it to produce and disclose what it has and knows about the things it must prove, and you will ask in a way that prohibits your opponent from surprising you at trial with new documents or testimony.

What You Want to Learn through the Fact-Finding Process

The fact-finding process in a lawsuit is called discovery. Your objective through discovery is to demonstrate that your opponent doesn't have the facts necessary to prove its claims against you. As you collect information and documents from your opponent, you will want to pay close attention, not only to their content, but also to what your opponent fails to provide. I sometimes refer to the fact-finding effort as a negative content audit—an analysis of the information that is missing.

In a negative content audit, you're looking for gaps of ownership and control of the Note, as well as your opponent's inability to prove important details about the Note. Keep a list of missing or incomplete information about:

- Who had physical possession of the Note, and when during its existence

- The terms and conditions of each alleged transfer, sale, or exchange of your Note all the way back to when you signed it

- The detailed circumstances involving any alleged loss or disappearance of the Note

- Your opponent's alleged authority to represent someone else if your opponent claims that someone else is the Boss of your Note

- The circumstances about the alleged Boss's interests in your Note, such as how, when, and from whom that company got possession of your Note, the agreements by which it obtained whatever interest it is alleged to have, any limitations of its rights regarding your Note and mortgage, and proof that it obtained its alleged rights from a company that was then the Boss of your Note.

This negative information (what your opponent can't prove) is the key to your legal rights.

Your Note represents a substantial amount of money. You and your judge, therefore, can reasonably expect and require the ownership and rights respecting your Note to have been thoroughly maintained with accurate and complete documentation. Your task is to help the judge see that your opponent's information is insufficient. If what your opponent gives you falls short of the legal requirements, your case should be decided against your opponent and in your favor.

The Uniform Commercial Code defines your opponent's burden. (See Chapter 11.) You can help your judge by pointing out what the UCC requirements are and where your opponent lacks meaningful evidence to prove it satisfies each of those requirements.

Informal Discovery—A Letter

Informal fact-finding can, and usually should, be done before a lawsuit begins. A letter requesting information is enough. Exhibit E, *Example—Informal Discovery*, gives you some text that might help you write your own letter.

Send it to the company that is making demands and threatening you, using whatever address it provides on the notice it sent. If that company says it is representing some other company(s), you'll want to send the letter to the other company(s) as well. Use certified mail, and request a return receipt. That way you'll have proof that the letter was sent, and proof that it was received or at least delivered.

Do not expect a meaningful answer to your letter before a court gets involved. I've seen many such letters sent, and the standard industry approach is to ignore them or to provide only conclusions or statements of confidence that are not supported by verifiable fact. The more I learn, the more I'm convinced that silence and canned responses mean the machine doesn't have the right to enforce the Note or to foreclose and take the targeted home. Each is evidence that your opponent doesn't have the information necessary to support its claims against you. Bear in mind that a response that doesn't provide all of the information requested by your letter is the same as no response at all.

I suggest that you send the letter even though we expect you will get no response or only words that are not supported by accompanying fact. You may say, "If I won't get a genuine response, why waste time and money sending the letter or letters?" Good question.

The answer is threefold.

First, and foremost, your opponent's silence or inadequate response lets you enter the lawsuit as the winner. (See Chapter 12.) Your opponent is required to prove its right to enforce the Note under the UCC if you ask it to. Your letter triggers that obligation.

The UCC says that your opponent's failure to provide complete answers and documents in response to your letter means (1) your opponent has no right to demand payment from you or to enforce your Note until and unless it provides genuine proof that it has those rights, and (2) that you have not breached or dishonored your Note by refusing to pay the demands previously made by your opponent. Whether or not you have missed previously scheduled mortgage payments isn't important, because the UCC says you don't owe anything to your attacker until, if ever, it proves under law a right to make demands related to your Note.

That little letter, and your opponent's failure to comply with its requests, puts you in the best possible position for entering the lawsuit. The foreclosure machine expects most courts to think of it as the wronged party, and deserving of your money or your home, just because it comes into court bellowing that you owe it money. But the Uniform Commercial Code of your state lets you say, "Not hardly!"

Your opponent's admission (its failure to respond to your letter) is legal evidence that you owe it nothing when the lawsuit begins. Receiving no response to your letter lets you truthfully and accurately state in the documents you file in court that you owe nothing to your opponent; that you have not breached or dishonored your Note by not paying whatever amount your opponent demands; and that your opponent, by its own refusal or inability to provide the information requested, has admitted that it has no right to demand payment from you or to threaten foreclosure. Your statement is accurate under the UCC and it also sets the stage for the legal matters before your judge, at least regarding the foreclosure fundamentals addressed by this book.

By focusing on the UCC and the benefit of having issued the letter, you put yourself in a strong defensive and offensive legal posture. You, not your opponent, will be the one to define the applicable law and factual requirements that govern the question your judge must address when deciding the case—whether your opponent has an actual right under the law to demand payments from you under the Note you executed. If it does not have that right, it also has no right to take your home to satisfy the debt you do not owe it.

Starting the suit with the UCC having defined your opponent as the loser is a good way to present the legal dispute to your judge. It lets you begin the lawsuit a step ahead of the foreclosure machine. A one-step lead might very well be enough advantage to defeat your opponent's claims.

What better way to introduce yourself to your judge than to show with the backing of the law that you are the winner? Sure, your opponent will have an opportunity during the case to produce facts that might show it has controlling rights. But unless that proof comes forward, your opponent has lost. Its only way to get past loser status is to prove its case against you pursuant to the strict requirements of the UCC. That is exactly the position in which you want your opponent when the case begins. It's the position that gives the most difficulty to the foreclosure machine.

The second reason for sending the letter is that having sent it will show your judge that you are a reasonable person. Your informal and courteous request for facts will demonstrate that you, at least, have made a good effort to avoid unnecessary or meritless litigation. You will have taken a responsible and adult step in response to threats thrown at you by your opponent. Your opponent said, "You either pay or else." With the letter, you're asking it to prove its right to make such demands. No person, including your judge, would do less in your situation.

Your opponent's failure to respond to your letter fully and with genuine proof means that you haven't received the information required by the UCC and might not owe your opponent anything. Your right to demand such proof is part of the UCC's way of protecting you from mistaken or fraudulent demands by a company that has no legal right to your money. Your opponent's silence or inability to provide the information you requested gives it the appearance of being a disrespectful and arrogant bully. How rude to demand money from a person under a threat of taking their home and then to refuse to make a reasonable response when asked to demonstrate the authority, if any, backing up those threats.

When you give the machine the informal opportunity to prove its right to your money or home, and it ignores your request or gives only a self-serving or condescending answer that doesn't provide the information you requested, you and the judge have good reason to be suspicious. Each time during the trial the foreclosure machine objects to being required to comply with your formal discovery, as it will do, you and the judge should wonder if the continuing pattern of not responding is a tacit admission that the machine can't prove its claims. Each new suspicion is good litigation value for you, and it is cheap and easily obtained value, costing only postage and a little time—the informal letter.

A judge has the responsibility to decide how much importance to assign to each bit of evidence in the dispute. Included in the whole body of evidence is the fact that your opponent, for some reason, did not or could not make a reasonable response to the letter you sent. Times will arise when your opponent will want the judge to give it the benefit of the doubt and to give something it offers as proof more evidentiary weight or importance than strict logical or legal analysis require. The lingering question about why the machine did not make a simple and forthright response to your letter might be that little bit of doubt that clinches your judge's distrust of your opponent during the trial.

The third reason is that you would like to know if the company threatening you actually has solid evidence that it has the right to demand payments under the Note and to foreclose. No one wants to waste time and money in litigation that has no upside. If your opponent's response to your letter satisfies you that it actually has the legal right to enforce the Note, you may want to re-evaluate whether fighting the foreclosure machine is to your advantage.

Use your opponent's inadequate response as comfort, and as solid evidence under the UCC, that you are not in default under your Note and that your opponent has no right to make demands or to foreclose—that you are the winner in the case. Your opponent will get the chance to prove otherwise during the lawsuit, but it will have to do that from the posture of a loser who is trying to overcome that status. I recommend, therefore, that you send that kind of letter.

Formal Discovery—Admissions, Interrogatories, and Production of Documents

The foreclosure machine is impressive and powerful when picking on the weak and uninformed. Its attorneys show up wearing nice suits and speaking nifty-sounding words that often have little to do with proving that it has the right to demand payments under the Note or to attempt to foreclose. The court's rules of discovery are the equalizing force available to you as soon as you are in a lawsuit. Formal fact-finding is a powerful tool that you can use to help the judge focus on what is really important and to force your opponent to "prove it" or "lose it."

Formal discovery takes place after the lawsuit has begun. It is conducted in accordance with the rules of your court. The court's rules of discovery give you an opportunity to learn the facts on which your opponent's case against you will be based. The rules vary from court to court, but you will typically be permitted to ask your opponent to admit things, to explain things, to produce documents, and to be available to testify under oath in a deposition.

The rules of the court will define the variety and scope of things you are permitted to demand from your attacker. Those rules may sometimes seem petty and picky—for instance, they may restrict the number of pages you can submit to the court and even specify that you use paper that has been hole-punched or has special borders. It's important, though, that you conform to the rules, whatever they are. Just remember that the rules are there to help the judge do his or her job.

In some courts you'll have state or federal rules of discovery to abide by, plus local rules that describe your court's specific preferences about how your discovery is done. If your court has two sets of rules, do your best to stay consistent with both sets. You can get the rules of discovery online, at your attorney's office, in a court library, from a legal aid office, at a local law school library, or from the clerk of the court.

Rules of discovery define when your opponent is required to respond to your fact-finding work. The operative word is "required." In a court battle, rules of discovery require proper responses. Bad things can happen to the party that does not play by those rules. The machine is not under much, if any, obligation to answer your questions informally, but after the litigation begins your opponent must comply with your formal discovery or else risk having the case decided against it due to its refusal to abide by the court's rules.

Exhibit F, *Examples—Formal Discovery,* demonstrates the type and scope of discovery I would use if I hadn't retired from the practice of law and my client was in a foreclosure suit trying to save his or her home. Exhibit F also contains a summary of the reasons for using formal discovery and provides sample requests for admissions, interrogatories, and requests for the production of documents.

Attorneys have different ways of engaging in fact-finding and different views about how best to use the discovery process. Don't be surprised if your attorney's method is different from mine. My approach, however, helps me stay focused on the foreclosure fundamentals and allows me to organize the process and the information in a way that I think better engages a judge, so he or she is less likely to overlook important matters.

Formal discovery encompasses three types of written requests that you can make of your opponent.

First, you can ask it to admit certain facts that will help your case. This is called a *request for admissions.*

If it denies the facts, or objects to the request, you can ask it to explain why. A *request for an explanation* is also called an *interrogatory.*

Finally, you can submit a *request for the production of documents,* asking your opponent to show you documents that relate to what it must prove.

Requests for admissions, interrogatories, and requests to produce documents are made in writing. You can also verbally ask questions and discover facts that you need during a deposition or formal questioning of a person before a court reporter, who takes down the questions and responses word for word.

Written discovery is often the least expensive and most thorough way to get the kind of information you need to defeat the foreclosure machine in a foreclosure lawsuit.

The documents you get through formal discovery will give you most of the information you need to help your judge see that your opponent cannot prove its right to make demands about your Note and mortgage. Equally important is the lack of documents. The negative content audit—an analysis that I described earlier in this chapter—can tell you more than the material your opponent actually provides.

Did I mention that you should not trust statements made by your opponent or assume anything unless proven with fact? The truth will often be different than the picture painted by your opponent's claims and statements. Think of discovery as something like a watermelon. Work is required before one can get through the rind and into the sweet meat of the fruit. Discovery is the same way. As we make requests for admissions, explanations, and documents, we anticipate that the opponent will do its best to evade the truth with a tough exterior shell. We engage in formal discovery expecting that we have to do the work to get to the sweet meat of what is true. Formal discovery makes that effort easier and more effective.

➤ *Requests for Admissions*

Requests for admissions drive my approach to formal discovery. The opponent is presented with a list of statements and requested to admit or deny each. The statements are crafted to be things we would like the opponent to admit as true, because those admissions would prove the opponent has no right to demand payments under the Note and no right to conduct a foreclosure.

For example, if the opponent claims a right to demand money under your Note, the requested admission might be, "Please admit that you have no ownership interest or any other interest in the Note." Having no such interests, of course, would mean your opponent has no right, on its own behalf, to make any claims related to your Note. If the response is an "admit," then you have what you want to help you persuade the judge to rule in your favor. Your opponent's own words or admissions can be the strongest evidence upon which to demonstrate your winning case.

➤ Requests for Explanations and Documents

The opponent, of course, rarely gives a simple "admit" in response, so requests for explanation (also called interrogatories) and requests to produce documents are used to help get closer to the truth.

If the answer to your request for admission is "deny" or "objection"— that is, any answer other than "admit"—an interrogatory can be used to demand that the opponent do two things: (1) explain why it did not simply admit the statement was true, and (2) identify whatever documents it relies on as a basis for not admitting the truth of the particular statement in your requested admission.

Requests for production of documents are used to make the opponent produce its files and documented information. A properly drafted request for production will cover physical and digital or electronic documents alike. Because the opponent will want you to see only the documents that are most favorable to its case, a request for production should ask for all documents and communications possessed by your opponent that relate in any way to your Note or mortgage.

➤ Summary of Formal Discovery

A recap of my formal discovery outline, at least regarding written matters, is as follows:

Request for Admissions

- Select statements that, if admitted to be true, help prove that your opponent does not have fundamental foreclosure rights.

- Ask for admissions about other things that will be helpful to the rest of your case if your legal theories are broader in scope than the foreclosure fundamentals discussed in this book.

Request for Explanations (Interrogatories)

- Ask for explanations of each response to requested admissions that is anything less than a straightforward "admit."

- Ask your opponent to identify each document it claims as support for the explanations it provides.

- Ask for explanations about other things you want to know.

Request for Production of Documents

- Ask for all documents identified by interrogatory responses.

- Ask for all documents related to or involving your Note and mortgage.

- Ask for all documents involving communications with any person or company about your Note and mortgage.

Depositions

Depositions are a form of formal discovery that can be very helpful in showing that your opponent does not have solid facts with which to win its case. A deposition generally takes place in a location other than the courtroom, with representatives of both sides of a legal dispute in attendance, even if only via phone. A person who has information relevant to the case responds to verbal questions under oath, while a court reporter records the testimony. The written transcript of the deposition can be admissible as evidence, just as if the witness were answering the questions in the courtroom.

The person to be deposed, who is referred to as the deponent, can be required to bring documents, but there is not much time during a deposition to thoroughly review documents produced by the deponent that have not previously been seen. When a deposition is used to gather documents, it often is done with an expectation that the papers will have to be reviewed at a later time.

You may find that fact-finding in a foreclosure is more efficient and effective if you deal first with written discovery. Then evaluate what you've learned about your opponent's missing or questionable circumstances. After that, depositions can be conducted if the results of the negative content audit suggest a deposition is warranted. If the explanations and documents obtained from the opponent are enough to persuade your judge that the opponent should lose, depositions may not be necessary.

However, you may want to further investigate information that your opponent has produced. Or you may need to obtain additional evidence to help demonstrate that your opponent can't identify the Boss of the Note, or that it can't substantiate its relationship to the Boss, or that the trustee who is conducting a nonjudicial foreclosure is acting upon instructions received from the wrong company. In these and other situations, you and your attorney might decide to depose someone. A review of the documents in your possession and answers to your discovery requests will be good guides to what depositions, if any, might be useful.

STAY CALM AND FOCUSED

Often I use the word *demand* when speaking of the requests issued in formal discovery. Technically, because the law gives you the right to force certain answers and documents from your opponent, these requests are demands. Formal discovery, however, is, or at least should be, a civil and courteous activity. Yelling, screaming, pounding your fist on a table, and similar antics are not effective ways to persuade a judge about the merit and worth of your objections to being foreclosed. In fact, my experience has shown that judges doubt the credibility of people who are too emotional, and that refers equally to the machine's attorneys.

Your case is one of thousands with which the judge is dealing. The best and most effective way to help the judge hone in on the most important legal issues and facts is to use clear and concise arguments of law and fact. A judge does not have time for rambling. He or she is extremely busy and can get turned off by anything that seems to be wasting time. Short and to the point is best, and emotions should be left at home. Otherwise, you will have played into the hands of the attorneys representing the industry's machine. They would like nothing better than to have you concentrate on your anger or hurt rather than the legal issues and facts important to your case. Anything that distracts you is a plus for them, so don't let it happen.

Expect your opponent to object to your formal discovery and to conjure up all kinds of high-sounding reasons why it should not have to comply with your requests. Every objection, excuse, and delay should heighten your motivation to keep pushing forward, because each one is a good sign that your opponent can't prove its assertions and claims. If it has good law and fact to support its alleged Boss rights, expect that evidence to surface quickly without a lot of difficulty or games.

Formal discovery is a great instrument with which to prick your opponent's thin skin of credibility. By the time the litigation has commenced, the machine will have already ignored or refused to comply with your informal fact-finding efforts. Its choice to not provide proof of its rights in response to your informal discovery letter will have planted the seed that the machine might not actually have the rights it asserts. Each time it attempts to throw up a roadblock rather than show real evidence, you can help the judge see that the machine is stalling and that its claims against you are baseless.

On one level, your opponent's legal maneuvering games are frustrating. On a higher plane, view them as opportunities. To the extent you can, look at each new set of roadblocks as a positive event. Each new stall and delay tactic will be your guide to involve the judge as you ask for an order compelling your opponent to comply with formal discovery. Each time you appear in front of the judge is an occasion for you to highlight the foreclosure fundamentals of fairness and to remind the judge that your attacker, not you, has the burden of proof regarding those most basic legal purposes, especially since it is trying to take your home.

Even if the judge does not state it outright, he or she will be wondering about the validity of your opponent's alleged rights with each new attempt it makes to avoid putting forward the requested information. The more the machine's popinjay engages in legal maneuvering rather than producing facts it should have readily available, the more your opponent risks alienating the judge's impartiality.

Remember, your goal is to show that your attacker loses because it does not have facts that support its claims. Even if your curiosity is aroused about who might be the real Boss of your Note, let it go and do not concern yourself with that matter. The most important question is whether your opponent is the real Boss or the servant of that Boss regarding your Note. Maintain your sights on helping the judge see that your opponent doesn't have Boss rights. Win the fight you are in before worrying about other things.

BEGIN YOUR FACT-FINDING PROMPTLY

I strongly recommend that you begin the formal discovery process as soon as the rules of your court permit you to do so. There are several reasons why this matters. First, diligence sends a good message to the judge about your sincere intentions in the case. Second, you want to know as quickly as you can whether the machine has genuine facts to support its claims. Third, your formal discovery is a measure of insurance against your opponent's efforts to win the legal fight without having to first prove it has facts to support its assertions.

Regarding this third point, judges can bring a case to a halt if the facts are clear and the law that applies to those uncontested facts indicates that no more time need be spent on that particular legal dispute. One tactic that parties to a lawsuit can use to achieve such a shortcut is a motion seeking summary judgment. Your opponent could, for example, file a motion for summary judgment telling the judge that the information summarized in its motion constitutes the only facts necessary for the judge to rule against you, at least regarding those parts of your case being attacked by your opponent. The information your opponent puts in the motion would, of course, rarely be sufficient to prove its right under the UCC to enforce the Note.

A motion for summary judgment is typically denied, however, if filed before formal discovery is completed. You do not want your case to be ended in your opponent's favor before your opponent is required to show what its files contain. Active and dedicated fact-finding is your best way to avoid having to deal with the machine's motions that allege certain things are true or complete before you actually have enough information to counter such claims or to rebut and defend against misstated, inaccurate or outright fraudulent claims made by your opponent.

If you wait to start formal discovery until after your opponent files a motion seeking a quick end to the lawsuit, your opponent will likely argue that your newly raised concern about discovery is not genuine, but is instead only an improper litigation ploy or delay tactic. Do not give your judge any reason to accept that type of argument. Go into the case with a commitment to making your opponent prove everything necessary under the foreclosure fundamentals. Be resolved to make your opponent show whatever it thinks supports its case before the judge makes a decision that could hurt you. Formal discovery is a powerful tool—one that should be turned on as soon as the lawsuit starts.

GUARD AGAINST THEME-SPINNING

Active discovery effort is also a good way to combat theme-spinning. Your opponent, seeking sympathy from the judge, will likely use its tricks and wiles to create a theme it will spin throughout the proceedings, a story it will repeat as often as allowed. The particular words will vary, but here is the kind of picture of you that your opponent is likely to paint for the court:

Although the Borrower's poor financial circumstances might be sympathetic, he has no evidence to support any further delay of the foreclosure. The Borrower is just another professional debtor who stopped making mortgage payments and is now in court looking for a handout in the form of more free rent, at least for as long as he can get the court to let this case drag on. The Borrower is abusing the legal system for his own personal gain. He knows we are right but he has chosen to use cheap theatrical tactics to delay the inevitable. In fact, this legal fight is nothing more than the Borrower's emotional grudge. He may need anger counseling or a soup line for the indigent, but he should not be wasting the court's time any further.

Take a moment to think about the story the judge was just told. Any concern the judge is going to wonder about your motives? Any embarrassment or discomfort about the picture of you that your opponent just painted? Sure. You wouldn't be human if you didn't feel bad when things like that are said about you. Appreciate how easy it could be for a judge to lose focus when hearing that kind of yarn, especially if it is repeated over and over during the case.

Do not get sidetracked, however. Get rid of the emotion and remember that you have a story of your own. You are in court because your opponent has demanded your money under threat of foreclosure, and it has refused or been unable to prove any right to either. You're there to protect your rights and your home. Your story will persuade the judge to discount the misleading tale told by your opponent and listen instead to the law and facts.

Your opponent's theme-spinning is designed to mislead the court into thinking the evidentiary burden is your problem. When that happens, explain to the judge that it is your opponent's duty and obligation under the UCC, not yours, to prove its rights in relation to the Note. Remind the judge that your opponent's failure to respond to your letter (the informal discovery previously discussed) as required by the UCC means you owe it nothing, and that your Note is not in default or breached simply because you refuse to pay money to a company that has not shown any right to it. Your opponent's effort to spin a negative story about you is an opportunity for you to help the judge see who actually has the tarnished reputation and argument.

LET THE JUDGE HELP IF THEY DON'T COOPERATE

Don't expect your opponent to comply with your demands for discovery, even though the law says it must. The foreclosure machine will use one excuse after another to avoid having to show all of its cards. It will play games to keep you from seeing what information it has. More often, your opponent's tactics will be an attempt to hide the fact that it can't prove it is the Boss or the Boss's servant per the UCC requirements. You will be well served to think of each objection or failure to comply by your opponent as further evidence that it doesn't have the necessary proof.

Be strong and resolute in your insistence that your opponent must provide everything you demand through the formal discovery process. Do not give in or let your opponent off the hook. If you keep quiet in the face of its refusals to comply, this is likely to be construed as your acceptance or agreement that your opponent does not have to cooperate with the court's rules of discovery. That is not the message you want to send to the judge.

If your opponent's refusals and delays persist, get your judge involved. Ask him or her to compel your opponent to comply. Terminology varies from court to court, but each court has rules you can use to force your adversary to disclose everything it knows that is important to your defense or claims.

At some point, your opponent may state that it has no more information or documents to give you. The court won't require it to produce what it says it doesn't have. If your opponent claims it has given everything you requested, then get that in writing from your opponent or else ask your judge for an order that prohibits your opponent from surprising you later with any additional information or documents. If your opponent claims to have no more information, then its entire case against you should be limited to the facts and documents it has disclosed, and it should not be allowed to later add something else.

You can persuasively demonstrate the correctness of your request to your judge by pointing to your court's rules, which will give broad discretion in what you want from your opponent. You have the UCC and case law interpreting the UCC, which place the burden of proof on your opponent since it is trying to enforce your Note against you. You also have the legally recognized need for you to learn the details and actual substance of your opponent's asserted claims when being attacked that way. (See Chapter 11.)

If you sent the informal discovery letter I mentioned earlier in this chapter, don't forget to remind the judge that, by failing to respond to the letter or giving a shoddy response, your opponent has already admitted that you don't owe it anything. Mentioning that letter strengthens the importance of the UCC in your case. It also highlights the definite need for genuine proof of Boss status from your opponent, since it earlier did not have proof that it was the Boss or the Boss's servant.

Be prompt in filing your motion to compel your opponent's cooperation. If you delay too long, you might lose the right to do so under your court's rules. Don't bother your judge too soon if your court's rules require you to first attempt an informal resolution with your opponent. But if you come to a standoff, don't dally around.

Each time your opponent forces you to assert your discovery rights in court, it gives you a new opportunity to tell the story you want the court to understand—that the fairness principles of the UCC rules require your opponent to prove its right to enforce your Note before you have any duty to pay it anything or let it take your house. Not all judges are familiar with the UCC, so use each hearing as an opportunity to educate your judge and also to create a clear record that you have requested what is due you under the law.

Judges are accustomed to helping resolve discovery disputes. Get your judge involved if that's the only way you can make your opponent provide the information you've requested through the formal discovery process or else admit it has nothing else. Formal discovery is your opportunity to collect the factual information you need to focus the court's attention on your real story and drive home the important principles and merit of your legal case—use it.

Remember that what your opponent doesn't have or doesn't show you is the strength of your case against it. Obtain whatever facts and data it has about your Note and mortgage. Then do your negative content audit to locate gaps and missing facts that your opponent should have been able to prove in order to have the right under the UCC to enforce your Note.

The foreclosure machine has a terrible record in court when it's actually required to back up its hot claims with genuine facts. Its poor performance when it has been under the gun is good reason to be hopeful. Give your opponent the chance to fall flat on its face by your use of informal and formal discovery.

CHAPTER 11

RULE 3:
MAKE THE MACHINE PROVE ITS
RIGHT TO FORECLOSE

*"Laws are not masters but servants,
and he rules them who obeys them."*
Henry Ward Beecher
(1813-1887)

We do not have to make payments that we do not legally owe. Every month, however, borrowers targeted for foreclosure make payments and even give up their homes to people to whom they owe nothing. This has happened too frequently over the past several years, and it will continue for borrowers who do not use the law to their advantage.

A law with which the mortgage finance industry is all too familiar, and which you need to learn about, is the Uniform Commercial Code, or UCC. This chapter explains the importance of what the foreclosure machine already knows, and what it hopes you will not learn.

Bear with me in this chapter. The discussion covers complex points of law, and, by necessity, it contains a certain amount of legalese. But what you'll learn goes to the heart of your case against the foreclosure machine. I think you'll have a lot more success if you learn and apply these concepts and rules of law.

Let's begin with the Boss concept.

THE IMPORTANCE OF THE BOSS

Only one person or company has the legal right to enforce the Note when mortgage payments are late or not made. That "one" has the sole and legal right to receive payments due under the Note, to make demands for delinquent payments, to sell or give the Note away, to modify the terms of the Note with the borrower's consent, and to fully discharge or settle the borrower's obligation under the Note. That "one" exerts full dominion over the Note, including the right to tear it up or destroy it if desired. Laws and documents often differ as to the word or phrase they use to refer to the "one," and these variations in terminology are often and intentionally abused by the industry's machine. To avoid confusion, you and I will refer to this one person or company with genuine control over your Note as the Boss.

When you bought your house, or perhaps later when you refinanced it, you signed a Note promising to repay your loan and to make the mortgage payments for the benefit of the lender with which you dealt. That lender became the Boss of the Note, per the UCC, when you signed and delivered the Note. The Note contained language authorizing the Boss to sell the Note to someone else if it chose to do that, or it did not prohibit such dealings. The identity of the Boss of your Note, therefore, could have changed after you signed the Note.[74]

Most residential real estate loans created from the late 1990s through 2008 were sold and resold in the secondary mortgage market, as this period was the heyday of mortgage-backed securities. If the first sale of the Note was made in full compliance with the UCC, the buyer would have become the new Boss of the Note. If that first buyer subsequently sold the Note in full compliance with the UCC, the second buyer would then have become the Boss. If a third buyer later purchased the Note in full compliance with the UCC, the third Buyer would have become the new Boss, and so on, and so on.

If, however, a sale in that chain did not follow the strict UCC requirements, the Note ultimately could have been left without any Boss at all. That's correct: failure to comply with the UCC could have terminated an earlier Boss's rights under the Note and left the Note without a Boss. A transaction, for example a sale, could also have created a new owner of some or all of the value of your mortgage loan, but with no change in who was the Boss. In that event the buyer may have mistakenly thought itself the new Boss when in fact it obtained no Boss rights at all because of the UCC law of negotiable instruments.

Because you were not involved in the sale or exchange of your Note by your lender or its successors, you would not have received complete, if any, information about a change in its ownership or control. You would not have received information sufficient to let you or any attorney know whether each or any of the transactions had been done in full compliance with the UCC. You have never been in a position to know the true identity of the Boss of your Note except on that one day when you signed and delivered your Note and mortgage to your lender. Do not delude yourself into thinking otherwise. You received instructions, which may have changed from time to time, telling you where to send mortgage payments. You assumed that those instructions came from the Boss or the Boss's servant or agent.[75] (See "The Boss's Representative or Agent" later in this chapter.) You assumed that each payment you made actually reached the Boss and that the Boss gave you credit for the payment, thus lowering the remaining loan balance still due.

The first time you received a notice about a missed mortgage payment, you assumed the notice was an authorized communication from the Boss of the Note, or maybe the Boss's servant. When things really got bad and the notice turned into a demand for money combined with a threatened foreclosure, you still assumed the Boss was involved.

You never received a notice that said, "Oh, by the way, I do not represent the Boss of the Note, and by law I have no right to collect any payment from you. But, hey, send your money to me anyway, because if you don't I'll foreclose and take your house, whether or not that is actually a violation of your rights regarding the Note and the mortgage." But if the foreclosure machine were totally honest, that is the kind of notice it should have sent out to millions of borrowers. If the notice carried a disclosure like that, you would have begun to rethink the assumptions you had been making all along.

Let me again emphasize the basics. Only the Boss of the Note has a right to the payments you made. Only the Boss has the legal right to make demands under the Note if the payments have not been received in a timely manner. The Boss is the only one with the right to declare a default that can lead to a foreclosure of your house. If the Boss has not declared a default under the Note within the meaning of default as discussed in Chapters 4 and 8, foreclosure of the pledged collateral—that is, the mortgage against your house—is not proper. This is true whether you are dealing with a judicial or nonjudicial foreclosure.

When the foreclosure machine tries to take your house, it certainly implies that it is the Boss or that it can legally assert the rights of the Boss. But what if the machine is wrong? What does it mean if the machine can't prove it is the Boss or the Boss's servant? That means it has no right to your money and no right to foreclose. At least, that is my understanding based on my research and analysis.

If your opponent can't prove it has a right to Boss status, that also means that you may have been sending mortgage payments to the wrong company in the past, that any new payments you make in answer to the machine's threat may go to the wrong company, and, that if your home is foreclosed, the sales money may not get to the Boss, either. If there is still a Boss of your Note, and it did not receive your payments, you may still owe that money. Making payments to the wrong company or companies does not relieve you of the obligations to the actual Boss. You would hate to have your home foreclosed, or to settle with the machine for a sum of money or debt restructuring, only to be sued later by the real Boss, who has not been paid, did not receive the foreclosure monies, or did not agree to whatever debt restructuring you thought had occurred. These are all possibilities and problems for you if you assume that the foreclosure machine at your door actually represents the one and only entity with the right to call itself the Boss of your Note at that time.

Confusion about the identity of the Boss of the Note happens. This is apparently a result of sloppy business practices within the mortgage finance industry since the late 1990s. Should your judge doubt that, you can point to cases in which more than one company claims rights to the same Note[76] and cases, like those cited in this chapter, in which the party claiming rights, as if a Boss of the Note, could not, when pressed for proof, support its claims.

Sometimes a foreclosure suit is decided without the court's requiring and obtaining admissible evidence about the machine's alleged right to claim Boss status, and the relationship, if any, between the party claiming the right to foreclose and that of the alleged Boss. Whenever this happens, it places at risk the interests of the borrower, the true Boss, and others who may acquire interests in the Note when thinking they are dealing with the real Boss. UCC analysis is a must if adjudication is to be accurate, meaningful, and of value as precedent for others engaging in foreclosure litigation. You need to do your part to keep these important issues before your judge.

The mortgage finance industry created the economic mess we now endure. It doesn't own up to its responsibility, and yet it aggressively beats up on borrowers who have been made delinquent by the industry's incompetence, greed, and indifference. The industry has effectively created a double moral standard. It says that borrowers who don't pay their bills are bad, while it approves, or at least doesn't disparage, its own members who treat obligations as things to be ignored when doing so helps their business.[77] The industry hasn't demonstrated concern for the borrowers it created who are now victims.

So it is up to you to correct your own situation. Use your opponent's information, and lack of information, to show that it is not, and does not represent, the Boss of your Note. That is how you "get in their face." That is how you avoid paying your money to, or having your home taken by, a company with no legal rights to either.

THE UNIFORM COMMERCIAL CODE
PROTECTS BORROWERS

An Introduction to the UCC

Our legal system upholds common-sense principles of fairness. For example, it supports and has put legal teeth behind the concept that a borrower is required to pay only bona fide legal debts and that the Boss of that legal debt, not someone else, is the only one entitled to enforce the obligations of the Note.

The Uniform Commercial Code, or UCC, now law in every state, is designed to implement these fairness principles. It contains protections for the borrower that simultaneously protect the Boss, and vice versa. The UCC rules are designed to help ensure that payments of the Note (including foreclosure proceeds if a home is foreclosed to help satisfy the obligation of the Note) go to the Boss, and also to protect the borrower from someone not entitled to enforce the Note.

The UCC applies to mortgage loans because the Note is, with only rare exceptions, a negotiable instrument under the Uniform Commercial Code and, therefore, subject to that old and well established body of law.[78] If your lender had the right to sell your Note or put it into the stream of commerce so it could be sold and traded by others, it is a negotiable instrument. Yes, when your Note is sold, traded, or exchanged by people you do not know, it is, at least legally, a lot like the check you write on your bank account.

The Uniform Commercial Code is your friend. It is the enemy of the foreclosure machine when the machine falsely or mistakenly claims rights derived through ownership or control of your Note. Evaluating your attacker's claims in terms of the strict requirements of the UCC is the way to learn whether your opponent actually has any rights regarding your Note.[79] The UCC establishes the ground rules that can shield you from bogus threats coming from those who lack legal right to make those demands under the UCC.[80]

During a state's adoption of the Uniform Commercial Code, the renumbering system of its parts and other superficial differences may have occurred as the state incorporated the UCC into the state's already existing body of laws. For example, the UCC's Article 3, § 3-301, *Person Entitled To Enforce Instrument,* is § 55-3-301 of the New Mexico Statutes; § 28-3-301 of the Idaho Statutes; § 3301 of the California Commercial Code; § 73.0301 of Oregon's Commercial Transaction Statutes; and 12A:3-301 of the New Jersey Statutes. (The symbol §

stands for the word *section*. The number that follows it identifies the relevant section of the statute in question.)

My UCC references are to the version of this code that was approved by the Uniform Law Commissioners, in collaboration with The American Law Institute, and then recommended for adoption by the states. A copy of this form of the Uniform Commercial Code can be viewed online at www.law.cornell.edu/ucc. Article 3—*Negotiable Instruments* is the part of the UCC you will use most. A copy of that portion of the UCC can be viewed at www.law.cornell.edu/ucc/3.

Compilations of the UCC by state, including variances or proposed revisions, can be located online or in the legal or business sections of public libraries or libraries in law schools or courts.[81] You can also compare the text of the UCC as available online or in this book with the text of your state's form of the UCC for the same section. The organization and content of the UCC among the states is highly standardized, however, especially with regard to the portions of the UCC most applicable to residential foreclosure matters.

The substance of the UCC also is highly uniform and constant among the states, and intentionally so, because it is law designed to nurture, protect, and standardize commerce across state lines and within state boundaries. Protecting the borrower and the Boss is important to the viability of trades and exchanges of negotiable instruments in the United States. The laws protecting their rights are also barriers to fraud and mistakes that could hurt buyers of negotiable instruments. For example, the UCC provides the means by which a prudent buyer can usually tell if the seller has the legal right to sell a negotiable instrument such as your Note.

The Uniform Commercial Code, when people take time to use it, is a type of insurance for those making, buying, and selling Notes, somewhat akin to real estate title insurance that gives additional protections and comforts to people who buy and sell real estate. The UCC is law designed to foster commerce by protecting your interests, the interests of the Boss (that is, the only one entitled to sell the Note), and the rights of prospective purchasers of the Note.

Some Provisions of the UCC and Related Case Law

The content of the UCC and related case law reflect concerns for the protections afforded to a borrower who issues a Note or other negotiable instrument. Here are some examples:

> "[T]he payor of a [N]ote exposes himself or herself to double liability if he or she makes payment to someone other than the [Boss] of the instrument, *unless the other person to whom*

payment is made is an agent of the owner of the [N]ote." (Emphasis added.) *In the Matter of Foreclosure of a Deed of Trust Executed by Woodard,* 185 N.C.App. 159 (NC Ct.App. 2007).

"The purpose of the possession requirement in Article 3 [of the UCC] is to protect the Debtor from multiple enforcement claims to the same [N]ote." *Marks v. Branstein,* No. 09-11402-NMG (USDCt D. MA 2010) and, also, *In re Kemp,* No. 08-18700-JHW (Bankr. D. NJ 2010). Here, "possession" refers to physical possession of the Note with all of the markings and attachments to it, as contrasted with what someone says is a copy of the physical Note.

Part (c) of UCC § 3-203, *Transfer of instrument; rights acquired by transfer,* provides that even a person in possession of the Note cannot enforce it if the Note was not properly indorsed and delivered to that person. (The UCC spells indorse with an "i" rather than an "e" as in most dictionaries.)

Part (d) of UCC § 3-203, *Transfer of instrument; rights acquired by transfer,* attempts to eliminate risks of multiple claimants under the same Note by providing that a possessor of the Note who did not acquire 100% of all rights and entitlements under the Note is a transferee who "obtains no rights." For example, someone who can prove only a partial interest in the Note, or who might only be holding onto the Note for someone else, does not have a right to enforce the Note.[82] That is, only the one Boss of the Note can direct enforcement of the Note, and there can only be one true Boss.

Part (b) of UCC § 3-309, *Enforcement of lost, destroyed, or stolen instrument,* provides in relevant part that "The court may not enter judgment in favor of the person seeking enforcement [of a lost, destroyed or stolen Note] unless it finds that the person required to pay the instrument is adequately protected against loss that might occur by reason of a claim by another person to enforce the instrument."[83]

UCC § 3-501(a) states that only the one entitled to enforce the Note or its servant may make demands for payment.[84] § 3-501(b)(2) states that, upon your request, whoever is making the demand must exhibit the Note, identify itself, and, if alleging to represent the Boss, then prove its authority to be the servant. The borrower "is given the right to make these demands for his [or her] own protection."[85]

Right to enforce a Note requires strict compliance with the UCC in order to achieve the protective policies under the UCC. See, for example:

- *Adams v. Madison Realty & Development, Inc.*, 853 F.2d 163 (3rd Cir. 1988): This decision notes that strict compliance with the UCC protects each intended owner of the Note as it gets passed about.

- *Cogswell v. Citifinancial Mortgage*, 624 F.3d 395 (US Cir.7th 2010): Ruling against the foreclosure machine, the court raised the concern that the machine's failure to prove compliance with the UCC requirements created a reasonable concern about whether the "[N]ote was actually held by another who would be entitled to enforce it against the property owners."

- *Norwood v. Chase Home Finance*, No. A-09-CA-940-JRN (USDCt. W.D. TX 2011): "The rationale for the strict requirement of possession [of the physical Note] is to protect the obligor from being subject to multiple demands for payment on a single [N]ote. ... Without procedural safeguards, multiple parties could force the debtor to pay the [N]ote. If the original [N]ote is a prerequisite for enforcement, however, then a later party faces a significant hurdle before it may enforce the [N]ote."

- *Bank of America v. Miller*, 2011-Ohio-1403 (OH Ct.App.2nd 2011): "[I]t becomes essential to establish that the person who demands payment of a negotiable [N]ote, or to whom payment is made, is the duly qualified holder. Otherwise, the obligor is exposed to the risk of double payment, or at least to the expense of litigation incurred to prevent duplicative satisfaction of the instrument. These risks provide makers with a recognizable interest in demanding proof of the chain of title."

Some Judicial Concepts You Should Know

Sometimes the fairness principles that protect you from claims of those who are not the Boss surface when a court addresses common judicial policies, such as:

- *Judicial standing*—whether the plaintiff (that is, the party who starts the lawsuit) has sufficient connection to the Note to justify invoking the court's jurisdiction, or control of the case, when making claims against you[86]

- *Real party in interest*—whether your opponent is actually the one to whom you legally owe money under the Note[87]

- *Joinder*—whether the essential persons are actually parties to that particular lawsuit so full adjudication of all closely related legal issues can be raised, thereby affording the borrower and the Boss the opportunity to raise all of their claims and defenses with a view of obtaining the most meaningful and complete adjudication possible[88]

- *Finality, or judicial economy or efficiency*—whether the borrower and the Boss should be in the same lawsuit so the dispute about what if anything is owed can be fully resolved once and for all times without risk of burdening the borrower, the Boss, or the judicial system with unnecessarily extended or additional litigation[89]

When courts address these judicial policies in relationship to a real estate foreclosure, UCC law is necessarily invoked, even if not specifically mentioned. This is because correct decisions about those policy issues typically revolve about the question of who has rights to enforce the Note. In other words, is your opponent actually the Boss?[90] The only way to know whether your opponent has the right to enforce the Note (or the mortgage, which has no validity independent of the Note)[91] is to force it to prove its relationship to the Note, and in minute detail going back to the lender who was the first Boss of your Note. That relationship, whether or not it exists, can only be defined with analysis pursuant to the UCC.

Each time the court deals with an issue that involves one of these judicial policies, the UCC's strict definition of the Boss should be placed before the judge. Strengthen your case by making certain that you raise the fairness principles of the UCC and that the judge looks at them as he or she makes decisions involving judicial standing, real party in interest, joinder, finality and judicial economy.

The UCC Also Protects the Boss

I think your judge should be reminded that his or her decision involves more than just your dispute with your opponent. An incorrect decision can hurt both you and the true Boss of your Note. An incorrect decision can also send the wrong message to those who deal in negotiable instruments like mortgage loans and are looking for excuses to ignore the plain language of the law.

In addition to protecting you, the UCC simultaneously protects the Boss. As noted earlier in this chapter, your obligation under the Note is not reduced or discharged if you pay the wrong person, or if the wrong person gets the foreclosure proceeds from selling your house. The UCC intends that the Boss should be solely in charge of your Note. Its incorporated fairness principles for the Boss keep you on the hot seat to be certain your payments get to the right person, including proceeds from a foreclosure.[92]

Even if a court mistakenly rules that your opponent has the right to payments or foreclosure, you could nevertheless be liable to the real Boss of the Note. For example, UCC § 3-602 subjects the borrower to continuing liability and the risk of extended litigation with the Boss should the borrower make Note payments to or permit its home value to be taken by someone other than the Boss.[93] Your obligation under the Note is clearly discharged to the extent your payments go to "a person entitled to enforce the [Note]," as stated by § 3-602(a)(ii), but you may still owe that money to the Boss if the wrong person gets your payments. Making sure your payments go to the right person is important. This is a legally recognized concern when the issue of who has the right to enforce a Note is raised.[94] A court order in favor of a person who is not the Boss of your Note does not necessarily protect you if the disgruntled and real Boss later decides to make you pay your obligation under the Note.

The documents you submit to the court should help the judge remember the underlying fairness principles that are incorporated in the Uniform Commercial Code. If you don't remind the judge that the UCC is designed to protect you and the Boss from claims by people lacking the right to enforce the Note, your judge may get too involved with details and lose sight of the broad purposes of the UCC and its strict requirements when defining who has the sole legal right to enforce and make claims related to your Note.

You have no choice but to push your opponent to prove its alleged Boss-type rights. You're at risk of more headaches and debts if you don't.[95] This pressure on you is the UCC's attempt to help take care of the Boss.

I think it is common for the wrong company to allege Boss status in a foreclosure-related lawsuit. How often such mistakes or fraud have occurred can't be accurately computed. Only a tiny portion of the millions of foreclosures in the past few years resulted in contested litigation. The mass of judicial foreclosures placed no burden on the machine to actually prove its right to take the targeted homes. Most foreclosures were the nonjudicial type, in which no judge was ever involved and no facts were preserved in public records regarding the propriety or legality of those foreclosures. Typically, a company showed up, demanded payment under threat of foreclosure, and the homeowners walked away without ever demanding proof that the attacker had the rights it claimed.

Published court decisions in which the foreclosure machine prevailed have rarely involved genuine UCC analysis. Often, the reason is that the borrower in those cases didn't know about the UCC or failed to put the foreclosure fundamentals clearly at issue.[96]

Successes by borrowers, on the other hand, have frequently involved some level of analysis of Boss rights according to the UCC. Those questions may have been raised either by the borrower or the judge, and either directly as a UCC question of law or indirectly as a determination involving a judicial policy such as judicial standing or real party in interest.[97] As a result of my research, I am convinced that borrowers will realize substantial gains if they challenge the machine to actually prove a right to make demands regarding the Notes.

You are not required to pay the wrong claimant under the Note, and that is one of the UCC protections for you. However, if your payments or home go to any person other than the one true Boss, you face the risk of another lawsuit and more collection headaches. That is an intended pressure for the benefit and protection of the Boss of your Note. These are serious matters for both you and the Boss. The judge needs to understand that letting the wrong person take your money or home can hurt the Boss and also can expose you to more problems. However, the risk of an incorrect decision can be minimized by adherence to the strict UCC requirements. Both judicial precedence and UCC authority are available to help you explain this to your judge.

THE UCC AND THE BURDEN OF PROOF

As noted above, the UCC, which has been adopted by all fifty states, defines the Note as a negotiable instrument.[98] Because this well-established body of law controls negotiable instruments, it therefore defines who has the right to enforce your Note. The UCC makes it clear that you owe your opponent nothing unless and until it produces real proof that it has the right to enforce your Note—that is, proof that satisfies the strict tests of the UCC. This is how the law helps protect you from someone who has no right to your money or home.

Your court's rules place the burden of proof on the party claiming the right to enforce your Note, but the UCC is even tougher. Your opponent must prove that it is the Boss or the Boss's servant or else lose its case against you.[99]

The UCC authorizes you to demand information from your opponent and simultaneously places a heavy burden on it to comply with your request. If your opponent doesn't cooperate, it has no right to demand payment from you, and no right to your money also means no right to take your house.

Here are examples of what the UCC requires from a person claiming the right to enforce your Note:

> ➤ UCC § 3-203(b) vests in the transferee (the person to whom the Note is transferred) the rights of the transferor (the person who held the Note and is transferring it to a new holder) to enforce the payment obligations of the Note. This would permit, for example, a person in possession of the Note to claim Boss status when it couldn't otherwise qualify as a Boss. Qualifying as Boss under this part of the UCC is difficult. The required proof would consist of showing that the prior company was the Boss at the time of the transfer and that it intended to deliver all of its Boss powers when it gave up possession of the Note. Thus, the proof would have to establish the transferor's right to Boss status by analysis of those rights all the way back to your lender, and clear evidence would have to be provided as to the reasons and intents of that transferor when giving up possession.[100] If applicable, this section creates a possible Boss status as a "non-holder in possession" under UCC § 3-301(ii) discussed later in this chapter.

> ➤ UCC § 3-308(b) provides that a person who actually produces the Note is entitled to payment, but only if that person "proves entitlement to enforce the instrument under Section 3-301."[101] In this section and many other UCC sections, references to "enforce" mean the strict Boss status requirements of UCC § 3-301, discussed more fully later in this chapter.

> ➤ UCC § 3-309(b) involves enforcement of a lost, destroyed or stolen Note. It states that the person seeking to enforce the Note "must prove the terms of the instrument and the person's right to enforce the instrument." Recall that under the UCC the word *instrument* means the Note. Observe that this section also requires proof of the "right to enforce," that being the difficult Boss status requirements of UCC § 3-301.

> ➤ UCC § 3-501, *Presentment,* states that only a person with the right to enforce the Note has a right to make demands under

it.[102] Are you beginning to appreciate the importance of the "right to enforce"?

➤ UCC § 3-501(b)(2) states that, upon your demand, "the person making presentment"—that is, the person demanding payment of the Note—must exhibit or present the Note. Pursuant to this part of the UCC, your opponent has no right to demand payment from you until it has produced the physical Note. A copy is not enough. The only exception occurs when your opponent asserts a right to enforce the Note pursuant to § 3-309 (related to an alleged lost, destroyed, or stolen Note) and provides all of the proof that § 3-309 requires.

➤ UCC § 3-501(b)(2) further states that the person making presentment also must, upon your demand, give reasonable identification, and, if presentment is made on behalf of another person, provide reasonable evidence of authority to do so. In other words, your opponent has to identify itself, meaning prove its right to enforce your Note or else its authority to act on behalf of someone else who has that right. If your opponent claims to be the servant of the Boss, you are entitled to see proof that the company your opponent identifies as the Boss really has that status under the UCC. Your opponent must also prove that it is doing that Boss' bidding regarding your Note as a result of a clear instruction about your Note from that alleged Boss.

Until you've received all of this information from your opponent, you have not dishonored or breached the Note by not paying the demanded money to the company that has not proven its right to make that demand. The law does not require you to pay money to a company that makes demands but refuses to, or cannot, prove it is owed your money.

Furthermore, until all of that information and proof is provided, you haven't been told by the Boss or its representative that anything is due under the Note—that is, "presentment is not effective until the presenter has reasonably satisfied all proper counter-demands of the person to whom presentment has been made."[103] Unless you get complete proof that your opponent has a right to enforce the Note, therefore, the notice of delinquency or default you received is meritless—only the one true Boss of your Note has the right by law to say when and how much, if anything, you owe related to your Note. The real Boss could be mistaken or a crook, so you don't want to take its word about such matters, either. No person other than that Boss, however, has any business or right to say what the Boss thinks or wants to do regarding your Note.

➤ UCC 3-602(b) states that the borrower's obligation to pay anything on the Note, including letting his or her home be taken as payment, is subject first to the duty of the attacker to give proof of its rights. This section states, "Upon request, a transferee shall seasonably furnish reasonable proof that the Note has been transferred." In essence, this is a requirement that the person claiming the right to enforce the Note must prove it has that right when requested to do so. If the person can't provide that proof, or refuses to respond to the request, the borrower doesn't owe anything to that person. Observe, that this provision requires your opponent to provide real proof—not opinions, guesses, or self-serving conclusions. You can make your request before a lawsuit begins via an informal letter, as discussed in Chapter 10, and by a letter or formal discovery during the course of your lawsuit.

Numerous court decisions and other legal authorities address the UCC's fundamental fairness principles. These legal sources support the idea that the burden of proof is placed on the person who is demanding payment from you or threatening to foreclose. A few examples are provided below:

" ... [T]o protect the Debtor from multiple enforcement claims to the same [N]ote ... the maker of the [N]ote must have certainty regarding the party who is entitled to enforce the [N]ote. From the maker's standpoint, therefore, it becomes essential to establish that the person who demands payment of a negotiable [N]ote, or to whom payment is made, is the duly qualified holder. Otherwise, the obligor is exposed to the risk of double payment, or at least to the expense of litigation incurred to prevent duplicative satisfaction of the instrument. These risks provide makers [i.e., borrowers] with a recognizable interest in demanding proof of the chain of title. Consequently, plaintiffs here, as makers of the [N]otes, may properly press defendant to establish its holder status."[104]

Discussing requirements of UCC § 3-301(ii), the federal bankruptcy court concludes that a person claiming status as a "non-holder in possession of the instrument who has the rights of a holder" must "prove the transaction" by which it claims to have obtained such rights, must prove the transferor had the right to enforce the Note at that time, and must produce the physical Note. Further, the court noted that mere ownership of the Note did not establish the right to enforce the payment obligations under the Note and that even if possession of the Note was demonstrated, the court was not allowed to assume without proof that the other requirements had been satisfied. *In re Wilhelm*, 407 B.R. 392 (Bankr. D. ID 2009). Notice that neither possession nor ownership is sufficient to establish the "right to enforce" your Note.

"In addition to authenticating the [N]ote, MERS must show that it is entitled to enforce the [N]ote. Only the holder of a negotiable promissory [N]ote (with minor exceptions not relevant in this case) is entitled to enforce the [N]ote. *See* CAL.COM. CODE § 3301. The holder enforces the [N]ote by making a demand for payment. *See id* § 3501(a). The person making a demand shows its right to enforcement by showing the original of the promissory [N]ote. *See id,* § 3501(b)(2)." *In re Vargas*, 396 B.R. 511, 517 (Bankr. C.D. Cal. 2008). As discussed later in this chapter, the physical Note, not just a copy, must be produced if your opponent claims to have the right to enforce it and does not claim that the Note was lost, destroyed or stolen.

"The rationale for the strict requirement of possession is to protect the obligor from being subject to multiple demands for payment on a single [N]ote. *See Camp,* 965 F.2d at 29 (explaining that mere possession is insufficient because a later party may demand payment). Without procedural safeguards, multiple parties could force the debtor to pay the [N]ote. If the original [N]ote is a prerequisite for enforcement, however, then a later party faces a significant hurdle before it may enforce the [N]ote." *Norwood v. Chase Home Finance,* No. A-09-CA-940-JRN (USDCt. W.D. TX 2011).

"[W]here the negotiable instrument sued upon is in the possession of the plaintiff, the original of the document, normally, must be produced since it is the best evidence of the obligation." *Nadjarian v. Rose,* No. PC/05-5213 (RI SuperiorCt. 2009). That is, if your opponent claims to have the physical Note, the only way to fully protect your rights is for you to demand to see and then examine all of that document, which will likely be different than when you gave it to the lender.

"In a foreclosure proceeding under a power of sale [i.e., non-judicial sale], the lender bears the burden of proving four elements that must be established in order for the clerk of court to authorize the mortgagee or trustee to proceed with the foreclosure: (i) valid debt of which the party seeking to foreclose is the holder, (ii) default, (iii) right to foreclose under the instrument, (iv) notice to those entitled to such ..." *In the Matter of the Foreclosure of a Deed of Trust Executed by Adams,* No. COA09-1455 (NC Ct.App. 2010). For more information about the importance of the UCC in nonjudicial foreclosure situations, see the discussions later in this chapter and in the section called *Avoid "Show Me the Note" Difficulties* in Chapter 12.

"[I]t becomes essential to establish that the person who demands payment of a negotiable [N]ote, or to whom payment is made, is the duly qualified holder. Otherwise, the obligor is exposed to the risk of double payment, or at least to the expense of litigation incurred to prevent duplicative satisfaction of the instrument. These risks provide makers with a recognizable interest in demanding proof of the chain of [ownership and control]." *Bank of America v. Miller,* 2011-Ohio-1403 (OH Ct.App.2nd 2011).

"The official commentary to this section explains that while the transferee of an instrument may enforce the instrument without being its holder, the transferee, unlike a holder, is not entitled to the presumption of the right of enforcement, and must prove the transaction through which the instrument was acquired. UCC § 3-203, § 2, cmt. 1 (1999)." *In re Thomas,* No. 10-40549-MSH (Adv. Pro. No. 10-04086) (Bankr. D. MA 2011). This case is discussing the state of Massachusetts's equivalent of UCC § 3-203(b). Keep in mind also that, in this context, *holder* refers to the person who qualifies as a Boss pursuant to the UCC, not simply a person with the Note in hand. A person in possession of the Note may have no right to enforce it pursuant to the UCC.

"Person seeking to enforce ... *must* identify the person entitled to enforce the [N]ote and establish that that person has not been paid," and "Determining to whom a [N]ote is payable requires examination not only of the face of the [N]ote but also of any indorsements. This is because the party to whom a [N]ote is payable may be changed by indorsement."[105] Also, regarding application of § 3-203(a): "[T]he person in possession of the [N]ote *must* also demonstrate the purpose of the delivery of the note to it in order to qualify as the person entitled to enforce."[106]

(Emphasis added.) *Report on Application of the UCC to Selected Issues Relating to Mortgage Notes,* Permanent Editorial Board for the Uniform Commercial Code.

"BOSS" PER THE UCC

What Is a Boss?

I selected the term *Boss* for the purpose of introducing the Uniform Commercial Code's importance to your court fight against the industry's foreclosure machine. The authority, control, and trump rights associated with the word Boss are helpful concepts when thinking about your Note and determining whether your attacker has the legal right to be making demands related to the Note or mortgage (a document that has no importance apart from the Note).

The UCC, however, does not mention *Boss* at all. Nor does it provide a single defined word that encompasses all the rights and entitlements of the Boss, even though the Boss concept is a good way to relate to the many words and parts of the UCC.

Your opponents will not likely mention *Boss* either. The foreclosure machine, when trying to imply or intimate that it is the Boss of the Note, or that it represents the Boss, will toss around terms like *beneficiary, lender, owner, creditor, trustee,* or *holder.* Sometimes it will even claim to be in *possession* of the original Note, as if the use of any of these words or claims magically gives your opponent the right to enforce the Note. Even ownership of the Note is not a prerequisite to having the right to enforce the Note.[107] There is no open-sesame magic, and no words that automatically mean your opponent has the right to make demands related to the Note.

Ignore, therefore, whatever label your opponent uses to refer to its alleged rights. Instead, concentrate on the tests of the UCC. Substance, not labeling, is the only thing truly important when applying the UCC. Your opponent must either prove that it is the Boss or the legitimate representative of the Boss, or else it has no right to make demands for payments or to allege that you are in default.

Even the words of the contracts you executed, those being the Note and the mortgage, do not trump the UCC when it comes to deciding who by law holds the status of Boss of your Note.[108] For example, suppose the terms of your Note attempt to define the Boss differently from the UCC, or the Note or mortgage refers to the successor lender as then having all the rights of the original lender—this makes no difference.

The UCC, not the text of the Note or the mortgage, defines the Boss of your Note. Being a negotiable instrument triggers the rules of the UCC, which include defining the rights of the lender and its successors regarding the enforcement of the obligations of your Note.

A good judge will look beyond labels and will apply law as indicated by the facts and the meaning reasonably assigned to those facts in the context of the law and policies underlying it.[109] Your discovery demands and your evaluations of the information that your opponent produces will show what it can and cannot prove. Facts, not your opponent's calculated words, determine whether it has a right to enforce the Note. Keep your eye on the requirements of the UCC and you'll be able to see past the machine's subterfuge.

I will continue to use the term *Boss* for two reasons. First, because it reflects a correct concept, and second, because it is easier to use Boss as an instructive tool than to talk about the various ways a person can become the Boss pursuant to the interactive pieces of the Uniform Commercial Code. I will also use references to the basic UCC document, the one that has been assimilated into each state's body of law. As I've said, the numbering and labeling used in this book may vary from how your state numbers and labels the same UCC text, but you will not have difficulty identifying your state's complement to the sections I discuss once you get into that activity. In your litigation, you and your opponent will, of course, refer to the UCC in the way specifically set out by your state's statutes.

Let me emphasize that only one person has the right to enforce your Note. The UCC is a body of law designed to give the right of enforcement to the one person who most fairly, in the eyes of those who created that law, is entitled to that stature. To underscore that there can be only one Boss for each Note, UCC § 3-203(d) provides that "If a transferor purports to transfer less than the entire instrument, negotiation of the instrument does not occur. The *transferee obtains no rights under this Article* and has only the rights of a partial assignee." [Emphasis added.] A person who doesn't receive complete ownership of and full rights to the Note when it obtains possession of the Note can't be the Boss. A Boss has everything or nothing, under the UCC, and there are no exceptions.

The one-Boss concept is there to protect you from possibly paying the wrong person. It simultaneously protects the Boss from some interloper trying to take what is owed to the Boss. The identity of the Boss can change with each sale or exchange of the Note, as was so common within the industry during the late 1990s through 2008. At each point in time, however, there can be only one Boss—or possibly even no Boss at all, depending on how botched a sale or exchange within the chain of ownership and control might have been.

Understand that the Boss can make whatever arrangements it wishes with others regarding sharing the proceeds or benefits of the Note, including sharing in possible foreclosure proceeds. But the Boss is the only person entitled to make those arrangements. Likewise, the Boss, and no one else, is the only person or company with the right to engage a servant to help it manage its interests in the Note and related mortgage. A Boss's creditor may have legitimate claims against the Boss for money it gets from enforcing your Note. That creditor, however, is not the Boss as defined by the UCC and has no right to pretend otherwise, no right to enforce the payment obligation of your Note, and no right to foreclose your home.

A Definition of the Boss—the UCC's Starting Point

Now we need to look at the UCC to learn how it defines the person with Boss-type authority over the Note. In other words, the person who is:

- The one with legal authority to enforce the Note—that is, to collect the amounts owed under it

- The one legally entitled to payments under the Note

- The one entitled to foreclosure sale proceeds should your home be foreclosed to satisfy your obligation under the Note

- The one with the authority to declare a default under the Note as a necessary precursor to initiation of a foreclosure, whether in court or by non-judicial process[110]

Obtaining a technical understanding of Boss under the Uniform Commercial Code begins with UCC § 3-301, which states the following:

UCC § 3-301. Person Entitled To Enforce Instrument

"Person entitled to enforce" an instrument means (i) the holder of the instrument, (ii) a non-holder in possession of the instrument who has the rights of a holder, or (iii) a person not in possession of the instrument who is entitled to enforce the instrument pursuant to Section 3-309 or 3-418(d). A person may be a person entitled to enforce the instrument even though the person is not the owner of the instrument or is in wrongful possession of the instrument."[111]

A brief comment about the last sentence of § 3-301 is warranted. It won't likely have any importance to your case, but I thought you might like to know what the UCC is getting at by having added it. Don't worry about the possibility that your opponent will be permitted to enforce the Note if, for example, it was stolen from a rightful owner or was acquired in some illegal or immoral way.

Inside a court of law, your opponent will be required to prove its relationship to the Note. In other words, it will have to answer such questions as: Is it the Boss or a duly appointed agent of the Boss? How and when did the alleged Boss obtain possession of the Note, and under what circumstances? From whom did the alleged Boss obtain possession, and what relationship to the Note did that person have per the UCC? If your opponent admits having wrongfully obtained possession of the Note or it says a thief is in the chain of title, rest assured the judge will not let your opponent enforce that Note.

The last sentence is in § 3-301 to help clarify the commercial aspect of a negotiable instrument, and it places a higher responsibility on the owner of the Note to protect its property. For example, consider a situation where there is a purchaser of the Note who is totally unaware that it was stolen. The UCC says the innocent buyer has the right to enforce the Note rather than the Boss who failed to protect the Note against theft.

You won't be facing an opponent who seeks to enforce the Note while admitting to having acquired it illegally or wrongfully. Nor will you face an opponent who asserts Boss status under a claim of having innocently acquired possession of a Note that was stolen or wrongfully taken from a previous rightful owner. Any company that would try to claim Boss status for a stolen or improperly obtained Note has a terribly difficult burden of proof about too many things to go there. That last sentence clarifies that ownership is not a requirement of Boss status, but the rest of that last sentence will not likely have any importance in your lawsuit.

Typical of statutory law, many of the words used in the UCC are defined by other statutes and by case law that has developed over time. A few explanations may help you more comfortably absorb the UCC's legalese. For example, think *Note* when you see *instrument*.[112] The word *enforce* can be understood to mean the legal right to all of those Boss-type powers and entitlements I itemized above. The word *person* is used broadly to address an individual or a legal entity, which might be, for example, a corporation, a partnership, a trust, a government agency, or a limited liability company.[113] When I write the word *person*, I use it in that broad sense as well, unless the context clearly indicates otherwise.

THE THREE TESTS
THAT DETERMINE BOSS STATUS

UCC § 3-301 sets forth three tests to determine if a person is entitled to enforce an instrument or Note. A person who satisfies any of these three tests is the Boss at that time. If a Boss sells or transfers the Note, a successor Boss may arise, but only if that next person in the chain of rights then satisfies part (i), (ii), or (iii) of § 3-301.

The three tests are mutually exclusive, so a person who can satisfy part (i) cannot also satisfy (ii) or (iii). Likewise, a person who cannot satisfy part (i) may be able to qualify as a Boss pursuant to part (ii) or (iii). Anyone who cannot prove status pursuant to one of these three tests is not the Boss.

Furthermore, a person is no longer the Boss if that person transfers its rights as Boss to another. A person who is the Boss can also waive or abandon that position by agreement with others. A person who claims Boss status due to special relationship with an alleged Boss must first prove that alleged Boss satisfied these UCC tests, and then must prove the legal relationship that lets that claimant act like the Boss regarding your Note. These simple truths are stated here to help you evaluate the meaning of what your opponent cannot prove with the documents and information it produces in response to your fact-finding.

Remember, your objective is to demonstrate that your opponent can't prove it is the Boss or the Boss's servant. You may never learn who the Boss really is, but you don't need to know that in order to defeat your opponent in court.

Compliance with parts (i) and (ii) of § 3-301 requires current physical possession of the original Note, but part (iii) does not. If your opponent actually has physical possession of the Note, it must satisfy the tests of parts (i) or (ii) to enjoy Boss status. If the opponent does not have possession of the Note, then analysis under part (iii) will control whether or not it has Boss status for itself or for whomever it might claim to be representing. Part (iii) is, however, also tied to possession, because the person claiming rights under part (iii) has to prove that it or its successor properly held physical possession in the past. Physical possession is, therefore, a key element that must be proven by anyone asserting the right to enforce a Note, whether or not the person claiming Boss status currently has possession of the Note.

As mentioned earlier, reason exists to be hopeful that the machine won't be able to prove physical possession of the Note or strict compliance with the UCC, because of the mortgage finance industry's sloppy business practices in those years when its emphasis was so heavily on selling mortgage-backed securities.[114] Likewise, evidence exists that the managers of investment pools that purchased the millions and millions of mortgage-backed securities often did not take possession of the Notes or personally inspect those Notes to check for even rudimentary compliance with the UCC requirements.[115] Whether the foreclosure machine represents itself, a bank, or an investment fund, its difficulties will be the same. The machine must prove a proper chain of possession of the Note and authority per the UCC, or else it has no right to enforce your Note.

What the UCC means by the three ways a person can qualify to enforce the Note are discussed below. In addition, Exhibits D, *Checklist—Investigation of Boss Status;* E, *Example—Informal Discovery;* and F, *Examples— Formal Discovery,* which you will find in the back of this book, are provided to demonstrate how the UCC rules get incorporated into the effort to make the machine prove whether it has the right to enforce your Note or to foreclose your home.

UCC § 3-301(i)— Holder of the Instrument

UCC § 3-301(i) recognizes a person's right to enforce a Note if that person is "the holder of the instrument." Unfortunately, no single definition or section of the UCC supplies the complete meaning of this little phrase. Understanding what the UCC means by it requires the aid of other parts of the UCC.

UCC § 1-201(21) defines what a holder is after the person achieves that status. But to learn how a person becomes a holder, and to find out the limitations of enforcement rights that apply to the types of persons who could become a holder, one must study UCC §§ 3-109, 3-201, 3-203, 3-204, and 3-205. Not every holder has the same enforcement rights. For example, a thief or a person who found a lost Note could be a holder, but he or she would have no rights to enforce the Note. Also, some holders are subject to claims and defenses that the borrower could raise against the original lender or its agents, while a holder in due course is freed from liability for most of those types of claims and defenses. You'll get a better feel for the differences as we look more at the concept of "holder of the instrument," just one of the three classes of persons who can enforce a Note.

Because piecing together what *holder* means can be a little daunting, you may find it helpful to think of holder in the way I define it in order to help me keep the interactive elements in focus:

> A *"holder of the instrument" is a person in physical possession of the Note, having received it from a previous holder who, at that time, had the sole right to enforce the Note and who voluntarily delivered the Note with the intention of transferring all of the transferor's interests in the Note, including the right to*

enforce it, to the transferee, said Note having been indorsed by the person who was the Boss at the time of the indorsement to be payable specifically to the recipient, or else payable to whomever has possession of it.

This definition is of my making. It helps me remember to check the many UCC requirements for Boss status. It describes a holder who would have the right to enforce your Note if you came across that person in a foreclosure lawsuit, and is not about holders who might not be a threat. You may think it too wordy, but the more you look at all of the legalese used to define the little six-letter word *holder*, the more tolerant you may be of my mnemonic device.

Keep in mind that your opponent may say it is a holder. Use of that label, however, does not a holder make. You are not up against a holder if your opponent can't prove all of the crucial factors that define that status under the UCC. So learning the correct definition is, therefore, important to your ability to ferret out those who mistakenly or intentionally claim this type of Boss status when in fact a true holder is not involved.

UCC § 1-201(21) provides this definition: "Holder...means: (A) the person in possession of a negotiable instrument that is payable either to bearer or to an identified person that is the person in possession ..." The UCC emphasizes possession, which means actual physical possession of the Note, not a copy and not someone's word that they have possession. A person can't be a holder under the UCC without actually having the original Note in their possession.[116] If your opponent claims to be the holder, or it claims to represent the holder, but for any reason it cannot or refuses to produce the physical Note, you should conclude that it is not the holder of your Note and you should ask your judge to make the same conclusion.

The language about "payable either to bearer or to an identified person that is the person in possession" requires a look at how the Note is indorsed. In other words, was it made payable to just whomever had possession or to a specific person? Did a prior Boss of the Note properly designate who should take over the Boss rights when the ownership changed? The original lender to whom you gave the Note was the first owner and the first to qualify as a Boss under the UCC because it was a holder per 3-301(i). Most likely, there have been several subsequent owners as a result of routine sales and exchanges of your Note. As previously discussed, the UCC test does not require ownership or define Boss in terms of whoever claims to be an owner of your Note. Just having some interest in the Note and mortgage is not enough. Each sale or transfer of your Note requires looking to the UCC for guidance about two key points: (1) whether each next person claiming rights in your Note is actually a Boss, and (2) whether your opponent is actually recognized under the UCC as being or representing the current Boss in what could be a line of many Bosses over time.

UCC §§ 3-204[117] and 3-205[118] contain the basic indorsement rules that arise in a typical foreclosure setting. Like the check you might make out to Mrs. Smith, how she signs the back of that check has a lot to do with who ultimately has the right to cash the check at your bank. Lack of indorsement, or indorsement by the wrong person, can defeat your opponent's claim that it has Boss status or represents the Boss. If, for example, your lender indorses the back of your Note as "payable to Company X" and your opponent is not Company X or the servant of Company X, your opponent does not have the right to enforce your Note.

UCC § 3-204 states that an indorsement is a signature or other words signed onto the Note or a paper affixed—that is, attached—to the Note.[119] An indorsement is something that some person in the possession of your Note, not you, puts on or attaches to the Note.

This rule shows why your opponent must produce the actual Note and not be permitted to simply show a copy of what you signed or copies of papers it claims are the indorsement(s). A Note may consist of one or many pages. The UCC does not specify which side of the paper or where in the Note an indorsement can be made, so an indorsement could be attached or affixed to the front or back of any page. You need to see the original Note so you can thoroughly inspect each page. Without the actual Note, you have no way to verify what, if any, indorsement papers have been affixed or attached to the Note and whether they are in compliance with § 3-204.

If your opponent objects to being required to produce the Note, you will want to help your judge understand the necessity of seeing the actual Note in order to determine what, if any, indorsements are on or affixed to it. Explaining the risks to you and to the real Boss if your opponent claims to have the physical Note but can't actually produce it can be a helpful part of your explanations to the judge.[120] Your explanation supported by UCC §§ 3-301(i) and (ii), 3-308(b), 3-501 and 3-501(b)(2) should help persuade your judge to make your opponent display the Note for your inspection. Anything less than letting you actually inspect the physical Note should be viewed as evidence your opponent doesn't actually have it.

What impact, if any, an indorsement has is set out by UCC § 3-205. An indorsement by a person who is not already a holder or payee is a nullity—that is, it is legally invalid—and therefore has no effect on who may enforce the Note.[121] This is called an *anomalous indorsement*. If an indorsement was made by a person not in the chain of ownership and control of the Note, that indorsement is merely scribble on the Note or wasted paper attached to it. Likewise, if a person who was previously a holder but is not a holder at the time of indorsement—for example, because it had previously transferred all of its interests in the Note to someone else—that person's indorsement is also a nullity.[122] When asking whether an indorsement was made by a holder, the inquiry must be joined with, "Was that indorser[123] a holder with the right to enforce the Note at the time it made the indorsement?"[124]

An indorsement that identifies the person to whom the Note is payable is a *special indorsement*,[125] also referred to as a Note that is *payable to order.*[126] You can think of this as an abbreviated way of saying "payable to the order or demand of the person specified by the indorsement." If the indorsement does not specify a particular payee, it is called a *blank indorsement.* A signature of the specified payee, with nothing more, can be a blank indorsement. That would make the Note *payable to bearer.*[127]

A Note payable to bearer can be converted into one that is payable to order, and vice versa.[128] This possibility is yet another reason to insist on seeing the physical Note. Otherwise, your opponent could show, for example, a copy of a blank indorsement even though the Note was later indorsed on a different page to be payable to the order of a specific person. Seeing the physical Note is a must, regardless of whether your opponent claims to be the Boss or the legal representative of the Boss. Making your opponent show the physical Note is the best way to protect you as a borrower and also to protect the interests of the true Boss of the Note. (See Chapter 12.)

UCC § 3-205 also provides that neither a special indorsement nor a blank indorsement is valid unless it was made by the then holder of the Note. Each indorsement on the Note should make you question whether the indorser was in fact the Boss or holder at the time the indorsement was made. If the person indorsing the Note didn't independently qualify as a holder of the instrument at that time, that person's indorsement is invalid.[129] Taking possession of a Note without a proper indorsement means no Boss rights have transferred at that point. There are exceptions, as indicated in UCC §§ 3-301(ii), 3-203(b) and 3-203(c), but unless all of those requirements are alleged and proven, the person in possession of that Note is not the Boss. The chain of ownership and control of the Note is important to a determination under the UCC as to whether your opponent can, in fact, prove it has genuine Boss status.

The foreclosure machine frequently produces self-serving affidavits and declarations that say it has the Note. Do not give in: be diligent and demand to see the physical Note. The UCC gives you the right to make that demand and places your opponent at a substantial disadvantage if it does not comply. (See *Avoid "Show Me the Note" Difficulties* in Chapter 12.)

UCC § 3-201, *Negotiation,* § 3-203, *Transfer of Instrument; Rights Acquired by Transfer,* and § 1-201(15), *Delivery,* also bear on what § 3-301 means by *holder of the instrument.* UCC § 3-201 tells us that a person other than the borrower (that is, the issuer or maker) becomes a holder through negotiation,[130] which means transfer of possession if the Note is payable to bearer. When the Note is payable to a specific person, the transfer of the Note to someone else must include indorsement by that specified person.

Transfer is the new word introduced by § 3-201. It is explained by § 3-203,[131] which tells us that the Note is transferred by delivery "for the purpose of giving to the person receiving delivery the right to enforce the instrument."[132] UCC § 1-201(15) defines delivery as a "voluntary transfer of possession."[133] UCC § 3-203(d) also provides that the transferor must intend to relinquish 100% of its rights in the Note to the transferee, or else the transferee obtains no rights to enforce the Note.

I find § 3-203(d) particularly interesting. A person who gets less than 100% of the interests in the Note gets no enforcement rights at all. That person may have some right to share in collection proceeds with others, for example, but the rule is clear—all rights or else no right to enforce the Note as its Boss. The details involving the how and why a person gets possession of the Note are, therefore, extremely important.

A person, even if in possession of the physical Note, may not have any right to enforce it because that person did not obtain all of the Boss rights, rights involving its value and control. Examples of when the person might buy or get possession of the Note but not acquire all of the Boss's rights would be as follows:

- An agreement with the previous person in possession of the Note limited the enforcement rights of the successor by dictating the details about how, when, or by whom enforcement is authorized.

- An agreement with the previous person in possession of the Note limited how much money the successor can pocket if any money is collected by enforcing the Note.

- An agreement with the previous person in possession of the Note established that the recipient only had the right to hold onto the Note for the benefit of someone else.

- The Note was received under an agreement that dictated who had the right to service that mortgage loan, whether the services involve, for example, accounting, collections, borrower communications, or foreclosure services.

Therefore, when your opponent can produce the physical Note, you must investigate all agreements it has with any others regarding your Note. Even if your lender reserved the right to service the Note when it was first sold to some other person, that fact may be enough to negate your opponent's ability to prove it has 100% of all legal and financial rights in the Note, and, accordingly, enough to negate its right to enforce your Note.

These parts of the UCC show that, for a person to become a holder, negotiation must occur, meaning voluntary delivery of possession with an intention that the recipient will thus receive all of the rights to and ownership of the Note. If the prior holder of the Note did not intend that someone else might get it, as in the case of theft or the finding of a lost Note, no delivery or transfer would have occurred per the UCC. Thus the new possessor of the Note—in this example, the thief or the finder—could not be a holder, regardless of what indorsements were on the Note when the new person took possession.[134]

Likewise, if the holder's signature is forged or if the holder's agent exceeds his authority in signing the indorsement, this constitutes a failed negotiation.[135] Even though § 3-201(a) suggests that holder status can occur when the prior holder has "involuntarily" transferred possession, other provisions of the UCC deprive enforcement rights for those taking possession without the consent and knowledge of the prior holder of the Note. Remember, therefore, that some holders have a right to enforce a Note and others do not.

If the chain of possessors of a Note includes a person who was not a holder as defined by the UCC, anyone in possession thereafter may also be denied the status of holder, and not permitted to enforce the Note. Through your formal and informal discovery, you should maintain pressure on your opponent to prove not only how it obtained possession of the Note, but also the circumstances by which each alleged prior holder obtained and gave up possession of the Note and all arrangements your opponent has with others regarding anything to do with your Note. Remember that mere possession of the Note does not prove Boss status under the UCC.[136]

UCC § 3-203(b) provides that transfer of the Note vests in the transferee any right to enforce the Note that had been held by the transferor. If a prior possessor of the Note does not have the right to enforce the Note pursuant to § 3-301(i) or (ii), which are the current-possession-related mechanisms for enforcement rights, then the transferee obtains no right to enforce the Note. If the transferor has enforcement rights and the change of possession was a voluntary act for the purpose of transferring all interests in the Note to the transferee, then the transferee has the enforcement rights of the transferor. Your opponent has an extremely difficult burden of proof when it claims rights of the prior transferor. (See Chapter 12.) Special rules regarding application of § 3-203 to questions about rights of a holder in due course will be discussed later.

A brief comment about UCC § 3-203(c) may be helpful for some borrowers who face the situation in which the opponent has the Note but it was not properly indorsed by a prior holder. UCC § 3-203(c) states that the new person in possession does not have the right to enforce the Note until it is properly indorsed by that prior holder. This keeps alive the possibility that the person currently in possession will eventually have the right to enforce the Note, but it won't have that right until the correct indorsement is obtained. This section of the UCC does not relieve the burden of proof from the person trying to enforce the Note. That person must prove, first, that the lack of the indorsement was unintended or inadvertent, and second, that the person from whom the late indorsement is obtained was actually the holder at the time the indorsement should have been placed on the Note. This is a special law for special circumstances and most of you will never run into this situation.

As you can see from what I have outlined above, the term *holder* can only be understood by interactive use of several sections of the Uniform Commercial Code. The simple definition of 1-201(21) does not tell the entire story. Yes, it states the basic profile of a holder, but the other sections describe how, and if, a person can obtain that technical profile.

Now that you have seen a bit of the details that lead to the UCC's definition of holder, my coined definition may seem more friendly and useful. Remember that my version is about the holder who may have a right to enforce the Note, not the other holders. It is worth repeating with the addition of references to the UCC parts upon which it is based:

A "holder of the instrument" is a person in physical possession of the Note, having received it from a previous holder who, at that time, had the sole right to enforce the Note and who voluntarily delivered it with the intention of transferring (§§1-201(21), 3-201, 1-201(15) and 3-203) all of the transferor's interests in the Note (§ 3-203(d)), including the right to enforce it, to the transferee, said Note having been indorsed by the person who was the Boss at the time of the indorsement to be payable specifically to the recipient, or else payable to whomever has possession of it (§§ 1-201(21), 3-204 & 3-205).

Your fact-finding work will focus on using the discovery process to gather the documents and information available to your opponent and then assessing whether its facts actually prove that it is the Boss of your Note or the Boss's servant. For your opponent to be a holder of the instrument, its evidence must detail the ownership of the Note, including:

- Each sale and transfer must be documented regarding when, by whom, and all of the related agreements, all the way back to your original lender.

- Indorsements must be on or affixed to the Note.

- Indorsements must have been made at the time the indorser was actually the holder of the Note, unless the exception of § 3-203(c) applies (which also requires strict proof).

- The indorsement must be either payable to bearer or to order. In the latter situation, it must be specifically payable to your opponent or the Boss it claims to represent.

- Each transfer in the chain of ownership and control must have entailed the entire relinquishment of all rights in the Note by the transferor.

On this last point, the foreclosure machine sometimes plays games with borrowers and the courts by having possession that was never intended to vest all of the rights of the Note in that foreclosure shop.[137] The machine sort of borrows possession under an undisclosed agreement with whomever had the physical possession (which could be a person without a right to enforce the Note), and then it asserts in court that it is the holder and can produce the physical Note. The machine may admit its ploy on direct examination, but it often keeps silent about the ruse it has contrived unless it gets caught. This deceptive tactic is part of an attempt either to hide the identity of the Boss so it does not get entangled in the litigation, or to avoid having the enforcement rights of that accommodating transferor investigated. None of the companies that participate in this type of cover-up may have the right to enforce the Note.

Because the machine uses tactics like this, in every instance in which your opponent claims to have physical possession of Note, you should respond with questions and demands for the production of facts. Insist on proof about how, and under what agreement or circumstances, the possession was obtained and held by each name appearing in the alleged chain of ownership, possession, and control of the Note.

Getting past your opponent's claims and self-serving conclusions can require diligent work. Carefully trace the details in the documents you obtain in response to formal discovery, for as some published court decisions show,[138] the details can be very important in persuading the judge that your opponent has not proven its burden with clear and convincing evidence.

Review documents and try to reconstruct the chain of ownership and rights. Make note of missing dates, unexplained time gaps, lack of proof about what happened with each new alleged transfer or exchange of your note, lack of agreements about each of those transfers, and any circumstances that make you suspect that a complete and UCC-compliant chain of ownership and control doesn't exist. Creating diagrams of names, dates, and circumstances, much as you would have done for classroom exercises in school, can be very helpful when going through the papers, admissions, and explanations your opponent will provide through your formal fact-finding process. If your opponent's facts fall short of proving that it or the Boss it alleges to serve is the holder of the instrument, the machine should lose.

"The devil is in the details" is a common phrase that alerts us to look beyond surface appearance. Pushing your opponent to prove its statements and claims with genuine and relevant fact is the only way to get to the truth. Let the details be your angel and your opponent's devil.

UCC § 3-301(ii)—Nonholder, in Possession, with Rights of a Holder

The wording of § 3-301(ii), "a nonholder in possession of the instrument who has the rights of a holder," basically refers to a person who is not a holder pursuant to the requirements of § 3-301(i), but who has physical possession of the Note and the right to enforce the Note as if it were a holder. If your opponent can't prove it is a holder of the instrument pursuant to § 3-301(i) but it has physical possession of the Note, then the question may arise about its rights under § 3-301(ii).

Generally, the status of nonholder in possession is derived from having legally succeeded to the enforcement rights that were previously held by another person. For example, the person possessing the Note might have obtained it as a result of a legal seizure of the previous holder's assets, a corporate merger, or the termination of a corporation's or partnership's existence. Or the person could have paid the obligation the holder thought due under the Note, thereby being subrogated (meaning put in the place of the holder) respecting the holder's right to enforce the Note.

This section of the UCC has also been interpreted broadly to permit an enforcement right under other situations recognized by law where the successor has the rights of its predecessor.[139] The key concept is "recognized by law"—not what might be assumed by a borrower. In some cases, a court decided the foreclosure machine had the right to enforce the Note pursuant to § 3-301(ii) based on little more than the admission of a borrower who assumed the opponent was a successor to a prior holder and told the judge this, even though the borrower didn't have facts to support such a statement. You should learn two lessons from this. First, never make assumptions for which you don't have factual support. Second, always require your opponent to prove with genuine facts that it has enforcement rights per the UCC.

Neither possession in and of itself nor ownership of the Note are sufficient to establish the right to enforce the Note under § 3-301(ii). Your opponent must prove the transactions by which it came into possession of the Note.[140] If your attacker is not a holder pursuant to § 3-301(i) and it alleges a right to enforce the Note pursuant to part (ii), it must prove four things:

1. That it has physical possession of the Note, which is available for inspection by you and the judge;

2. How, when, and based upon what facts it succeeded to the rights of the prior Boss of the Note (for example, as a legally recognized successor in interest, or via a legal seizure of the Note from its holder, or by whatever theory your opponent asserts);

3. That the person alleged to have been the prior Boss actually was a Boss pursuant to the UCC at the time your opponent was deemed the successor; and

4. That it obtained 100% of all economic and legal rights and interests in the Note, and not just some or even most of them.

Your opponent has to prove each of these requirements or else it has no right to enforce the Note under § 3-301(ii) of the UCC. In fact, with respect to this and all parts of the UCC that deal with who has the right to enforce the Note, a person has either complied fully and exactly with the UCC requirements or else that person does not have the right to enforce the Note.[141] UCC compliance, unlike a game of horseshoes, is not a game that can be won by simply being "close enough."[142]

§ 3-301(iii) - Not in Possession but Entitled to Enforce

UCC § 3-301(iii), "a person not in possession of the instrument who is entitled to enforce the instrument pursuant to §§ 3-309 or 3-418(d)," involves the right to enforce the Note by someone who does not have actual possession of it but who is entitled to enforce it if the person's circumstances clearly satisfy one of the two referenced UCC sections. Of the three ways a person can qualify to have the right to enforce the Note pursuant to § 3-301, part (iii) is the only way possible for someone who does not have physical possession. This part (iii) test, however, requires proof of a prior holder status, which in fact does require proof of prior physical possession.

UCC § 3-309, *Enforcement of Lost, Destroyed, or Stolen Instrument*,[143] is available to a person who was a holder of the Note per the UCC but who no longer has the original Note because it was lost, destroyed, or stolen. If your opponent claims the right to enforce the

Note pursuant to § 3-309, you must require your opponent to put forward facts that prove three things:

1. That it had the right to enforce the Note pursuant to 3-301 at the time the Note was lost, destroyed, or stolen; or that it acquired rights to the Note from the person entitled to enforce the Note pursuant to § 3-301 at the time the Note was lost, destroyed, or stolen;[144]

2. That the loss of possession was not caused by voluntary transfer or legal seizure; and

3. That possession cannot be reasonably regained.

These requirements, just like those for §§ 3-301(i) and (ii), demand a lot of proof from your opponent. UCC validation is, by its very nature, a fact-intensive inquiry.

The foreclosure machine, when claiming rights to enforce under this part of § 3-301(iii), has often alleged that it looked for the original but could not locate it. I could honestly say I didn't find a Rolls Royce at my house today even though I looked for it. My search, of course, doesn't mean that I ever owned one. Likewise, compliance with the UCC requires more.[145] Your opponent must prove that it actually had possession of the Note and what happened to it or that it obtained Boss rights from a person with verifiable Boss authority who previously qualified per § 3-309.

Also, if your opponent was previously the holder, it may not enforce the Note under § 3-309 if it lost possession either voluntarily by a transfer to another or involuntarily via a lawful seizure.[146] For example, did your opponent sell the Note, or deliver it to one of its creditors to satisfy a debt?

If your opponent introduces an affidavit or certificate attesting to unsuccessful efforts to locate the Note, be extremely careful. Make certain the information clearly and believably supports each and every requirement of § 3-309. Also, push for the opportunity to question, either at trial or via deposition, the person who provides that written testimony, so all relevant facts can be investigated thoroughly. In other words, don't accept as legally significant or truthful any written testimony introduced by the industry's foreclosure shop.

If your funds are too low to permit you to conduct a deposition of the person whose affidavit the machine wants to use, do not despair. Affidavits are not usually admissible at trial. If your opponent wants to get that information before the Court, it will need to have the person testify in person. At that point, you can question the person about the circumstances involving the Note that is alleged to have been lost, destroyed, or stolen. If, under questioning, that person shows he or she doesn't actually know what happened and doesn't know if the Note was actually ever in your opponent's physical possession, the testimony will hurt your opponent's case and help yours.

The second possibility under 3-301(iii) involves § 3-418, *Payment or Acceptance by Mistake.* This section points to portions of Article 4, *Bank Deposits and Collection,* of the UCC. I have not seen § 3-418 applied in any foreclosure lawsuit to date. Its application appears to be limited to negotiable instruments that are routinely created and processed through the banking system rather than Notes created in mortgage loan transactions.

UCC § 3-301—A Concluding Remark

UCC § 3-301, as outlined above, sets forth the three ways, and the only ways, a person can become the Boss of the Note. To win in court against the foreclosure machine, you must consistently require it to show what it has and knows about the Note and any alleged Boss the machine claims to represent. Your opponent must answer your pesky questions about how, when, where, how much, and why with reasonable explanations and documentary proof, or else it should lose.

When the case is over, if your opponent fails to carry its evidentiary burden, you may be no closer to knowing the identity of the Boss of the Note. That does not matter. Beat the company attacking you and you will have done well. One step at a time is the path to success.

THE BOSS'S SERVANT OR AGENT

It is noteworthy that none of the three enforcement tests of UCC § 3-301 grants Boss status to an agent or servant. These enforcement rights must first be proven to exist for the Boss. If a Boss exists, then your opponent and the Boss are required to provide strict proof that shows the exact nature, authority, and scope of the alleged agency relationship respecting your specific Note.

What Is an Agent ?

An agent is someone who has been authorized by another party—the principal or master—to perform certain actions on its behalf. The agent could be designated by any of several names, such as agent, servant, representative, or loan servicer.

The Boss has a right to designate another person or company to do its bidding regarding your Note. It can appoint a servant to help manage the

Boss's interests in the Note, send out notices, discuss possible solutions should a dispute arise with you, commence foreclosure in the event of a default, and so forth. The servant has no legal rights regarding the Note except as expressly directed by the Boss, and this is so no matter what the servant is called. Labels like loan servicer, agent, or servant mean the company has no authority unless the Boss says otherwise. A servant can't create its own authority.

If your opponent can't prove its master is the Boss of your Note, questions involving the claimed master-servant or principal-agent relationship become moot and unimportant. No Boss means no right to make demands under the Note, and no right to foreclose, because the Note is not in default and you owe nothing to your opponent or the company for which it works.

As a practical matter, you have limited time to gather your facts during the lawsuit, so you'll want to demand that your opponent prove its master has Boss powers and, at the same time, also prove the opponent's relationship with that alleged Boss. You have a right to receive all agreements, communications, and documents that have gone back and forth between your opponent and the alleged Boss. Look at them and see if they actually prove Boss status consistent with the requirements of the UCC. Those documents must also show that the alleged Boss actually instructed your opponent to start collection efforts regarding your Note or the foreclosure process.

Sometimes there is an intermediary servant layer involved. A master servicer for a company will assign various tasks and duties to other companies rather than perform all of the work itself. If your opponent claims its master servicer gave it instructions, then you need to see at least three sets of agreements and communications. You want the ones between your opponent and the master servicer, those between the master servicer and the alleged Boss, and those between the alleged Boss and your opponent.

When looking at a servicing or servant agreement, keep in mind that the servant often has no right to delegate its duties to other sub-servants unless the Boss expressly authorized such delegation. If the Boss appointed, for example, Wells Fargo as a master servicer but did not expressly authorize Wells Fargo to designate a change of trustee in a deed of trust, Wells Fargo probably has no right to designate a new trustee.[147] When dealing with an opponent that claims to be servant for some other company, look at the agreement that is supposed to define the servant's authority. Don't assume it has more rights or powers than what the agreement clearly says. That is not how master-servant arrangements work in the mortgage finance industry.

Anyone can claim to be the agent of someone else. The foreclosure machine regularly implies or says it is the agent of the Boss. The only way for the machine to prove that, however, is for the alleged Boss to show up and confirm the existence of a master-servant arrangement regarding your Note, and to define, with contractual proof, the nature and scope of the arrangement.[148] The company claiming servant status can't prove such a relationship using only its own self-serving statements or papers. Your opponent can have its staff say what it wants them to say, or it can produce affidavits allegedly from the Boss, but neither is enough.

Stick to your guns and push to get whatever written agreements exist. Otherwise you can't be certain what the real relationship is, when it was formed, and whether it actually applies to your Note and mortgage. If you have any doubt that you're getting all of the documents, communications, and agreements that have passed between your opponent and its alleged master, ask the judge to make the alleged master join the lawsuit. That is the only way to be sure you can use the full force of discovery, and the only way to be sure that you get more than simply what your opponent wants to give you after filtering what it lets you see. (See *Joinder of Real Parties in Interest,* below.)

If your opponent asserts that there is only a verbal arrangement or attempts to get by with no more than summaries of the alleged agreement, that is evidence of something being hidden. Businesses like banks and Wall Street finance companies are distinguished, in part at least, by using lots of paper to document arrangements, not verbal agreements. Remind your judge of this reality when seeking his or her help to obtain full compliance with your discovery demands.

A Note and mortgage represent a large dollar asset. Common sense tells us that a real Boss is going to have more than a verbal deal with some lackey when the asset involved represents so much money. Expect and demand to see the written agreement that pertains to your Note and mortgage. Your opponent's failure to produce such evidence should be viewed as suspicious and evidence that it doesn't actually represent the other company regarding your Note and mortgage.

If your opponent claims the right to enforce the Note on its own behalf and not as a servant of some other company, then you don't need to investigate agency matters. If, however, it is unclear whether your opponent is claiming Boss or servant status, then your discovery should require your opponent to state whether it is acting as servant for some other company and, if it is a servant, to provide copies of all documents and communications sent or received from the alleged master that involve your Note or mortgage in any way.

If your opponent begins by claiming Boss status but later changes its story to being a servant of an alleged Boss, your discovery work won't change, but you will have received added evidence that may be of help when you are in front of the judge. Your opponent will have, by its changed position, admitted dishonesty or incompetence, both of which demand that whatever it says can't be trusted by you or your judge. The changed story should also be sufficient grounds for requesting more time for discovery if you need more fact-finding time.

You should make note of any change in position about an important matter and share it with the judge whenever the machine objects to your requested discovery and whenever the machine asks the judge to take its word for anything. Your opponent typically will want discovery to be abbreviated, and to have the right to say and imply that it has evidence without showing it. Flip-flops and waffling about its position are good indicators that your opponent's judgment is, at best, flawed about what is or is not important. Challenge its credibility each time you have an opportunity to address your judge. Help your judge keep track of your opponent's indiscretions. And use your opponent's tarnished reputation to keep pressure on it to comply fully with all of your discovery demands.

Trustee Under a Deed of Trust

A trustee under a deed of trust has no authority to decide on its own that a default exists under a Note or to initiate a foreclosure. At least, that kind of authority is extremely rare. Only the Boss of the Note has those rights. Read your deed of trust document and you will see what I mean.

Your state's nonjudicial foreclosure statutes will also require that whatever the trustee does must be consistent with the agreement between the borrower and the Boss, who will likely be referred to as creditor, lender, or beneficiary in the deed of trust document. The referenced agreement, of course, means the arrangement made by the lender and you in your Note and mortgage, and the UCC then defines who has the right to enforce the Note and thus control the mortgage.

The trustee is a type of agent or servant. Whoever gives the trustee instructions to start a foreclosure must be the Boss or a duly appointed servant of the Boss. The trustee's authority is typically set out by the deed of trust or trust deed, or whatever title is used in that state for the document that creates the lien against the borrower's home and can be used in a nonjudicial foreclosure. That document usually requires the lender or its successor to do certain things that then trigger the trustee's right to commence the nonjudicial foreclosure process. As you now know, the identity of that lender or successor is controlled by the UCC because the Note is a negotiable instrument.

Frequently, state law defines the trustee as having duties to both the Boss and the borrower in order to help ensure that only a proper foreclosure might take place. The trustees, however, get their money from the machine, so you can imagine to whom they listen the most. Do not, therefore, trust any summary or affidavit issued by the trustee's office. What you'll want from the trustee is a copy of every document, email, fax, agreement, and anything else in the trustee's file regarding your Note and mortgage. You should have no difficulty obtaining the trustee's records.

Send a letter requesting copies of its entire file regarding your Note and mortgage. The trustee may give them to you upon request, or it may refuse in order to better accommodate the company paying its bills. You may have to enter the lawsuit without copies of the trustee's files but you can gain access to that information and documents through formal discovery. If the trustee wants to play games, your court's rules will help you force it to comply with your fact-finding. Look for those rules and use them.

If the trustee refuses to cooperate, you can also use that fact to help persuade your judge that your opponent and/or the trustee know they have violated your rights and are trying to hide information, thereby necessitating court assistance with getting to the truth. Why else would the trustee refuse to show its records when it is helping others take your home?

When reviewing the trustee's records, you are looking for information that indicates it commenced the foreclosure process without having been instructed to do so by the Boss. You also want to find any violations of the procedural rules of the nonjudicial process. Who instructed the trustee to commence the foreclosure process? What evidence does the trustee have that the person giving it the "start" instruction was the one true Boss or a servant of that Boss? Did the trustee even make any investigation as to Boss status? Did the trustee send out all of the notices required by your state's nonjudicial statutes, and to the correct addresses or publications?

You'll be conducting a negative content audit of the trustee's information and documents, much like the work you'll do when you get documents and information from your opponent. The trustee's information will frequently disclose that it has no meaningful basis for following the instructions that led to its commencement of the foreclosure. Less often, but it happens, the trustee will have failed to send out the required nonjudicial notices at the right time, to the right address, to the right people, or with the correct text. Look for what the trustee did not do right and use that to challenge the validity of the foreclosure you face.

Don't get concerned or intimidated if the trustee points to documents that have been formally filed in the public land records as the trustee's alleged authority to do what it has or plans to do. Papers can get filed by mistake and in furtherance of illegal actions. Any documents involving your Note or mortgage that a trustee or any company filed in public records are suspect and subject to being declared invalid by your judge if the Boss was not properly involved. For example, the records might include assignments of your mortgage, or changes in the designated trustee, or notices about an upcoming foreclosure. These are not legal and binding if your opponent fails to prove that they were properly created or directed by the Boss of your Note. Public records are just more papers that need to be evaluated in light of the foreclosure fundamentals.

When ShellGame-MERS Is Involved

The question of agency is particularly important when ShellGame-MERS (Mortgage Electronic Registration Systems, Inc.) appears in the chain of title of your mortgage or deed of trust. As discussed in Chapter 4, ShellGame-MERS has no ownership or beneficial interest in any Note or mortgage. That means that the law and facts are well established that ShellGame-MERS never has independent authority to sell, assign, transfer, exchange, enforce, or otherwise do anything with a Note or mortgage. ShellGame-MERS, therefore, can't be properly involved unless in the role of servant for the Boss. Challenging ShellGame-MERS to prove its involvement has been duly appointed and directed by the Boss of your Note is the legal field upon which you can anticipate success when fighting back.

The mortgage finance industry and its foreclosure machine use the name of ShellGame-MERS in ways that impact the validity of a foreclosure. This is true whether the borrower has a mortgage or deed of trust. If ShellGame-MERS is mentioned in your mortgage, your opponent will either be ShellGame-MERS or a company that has to prove that its alleged Boss rights depend on something done in the name of ShellGame-MERS.

ShellGame-MERS doesn't pretend much anymore to be the party conducting a foreclosure. I think that's because it has suffered too many embarrassments when challenged in past lawsuits, and also because, as an actual party in a lawsuit, it exposed the industry's folly to heightened discovery. If the true nature of its existence and operations were too often exposed to the public, the presence of its name in mortgages would lead to increasing foreclosure challenges and losses for the machine. ShellGame-MERS will not likely be a party in your lawsuit.

The industry and its machine continue, however, to press a claim that ShellGame-MERS is in fact an agent for the original lender and for every successor to the lender who is also a member of the MERS System. The argument is that membership in the MERS System creates an ongoing agency relationship between ShellGame-MERS and each successor of the lender's interests in the Note and mortgage. That story has been accepted by most courts when it has gone unchallenged by borrowers, who typically didn't demand proof that ShellGame-MERS was authorized to represent companies alleged to have been Bosses at different times in the life of the Note.

One federal court, however, actually took time to read the *MERS Rules of Membership* and found that no such agency appointment existed, and that ShellGame-MERS obtained no independent authority to act as an agent of successors, even those who adopted the MERS rules.[149] There is no genuine evidence that ShellGame-MERS receives carte blanche authority to do what it wants with the Notes and mortgages owned by companies because of those so-called MERS Rules of Membership.

At other times the question of whether ShellGame-MERS had authority to foreclose or to act on behalf of some alleged master were resolved upon a mistaken assumption that the borrower, upon executing the mortgage document, had appointed ShellGame-MERS as agent of the original lender and also every successor to that lender. The borrowers in those cases didn't know how to raise an effective challenge to the foreclosure, and they were no match for the polished legal beagles of the machine. Those assumptions were wrong because only a principal—that is, the Boss—has the power to appoint its servant. Your state law will corroborate that statement if you do a little research.

The mortgage document is executed by the borrower, not by the lender and not by any unknown person who might succeed to the lender's interests in the future. Obviously, the borrower is not a representative of the original lender or any successor. The borrower has no authority to create an agency relationship between those persons and ShellGame-MERS. A borrower never has the authority to appoint ShellGame-MERS as servant for any company.

At most, the borrower who signs a mortgage document that mentions ShellGame-MERS can be viewed as having acknowledged that the lender or some successors might appoint ShellGame-MERS to be a servant. However, that simple acknowledgement cannot possibly create an agency relationship between persons whom the borrower does not represent. The U.S. Supreme Court has ruled that a borrower cannot appoint, through a loan transaction, a servant to act on behalf of future unidentified persons.[150] Nothing you signed at your loan closing gave you the power or authority to appoint ShellGame-MERS as servant for anyone. It is a ridiculous concept that should be easily rebutted if your opponent tries to use it.

If the machine argues that ShellGame-MERS was a servant of a prior Boss of your Note, you must make it prove two things. First, it must show that the company ShellGame-MERS was allegedly serving was in fact the Boss of the Note and mortgage at the time ShellGame-MERS alleged to have sold, transferred, or assigned the Note and/or mortgage to some other company. Next, it must produce evidence proving that ShellGame-MERS was acting as that prior Boss's servant when the subject documents were being signed in ShellGame-MERS's name.[151] And because ShellGame-MERS is involved, your opponent must also prove that it was actually ShellGame-MERS that used its name, not some clerk or employee of another company that was acting on its own and without any direction from ShellGame-MERS regarding your Note and mortgage.

As I've said, your opponent has the burden of proving that its claimed Boss status can be traced all the way back to the lender's rights, through as many intermediary companies as are involved in the chain of ownership and control of your Note. If your opponent relies on a piece of paper showing that ShellGame-MERS assigned or transferred your Note and mortgage to some other company, you should be making a mental list of questions for your opponent to answer and document with genuine proof.

For example, what evidence does your opponent have that the company for which ShellGame-MERS was supposedly working actually had Boss status at that time? Is there any evidence that the company actually communicated with ShellGame-MERS about your Note and mortgage? What evidence does your opponent have that ShellGame-MERS, not some other company using its name, actually responded to that earlier Boss's instruction regarding your Note and mortgage? Look for the information that your opponent should, but doesn't, have about these matters. Those gaps and missing bits of proof are the straws that can break the machine's back.

Joinder of Real Parties in Interest

If the machine alleges that some other company is the Boss, look to your court's rules regarding what is called "real party in interest" or "standing." These are two of the judicial principles I mentioned earlier in this chapter. (See Chapter 12 to learn more about these concepts.)

If the suit was filed against you, the servant lacked standing and the suit should be dismissed upon your request, or else the servant should exit and its alleged master (that is, the alleged Boss) should become the plaintiff attacking you. Of course, there is no need for an admitted servant to be in the lawsuit when you can deal directly with the company claiming to be the Boss, unless you want the servant there so you can sue it for wrongs it committed.

If you start the lawsuit and later learn about an alleged Boss, you should ask the judge to make it a party in your case. A person standing in for someone else as a servant is not considered to be a real party in interest.[152]

Do you want the servant in the case you start? The answer will probably hinge on the importance of the legal claims you have against the servant regarding its conduct towards you. If your case is mainly an effort to stop a wrongful foreclosure, but not an effort to get back money from the servant, you will probably be better off with only the alleged master in the fight against you. The court will probably dismiss the servant on your request and make it leave the lawsuit, whether based on a standing or a real party in interest reasoning. Unless you have a really good reason, why have two opponents picking on you during the lawsuit if your fight is actually only with the alleged master? If, however, you believe the servant owes you something and the law will make it pay, holding it in as a party would make sense.

If a company admits to being a mere servant for an alleged master, you want the master in your lawsuit so you can make it prove all of the complicated and difficult matters of proof regarding the UCC requirements. You don't want to be limited to the middleman servant's information about its master, because that information may be incomplete and filtered to protect the master. You want everything to come directly from the master, and you want full access to everything the alleged master has about your Note and mortgage.

Beat that alleged master in court and you will have dispensed with it and with any possible claims its servant company might try to assert later. The servant, even though ousted from your suit, had its day in court when you argued to the judge that it had no business remaining in your lawsuit. That is, the servant will most likely be prohibited from later concocting a new story about why it should be permitted to take your money or house.

When facing a lawsuit with you, the alleged master company may say the servant company is wrong and there is no master-servant relationship. The alleged master may even state that it has no legal interest in your Note and mortgage. In that event, you will have successfully eliminated that alleged Boss's right to pick on you, and at the same time you will have demonstrated that your opponent must lose. Your opponent's claim to being a servant means it has no direct interest in your lawsuit. Your opponent's inability to point to an alleged Boss for which the opponent claims to work would mean it also has no indirect interest in your Note and mortgage. Thus, this type of scenario would mean that your case should be concluded in your favor and against both the servant and its alleged master.

WHAT IF THE BOSS IS IDENTIFIED?

If the genuine Boss actually appears in your case, do not assume your case is lost. You may still get results you can classify as a win. Additional questions of fact and law rise in importance if the alleged Boss is actually a party in your lawsuit. The next two topics can only be addressed with the true Boss of your Note, not with a servant and not with a company that erroneously claims Boss status.

Accounting Issues—How Much Is Owed and to Whom

How much money, if any, you owe to the Boss cannot be known until the Boss is identified. This is because any accounting information provided or asserted by the machine is meaningless until and unless it can be demonstrated to be the actual account information on the books of the one and only Boss of your Note. If your opponent is not the Boss, it can talk all day about how much you owe, but those words mean nothing because your remaining obligation under the Note is solely a matter between you and the Boss. Your opponent's comments under those circumstances must be understood as the statements of a stranger to your Note and mortgage—statements by a company that has no stake in either.

As soon as the alleged Boss is identified, you will want to exercise your formal discovery against it. Your objective will be to force it to produce its records and information regarding its rights in the Note, if any, and its accounting of payments received respecting its ownership of the Note. The extra information may show that your obligation under the Note has already been paid off.

Several things could have happened that only the Boss knows about but which could have reduced your obligation under your Note. For example, an insurance policy protecting the Boss against loss regarding your Note could have been paid off. An indorsement warranty claim may have resulted in payment to the Boss by a person who previously indorsed the Note and became liable to subsequent holders pursuant to UCC § 3-415; that provision of the law makes an indorser liable along with the borrower for the obligation under the Note under some circumstances.[153] Another possibility might be that your Boss sued or threatened to sue whoever sold it your Note and mortgage, based on a claim that the value or details of your Note were misstated or falsified. If that legal threat or lawsuit ends in a settlement payment to the Boss, that, too, should reduce or eliminate the amount you owe under the Note.

The details of payments to the Boss may show that it actually lost its Boss status when it got paid. For example, if an indorser has made good on its obligation to the Boss, then pursuant to § 3-412 the obligation under the Note is payable to that indorser, not to the Boss.[154] Likewise, if an insurer has paid all or some of the obligation, then it, not the Boss, may be the one who is legally entitled to enforce the Note pursuant to subrogation rights.[155]

A full accounting is how you learn whether the company you think is the Boss is still entitled to enforce your Note or if that right has moved to someone else because of dealings about which you are unaware. If you have to make mortgage payments to anyone, or if anyone gets to foreclose on your house, you want to make sure the right person gets those benefits. If the accounting information indicates that some other person may have the right to enforce your Note, that may be all you need to defeat your opponent or opponents in the current lawsuit.

Your opponents will probably lose all interest in continuing to fight with you once they learn they can't get anything. That lawsuit should be over. Whether or not you have another fight with the newly identified and possible Boss will be a matter to address in the future, but it's not a fight you have to start. The newly identified company that seems more likely to be the Boss might have also done something to terminate its Boss status. Therefore, take care of the immediate threat represented by your opponent or opponents and deal with the future as it develops.

Holder in Due Course

If a Boss is identified in your lawsuit, the type of status it has as a holder might be important, depending on the specific facts of your case. Here's why.

When you took out your loan, you dealt with the lender and its agent. One or both may have violated your rights by misrepresenting important facts, falsifying your loan papers, promising to refinance the loan in the future, or doing something else that violated state or federal laws designed to protect you. The lender and the agent may no longer be in existence or may be judgment proof—that is, so poor that suing them would likely cost you more than you could realistically expect to recover from them. However, you may be able to reduce or eliminate the amount of your obligation under the Note because of wrongs committed against you during the loan process. If you think you have a good legal defense or claim relating back to the creation of your Note, you can assert them against the person with the right to enforce the Note, but not if that person is classified as a holder in due course under the UCC.

The Uniform Commercial Code defines a holder in due course as one who takes an instrument for value in good faith, absent any notice that it is overdue, has been dishonored, or is subject to any defense against it or claim to it by any other person. Arguments about the status of holder in due course frequently center around two points: (1) when the Boss learned, or should have learned, that you had legal claims that could have been asserted against your lender or its agent, and (2) how much that Boss knew about delinquencies or possible defaults of your obligations under the Note and mortgage before the Boss acquired its interests in them. If your lender or its agents violated laws, or did things that created legal defenses or claims you could have used against them had they tried to enforce your Note, you will want to remember that you may be able to assert those legal issues against the Boss, should it appear. Then the concept of holder in due course might be important for you.

Your discovery can lead to information that is important in determining whether a person can actually be viewed as a holder in due course, should that person prove it is the Boss. You can simultaneously investigate your opponent's alleged Boss status and whether it might possibly be a holder in due course. The level of detail required for either your opponent or an alleged master to prove it has Boss status is often enough to determine whether a Boss is a holder in due course. The way that I suggest you use discovery pretty much requires your opponent to disclose the information you might also need should "holder in due course" later become an issue in your case.

Of course, if your opponent is not the Boss or the servant of the Boss, your opponent will lose and you will not need to argue about questions regarding the account balance or whether someone is a holder in due course. That's why *Fighting the Foreclosure Machine* focuses primarily on helping you and others defend against mistaken and fraudulent claims by persons alleging Boss status. I don't attempt to provide a comprehensive discussion about the topic of holder in due course in this book. It is not essential material for all borrowers fighting the foreclosure machine. It is also a large topic which is better saved for another day and another book or paper. If, however, this topic becomes important to you, the additional information below can help guide your studies and legal analysis.

UCC § 3-302, *Holder in Due Course,* sets out the basics that must exist for someone to qualify as a holder in due course—namely, the person has to have acquired your Note for value; the person has to have acquired it in good faith; and, at the time it acquired an interest in your Note, the transferee had no information suggesting there were any disputes, delinquencies, or other enforcement issues involving your Note. UCC § 3-302 is modified, enlarged, and defined by several other parts of the UCC, so your study will also take you to them. For example, you would want to look at the following:

- § 1-201(20)—defines "good faith"

- § 3-202—defines "notice" and "knowledge"

- § 3-106(d)— applies if your Note or an indorsement on it includes verbiage alerting others that you have a right to assert claims against the lender and its successors

- § 3-203(b)—vests enforcement rights of a transferor upon the transferee, but with limitations if an otherwise "holder in due course" perpetrated wrongs respecting the Note

- § 3-203(b)—also does not transfer holder in due course status to a subsequent holder[156]

- § 3-303—addresses what is meant by taking the Note for "value"

- § 3-305—describes defenses and claims the payor or borrower cannot assert against a Boss who is a holder in due course

- § 3-306—describes claims to the Note which defeat holder in due course status if known about prior to transfer

- § 3-308—requires the Boss to prove its status, including that of a holder in due course, if it tries to avoid defenses and claims available to the borrower (if an opponent claims status as a holder in due course, it has this added evidentiary burden of proving with facts all elements of that status)[157]

If, therefore, the real Boss is present in your lawsuit, it may be subject to your right to reduce or eliminate your obligation under the Note because of wrongs you may have suffered during the loan creation process. If that Boss knows too much about problems regarding your Note before it acquires your Note, the Boss is probably not a holder in due course.

I suggest that you not worry about a Boss appearing in your case until one actually shows up,[158] and then don't be too hasty to concede defeat. That's the time to demonstrate what, if any, amount is still owed under your Note, based on what you have learned through discovery, and that's also the time to question the Boss's alleged status as a holder in due course for the purpose of holding it liable for damages owed you by your lender

The accounting and holder-in-due-course matters are important only if your judge concludes that your opponent is the Boss of your Note. Court rules, however, often require you to raise these issues early in the lawsuit, before you know if your opponent can prove Boss rights. Pleading in the alternative is often how people do that. You would first state that your opponent lacks authority to enforce your Note. You would next state that if the court thinks otherwise, then you maintain that you owe your opponent nothing and that it is liable for the predatory wrongs you suffered when you took out your loan. Your wording would, of course, be more eloquent and specific as to your circumstances. Pleading in the alternative is a common technique when asserting matters that cannot both be true at the same time.

CHAPTER 12

RULE 4:
DON'T GIVE THE MACHINE AN EASY WIN

PRESENT YOUR STORY WITH CARE

When you file a complaint with the court against your opponent, or when you file counterclaims in response to your opponent's complaint against you, you are in essence telling the judge a story. At the same time, your opponent is spinning a different tale. Even though both stories concern the same situation, they look at it from different angles and portray it in different lights.

The judge has the task of determining whose version of the story is correct. He or she will then decide what the ending should be—that is, whether you or your opponent will prevail. The judge will base that decision on the facts and evidence presented by both sides, as well as the relevant statutes and the case law that applies to your particular case.

In presenting your story to the judge, you have two objectives. You want the story to be clear, compelling, and persuasive. You also want to have the opportunity to present it fully, without being short-circuited on procedural grounds or by your opponent's use of legal tactics against you. The various sections of this chapter are intended to help you put your story forward effectively and to anticipate and avoid some of the possible pitfalls you may encounter.

What you file will, of course, need to reference your own state's version of the UCC. If your Note or mortgage contains text on which you want your judge to focus, then help the judge find it by making that document an exhibit to your filing with the court and providing a clear reference to the text in question.

Your story should be persuasive and make it easy for the judge to see the factual and legal foundation upon which it is based. Exhibit B, *Example—Foreclosure Fundamentals Woven into the Story,* which is discussed in Chapter 8, is an example of how a story was persuasively told using easily followed references to facts stated in a complaint and exhibits attached to that complaint. It also demonstrates how one borrower wove specific legal references into the story so the judge could more easily see the path on which that borrower was positioned.

Make use of whatever you think is helpful or relevant from the examples, exhibits, and comments in this book. The information I've provided relates mostly to the UCC-driven foreclosure fundamentals that are at the heart of *Fighting the Foreclosure Machine*. It's up to you and your legal adviser to decide what information is helpful and how you will present the information you want your judge to see. The legal theories you use in your lawsuit may extend beyond the foreclosure fundamentals I discuss. Weaving what I call the foreclosure fundamentals into a larger cloth should not be that difficult.

The Importance of Accuracy

Accurately state your facts, especially those so crucial to engaging the judge in your story and your fight. Your earliest filings with the court need to be correct in order to set the stage for what will follow.

Many court cases have been unfavorably resolved against borrowers because they misstated the facts. The foreclosure machine did not have to prove it won because those borrowers had already proved they lost by the mistakes they made when they stated the facts incorrectly. For example, the borrower may have admitted being in default under the Note when, in reality, no default existed. Or the borrower may have acknowledged that he or she owed money to the opponent, or that the opponent had the right to enforce the borrower's Note.

In those cases, the borrower, not the foreclosure shop, proved that the foreclosure was legal. Those court losses can be traced to errors in the borrower's statement of the facts. Accuracy is extremely important. Do yourself a favor: make sure your judge gets correct information.

Some ways of stating the facts are better than others when you're trying to introduce the judge to the legal issues that are so crucial to a correct adjudication. My suggestions and comments, of course, reflect my understanding of the circumstances in which borrowers typically find themselves. If you think your situation is different, by all means tell the judge what you believe to be true and correct. That is your duty when dealing with the court. Be careful, however, to distinguish between what you actually know and what you can only guess.

A guess that you owe something to your opponent or that it has any right to demand money from you under threat of foreclosure is a mistake you must avoid. Remember, only the Boss of your Note has the right to make demands or to seek foreclosure. Until the company sending the demands and threats proves itself to be that Boss or the Boss's duly appointed servant regarding your Note, that company has no credibility and you should not think otherwise.

Your judge knows only what you and your opponent put in the court's record. You want your judge's decision to be accurate, so you must make sure you give your judge correct information.

The section that follows talks about how to make accurate statements of fact and gives examples of how to present the information. The discussion and examples concern topics with which borrowers have had particular difficulty in the past.

The "Upon Information and Belief" Statement

"Upon information and belief" is a phrase frequently used when starting a lawsuit. If you sue to stop a foreclosure, you will likely use this phrase or something very much like it. If you think your home was wrongfully taken in a nonjudicial foreclosure, and you seek to obtain money damages, have your home returned, or establish that your opponent has no right to evict you, then the complaint you file with the court will probably include an "upon information and belief" type of statement.

Attorneys use this kind of phrase all the time. It's a way of stating what you think will be proven once all the facts are on the table—that is, after the formal fact-finding is concluded, after your opponent has presented whatever things it thinks are important, and after testimony is presented to the judge at trial.

Each time you write "upon information and belief," your judge will understand the statement to be your estimate of the facts the judge will see as the case moves along. It is your projection of what the facts will establish, based on what you think reasonable in light of the information that has come to your attention up to that point. Your sources of information may be newspaper articles, TV shows, books, chitchat with friends, the Internet, in-depth research and analysis conducted by you or others, or even mere speculation about which you have a "feeling."

Understand that "upon information and belief" does not mean you have all of the information in hand with which to immediately prove those projected facts. It is not your personal promise that you can absolutely prove everything stated in the "upon information and belief" statement. Its use alerts your judge and your opponents to the possibility that you may not be able to prove those things, but that you hope those proofs may be available when you need them during the lawsuit.

An "upon information and belief" statement that says no more than "Company XYZ has no right to foreclose" does not help a judge understand why you should win your case. That statement simply tells the judge the legal conclusion you want your judge to make in your favor. It contains no facts to help the judge understand why the conclusion you seek makes any sense. Providing a factual background, even if those facts are speculated via "upon information and belief," is how you introduce the judge to the story of why you should win. The "upon information and belief" statement lets the judge get a feel for the type of facts you hope can be proven in support of the result you want from the lawsuit. Just like a joke isn't funny unless a story comes before the punch line, your case makes no sense unless you give the judge something to work with. When you fail to do that, you risk having your case get dismissed or decided in a way that's not in your favor.

Use "upon information and belief" to help lead your judge to the legal conclusion you want. It lets you give a more complete story before you've had a chance to gather facts from your opponent. Your judge will better understand your side of the dispute and be more sympathetic with where your story leads when you use this technique.

A statement of fact that can help your judge's understanding and your cause might be, for example: "Upon information and belief, I have no obligation to pay anything to XYZ; it is not a successor in interest to my Note or my mortgage; and it does not represent any company to which I owe anything regarding my Note and mortgage." A statement of fact like this can lead the judge's thinking toward the conclusion you desire, even though the sentence doesn't actually say what you want the judge's ruling to be. Everyone, including your judge, knows it would be wrong to let a person take your home if you don't owe that person anything.

When the lawsuit starts, you don't have all the facts that prove your opponent has no legal authority to do what it has done or threatens to do. You must, therefore, let the judge know about the facts you hope your opponent cannot prove. The "upon information and belief" statement is a good tool for that purpose. Some examples of how to use it are presented below. For more, refer to Exhibit C: *Examples—Responses And Claims.*

➤ *Your opponent is not the Boss or the Boss's servant.*

You can't possibly know the identity of the Boss prior to the lawsuit. Your opponent will not have provided sufficient information for you to know whether it is the Boss or the Boss's servant. All you can possibly know when the lawsuit starts is that your opponent claims to have rights that belong only to the Boss.

Your money and your home are not for the taking by any person or entity who doesn't first prove you actually owe it something—that's what fairness and justice are about. An imposter trying to get what is yours needs to be driven away, and that's where a judge can be of help.

Unless you have unequivocal proof, not guesses or assumptions, that your opponent is the Boss or the Boss's servant (see Chapter 11), your complaint or answer to a complaint should include something like this:

"Upon information and belief, I have no agreement with my opponent; it is owed nothing by me; and my opponent does not own or control any interest or right in my Note that permits it to enforce my Note in accordance with the constraints of this state's UCC. Furthermore, these facts apply equally to any company for which my opponent might claim it is working to take my home."

➤ The Note is not in default.

Many borrowers have lost in court because they started off by stating they were in default under the Note. Those borrowers were ignorant of the legal meaning of *default*. They did not have your advantage of having the information in Chapter 4 in the section called *Default—What It Means In Foreclosure*. They mistakenly equated missed or late monthly payments with that word. When they admitted being in "default," they made the judge think they were saying their opponent must be the Boss of the Note, with the right to demand payments under threat of foreclosure. Those borrowers pretty much sealed their fate when they told the judge something that was not true and was so helpful to their opponent. You now know better, so do not follow in their footsteps.

Unless you have unequivocal proof, not guesses or assumptions, that your opponent is the Boss or the Boss's servant, your complaint or answer to a complaint filed with the court should state something like this:

"Upon information and belief, my Note is not in default, I have received no presentment per the constraints of this state's UCC to the contrary, and I owe nothing to my opponent or the company for which it is working."

➤ The balance owed under the Note is unknown and may have already been paid off.

You know only one side of the story about the payment history of your Note. You may know how much you have paid over the years and how much the Note states is due from you. But without the aid of formal fact-finding in a lawsuit, you surely do not know how much money the Boss has been paid on your Note by others, or how much it will receive from others. Payment might have been made by an insurance company, a previous indorser of the Note who became liable on the Note along with you, or a person who settled a lawsuit or potential lawsuit involving your Note.

If your opponent can prove it is the Boss or the Boss's servant, the facts may show that the debt of the Note has already been paid in full and that your opponent is trying to get more money than what is actually owed under the Note. A Boss who has been fully paid no longer has any claim under your Note, no right to enforce it, and no right to foreclose.

Formal fact-finding pursuant to the court's rules of discovery can help you learn about such matters, but not unless the Boss of the Note is actually identified by your opponent. Only the Boss can give a complete accounting. Whatever any other person says about the remaining balance is not relevant.

Don't assume that just because you haven't paid all of the monthly payments you thought were due that your opponent is owed anything. Before it can demand payment from you, it must first prove who the Boss is. If the Boss is someone other than your opponent, then your opponent must prove it is the legal agent of the Boss. If it cannot prove the required Boss status, the amount due, if any, is not even important because your opponent will lose and that satisfies your objective in your lawsuit.

If your opponent can prove proper Boss status, it must also prove how much is still owed, if anything. It must provide a full accounting of every receipt and disbursement related to your Note from its inception. If it does not or cannot, the Note has probably been paid off, and you should ask your judge to make that same conclusion. There can be no justification or rationale for guessing about something that important if the Boss cannot prove what balance, if any, is still due.

Unless you have unequivocal proof, not guesses or assumptions, that your opponent is the Boss or the Boss's servant, and equally certain proof of the amount now due, you cannot possibly know that the obligation of the Note even exists anymore. Your complaint against your opponent or your answer to a complaint it files against you should state something like this:

> "Upon information and belief, I owe nothing to my opponent; I have seen no evidence or presentment that any amount is still due under my Note. Furthermore, I maintain that the balance due under my Note is not relevant to the controlling question of whether my opponent has any right by law to enforce my Note pursuant to this state's UCC."

> ➤ *Each purported assignment, sale or transfer of your mortgage or Note was invalid and conveyed no right to enforce your Note.*

Only the Boss of the Note has the right to assign, sell, or transfer the Note or mortgage to someone else, or to have its servant do those things. Suppose there have been three alleged sales, assignments, or transfers of your Note. Each one was proper if, and only if, directed by the Boss of the Note at that time. The same is true for any assignment of the mortgage.

Refresh your memory about the UCC requirements regarding identification of the one true Boss once the Note has changed hands (see Chapter 11), and you will better appreciate the complexity of the UCC requirements. That review will underscore the fact that you don't have enough information to know the identity of the Boss. You may never know the identity of the current Boss of your Note, but you can be certain that no exchange, sale, or transfer of your Note or mortgage was valid without having been made by whoever was the Boss at the time that any such transaction occurred.

The foreclosure machine may try to fool you and the judge by using the name and signature of a prior Boss to create documents intended to help take away your home. The original lender, for example, may have been the Boss of the Note in 2005, but not in 2011 when your opponent alleges that the lender assigned the Note and mortgage to some other company. That original lender may have sold your Note the same day you signed it and, thereby, lost its status as Boss.

"Once a Boss, not always a Boss" is a fact under the UCC. Every transaction involving the Note or mortgage must be proven to have been an act of the Boss at that time: no exceptions. Even if your original lender now claims to have possession of the Note, its status as the current Boss must go through the same fact-finding and analysis as any other person claiming Boss status. It must prove how, when, and under what circumstances it obtained its current possession. It must also prove that it holds absolute rights in the Note and mortgage, versus only being a puppet for some undisclosed company that may have no rights to enforce the Note. For example, the original lender could have sold the Note the same day you signed it and then received possession of the Note later solely to help some other company take your home. Caution is warranted because the machine has played that type of deceitful game in foreclosure cases.

If your opponent claims or implies that its rights against you involve any sale, purchase, transfer, or assignment of your Note or mortgage, an accurate response is this:

> "Upon information and belief, I deny that any past transaction involving my Note or mortgage created in my opponent a legal right to now make demands on me for payment related to my Note, declare my Note in default, or otherwise enforce my Note per this state's UCC, and my opponent has refused to provide genuine evidence to the contrary. Accordingly, I owe my opponent nothing, I owe nothing to whatever company my opponent may allege to be serving, and my opponent has no right to prosecute a foreclosure of my home when I owe nothing to it or whatever person for which it may be working."

This is a correct and accurate statement unless you actually have unequivocal proof, and not guess or assumption, to the contrary.

Even if the machine's story seems plausible on the surface, remember to challenge each and every exchange of your Note or mortgage, and to demand thorough and substantiating evidence about each. The foreclosure machine will slant its explanations and stories to appear plausible—that is what it does. Only dedicated fact-finding can demonstrate which, if any, of the statements it makes are true and sufficient to the tests under the UCC. If it fails to produce convincing evidence, it should lose.

➤ *MERS has no valid involvement with your Note.*

If MERS is mentioned in your mortgage, your opponent should have big difficulties. As previously noted, I call it ShellGame-MERS because it appears to be an empty shell that is little more than a pawn for whatever loan servicer wants to use its name. Formal fact-finding should disclose that it has not actually made any valid assignment or transfer of your Note or mortgage.

Extra evidence highlighting the shortcomings of ShellGame-MERS will be available in my soon-to-be-released book, *ShellGame-MERS: Contrived Confusion.* In the meantime, adherence to the foreclosure fundamentals will help disclose the ruse that occurs when the industry's foreclosure machine uses the name of ShellGame-MERS.

Any alleged assignment or transfer of the mortgage by ShellGame-MERS to any other company must be invalid, because ShellGame-MERS is never the Boss of the Note, nor does it represent the Boss of the Note. Neither ShellGame-MERS nor your opponent can likely prove otherwise if put to the test. Therefore, unless you know something I don't know, each and every claim that ShellGame-MERS ever passed on an interest in the Note or mortgage to some other company should be met with a statement like this:

"Upon information and belief, I deny that MERS had any ownership or beneficial interest in my Note and mortgage. Furthermore, I maintain that it never made an assignment or transfer of either in response to the instructions of a company then having the right to enforce my Note pursuant to this state's UCC. Accordingly, any purported assignment or transfer from MERS to any company was invalid and transferred no rights or interests in either."

➤ *The attempt to foreclose is invalid because the identity of the Boss is unknown.*

Your case commences without your having received proof of the identity of the Boss. Having read Chapter 11 places you in a better position to understand the fact-intensive nature of Boss status and to recognize that you have not seen the type of evidence necessary to classify your opponent as a Boss or a Boss's servant. If you engaged in informal discovery with a letter like the one in Exhibit E, you understand even more that your opponent has not shown itself to be entitled to exercise the rights of a Boss of your Note. This fact alone negates the alleged validity of any foreclosure attempt, and it places a heavy burden on your opponent to prove up a lot of details as your fact-finding progresses.

The interactive legal authorities of your Note, your mortgage, and your state's foreclosure laws (including its UCC) do not sanction foreclosure by anyone other than the Boss or its servant. Spend a little time looking at the foreclosure laws of your state and you will see that the statutes and the case law interpreting them make clear that foreclosure is only proper when an obligation is owed by the borrower who pledged his or her home as collateral, and owed to the person who has elected to commence the foreclosure. Those laws necessarily force the controlling issue back to the UCC. What counts is whether your opponent can prove that your obligation under your Note is owed to it or the company for which it may claim to be working.

If your opponent has not proven unequivocally that it is the Boss or the Boss's servant respecting your Note, foreclosure cannot be legal. In that event, an accurate statement for your complaint or answer to a complaint might be this:

"Upon information and belief, I owe my opponent nothing; I owe nothing respecting my Note to any company for which my opponent might work; and it has no right to enforce my Note pursuant to this state's UCC. It therefore has no right to take my home via foreclosure under a mistaken or fraudulent claim that it has the legal right to collect an unsatisfied debt owed by me."

If your mortgage is a deed of trust, the statement might be this:

"Upon information and belief, I owe my opponent nothing; I owe nothing respecting my Note to any company for which my opponent might work; it has no right to enforce my Note pursuant to this state's UCC; and it has no right to trigger the power of sale under my deed of trust for the purpose of taking my home via foreclosure under a mistaken or fraudulent claim that it has the legal right to collect an unsatisfied obligation owed by me."

➤ *Any action by a trustee or foreclosure administrator in pursuit of a nonjudicial foreclosure must have been improper.*

If you've received notices and threats from a trustee or foreclosure administrator as part of a nonjudicial foreclosure, such a person has no authority to do anything without first having received instructions from the Boss of your Note. (See Chapter 11.) Only the Boss can trigger foreclosure under the terms of the deed of trust, and only the Boss can declare a default or commence collection activities related to your Note. The trustee rarely has authority to start a foreclosure process on its own.

Any notice, therefore, that allegedly comes from a trustee or foreclosure administrator must be invalid, because no default has been declared by the Boss of your Note, no amount has been proven by the Boss to be due, and whatever instructions led to the issuance of those foreclosure notices must not have been given by the Boss. The state's nonjudicial foreclosure procedures also may have been violated on various technical grounds, but the "no Boss, no foreclosure" fundamental principle will always apply, pending actual proof of the identity of the Boss and the role, if any, it played in starting the nonjudicial foreclosure process.

When you don't know the identity of the Boss, an accurate statement for your complaint or answer to a complaint would be this:

"Upon information and belief, the threatened foreclosure is in violation of my rights because the power of sale pursuant to my deed of trust has not been initiated by the person entitled to enforce my Note pursuant to this state's UCC, or that person's servant; the alleged trustee did not receive instructions to commence this foreclosure from the person to whom the obligation of my Note is owed, or that person's servant; and I do not owe anything to the person for whose benefit the threatened foreclosure is allegedly being conducted. Accordingly, the threatened foreclosure violates the terms of my Note and deed of trust, and it violates this state's nonjudicial foreclosure law, which necessarily requires application of this state's UCC regarding the issue of who has a right to enforce my Note."

> ➤ *Your opponent has admitted that you owe it nothing and it has no right to foreclose.*

If, prior to the commencement of your lawsuit, you engaged in informal discovery by sending your opponent the type of letter discussed in Chapter 10 and Exhibit E, you probably did not receive a response that contained genuine facts sufficient to prove that your opponent is the Boss or the Boss's servant with respect to your Note. That lack of response means your opponent has admitted that you owe it nothing, and that it has no right to make any demands under your Note. (See Chapter 11.) This adverse admission lets you start the lawsuit at the top of the hill and puts your opponent at the bottom with a long climb ahead.

An accurate statement in your complaint or answer to a complaint about this occurrence should be something like this:

"Upon information and belief, my opponent has refused to, or cannot, produce evidence that it has any right to enforce my Note, for itself or any other person, even though I requested that proof from my opponent. Accordingly, my opponent has admitted pursuant to this state's UCC that I owe it nothing, that it has no right to make demands related to my Note, and that I did not dishonor my Note as a result of refusing to comply with my opponent's unsupported and mistaken or fraudulent demands. Furthermore, I maintain that, because I owe nothing to my opponent, or any company for which it works, it has no right to foreclose on my house because it can show no unsatisfied obligation that is secured by my mortgage."

DEFEND AGAINST A MOTION TO DISMISS

Routine litigation practice includes trying to win cases on procedural grounds in order to avoid a full evidentiary trial. So don't be surprised if your opponent files a motion to dismiss, or a demurrer, as it is also called in some places. A motion to dismiss tries to persuade your judge that your claims or assertions do not involve matters that warrant the court's time and attention. If the court approves the motion, some or all of your claims against your opponent can be eliminated. Winning a motion to dismiss is a big plus for the machine because it will have saved time and money, and avoided having to prove that you actually owe it anything.

A motion to dismiss is typically filed early in the lawsuit. The machine regularly files this type of motion before it has been required to produce any evidence in the discovery process, and before it is even required to answer your formal challenges. A motion to dismiss asks the judge to throw out or dismiss claims which are alleged to have no legal merit in fact or law.

The test used to evaluate the legal sufficiency of the party's claim is similar in state and federal courts. Drafting your complaint or answer to avoid a quick dismissal of your claim often entails little more than making certain the facts you allege actually support your legal theories.[159]

You want the judge to rule that your opponent does not have the right to make demands under your Note and that it lacks the legal right to foreclose. A motion to dismiss, however, will likely be successful if your complaint says no more than, "My opponent lacks the legal right to enforce my Note," and, "My opponent has no right to take my home via foreclosure." These two statements are conclusions, neither of which is supported by any allegation of fact.

Defending against a motion to dismiss is not that hard. The idea is to avoid arguing only platitudes or legal conclusions. Instead, shore up your conclusions with allegations of fact that demonstrate to the judge that your case is more than just hot air.

The following are sample statements that can help your claims withstand a motion to dismiss. These examples are written as if the borrower issued a letter seeking information from its opponent prior to the lawsuit's beginning. (See Chapter 10 and Exhibit E.) The statements you use in your complaint or your counterclaim against your opponent will, of course, be supported by your facts, references to documents you attach as exhibits, and citations of law specific to your state and your situation, but I hope you will find these examples useful. Along with whatever else might be in your complaint or counterclaims against your opponent, the parts of the story involving UCC-driven law might be as follows:

- "Upon information and belief, my Note has been sold, assigned, exchanged, traded, or otherwise transferred many times since its creation."

- "Upon information and belief, my Note is a negotiable instrument pursuant to UCC § 3-104 of the Uniform Commercial Code. As such, only the person qualified by UCC § 3-301 has the right to enforce the Note, and necessarily the right to enforce my mortgage, which is only incidental to my Note."

- "My opponent has failed to, or cannot, provide verifiable and complete information explaining how it acquired or obtained an interest of any kind in my Note, even though I requested such proof. A copy of my Letter is attached as Exhibit "A." Upon information and belief, therefore, I deny that my opponent has any interest in my Note, whether as owner, possessor, or person with a right to enforce my Note pursuant to UCC § 3-301."

- "My opponent has refused to, or cannot, identify the person who has the right to enforce my Note pursuant to UCC § 3-301, even though I have requested such proof. A copy of my Letter is attached as Exhibit "A." Upon information and belief, therefore, I deny that my opponent is an agent or representative of any person actually having the right to enforce my Note."

- "My opponent has failed to, or cannot, provide information regarding the balance, if any, due under my Note, even though I requested that information. A copy of my Letter is attached as Exhibit "A." I have received no information regarding the balance due, if any, under my Note from any person having demonstrated the right to enforce my Note pursuant to the strictures of the UCC. I, therefore, do not know if any amount is still due, and I have not received any presentment respecting my Note, as defined by UCC § 3-501. Upon information and belief, therefore, I deny that any balance is due under the Note, and, furthermore, I maintain that questions or answers about the amount still due, if any, under my Note have no bearing on the crucial legal issue of whether my opponent has any right to enforce any obligation under my Note."

- "Upon information and belief, I deny that any default exists under the Note or that the Note has been dishonored or breached pursuant to UCC 3-502 as a result of my having refused to comply with the unsupported claims of my opponent. Furthermore, I maintain that no discussion of

207

default or dishonor bears on the question of law as to whether my opponent has any right to enforce my Note pursuant to this state's UCC."

- "My opponent has failed to, or cannot, provide the chain of ownership and authority respecting my Note since its creation, including the circumstances and details of each alleged transfer, sale, or exchange, even though I requested same. A copy of my Letter is attached as Exhibit "A." Upon information and belief, I therefore deny that my opponent has any legal interest in my Note, that I have any obligation to it pursuant to my Note, or that it even knows a person with the right to enforce the Note."

- "Because my opponent has failed to, or cannot, provide any evidence that it has a cognizable interest of any kind in my Note, that it has the right to enforce my Note, or that it even knows the identity of such a person, upon information and belief, I therefore deny that my opponent has demonstrated any condition or circumstance that would have permitted it to declare a default or accelerate any obligation under my Note."

- "Because my opponent has failed to, or cannot, provide any evidence that it has an identifiable interest of any kind in my Note, that it has the right to enforce my Note, or that it even knows the identity of such a person, upon information and belief, I therefore deny that my opponent has demonstrated any condition or circumstance that would have permitted it to initiate a foreclosure under the terms of my mortgage."

- "The Uniform Commercial Code requires anyone making demands under my Note to first prove a right, recognized under the UCC, to enforce the Note. My opponent has failed to do that, and its failure, for whatever reason, is a tacit admission that it has no right to enforce my Note and that I do not owe anything to it or any company for which it is acting as servant. Now it seeks to avoid discovery by having filed this motion to dismiss. Its motion is further evidence that it cannot or refuses to prove it has any rights respecting my Note and mortgage."

The above examples are longer than simply saying, "My opponent is wrong and should lose," but longer is better. This series of statements gives facts that help the judge understand why your conclusions of law are being made and why your case is plausible and deserving of more time in court. Allegations of fact, including those made "upon information and belief," help build a solid barrier against dismissal should your opponent file a motion to dismiss your claims.

DEFEND AGAINST A MOTION FOR SUMMARY JUDGMENT

A motion for summary judgment is a little different from the motion to dismiss discussed above. Your opponent would file a motion to dismiss arguing that, even if everything you filed is true, you should still lose. Its motion for summary judgment will say that, based on its version of the facts, you should lose. A motion to dismiss requires the judge to concentrate on what you file. A motion for summary judgment, however, asks the judge to focus on what your opponent claims are the most important and allegedly uncontested facts.

A motion for summary judgment contends that no genuine issues of material fact are present and that the judge should, as a matter of law, rule in favor of the party that files the motion. It asks the court to decide who wins without need of a trial or the full presentation of evidence.

Your opponent is likely to craft a motion for summary judgment using what it claims to be the only important facts—that is, the ones that will serve its self-interest. It will assert that you do not object to the truth or accuracy of its selection of so-called facts. The foreclosure machine will use a motion for summary judgment in hopes that you will not be prepared to rebut or contest its motion. If successful, it will have defeated your claims without your judge ever learning how much your opponent cannot prove.

It can more easily get away with this tactic when the borrower has not taken advantage of the power of the court's rules of discovery to learn what evidence your opponent does not have. If that is your situation, you may not be able to effectively rebut its claims.

The more you know about what your opponent has in the way of evidence and information, the easier it is for you to help your judge see that your opponent does not have enough facts to support its claimed right to demand money from you or to take your home.

Remember, it is your opponent who has the burden to prove that it has the right to enforce your Note as its Boss or its Boss's servant. In the course of your formal fact-finding, you will be looking for any data or information that is essential to proving those claims, yet is missing from what your opponent shows. Your opponent is counting on you to be unprepared. If you've done your homework, you will be able to withstand its effort to avoid a trial that would look at all the facts.

Defeating a summary judgment motion requires showing the judge that there is more to the case than what your opponent claims. You need to demonstrate which of its alleged facts are not true, which are misleading in terms of the genuine issues, and the facts required by the UCC which the opponent has not shown, Point out the existence of other facts important to a correct adjudication, and give examples of how a jury could view the totality of facts and missing facts in a different way from the conclusion the opponent promotes. Help your judge understand that your opponent's hand-picked facts are not complete or sufficient to prove its right to enforce your Note under your state's UCC and that, contrary to your opponent's contention, there are genuine issues of material fact that necessarily have to be decided at trial so that the applicable law can be properly applied.

If facts important to a proper legal resolution are in dispute, the judge is not supposed to rule on the factual issues. He or she must deny your opponent's motion and let the lawsuit continue to a trial on the full merits, that is, the essential facts and law of the case.

A motion for summary judgment looks primarily at whether all of the important facts are already known and before the judge. If they are, the judge feels comfortable ruling on who wins that contest. If the facts are not all there, the judge is supposed to deny the motion.

The UCC-driven issues of your case depend heavily on facts. Boss status cannot be simply proven with an alleged assignment of the Note or an affidavit that your opponent is entitled to enforce the Note. The determination of Boss status requires looking at all of the factors involving transfers, sales, and assignments of your Note (see Chapter 11). Point out the fact-intensive nature of the UCC issues to your judge. Then explain what facts and information your opponent has not yet proven, along with your summary of discrepancies and conflicting information in what it has shown. That should be enough to demonstrate that genuine issues of material fact are still present, thus making the grant of summary judgment inappropriate. Everything that raises doubt about the accuracy, thoroughness or trustworthiness of your opponent's selected statement of facts is what you want your judge to see.

Another comment about litigation procedure is worth noting. A motion for summary judgment is usually thought premature and not ripe for a decision by the judge when fact-finding or discovery is in progress and not yet complete. Conceptually, the ongoing fact-finding may uncover genuine issues of material fact that would show any earlier approval of a motion for summary judgment to have been too hasty and incorrect. This is another reason to begin formal discovery as soon as the court's rules permit you to do so. If you put it off and then find yourself facing a motion for summary judgment, your judge may not give you more time for fact-finding. A motion for summary judgment is not very threatening, however, if you are in the midst of formal fact-finding when the motion is filed, or if you have not been able to begin discovery because the case is so new or because local rules prohibit formal-fact finding at that point in the process. Under those circumstances you can often defeat a motion for summary judgment by showing that it is premature, since you have not yet had an opportunity to commence or complete formal discovery.

As Chapter 10 emphasizes, aggressive fact-finding is a good protection against a premature motion for summary judgment. It is also the best way to keep pressure on your opponent and find the weakness in your opponent's armor of apparent confidence.

RAISE A "REAL PARTY IN INTEREST" CHALLENGE

"Real party in interest" is the label reserved for the person who has the substantive right being asserted in the lawsuit. In a foreclosure case, that substantive right is, at a minimum, the right to enforce the Note held by the Boss.

One judicial policy behind the concept of the real party in interest is to prevent people from suing about things and rights that do not belong to them. Another purpose of this rule is to put all persons with a genuine stake in the subject matter of the claim into the same lawsuit so that all of their rights and defenses can be addressed once and for all time in that one case. Deny that your opponent is a real party in interest and your court will have to address these concepts and the underlying protections to which you are entitled.

When the case starts, you know, of course, that your opponent has not proven that it is the Boss of your Note or that it can identify the Boss. In light of that failure, it is reasonable to allege that it is not the real party in interest. The allegation might be phrased like this:

> "Upon information and belief, my opponent has no legal interest in my Note or mortgage and no right to enforce either; I owe nothing to my opponent or to any company of which my opponent might claim to be servant respecting my Note and mortgage; and, furthermore, I deny that my opponent is a real party in interest in this lawsuit."

Denying that your opponent is the real party in interest makes that concept a jurisdictional issue in federal courts and in most state courts. This often means that the trial court and the appeals court have no right to rule in your opponent's favor without first making their own determinations, based on evidence before the lower court, that your opponent deserves the real-party-in-interest status.

As with all foreclosure fundamentals, the burden is on your opponent, not you, to prove it is the real party in interest regarding your Note and mortgage. Your challenges to its claimed status under the UCC also provide a good foundation for challenging its right to status as the real party in interest.

Some state courts can raise this issue on their own, but in other courts it is not an issue unless you bring it up. In your complaint or your response to a lawsuit, deny your opponent is the real party in interest, unless you have a really good reason not to. This should put you a step ahead regardless of your court's specific rules on this subject. Using this judicial rule is another way to force to the surface the foreclosure fundamentals stressed by *Fighting the Foreclosure Machine*.

Some courts require the real party in interest to be the Boss of the Note. Others permit a duly appointed servant or agent to conduct the lawsuit. The first hurdle for your opponent, of course, is to prove the identity of the Boss. If the Boss is not identified, any questions about who is an agent or servant are moot and need not be addressed. If your opponent claims to work for the alleged Boss, your opponent must thoroughly prove that agency relationship. (See Chapter 11.)

By challenging your opponent's status as the real party in interest, you effectively will be asking your judge to decide whether your opponent has the right to assert Boss powers. Your judge may even see something you miss that might help prove that your opponent's effort to foreclose must be denied by the court as a matter of law. I have difficulty imagining when a challenge to the machine's status as a real party in interest is not a good idea.

DENY THE PLAINTIFF'S JUDICIAL STANDING

A judicial concept closely related to real party in interest is that of *standing*. To have standing means that a party starting the lawsuit (the plaintiff) can justify its participation in the suit because it has a sufficient connection to the issues involved and can demonstrate that it will be harmed in some way if the suit is not resolved in its favor. If you are sued, you can and should think about denying that your opponent has judicial standing. By making this challenge you will also enlist the court's help in determining your opponent's relationship to your Note and mortgage.

Your judge will look seriously at a standing challenge because it goes to the heart of whether that court has the authority to hear your opponent's case against you. If your judge thinks not, the lawsuit will be dismissed. Whether your opponent would be able to file a new lawsuit would depend on how the judge dismisses the case.

Beating your opponent's lawsuit is the primary objective at hand, and it is something to celebrate should it happen for you. That is so even if the opponent is not barred from trying a foreclosure later. Reports say the foreclosure machine often gives up if once beaten in court.

In a foreclosure case, the plaintiff typically must prove several things regarding its alleged judicial standing:

- That the Note is in default

- That it or the company for which it works has the right to enforce the Note pursuant to the constraints of the UCC

- That it would be directly injured by the breach of the Note

- That receiving a judgment against you will help reduce its injury

If your opponent can't prove it is either the Boss of the Note or the Boss's servant with respect to your Note and mortgage, it can't prove that you owe it anything. If you owe it nothing, your judge will think that your opponent does not have any injury respecting your obligation under your Note, or any right to take your home. A challenge to standing could accelerate and make more prominent the fact-intensive, UCC-driven legal issues. That type of fight might even result in your opponent's suit being dismissed without the need for a full trial.

Federal and state court rules vary. Some courts require the plaintiff to prove it is the Boss of the Note and the title owner of the mortgage. Some permit the Boss's servant to initiate the suit. Others require that the Boss must be a party to and initiate the lawsuit in its own name. Resolving the question of standing, regardless of the procedural rules of your court, should help ferret out whether your opponent can identify the Boss of the Note. If it cannot, then its case should be dismissed.

Some courts maintain that the issue of standing may be raised at any time; it may even be raised for the first time when a case is appealed to a higher court. The rules of other courts require that challenges to standing must be raised early in the case or else the right to raise that issue can be lost. You can avoid the risk of losing the right to later challenge the plaintiff's standing by denying it in your answer to the complaint filed against you.

By denying the plaintiff's standing, you force that issue to be addressed at both the trial level and the appellate level of the court system. That is, your judge and the appeals court must find that standing was proper. If the lower court does not address the standing issue, or it makes a ruling that standing is present then, on appeal, you can ask the higher court to address that issue. If the appellate court rules that your opponent lacked standing, no ruling or order issued by the lower court would have any further validity.

Judicial standing and the right to enforce your Note are inextricably connected in a foreclosure lawsuit. Your doubt that your opponent is the Boss or the Boss's servant is sufficient grounds upon which to challenge your opponent's standing. Your having raised the issue in your answer to your opponent's complaint should ensure that your judge will also be looking more closely at your opponent's alleged rights.

AVOID "SHOW ME THE NOTE" DIFFICULTIES

Some courts in a handful of the nonjudicial foreclosure states have ruled against borrowers who presented weak and inaccurate facts joined with nonexistent or poorly stated legal arguments. The foreclosure machine was able to convince a few judges that the borrower's only objection to foreclosure was based on a simplistic and meritless claim. The machine maintained that the only legal issue presented by the borrower was whether the state's non-judicial foreclosure law specifically and expressly stated that the physical Note had to be produced before the foreclosure sale took place, even though, in reality, the law did not say this. In other words, according to the machine, the borrower's entire claim boiled down to one demand: "Show me the Note."

Unfortunately, the borrowers in these so-called show-me-the-Note cases typically did not file an objection to that interpretation of their entire legal argument. Nor did they contest the machine's statement of what the lawsuit was about. In some instances, the borrower may have filed a response that was incomprehensible.

These borrowers also granted Boss status to their opponents without requiring them to prove that they were the Boss or the Boss's servant. The borrowers did that by admitting that the Note was in default and that they owed money to the machine, or by filing documents with the court that let the judge think that they made that type of admission. The borrowers probably filed those incorrect statements of fact because they lacked knowledge and were too comfortable relying on assumptions and guesses.

What These Cases Might Mean for You

The so-called show-me-the-Note decisions are little more than examples of successes for the foreclosure machine when it beat up on people who were unprepared and unable to defend themselves. I don't think you'll be acting like the borrowers who lost those cases. That kind of decision should not pose a problem if you accurately state your facts and draft your complaint to defend against a motion to dismiss.

The foreclosure machine will try to twist whatever the borrower says. If your lawsuit is being conducted in one of the few states to have issued such show-me-the-Note decisions, your opponent will probably tell the judge that your entire lawsuit is effectively just another show-me-the-Note case that should be dismissed. Your statement of facts and presentation of the law applicable to your situation should, however, easily demonstrate to your judge that your case does not fit that pattern.

The show-me-the-Note decisions represented superficial issues for which equally superficial and extremely limited rulings were sufficient. Those cases never addressed the meat of the foreclosure law. They did not consider whether the state's citizens could have their homes legally taken by companies who were not owed anything by the homeowners targeted for foreclosure. In lawyer lingo, those cases have no value as precedent to a new case that presents different facts and different issues of law.

Nonjudicial foreclosure statutes do not say the Note has to be produced prior to the foreclosure sale. So what? Those statutes and the court cases interpreting them make clear that foreclosure is only proper when conducted to benefit the person owed an obligation by the borrower. The text of the nonjudicial foreclosure statutes varies among the states, but no state's foreclosure law condones or encourages the taking of a person's home by a company to which the homeowner owes nothing. The purpose of foreclosure is to take care of the person owed the obligation evidenced by the Note when there is a default and that person elects to commence collection of the debt that is owed to it. That person, of course, is the Boss according to the Uniform Commercial Code. Some statutes permit a servant to conduct the foreclosure, and that includes the services of a trustee designated to carry out a nonjudicial foreclosure as permitted by the terms of the deed of trust document. Of course, if a servant is involved, it must prove both the identity of the Boss and that the alleged servant is actually following instructions from that Boss regarding your Note and mortgage.

Your state's law may label the person entitled to foreclose as lender, creditor, mortgagee, beneficiary, trustee, or something else. Look deeply enough into your state's foreclosure statutes and the case law that interprets them and you will see that they are all labels used when the purpose of the law is to benefit the person entitled to enforce your Note, that is, the Boss. Only the person to whom you have a legal obligation regarding your mortgage loan is supposed to have the right to your payments or home if a foreclosure happens. Again, I have never heard of a state that knowingly permits or intends that a citizen can lose his or her home to a person or company not owed anything under the mortgage loan.

If your opponent relies on show-me-the-Note decisions in an attempt to defeat your complaint, you can most likely withstand that attack by distinguishing your circumstances from those in the show-me-the-Note case or cases to which your opponent points. Those cases typically involve a borrower who admits or is deemed to have agreed that it was in default of its Note obligation, and that the opponent was owed money. None of those cases actually addresses legislative purpose or the substance of the state's foreclosure law. They are little more than superficial judicial solutions to what were presented as superficial legal questions. If you've done your homework, you will clearly be able to show facts and law that make those earlier cases inapplicable to your situation. For example, you most likely will be denying that any default exists, that anything is owed to your opponent, and that the opponent has any right to enforce the Note. Your statement will contain allegations like these:

- The attempted foreclosure violates the terms of my deed of trust, which authorizes only the person empowered by the UCC to initiate the power of sale.

- It violates my state's nonjudicial foreclosure law because foreclosure is proper only if consistent with the agreements I made with my lender (i.e., your Note and mortgage).

- It violates that foreclosure law because the threatened foreclosure is not being conducted for the benefit of the person entitled to enforce the obligation of my Note, if any balance is still owed to that person, and I deny that any balance is due based on what I know.

Your presentation of facts and legal issues will lead your judge to important questions that require genuine legal analysis, as contrasted with the circumstances of the show-me-the-Note cases.

A North Carolina case provides a useful outline of when the nonjudicial foreclosure process is proper:

"In a foreclosure proceeding under a power of sale [i.e., a nonjudicial sale], the lender bears the burden of proving four elements that must be established in order for the clerk of court to authorize the mortgagee or trustee to proceed with the foreclosure: (i) valid debt of which the party seeking to foreclose is the holder, (ii) default, (iii) right to foreclose under the instrument, (iv) notice to those entitled to such ... " *In the Matter of the Foreclosure of a Deed of Trust Executed by Adams,* No. COA09-1455 (NC Ct.App. 2010).

This North Carolina case is not binding authority in other states, and North Carolina's foreclosure procedures are not the same as those of other states. But this is a well-reasoned and persuasive example of the things that should be proven for a nonjudicial foreclosure to be valid. As best I can tell, the four requirements correctly state the proper foreclosure requirements in every state that permits nonjudicial foreclosure.

Parts (i) and (ii) invoke a state's UCC, because that law controls the question of who has the right to enforce your Note. Part (iii) requires a review of the deed of trust to determine when foreclosure may commence as defined by your agreement with your lender. That effectively forces the question about the identity of the Boss, because only the Boss now owns the enforcement rights of your lender as provided by the UCC. Therefore, only that Boss is authorized to trigger a power of sale that will get a trustee started in the actual conduct of a foreclosure. Part (iv) means your opponent and the trustee are required to comply with the state-specified details of a nonjudicial foreclosure, such as public recordings of documents, publication and distribution of notices, content of the text in those notices, the timing of the different requirements, and communications with the borrower targeted for foreclosure.

If your opponent can't prove each of the four elements set out by North Carolina, your foreclosure should be stopped. If the foreclosure is already completed, it should be ruled wrongful, if time still remains within which to get the foreclosure overturned. If your opponent has not proven the identity of the Boss, your facts and statement of law for the judge will make clear that the foreclosure, whether threatened or concluded, violates all four parts of that test and is therefore not valid. You will, of course, direct your judge to your state's statues and court decisions. Exhibit B may help you explain everything to your judge.

Dealing with the Trustee's Role

A nonjudicial foreclosure involves a trustee or foreclosure administrator who conducts the foreclosure. If you are trying to stop a nonjudicial foreclosure, or you are suing to get something back after the taking of your home, your complaint will be more complete and accurate if it injects allegations regarding the role of the trustee who is conducting or who conducted the foreclosure. For example:

- "Upon information and belief, the alleged trustee attempting to foreclose my home does not know the identity of the person authorized by this state's version of the Uniform Commercial Code to enforce my Note [i.e., the Boss of my Note or the Boss]."

- "Upon information and belief, the alleged trustee was not appointed to that position by the Boss of the Note or its duly appointed agent, and, accordingly, the alleged trustee has no authority to initiate or conduct a foreclosure pursuant to the terms of my deed of trust and this state's nonjudicial foreclosure law."

- "Upon information and belief, the alleged trustee has made no effort to verify the identity of the Boss of the Note and has therefore breached its duty to that Boss and also to me by commencing and conducting the foreclosure."

- "Upon information and belief, the alleged trustee initiated the threatened foreclosure for the purpose of delivering the foreclosure sale proceeds or the title to my house to a person other than the Boss of the Note, contrary to the terms of the Note, the deed of trust, and this state's nonjudicial foreclosure law."

- "Upon information and belief, my deed of trust does not authorize the alleged trustee to initiate a foreclosure of its own volition, and yet it received no instruction to do so from the Boss or the Boss's servant. Accordingly, no power of sale has been triggered, so foreclosure is not valid or authorized."

- "Upon information and belief, I owe no debt to the alleged trustee or whomever it claims to be serving."

- "Upon information and belief, the alleged trustee did not initiate the subject foreclosure pursuant to the terms of the deed of trust and the Note secured by same, and therefore is participating in a mistake or fraud respecting the foreclosure of my home."

- "Upon information and belief, the alleged trustee has violated the nonjudicial foreclosure statutes by having initiated a foreclosure that is not authorized by the deed of trust or the Note it secures; by having taken its instructions to commence the foreclosure from a person who is not the Boss of the Note or the legal representative of such Boss; by having commenced the subject foreclosure when, in fact, the Note served by the deed of trust is not in default or dishonored; and by having commenced the subject foreclosure, not for the benefit of the Boss of the Note, but instead for the purpose of delivering the foreclosure sale proceeds or title to the house to a person other than the Boss of the Note, in violation of this state's nonjudicial foreclosure law."

- [If ShellGame-MERS is listed in your deed of trust and is alleged to have appointed the trustee.] "Upon information and belief, the appointment of the alleged trustee by Mortgage Electronic Registration Systems, Inc. (MERS) was invalid because MERS owns no economic or ownership interest in my Note and deed of trust, and, further, because MERS did not represent as servant or agent of the Boss of the Note when MERS purportedly appointed or gave any instructions to that alleged trustee. Accordingly, the actions of the alleged trustee regarding my deed of trust were made without authority pursuant to my deed of trust or this state's foreclosure law and were in violation of my rights."

When you incorporate text like this into your complaint, you will raise factual and legal issues that challenge the validity of the foreclosure.

Worthy of comment is that when you use this tactic, you clearly have not limited your challenge to the single claim that your opponent must display the Note because your state's statutes specifically say so. Your objections will have merit in fact and law. You will direct your judge's attention to the text of your deed of trust and Note that support your position, and to your state's statutes and interpretations of those statutes by your state's courts. You will show how the purposes of your state's foreclosure process are intended to benefit the Boss of your Note, and no one else. You will have greatly distanced yourself from the meager facts and almost unbelievably narrow legal issues that were addressed in the show-me-the-Note cases.

UCC § 3-301 identifies three ways a person could have the right to enforce your Note, and only two of those ways require current physical possession of the Note. That's why your entire demand is not simply, "Show me the Note," and why references to show-me-the-Note decisions have no relevance to your lawsuit. In fact, unlike those show-me-the-Note cases, your discovery efforts and your complaint clearly indicate that you're asking the judge to use his or her legal skills to actually address a more complex and significant issue—the purposes of your state's foreclosure process and their relationship to your claim that your opponent is trying to take your home when it is not owed anything by you. If you didn't get complete proof of Boss status in response to your informal discovery letter (Chapter 10), you will also have your opponent's tacit admission that you owe it nothing and that no default even exists. Exhibit B is an example of how one person explained this to a judge.

Your judge will see that you have raised a genuine dispute, backed by fact and well-reasoned law. He or she will more easily see the connection between the nonjudicial statutes and the UCC. Your judge will have difficulty accepting that a person should be allowed to take your money or home if you don't owe that person anything. That said, your judge should conclude that the old show-me-the-Note decisions don't have any application to your case.

DON'T ACCEPT THE WAIVER ARGUMENT

Some lenders add contract provisions, clauses or sentences in the Note or mortgage which have no legal merit. A waiver of rights under the UCC is not uncommon in loan documents. The lender knows the waiver wording rarely has legal significance if challenged, but the lender puts it in the document anyway because it sometimes can be used to take advantage of the unwary.

For example, some Notes contain language like "I and any other person who has obligations under this Note waive the rights of Presentment and Notice of Dishonor. 'Presentment' means the right to require the Note Holder to demand payment of amounts due." This is a misleading way of saying the borrower is agreeing that, in the future, he or she may have to pay a person who has no right by law to the payment. It is a way of saying that the borrower has forgone the protections of the UCC, and that the borrower accepts the risk of being sued more than once by different companies, each claiming the right to enforce the same Note.

Most borrowers have no idea what those words mean. I imagine judges and jurors could easily have different interpretations. Many borrowers, however, have lost disputes with the foreclosure machine because of such alleged waivers.

The courts in most states, maybe all, ignore waiver text in contracts except where the facts clearly indicate that the borrower understood the rights being waived and intended to abandon, relinquish or waive those rights. If your mortgage loan documents state that you waived something, check with your attorney. If the lender did not clearly explain what the waiver was about and you did not understand when signing, you probably didn't waive or give up any rights. If, as with the text of the above example, the meaning would have been unclear to a typical bank customer, that waiver verbiage probably has no legal significance. But you have to object to its use if it is raised by your opponent.

Lenders typically have all the power and control during the loan process. If your lender was in charge of your loan process and did not clearly explain the included waiver verbiage, you will likely not be held to have waived anything. Laws do not favor the abandonment or loss of legal rights. This is especially true when the powerful are trying to take advantage of the weaker. Assume an alleged waiver buried in your Note or mortgage has no merit, and check what your state's law says about the validity of such contract language.

The lender's use of such language without fully and openly explaining the risks for a borrower may also rise to the level of an unconscionable, unfair or deceptive business practice, especially if the lender made no effort to explain that it was asking you to give up fundamental rights. If your lender's use of such waiver language is a violation of your consumer or borrower rights, you may want to assert those violations against the Boss, should it actually appear in your case.

GET YOUR JUDGE INVOLVED

When you're challenging the validity of a threatened or concluded foreclosure, it is essential to engage your judge in the matters you think important to your success. A good way to start your lawsuit is to file a complaint if you are the plaintiff, or an answer if you are the defendant, that states the important facts accurately, is drafted to avoid summary dismissal, and denies that the opponent is a real party in interest. Weave your story to show the judge why what you want makes sense in terms of the facts and the law you are choosing to argue.

As I mentioned at the beginning of this chapter, Exhibit B, *Example— Foreclosure Fundamentals Woven into the Story,* is a sample from a Nevada case in which the borrower did a good job of showing how that state's nonjudicial foreclosure statutes required application of the UCC. It demonstrated the connection of the nonjudicial foreclosure statutes to the deed of trust; the deed of trust to the Note; and the UCC as the authority under which the right to enforce the Note was defined. It showed the judge that a nonjudicial foreclosure is valid only if the Boss is identified pursuant to the UCC, and then only if that Boss actually chooses to initiate foreclosure. It was also considerate of the pressures on the judge by directing his attention to specific law and to places where the important facts could be located among all of the papers piled before the judge.

Draft your legal document that way and you will increase your likelihood of success. Remember, borrower protections and principles of fairness are embedded in the foreclosure laws of every state. You can use these laws as a powerful weapon in your fight to defend your home. Keep your judge's attention on them, and on the foreclosure fundamentals you've discovered in this book. Tell your story in a persuasive and compelling fashion, and you stand an excellent chance of defeating the foreclosure machine or substantially improving your position.

PART FIVE

Parting Thoughts

CHAPTER 13

HELP OTHERS FIGHT BACK

MAKE YOUR VOICE HEARD

Each new court battle is a vote against the mortgage finance industry's misconduct and a vote for more responsible and fair treatment of borrowers and foreclosure victims. If enough such votes are cast, government authorities ultimately will be forced to respond to the problems that led to extensive predatory lending, wrongful foreclosure practices, and the sickened economy. They will have to deal with the people who handed these problems to us, people who obviously had too much authority and too little ability to balance the public good with their own personal agendas.

Being a foreclosure victim, in and of itself, makes you part of the U.S. statistics on displaced families and homeowners. As an individual, you have a small but important voice. When your voice is combined with the cumulative voices of all those who take up the gauntlet and fight back, it will be much louder and more easily heard by those in positions of influence.

The mere effort of fighting back in court, irrespective of the final result, can touch the callous heart of the industry by reducing its cash flow. One analyst estimates that the mortgage finance industry loses about $6 billion for each month its foreclosure machine is delayed.[160] Enough $6 billion incremental costs can amount to "real money" at some point, even by the mortgage finance industry's standards. An increase in the number of challenged foreclosures has value in stimulating internal bickering and litigation within the industry. Enough delays also will help spark public debate that can lead to better long-term solutions for our country and more fair and just results for foreclosure victims.[161]

Increasing numbers of court victories for foreclosure victims will send an even louder message. The industry will be seeking possibly 10 million or more foreclosures in the next few years. It is exposed to losing as much as $1 trillion—yes $1,000,000,000,000[162]— if only one-half of those foreclosures result in victories for the targeted borrowers. You can bet the industry will be closely watching the tally of borrower victories, even if, in its public statements to its stockholders and the media, it portrays confidence and makes accusations about misguided judicial decisions or mere technical flaws.

The industry wants that money for itself. It doesn't want to spend potential profits on litigation costs. It doesn't want to pay money to wrongly foreclosed buyers, investors who lost money on their mortgage-backed securities, or insurance companies who want reimbursement for claims they pay that are related to investment losses of those investors.

In order to reap the mountains of capital it wanted, the mortgage finance industry has effectively pitted investors, securities packagers, loan originators, insurers, and foreclosure shops against each other. The blame games, the finger-pointing, the efforts to bolster corporate and individual reputations, and the related legal battles will keep them busy for years to come as they try to minimize their own losses.

As increasing numbers of targeted borrowers refuse to bow to the tyranny of the foreclosure machine and, instead, stand up for their legal rights, their combined voices should lead to increased public discussion and greater momentum for rational and effective solutions. The government may lead the way, or private companies within the industry may choose to devise their own solutions in order to forestall too much governmental intervention and regulation.

If the voices of borrowers fighting back get loud enough, fairness and justice could follow, whether through private initiative, governmental intervention, or some combination of both. By adding your voice to the chorus, you can take pride in helping not only yourself and your family, but also millions of others hurt by the foreclosure machine.

SHARE YOUR INFORMATION

Sharing information about successes and failures in foreclosure lawsuits is important. Knowledge is power. The more you and other borrowers know, the greater your chances will be of getting something back from the mortgage finance industry and blocking its foreclosure machine. The foreclosure machine shares information among its shops in order to play its games more forcefully. Borrowers should also share more as a way of leveling the playing field. One purpose of *Fighting the Foreclosure Machine* is to help this happen—for you and others in your situation.

Please help someone else by sending me the rulings made and the final orders issued in your case, whether or not the result was good for you. If something worked well for you, other borrowers would like to know how you got your result. If something went badly, maybe others can avoid the same problem if they know what happened in your case.

Most often, information about final orders from a court is all that can be easily located online or in law libraries. Important rulings that happen during the years the case is in progress are not usually published, even though many of the rulings involve good legal arguments and analysis by the parties and the judges. In many courts, even the final orders are put in the court's file but are not published in ways that make the information available to help others. The only way to ensure that this information, whether negative or positive from a borrower's perspective, can be available for analysis and critique is if borrowers will share.

So if something happens in your case that might be good for others to know, please send it. Other borrowers will be doing that, and your help will be appreciated also. This is one more very significant way that you can make your voice heard.

My objective is to be helpful and to provide accurate information. If you see anything in this book or at our website that needs correction, updating, or clarification, please let me know. Your input is encouraged and welcomed. You can find the contact information for mail and fax at: www.FightingtheForeclosureMachine.com.

PART SIX

Exhibits

Exhibit A
Items to Be Organized for Your Attorney

All documents in your possession regarding the mortgage loan should be assembled, regardless of whether they are copies, or whether they are unsigned or signed. Your file might include, for example:

1. Note

2. Mortgage or deed of trust

3. All communications you sent to any company involving anything to do with your mortgage loan

4. All communications and notices of any kind you received from any company with regard to your mortgage loan

5. All communications and notices of any kind you received from any company regarding any threatened, pending or already completed foreclosure

6. All documents you obtain from others in response to your discovery, both before and after the lawsuit starts

Organizing the documents in chronological order is a good paper management approach and will help you locate the information in the file as it grows during the fact-finding part of your fight with the foreclosure machine.

Visual access to a particular document can be enhanced by the use of Post-it® Notes. Mark the Post-it® with the document's date (or approximate date, if that is all you have), and affix it so that the tag hangs over the edge of the paper. Arrange them according to date, in ascending or descending order as you and those you work with prefer. You will then have a pile of papers with little tabs sticking out that have dates on them, and those papers will be in date order, making them easier to identify and retrieve. When you have more than one document with the same date, you can add an identifying number to the Post-it Note; for example, 11/02/2001 #2 or 11/02/2001:2, as you prefer.

You will also be well served to make some type of control sheet (digital or manual) that briefly describes each document and records its date and, if it has one, its number. Your list might look like this:

1: 11/02/2001 – Promissory Note (signed)
2: 11/02/2001 – Mortgage (unsigned copy)
3: 11/02/2001 – Mortgage (signed), etc.

You will be getting additional papers once the fact-finding gets underway. When you do, record them on your list, add a Post-it® Note to each, and put it in chronological order with the others.

Avoid marking or writing on the documents. A paper may become an exhibit in your lawsuit. Doodling or handwritten comments can be confusing. If you want to take notes or mark up a page, use a copy or make your comments on a separate piece of paper. If your document already has added markings, don't worry. Try, however, to keep your papers as clean as possible in case they need to be shown to your judge or your opponent.

Yes, this system will require a little work, but once it is organized, adding new documents is not that difficult. The ease of locating a particular paper later will be well worth the organizational exercise.

The documents you already have give you a good place to begin the negative content audit I mention in the section of Chapter 10 called *How to Get the Facts You Need*. Start with what you have and build upon it as you get more information from your opponent. You can make a sheet or sheets that show the name of persons claiming involvement with your Note or mortgage and the dates their names first surface. Indicate when the name first appears in the documents you have and the number you assigned to that document.

Look for any company that uses or is identified by labels such as lender, bank, creditor, note holder, holder, beneficiary, mortgagee, loan servicer, loan manager, trustee, owner, or titles similar to these. These are the types of labels that suggest Boss or servant status. Do the same for each company that claims to be the successor or substitute for another company, and note on your list the label that a new arrival uses in each document that mentions it. Do not be surprised, for example, to see the word "lender" used in your Note and mortgage, and then see that subsequent documents no longer refer to the lender but rather to a creditor, beneficiary, owner, holder, or mortgagee. Your initial task is to identify who claims, or is said by others to have, the designated label(s) at a particular time. If, for example, ABC Bank is listed as "lender" in one document, as "loan servicer" in another, and maybe as "trustee" or "creditor" in yet another document, your list should include each label, date, and document number.

This exercise will help you map out who has claimed some relationship with your Note and mortgage, when they assert that they had that relationship, and in what alleged capacity. Your work will disclose who claimed what title when the Note and mortgage were handed over to your lender and who now claims the right to bother you about your Note or mortgage, either for themselves or on behalf of others.

Every change of name for any title or label indicates transactions or events happening behind the scenes that you do not know about and that your opponent must explain. Even if, for example, ABC Bank was your lender and it is the only company mentioned as being the owner, holder, beneficiary, creditor, or mortgagee, it still must prove its current status as Boss of your Note, because, in that instance, the machine may have intentionally used the same name to hide the fact that your Note and mortgage had changed hands. Pursue the same level of discovery demands, informally and formally, even if you are not sure your Note and mortgage were ever traded, sold, transferred, or exchanged with others. The discovery process is the only way you can possibly obtain information that is crucial to the controlling issue of whether your opponent can prove that it is the current Boss of your Note or servant to that Boss.

Your lists should also identify statements by any company that says it does not know who owns, or has the rights in, your Note or mortgage. That, too, might be important if, later, the same company claims to have sold or transferred your Note or mortgage to someone else prior to saying it did not know the identity of the new owner. The industry members may say one thing one day and something different later. You want to know the truth. Inconsistencies in what they say or the documents they display help demonstrate that your opponent cannot prove the identity of the Boss. Discrepancies may be the result of a mistake or intentional fraud, but you won't be able to accurately define the root of your opponent's problem until you are well into the lawsuit.

Your opponent has the burden of proving that all of the transactions and changes of ownership involving your Note and mortgage took place under circumstances that resulted in Boss status currently residing with your opponent or the company it claims it works for, and that all of these transfers were made in ways strictly consistent with the UCC requirements (See Chapter 11.). If, for example, US Bank says it is now the owner and person in full control of your Note, then you must ask it to show all of the documents and formal transaction papers that support what it says. A mere assignment document, of course, doesn't tell the full story. If it can't produce a UCC-thorough chain of proof, it should lose.

Each new document you get during your fact-finding work should be similarly organized and included in your lists. This document management approach will help you and your attorney identify changes and events that require explanation and that, if not explained, will help you persuade your judge that your opponent has dropped the ball and does not have the right to make demands or foreclose. Your organized file will be extremely helpful as you try to help your judge understand the facts.

Being organized may also help you locate good legal assistance at prices suited to your circumstances. Good organization of the documents you already have can be useful as you interview attorneys. The information they'll want to know will be easier for you to summarize and locate. The fact that you have things in such good order may give the attorney more confidence in your abilities and favorably influence his or her willingness to work with you. Offering to help keep the files organized during the litigation may also help you reduce your legal fees.

Exhibit B
Example—Foreclosure Fundamentals Woven into the Story

This exhibit shows how one borrower (we'll call him Steve) presented his story of borrower rights and protections under the law in a case before a court in Nevada. Steve had tried to stop a nonjudicial foreclosure of his home, but he was unsuccessful. After the house was sold, Steve sued the banks and companies involved in the foreclosure, asking that they repay him for the house they took from him. Steve's suit is still in court with unknown results at this time.

The defendants filed a motion to dismiss Steve's suit, asserting that his complaint had not stated any legal claims recognized under Nevada law. A motion to dismiss is typically filed before the defendants answer the complaint and before a borrower has the opportunity to engage in formal discovery. What follows are excerpts from the answer Steve filed with the court in objection to the motion to dismiss.

Steve did a noteworthy job of weaving the foreclosure fundamentals into the formal document he filed. He wanted to make sure his judge understood how his Note and mortgage (in this instance, a deed of trust) related to Nevada's nonjudicial foreclosure law and the UCC. He hoped to strengthen his case by showing how the foreclosure fundamentals interact to protect borrowers like him.

Steve's work is a good example of how the story can be told and how it needs to be supported with legal and factual citations. It may help you craft the statements of fact and law you want to put before your judge.

NOTICE: Nevada's UCC numbering system is different than the UCC references used in *Fighting the Foreclosure Machine.* The UCC references used in this book and other clarifications are inserted in brackets throughout Steve's story for your convenience.

EXCERPTS OF INTRODUCTORY ARGUMENT

Defendants admitted prior to the foreclosure and wrongful sale of my home and prior to the commencement of this lawsuit that none of them was owed any money by me, that no presentment had been made for payment of my Note pursuant to Nevada's Uniform Commercial Code (the UCC) (NRS § 104.1101, et seq.) *[UCC § 1-101, et seq.]*, and that I had not dishonored or defaulted under the Note by refusing to comply with the demands they made. I, in fact, denied and continue to deny owing any money and having any obligation to Defendants. (Complaint ## ___ & ___) [Specific parts of Steve's Complaint were cited in his Answer to a Motion to Dismiss (the Motion), but are omitted for purposes of this exhibit.]

My Note is a negotiable instrument pursuant to Article 3 of the UCC, and more specifically NRS § 104.3104 *[UCC § 3-104]*. Defendants do not assert otherwise even though they must clearly understand that my case against them involves, to a large extent, my claim that they have no rights under my Note pursuant to the UCC, including no right to make demands upon me as if any of them had a right to enforce my Note whether directly or under a claim as agent carrying out the wishes of some unidentified principal. (Complaint ## ___ & ___.)

The UCC defines the person having the right to enforce and make demands upon me regarding my Note. It is the law of Nevada, in force at all times relevant to this case, and clearly applicable to the facts stated in my Complaint. My home was sold in a foreclosure in which each Defendant was involved and through which they asserted a right to take my home because of an obligation they said I had to them regarding my Note. The UCC, applied to the facts stated by my Complaint, establish that the Defendants had no such rights. I had no obligation to any of them and they, therefore, clearly were wrong in making demands upon which they acted by selling my home in a nonjudicial foreclosure. For purposes of deciding the merit of their Motion, my stated case is to be viewed in the light most favorable to me.

Exhibit A to my Complaint is a copy of the Note as I delivered it to the lender, Defendant Company XYA. (Complaint #___.) That copy of the Note shows no indorsements, directly on it or attached to it, and therefore does not indicate that it was ever transferred, sold, exchanged or delivered by the lender to anyone else. That Exhibit A of my Complaint does not indicate that the Note was ever negotiated (NRS § 104.3201(1)) *[UCC § 3-201(a)]* or that it was ever transferred or delivered to another person (NRS § 104.3203 *[UCC § 3-203]* and NRS § 104.1201(2)(o))

[UCC § 1-201(15)]. Defendant Company XYA, however, told me it sold the note shortly after it was originated, and thereby disclaimed any right in the Note. (Complaint Exhibit 5.) If Defendant Company XYA has no rights to make any demands for payment from me respecting the Note, then an important question is "who does." I tried to learn the answer to that question before the foreclosure took my home, but Defendants without exception refused to or could not answer that question for me. (Complaint ## ___ & ___, and Exhibit 12.)

The UCC is designed to protect me from demands by those who have no right to enforce the Note, that is, no right to demand money from me and no right to sell my house under an alleged triggering of a power to sale when I don't owe them anything. While protecting me from unauthorized demands and threats, the UCC simultaneously protects national commerce involving negotiable instruments and the person actually entitled to enforce the Note from having my assets, money or home, taken by an interloper whether illegally or by mistake. Protecting my interests is how the UCC helps protect the interests of the person with genuine interests in enforcement of my Note. The intended protections of the UCC are recognized across America. See, for example, *In re Kemp,* No. 08-18700-JHW (Bankr. D. NJ 2010) ("From the maker's standpoint, therefore, it becomes essential to establish that the person who demands payment of a negotiable Note, or to whom payment is made, is the duly qualified holder. Otherwise, the obligor is exposed to the risk of double payment, or at least to the expense of litigation incurred to prevent duplicative satisfaction of the instrument."); *Wells Fargo Bank v. Sessley,* 2010-Ohio-2902 (OH Ct.App. 2010)(Noting an "underlying concern about multiple judgments on the same debt."); *In re Kang Jin Hwang,* 396 B.R. 757 (Bankr. C.D. CA 2008)(Weighing whether failure to join another party to the suit might leave the borrower subject to a substantial risk of incurring multiple obligations under the same Note.); (*5-Star Management, Inc. v. Rogers,* 940 F.Supp. 512 (USDCt. E.D. NY 1996) (Recognizing a policy to "protect the maker of the Note, who also issues a mortgage, from being exposed to liability twice in respect of the same underlying debt."); *Adams v. Madison Realty & Development, Inc.,* 853 F.2d 163 (3rd Cir. 1988)(Addressing the UCC requirement of "indorsement" when the Note is sold or transferred, stressing the importance of strict compliance with the UCC because, otherwise, it would be "unreasonable to impose upon the indorsee the risk that the present holder or a prior holder had negotiated the instrument to someone not in the apparent chain of title by virtue of a separate document."); *In the Matter of Foreclosure of a Deed of Trust Executed by Woodard,* 185 N.C.App. 159 (NC Ct.App. 2007)("[T]he payor of a note exposes himself or herself to double liability if he or she makes payment to someone other than the holder of the instrument, unless the other person to whom payment is made is an agent of the owner of the Note."); *Weingartner v. Chase Home Finance*, No. 2:09-cv-02255-RCJ-RJJ (USDCt D NV 2010)(Rejecting a MERS claim of independent authority to assign the beneficial interest in the underlying debt, the Court indicated a need to avoid the risk of "rival claimants to the same underlying debt." P. 5); and "The purpose of the possession requirement in Article 3 [of the UCC] is to protect the Debtor from multiple enforcement claims to the same note."), *Marks v. Branstein*, No. 09-11402-NMG (USDCt D. MA 2010) and, also, *In re Kemp*, No. 08-18700-JHW (Bankr. D. NJ 2010).

The right to enforce a Note requires strict adherence to the UCC in order to achieve its protective policies. Rather than my being subjected to false or mistaken demands by people saying that they have rights under my Note, the UCC is there to help me, and this Court, ferret out and deny takings of private property by those who, in fact, cannot or will not prove the right to enforce the obligation they say is owed. Taking my home is a serious matter and must not be condoned or permitted except when the person doing the foreclosure actually is enforcing an obligation owed to it or its principal. See, for example, *Adams v Madison Realty & Development, Inc.*, 853 F.2d 163 (3rd Cir. 1988)(Holding that strict compliance with the UCC protects each intended owner of the note as it gets passed about); *Cogswell v. Citifinancial Mortgage*, 624 F.3d 395 (US Cir.7th 2010)(Ruling against the foreclosure machine because of its failure to prove compliance with the UCC requirements created a reasonable concern about whether the "Note was actually held by another who would be entitled to enforce it against the property owners."); *Norwood v. Chase Home Finance*, No. A-09-CA-940-JRN (USDCt. W.D. TX 2011)("The rationale for the strict requirement of possession [of the physical Note] is to protect the obligor from being subject to multiple demands for payment on a single note. ... Without procedural safeguards, multiple parties could force the debtor to pay the Note. If the original Note is a prerequisite for enforcement, however, then a later party faces a significant hurdle before it may enforce the note"); and *Bank of America v. Miller*, 2011-Ohio-1403 (OH Ct.App.2nd 2011)("[I]t becomes essential to establish that the person who demands payment of a negotiable Note, or to whom payment is made, is the duly qualified holder. Otherwise, the obligor is exposed to the risk of double payment, or at least to the expense of litigation incurred to prevent duplicative satisfaction of the instrument. These risks provide makers with a recognizable interest in demanding proof of the chain of title.")

The protections incorporated into the UCC include NRS § 104.3501(1) [*UCC § 3-501(a)*] (that only the person entitled to enforce the Note may make demands for payment of it), NRS § 104.3308(2) [*UCC § 3-308(b)*] (that the person claiming the right to enforce a negotiable instrument must produce the instrument) and NRS § 104.3301(1)(a-c) [*UCC § 3-301(i-iii)*] (which sets out three tests of which a person must satisfy at least one in order to have the right to enforce the Note). The first two tests under NRS § 104.3301(1) *[UCC §* *3-301]* require physical possession of the Note, and the third requires tracing the claimant's alleged right to enforce the Note to prior and proper physical possession of the Note pursuant to the strictures of NRS § 104.3309 *[UCC § 3-309]*.

Anyone can say I owe them money, but only the one person who, at the time of that statement, satisfies one of those UCC tests has the right to enforce the Note—only that person has the right to make demands under the Note. The fact that only one person has the right at any time to enforce the Note is made clear by the UCC's failure to authorize more than one person to have the same enforcement right at the same time (except in the case of a servant carrying out the instructions of the principal respecting the specific Note, e.g., NRS § 104.3501(1) *[UCC §* *3-501(a)]*). That singular right of enforcement is also made more clear by NRS § 104.3203(4) *[UCC § 3-203(d)]*, which states that a transferee of the instrument (i.e., the Note) has <u>no enforcement rights at all</u> unless the transferor released and delivered the entire interests in the Note to that transferee.

Defendants have not alleged that the Note has been lost, destroyed or stolen, so neither NRS § 104.3301(1)(c) *[UCC § 3-301(iii)]* or NRS § 104.3309 *[UCC § 3-309]* are applicable. None told me that was the case before the foreclosure and commencement of this action, and the Motion makes no such claim. Therefore Defendants must be asserting that one of them had physical possession of the Note (or their principal, if that was the case, had it) or else they have no right to enforce the Note pursuant to NRS § 104.3301(1) *[UCC § 3-301]*. They do not have or they have chosen to not produce the physical Note —it is not proffered with the Motion and was not made available for my inspection prior to the foreclosure and prior to this suit. (Complaint ## ___ & ___.) NRS § 104.3308(2) *[UCC § 3-308(b)]* says Defendants have no right to payment of anything owed under the Note unless they produce the physical Note, which they did not do. NRS § 104.3501(2)(b) *[UCC § 3-501(b)(2)]* required Defendants to display the physical Note upon my request. (Complaint Exhibit 12). They did not do that before this case started (Complaint ## ___ & ___) and to this date have not yet even offered to submit the physical Note for inspection. Accordingly, for purposes of evaluating the sufficiency of my pleading, Defendants must be treated as if they have not and cannot prove that they have the Note, or that any of them is entitled to enforce the Note pursuant to NRS § 104.3301 *[UCC §* *3-301]*. The benefit of the doubt belongs in my corner at this junction of this new lawsuit and for purposes of deciding how to rule on the Motion before this Court.

Note that my request for information from Defendants prior to the foreclosure was not a simpleton demand to "show me the note." I requested information that could reasonably be used to determine if any of them had the right to enforce my Note, either directly or on behalf of some other person. The UCC, as noted above, does not always require possession of the physical note in order for a person to be vested with enforcement rights. My requests went to the heart of this question about what if any obligation Defendants might demonstrate I owed to any of them or whomever they might work for. The facts upon which any of them may have been entitled to enforce the Note was for them to produce, and that may or may not have required production of the physical Note. Their silence was a tacit admission that they had no right to enforce my Note under any test within the UCC.

The UCC is intended to protect borrowers like me and those with legal rights in the notes from fraud and mistakes. The UCC also places a burden on me should I not take reasonable measures to make sure I am not paying the wrong person or letting the wrong person take my home that was pledged as collateral for the Note. I only get discharged from obligations under the Note if I pay the person entitled to enforce the Note per the UCC (NV § 104.3601) *[UCC § 3-601]*. Defendants ask this court to subject me to the risk of still being liable to whoever has the right to enforce my Note, since none of the Defendants established such right in themselves. I did what I could to avoid the risk of multiple claims related to the single Note I issued. The Court needs to help protect me from that risk by letting this case move forward, especially in light of the fact that Defendants did not evidence any such enforcement rights as sufficiently pled by my Complaint.

Neither my Note (Complaint Exhibit A) or the related Deed of Trust (Complaint Exhibit B) required the lender to let me review or to even know about each sale, transfer, exchange, pledge or other transaction involving those documents after I delivered them to the lender. Even though I was not in the "loop" about details or occurrences of such matters involving my Note and Deed of Trust, I had obtained information that indicated my lender, Defendant Company XYA, had sold the Note and Deed of Trust to someone else shortly after the loan was made in December 2003. (Complaint # __ and Exhibit 5.) Defendant Company XYA disclaimed any interest in the Note and Deed of Trust and said it did not know who if anyone had them. (Complaint Exhibit 5.) Suspiciously, Defendant Company XYA could not say who it sold the note to, but that is the fact as demonstrated in my Complaint. My Note was made payable to Defendant Company XYA who was also the identified "lender" and "beneficiary" per the Deed of Trust, yet that company said it no longer had any interest in either document. Defendant Company XYA, nevertheless, participated in the taking of my home as evidenced by my Complaint. (Complaint ## __ & __.) Through the commencement of this lawsuit as stated above, I received no evidence from Defendants that any of them had proof as to the identity of who might have the right to enforce my Note or to thereby trigger a power of sale per the Deed of Trust. That is, I faced a foreclosure of my home being conducted by people who were strangers to my Note and Deed of Trust—who were wrongfully selling my home and taking the proceeds of the sale for themselves.

The drafters of the UCC must have understood that the maker/borrower is often in the position of not being able to independently know whether a person making demands for payment or alleging a default actually has that one singular right to enforce a Note. I was kept in the "dark" by those who took my home, and I suppose that is a common occurrence for borrowers. But the UCC affords me an opportunity to demand proof of enforcement rights before being required to comply with the demands of someone who cannot or will not prove it has a right to enforce my Note.

For example, upon my request the person making demands for payment must prove its right to do so (NRS § 104.3501(2)(b)) *[UCC § 3-501(b)(2)]*, and that includes producing the physical Note or else claiming and proving the enforcement right pursuant to NRS § 104.3301(c) *[UCC § 3-301(iii)]* if the person claims the Note was lost, destroyed or stolen per NRS § 104.3309 *[UCC § 3-309]*. Further, upon my request, a person making the demand must prove that it is a "transferee" of my Note as that term is defined by the UCC (NRS § 104.3602(2)(d)) *[UCC § 3-602(a)]*. I therefore requested that the Defendants, and each of them, provide proof that they were either the person entitled to enforce my Note or that they were in fact servants working for such person. (Complaint # __ and Exhibit 12.) None of them provided any evidence that they either had the right to enforce the Note or that they were working for a person entitled, per the UCC strictures, to enforce it. (Complaint ## __ & __.) Wells Fargo was identified by Defendant Company XYA and Defendant Company XYB as the "master servicer" along with a statement that they did not know who owned the Note and Deed of Trust. (Complaint # __ and Exhibit 5.) Wells Fargo actually disclaimed any right in my Note and Deed of Trust. (Complaint ## __ & __, and Exhibit 16.) Defendants, however, just ignored my request. (Complaint # __.) They were each, therefore, unable or unwilling to provide proof that any of them had a right to make demands related to the Note. Because the Deed of Trust is only added assurance of payment of whatever is owed under the Note, Defendants established they have no right to foreclose and take my house. (See, e.g., *Weingartner v. Chase Home Finance*, No. 2:09-cv-02255-RCJ-RJJ (USDCt. D. NV. 2010) p. 5; Complaint Exhibit B, Part A.)

My request of __/__/2010 (Complaint Exhibit 12) was made more than a month prior to the foreclosure which took place on __/__/2010. (Complaint # __.) Their silence, for whatever reason, means that no demand or presentment has been made upon me because only a person entitled to enforce the Note has the right to make presentment (NRS § 104.3501(1)) *[UCC § 3-501(a)]*. Defendants demonstrated by their failure to provide proof of any enforcement right that their demands, accusations and threats were not, therefore, made by the person or on behalf of the person entitled to enforce my Note per the UCC.

Accordingly, by not complying with their unsupported demands, I did not dishonor or default on the Note. (NRS § 104.3501(1) & (2)(c)(2) and NRS § 104.3502) *[UCC §§ 3-501(a) & (b)(2-3) and 3-502]*. I owed nothing to any Defendant prior to the foreclosure and prior to the commencement of this lawsuit and none of the Defendants had a right to enforce my Note or to foreclose and take my home under allegations of having the right to enforce my Note. (Complaint ## ___ & ___.)

Defendants, through their Motion, make comments about my Note and Deed of Trust and my relationship with the as yet unidentified person with a right to enforce them. Defendants allege that I was in default of the Note even though, as demonstrated above, I denied same in my Complaint. They produce no evidence to the contrary. They comment about what a person can expect as normal or customary when the person is in default of their Note. None of that chit chat is relevant. Their comments are not admissible evidence. Their comments about my relationship with whomever actually has enforcement rights do not elevate the Defendants' legal standing. If just talking about what we would want in life were enough, Warren Buffet's estate would legally be mine. Defendants' comments and pontification about my relationship with the one person who might actually have the right to enforce my Note must be understood as statements by interlopers and persons with no genuine stake in my Note and persons with whom I have no obligations respecting my Note. Defendants' arguments regarding such matters have no bearing upon the primary legal questions before this Court—whether Defendants can prove that any of them had a right to enforce my Note or to foreclose and deprive me of my home. They did not demonstrate any such rights prior to the foreclosure or prior to this lawsuit as sufficiently pled by my Complaint. (Complaint ## ___ & ___.) It remains to be seen whether they will be able to convince the jury I have requested that Defendants or any of them had a legal right to take my money or to foreclose on and sell my home.

We are not here to make assumptions or guesses. The fact that Defendants wrote demand letters and threatened to foreclose unless I paid them has yet to be proven to be anything other than mistake, extortion or fraud conducted under the disguise of a non-judicial foreclosure. The UCC is devoid of any provision permitting a person to gain the right to enforce my Note just by saying they have that right or by writing official-looking demand letters and notices. The right to enforce my Note is a fact-intensive matter that requires application of the UCC. Defendants have thus far proven only that none of them had a right to enforce my Note and that none of them represented any person with that right.

The legal authorities which, in combination, define my rights and the burdens of proof upon the Defendants are the content of my Note and Deed of Trust, and Nevada's nonjudicial foreclosure statutes which necessarily invoke application of the UCC. Lacking the right to enforce my Note means that none of the Defendants had the right to trigger the power of sale pursuant to my Deed of Trust.

Nevada's nonjudicial foreclosure process does not operate in a vacuum but affords relief should the debt or obligation require enforcement, i.e., the statutory scheme looks to the underlying agreements of the borrower and lender. The power to sale under a deed of trust is recognized as a legal right arising after "a breach of the obligation" for which the deed of trust was given as security. (NRS 107.080, including, e.g., parts (1), (2)(a)(2), (2)(c), and (4)). Likewise, the "trustee" conducting a sale under this statutory scheme must be empowered to do so per the deed of trust. (NRS 107.080, including part (4)). The trustee's role is to act for the benefit of the beneficiary who is the lender, holder or the one owed satisfaction of the related debt. (*Weingartner, supra,* at p. 2-3; and Deed of Trust (Complaint Exhibit B, Part C). Because my Note is a negotiable instrument, the UCC, as noted above, defines who has a right to enforce the Note, i.e., the person to whom any obligation is owed per the Note. My Deed of Trust also expressly provides that the lender/beneficiary (not someone else) must first give me notice of alleged problems under the Note, declare a default, afford me an opportunity to cure the alleged default, and, only thereafter, may the lender/beneficiary (not someone else) instruct the trustee to initiate foreclosure. (Complaint Exhibit B, Part 22.) Yes, I understand that the lender or its successor with enforcement rights could instruct its servant to handle such matters respecting my Note, but only that lender/successor has the right to issue such instruction. That means the UCC has to define who has the right to enforce the obligation under the Note, because my lender sold the Note and Deed of Trust soon after the loan was originated. (Complaint ## ___ & ___, and Exhibits 5 and 9.)

The importance of the Note is further demonstrated by the fact that the Deed of Trust is only incidental to the Note and not a separate obligation in and of itself. (*Weingartner, supra,* p. 5; and Deed of Trust (Complaint Exhibit B, Part A.). This, too, highlights the importance of the right to enforce the Note per the UCC. That right is a required precursor to execution under my Deed of Trust.

No Defendant claims in the Motion that the lender, Defendant Company XYA, had the right to enforce the Note during the foreclosure process, a process that actually resulted in the sale and taking of my home. Therefore, whoever has the right to enforce the Note following the apparent loss of that status by Defendant Company XYA must qualify per the UCC as the person entitled to enforce the Note. That is the environment within which a negotiable instrument resides. No such person stepped forward prior to the commencement of this suit and, even to this day, none of the Defendants have chosen to respond as required by the UCC with verifiable and genuine proof that they had either the right to enforce the Note or that they were the legal agent of such a person (NRS § 104.3501(1)) *[UCC § 3-501(a)]*.

Accordingly, as demonstrated above, I had no duty to pay anything to any of the Defendants and they, therefore, had no right to say that I was in default of my Note. Because there was no obligation owed to any of the Defendants, there was no default upon which any of them could have acted to initiate the power of sale pursuant to my Deed of Trust. (Complaint Exhibit B, Part 22.) That is, none of the Defendants had the legal right to instruct the trustee under the Deed of Trust to commence a foreclosure. Thus, their individual and cumulative conduct was not authorized by law and they did, in fact, take my home in violation of law and my rights.

Defendants took my house by a nonjudicial foreclosure. The Nevada statute permitting nonjudicial foreclosures did not negate Nevada's adoption of the UCC. There is no Nevada statute that says people can ignore the requirements of the UCC by just filing papers saying that they are going to conduct a nonjudicial foreclosure. Neither Nevada's UCC nor its nonjudicial foreclosure statutes state that a foreclosure is proper when conducted by persons unable or unwilling to prove the legal right to enforce the underlying Note, that same instrument for which the Deed of Trust was granted as additional assurance that the Note, not any other debt, would be paid. Nevada law is devoid of any such policy or express law. Nevada's citizens would be shocked with any ruling that holds that they have no right to verification that they actually owe something to the person threatening to take their home in a foreclosure.

If a foreclosure were in court, Defendants would be said to lack standing and not be the real parties in interest if they tried to foreclose with no more supportive evidence than what they gave me prior to this suit. There is no evidence that Nevada law is intended to permit foreclosures by people who cannot satisfy the protective purposes of those judicial policies and statutes regarding unsupervised, nonjudicial foreclosures. There is no Nevada law that says, when a person receives a notice of default, that the underlying merit of the claimed authority may not be subjected to scrutiny. Defendants want this Court to rule otherwise and to subject me and the citizens of Nevada to more foreclosures by persons not owed anything directly or for their principals. Nevada's UCC gives us the right to be sure before paying the wrong person and before having our homes taken by mistake or fraud. That test of enforcement rights establishes whether an actionable obligation is present for purposes of a nonjudicial foreclosure. Nevada intended its citizens to have these complimentary bodies of law and that is why neither its UCC nor nonjudicial foreclosure statutes has provisions stating anything to the contrary.

None of the Defendants established that any of them was entitled to enforce my Note prior to the foreclosure or my filing suit. That is fact and undisputed fact at the time this suit was commenced. (Complaint ## ___ & ___.) At that point in time, Defendants were mere interlopers having made demands and threats as if they were entitled to enforce my Note. The claims of my Complaint establish both the fact that they were each afforded the opportunity to prove a right, direct or indirect, upon which they might make demands under my Note and that they provided no such proof. Thus, they admitted that none of them was authorized by law (the UCC) to enforce or make demands related to my Note. Lacking such a right, each thus participated in a foreclosure which, in fact, took my home and which, under Nevada's nonjudicial foreclosure statutes, was unauthorized—not having been initiated by the person entitled to enforce my Note per the UCC. Thus my Complaint properly sets forth facts sufficient to support what I claimed. I am supposed to be given the benefit of the doubt under these circumstances for purposes of this Court's deciding the Motion.

The court should deny the Motion because the facts pled in my Complaint and the law applicable to same establish that Defendants had no right to make demands under the Note, had no right to threaten foreclosure as a remedy related to my refusal to satisfy those unsupported demands, presentment had not been made prior to this lawsuit, and I had not dishonored my Note by refusing to comply with Defendants' demands prior to this lawsuit. Unless and until Defendants prove otherwise, their own conduct of failing to provide me the proof to which I was entitled per the UCC must give me the benefit of the doubt as to the merit of my claims against them. As pled, I owed the Defendants nothing when this action was filed and I was not in default under any obligation with them. (Complaint ## ___ & ___.)

Granting their Motion would be tantamount to broadcasting that, in the State of Nevada, anyone could take someone's home without ever having to prove a debt was owed, that being the same debt for which the home was given as security. Nevada has no law that would support such a result. Nevada cannot possibly want its citizens subjected to foreclosures by people who are not owed anything by the people being foreclosed. Nevada's nonjudicial foreclosure process requires a bona fide obligation in default before letting homes be foreclosed, and that necessarily invokes its UCC to identify the one person entitled to enforce that obligation.

CONCLUSION

The Motion should be denied. My claims, right to pursue discovery and preparations for a jury trial should not be blocked. Defendants were owed nothing by me, and yet they foreclosed and sold my home. They had no right to enforce my Note and no right to trigger the power of sale of my Deed of Trust. As properly pled, I have demonstrated meritorious and factually supported claims against Defendants.

Exhibit C
Examples—Responses and Claims

Introduction

You are in control of what you tell the judge if you sue the foreclosure machine or if you respond when sued by it. You should always be certain that what you put before the court is accurate to the best of your understanding.

The following statements demonstrate one way to raise the UCC-driven foreclosure fundamentals in order to introduce to the judge the issues of law and fact that are present with most foreclosures. They show how I would present these fundamentals if I were under attack by the foreclosure machine. You may have a better way to state the facts and lay out the story for your judge. Hopefully, however, what I have provided will make your work a bit easier.

Use only those portions of the examples that you find accurately reflect your situation and the legal theories of the case you want to present to your judge. If anything is not correct for your situation, do not use it.

The concept is to use accurately stated facts to educate the judge while keeping the burden of proof on the opponent. I think this method is consistent with the requirements placed on your opponent under the UCC. It also reduces the likelihood of having your case summarily dismissed, as your opponent will most likely attempt. Accuracy regarding the UCC-driven basics should also build a sound foundation upon which to launch other legal claims or defenses if you have any.

The examples are written as a complement to the formal discovery that will follow. The judge should uphold the claims against your opponent unless it can put forward genuine evidence to the contrary.

Definitions

Some definitions are provided as a way to make the examples less cumbersome so you can better focus on the concepts being woven into these sample statements. The use of defined terms in pleadings is a way to avoid extensive repetition while also helping the story flow better. The definitions you provide when you file your own complaint or counterclaim will probably be more detailed than these teaching aids. For example, your definitions of "Note" and "Security Instrument" might reference the exact titles of those documents and the dates you executed them. I refer to the UCC but you will, of course, be making references to your state's version of the Uniform Commercial Code. For purposes of this exhibit, the following definitions are used:

"Lender" means the company you dealt with when you got your mortgage loan.

"Letter" means the informal discovery letter(s) you issue to your opponent prior to litigation actually commencing.

"Note" means the promissory note you executed and delivered to your Lender when taking out the loan.

"Property" means the home you are defending.

"Security Instrument" means the mortgage, trust deed, or deed of trust (by whatever name it carries in your loan documents) which you executed and gave to the Lender as additional assurance your Note would get paid.

"I," "Me," or "My" refers to you.

"UCC" means your state's version of the Uniform Commercial Code.

"Boss of my Note" means the person entitled to enforce your Note pursuant to the rules of the UCC, that being the person with the right by law to initiate and pursue collection activities for alleged breaches of the obligation evidenced by your Note.

Sample Statements

Statements like these can help to set the stage for the legal contest, at least as it relates to the basic UCC-driven foreclosure fundamentals. The examples below are not intended to set out grounds for any other claims or defenses you might choose to raise in your fight against the foreclosure machine. This exhibit also makes no effort to lay out history, party identification, or jurisdictional matters that you may deal with in the pleadings you file in court.

> *Samples for use in a complaint you file to initiate a lawsuit or a counterclaim you file against your opponent in response to its suit filed against you:*

1. My opponent has failed or refused to comply with the requests I made through my Letter to it. It has failed or refused to produce genuine evidence establishing that it or any person it knows is the Boss of my Note.

2. Upon information and belief, I deny that my opponent is the Boss of my Note or a servant of that Boss following instructions issued by that Boss respecting my Note and Security Instrument.

3. Upon information and belief, my opponent has admitted that my Note is not in default, that I owe it nothing, and that I have not dishonored or breached my Note by refusing to comply with the demands it made upon me.

4. Upon information and belief, my opponent is not the real party in interest in this case because it has no economic or beneficial interest in my Note and Security Instrument; because it lacks authority to discharge my obligation under my Note or to otherwise settle the dispute before this Court should settlement efforts be attempted during this lawsuit; and because it is not the Boss of my Note or that Boss's servant respecting my Note and Security Instrument.

5. My Note, a copy of which, as it existed when I executed it in *[year]*, is attached as Exhibit ___ hereto. It reflects no indorsements or allonges but, upon information and belief, it has been sold, exchanged, traded, assigned, or otherwise transferred since then.

6. Upon information and belief, my Note is a negotiable instrument pursuant to the UCC, and, accordingly, the right to enforce it is determined by that law.

7. Upon information and belief, I deny that my opponent obtained possession of the physical Note via a voluntary transfer of all the interests in my Note from a person who at that time was the Boss of my Note.

8. Upon information and belief, I deny that my opponent has possession of the physical Note, or even knows its whereabouts, and that it didn't have possession of the Note when it commenced this foreclosure process.

9.   Upon information and belief, I deny that my opponent can or is willing to produce my Note for inspection during this lawsuit.

10.   Upon information and belief, I deny having received notice that a default exists under my Note from a person who was at that time the Boss of my Note or that Boss's servant who was then following instructions of that Boss to so inform me.

11.   Upon information and belief, never having received notice of default from the Boss of my Note or its duly appointed servant, I deny that any condition exists under my Security Instrument that would trigger a power of sale or foreclosure of my Property.

12.   Upon information and belief, never having received notice of default under my Note from the Boss of my Note or its servant, I deny that any refusal on my part to make payments or to comply with any demand made by my opponent in any way evidences my dishonor of my Note, the creation of any delinquency, or a condition triggering any right to foreclose or use a power of sale under the Security Instrument.

13.   Upon information and belief, I deny that my opponent's ability to write demand letters and to make threats regarding my Note and Security Instrument establishes in any way that it has a right to enforce either.

14.   Even though my opponent has admitted that it has no right to enforce my Note and Security Instrument, I nevertheless maintain that I have never received complete accounting information from the Boss of my Note or its servant respecting the balance due, if any, on my Note. I have received no information about insurance proceeds, claim settlements, or indorsement warranty payments having been received or sought by the Boss respecting my Note. Lacking information to the contrary, I deny that any balance is still owed regarding my Note.

15.   Because my opponent is not the Boss of my Note or a servant of that Boss, I further deny that my opponent's comments or questions about my Note elevate in the least its legal status or right to enforce my Note pursuant to the controlling law, i.e., this state's version of the Uniform Commercial Code.

16.   Any interpretation of my Note that potentially subjects me to multiple claims regarding my Note was never intended and was never disclosed to me as being a possible result by the Lender. I never knowingly intended to waive or disclaim my right to only have to pay the one person entitled to enforce my Note, and the

Lender never discussed that possibility or asked me to make such a waiver or disclaimer. Any interpretation of my Note to the contrary would be a mistake, a violation of my fundamental rights, and not reflective of the intent and purpose of that agreement. Only the one true Boss of my Note as defined by the UCC for a particular time has any right to enforce my Note, and that is not my opponent.

17. Any interpretation of my Security Instrument that would permit a person other than the Boss of my Note to initiate and prosecute the foreclosure of my Property was never intended and was never disclosed or addressed by the Lender as a possible result. Therefore, any such interpretation of the purpose or intent of that document would be mistake, invalid and inconsistent with my rights and the agreement I made with Lender.

18. The Lender never disclosed or addressed that by executing its forms I would be construed to have relinquished my right to only pay my obligation to the person legally entitled to enforce it. That possibility was never mentioned by the Lender, and I never knowingly agreed to any such possibility. Further, I was never asked to, nor did I, agree to honor demands regarding my Note made by anyone who didn't prove the actual right by law to enforce my Note. Any assertion to the contrary by my opponent will be mistake or fraud, and inconsistent with the agreement I made with the Lender.

19. Upon information and belief, I have never knowingly agreed that any person other than the Boss of my Note would have the right to foreclose my Property pursuant to the Security Instrument I gave as collateral for my Note. The Lender never addressed or disclosed the possibility that, by signing its Security Instrument form, I would be authorizing a person not entitled to enforce my Note, and not owed anything by me pursuant to my Note, to take my home. That was never the intent or approved purpose of the Security Instrument. Any assertion to the contrary by my opponent will be mistake or fraud, as the facts to be revealed in this lawsuit will demonstrate, and inconsistent of the agreement I made with the Lender.

20. The Lender prepared, provided, and required that I use the forms which became my Note and Security Instrument. Any ambiguity or vagueness within either document must be construed against the Lender and its successor in order that my rights under those agreements be properly understood and applied.

➤ *If you are facing a nonjudicial foreclosure, the following additional parts may be helpful:*

21.   Upon information and belief, I deny the power of sale pursuant to the Security Instrument was ever initiated by action of the Boss of my Note.

22.   Upon information and belief, the alleged trustee has never been instructed by the Boss of my Note to initiate a foreclosure.

23.   Upon information and belief, the alleged trustee does not know the identity of the Boss of my Note, and, therefore, does not know the person authorized to issue instructions regarding the Security Instrument.

24.   Upon information and belief, the alleged trustee doesn't use internal policies or procedures that would permit it to determine whether the person engaging it to initiate the foreclosure process under my Security Instrument actually is the Boss of my Note or a duly appointed servant of that Boss.

25.   Upon information and belief, the alleged trustee initiated these foreclosure procedures of its own volition in violation of the express terms of my Security Instrument and this state's foreclosure law.

26.   Upon information and belief, the alleged trustee knows that public recording of documents does not ensure that the content is accurate, truthful or authorized by law. Accordingly, I deny that the alleged trustee acted, or is acting, in good faith to the extent it initiated and continues to conduct this foreclosure process alleging reliance on the fact that it can point to one or more documents which have been publicly recorded.

➤ *If your opponent starts the lawsuit, the following additional part should be considered:*

27.   Upon information and belief, my opponent lacks standing in this case, having no economic or beneficial interest in my Note, and no complete dominion over it, including no right to enforce my Note pursuant to the UCC.

➤ *If your opponent is the Lender, the following should be considered also because your Note was most likely sold in the secondary market and no longer owned or controlled by the Lender, who now may be involved only in some cooperative loan-servicing capacity:*

28. Even though my opponent was the Lender, upon information and belief, my Note was sold one or more times to others and my opponent no longer owns or has full dominion over my Note, including no right to enforce my Note per the UCC.

➤ *If your security instrument includes the name of Mortgage Electronic Registration Systems, Inc., i.e., what I refer to as ShellGame-MERS, the following additional parts should also be considered:*

29. Upon information and belief, Mortgage Electronic Registration Systems, Inc. (referred to in these examples as ShellGame-MERS) has no employees, no revenue, no assets of any consequence, no business operations, no electronic data system that tracks real estate loans in America, and no economic or beneficial interest in any Note, mortgage, or deed of trust.

30. Upon information and belief, ShellGame-MERS has no economic or beneficial interest in my Note and therefore has always lacked authority under the UCC to sell, assign, transfer, or otherwise deal in my Note or Security Instrument of its own volition or on its own behalf.

31. Upon information and belief, any document introduced by my opponent in this case that purports to be an assignment, declaration, transfer or affidavit executed by ShellGame-MERS was not executed by or pursuant to any instruction from ShellGame-MERS respecting my Note or Security Instrument and is invalid and has no legal effect regarding my Note and Security Instrument.

32. Upon information and belief, ShellGame-MERS has not received any instruction from, nor taken any action on the behalf of, the Boss of my Note respecting my Note or Security Instrument at any time relevant hereto. That is, ShellGame-MERS has never acted as nominee or agent of any Boss of my Note, and, accordingly, any alleged action by ShellGame-MERS respecting my Note and Security Instrument is invalid and of no legal effect.

33. ShellGame-MERS was not a party to the real estate loan process that resulted in my Note and Security Instrument. Accordingly, neither ShellGame-MERS nor anyone alleging to represent it has personal knowledge of the communications or negotiations that preceded or culminated in the creation of my Note and Security Instrument.

34. Upon information and belief, the Security Instrument was never intended to, and does not, grant any authority for ShellGame-MERS to take any action respecting the Security Instrument or my Note except upon clear and advance instructions of the then Boss of my Note. The Lender never said otherwise and I never knowingly agreed otherwise.

35. The Lender, not I, inserted the name of ShellGame-MERS into that Lender's Security Instrument form. I was never informed of the agreement between the Lender and ShellGame-MERS regarding any relationship they had or would have. Upon information and belief, I deny that ShellGame-MERS and the Lender actually had, at that time, any agency relationship respecting my Note and Security Instrument. I further deny that any such agency relationship was later made between the Lender and ShellGame-MERS.

36. Upon information and belief, I deny that ShellGame-MERS had any agency relationship with the potential future and unidentified successor to the Lender when I executed my Security Instrument. Further, I deny that ShellGame-MERS and any subsequent successor to the Lender, who also obtained the right to enforce my Note, established any agency relationship respecting my Note and Security Instrument.

37. By signing the Security Instrument form I did no more than acknowledge that the Lender had inserted the name of ShellGame-MERS into that document. I was never asked by the Lender or any of the then potential and unidentified successors to appoint ShellGame-MERS as agent for any of them. I have never been asked to, had the authority to, or ever accepted responsibility for, appointing an agent for the Lender or any of its successors respecting my Note and Security Instrument. Upon information and belief, I never knowingly granted any rights independently exercisable by or to ShellGame-MERS respecting my Note and Security Instrument or created in it any rights with successors to the Lender, whether or not such successors obtained the right to enforce my Note.

Conclusion

Once your pleading document is accurately stated, it and other sources of information can then help you present your story for your judge, much like the story told by Exhibit B. That type of story typically does not get told until motions and answers to motions arise in the lawsuit. However, the statements of fact and claims you make in your complaint or counterclaim become the foundation for that story, with more details and exact references of law to be built upon it.

Notice also how much strength your case acquires by your having issued the letter to which your opponent either did not respond or replied without the full information you requested. (See Chapter 10 and Exhibit E.) Silence or a shoddy response gives you so much with which to work, because it is your opponent's obligation under the UCC to prove the right, for itself or its master, to demand your money under threat of foreclosure. If you have used that informal discovery technique, your opponent should be at a substantial disadvantage when your lawsuit begins. Not issuing that type of informal discovery is not a mortal blow to your case, but the benefits of the letter approach clearly justify its use.

Exhibit D
Checklist—Boss Status
Investigation

Introduction

Only the Boss of your Note has the right to demand payment from you or to carry out a foreclosure. It is up to your opponent to prove that it is the Boss or that it is acting on the Boss's behalf as its agent or service.

The Uniform Commercial Code (the UCC), which is incorporated into the laws of your state, sets forth three ways that a person can become entitled to enforce the Note. To prove that it has Boss status, your opponent must provide genuine evidence that it meets one of those three definitions.

Chapter 11 goes into detail on the importance of the Boss concept and the role of the UCC in defining the Boss and protecting the rights of both the Boss and the borrower. This exhibit is intended to provide a helpful summary of that information.

Burden of Proof: Your opponent is under a heavy burden to prove the facts that would let it claim Boss status for itself or its master. Use informal and formal discovery (see Chapter 10) to keep that burden on its back.

Negative Content Audit: As discussed in Chapter 10, you beat your opponent by pointing out for your judge the required information your opponent has not produced. A negative content audit involves examining the documents and information your opponent provides via the discovery process to see what essential facts are missing. Focus on what your opponent cannot back up with genuine proof.

Its words and assurances are not evidence. If what it says, however, is contradicted by genuine evidence, then your opponent's words, whether by its attorney or its witnesses, suggest that your opponent, because of mistake or fraud, doesn't know the real facts.

Negative information—that which your opponent cannot prove—is the key to your lawsuit. The UCC defines the facts it must prove. You want to look for gaps in the information it provides and any missing or unexplained facts.

Summary—What the UCC Says about Boss Status

NOTICE: UCC section numbers in brackets refer to the sections in which a preceding word is defined or the preceding concept is explained. Recall from Chapter 11 that your state's version of the UCC may use a different numbering or labeling system.

WHO IS THE BOSS OF THE NOTE?

UCC § 3-301: Three ways a person becomes entitled to enforce the Note

➤ Physical possession is important for all three ways.

- Current possession is required for § 3-301(i) and (ii).

- Past possession is required for § 3-301(iii).

- Status of each prior transferee of a Note is necessary to understanding whether the person currently asserting Boss status actually has the right to enforce the Note.

§ 3-301(i): "Holder of the instrument"

Overview: A "holder of the instrument" is a person in physical possession of the Note, having received it from a previous holder who at that time had the sole right to enforce the Note and who voluntarily delivered it with the intention of transferring [§§1-201(21), 3-201, 1-201(15) and 3-203] all of the transferor's interests in the Note [§ 3-203(d)], including the right to enforce it, to the transferee, said Note having been indorsed by the person who was the Boss at the time of the indorsement to be payable specifically to the recipient or else payable to whomever has possession of it [(§§ 1-201(21), 3-204 & 3-205]. Remember, this is an aid I created, so you will not find this summary in your state's UCC.

➤ Your opponent must prove:

- Physical possession of the Note. This is the only way you can inspect the entire Note—front, back, endorsements, and allonges (if physically attached; paper-clipped pages or loose pages separate from the Note do not count).

- Proper indorsement, by a person who was a holder when the indorsement was made. (e.g., a person who was the Boss only in 2005 cannot be an indorser in 2007. Exception is per § 3-203(c), where transferee has the right to make its transferor indorse the Note.)

- Facts evidencing that the transferor intended to voluntarily deliver 100% of its rights, including the right to enforce the Note, to the transferee, and that the transferor retained no rights of any kind in the Note. Remember, only a Boss can transfer Boss status, and then only if it transfers 100% of all rights and interests in the Note.

➤ "Holder" profile is defined in § 1-201(21), but right to enforce means more. Other UCC parts define which person in possession of the Note may enforce it. Facts that supersede physical possession must be proven because mere possession does not, in itself, prove Boss status.

- What information did your opponent obtain to assure itself that the person who transferred the Note to your opponent or its master was actually the Boss at the time of that transfer? You need to ask for every paper or digital record your opponent has regarding this question. Your opponent may not have inquired about prior Boss status, which, in itself, means that your opponent cannot know whether it or its master has the right to assert Boss status.

- Even if your opponent has paper alleging that all rights to your Note were assigned to your opponent or its master, where is the contract that resulted in the creation of that assignment or transfer document? The contract may show a side agreement that is inconsistent with the text of the assignment. For example, the contract may say the opponent or master is only holding the Note for another person, or that the transferor is retaining some interest in the Note and not therefore transferring 100% of all rights, or the transferor does not warrant or guarantee that what it transferred constituted the right to enforce your Note.

➤ § 3-201(a) states that "negotiation" by "transfer" is necessary to "holder." Status.

- "Transfer" per § 3-203(a):
  - Requires voluntary delivery [§ 1-201(15)].
  - Purpose is to give enforcement right to the transferee.

- Requires giving 100% of rights in Note [§ 3-203(d)].

- Look at the contract that resulted in the alleged transfer to learn more about the deal between transferor and transferee. Retained servicing rights or share of collection proceeds, for example, are inconsistent with the 100% rule. If there is no contract, this would indicate your opponent cannot prove the details of the transfer.

- "Negotiation" makes a new "holder:"

  - The only exception is per § 3-203(b). If the possessor of the Note cannot prove a proper "negotiation," it may claim the enforcement right held by the transferor. The burden of proof requires the maximum evidentiary foundation regarding rights possessed by the transferor, how it obtained those rights, who from, under what agreement, and what the transferor, not the transferee, intended when the transfer was made. This section is one way a person may be able to claim Boss status as a nonholder in possession under § 3-301(ii), discussed more below.

➤ § 3-201(b) states that, if the Note is payable to a specific person, indorsement by that person must be on or physically affixed to the Note.

➤ § 3-201(b) states that, if the Note is payable to bearer, transfer of possession is required, and that means voluntary intention to convey 100% interests in the Note to the transferee. Remember that possession alone, even of a bearer Note that is indorsed in blank, does not prove Boss status. Your opponent must still provide complete information about the full chain of ownership and control to know if the person currently in possession is the Boss. Your opponent's lack of chain information is evidence that the current possessor can't prove it has Boss status.

➤ Indorsement requirements:

  - § 3-204(a) states that "indorsement" has to be on the Note. The exception is called an allonge, that being an indorsement on a piece of paper that is physically "affixed" or attached to the Note. A writing or signature on a separate, unattached paper does not qualify.

- § 3-205 defines three types of indorsements: "special indorsement," "blank indorsement," and "anomalous indorsement."

  - Only the holder at the time of indorsement can make a valid indorsement. That is, only a Boss can transfer Boss status.

  - "Anomalous" means the indorsement was by a person who, at the time, was not the Boss of the Note, and, therefore, this is not an indorsement that could transfer any rights.

  - "Special" indorsement makes the Note payable to an identified person. Only that specific person can transfer Boss rights, and only if, at the time of indorsement, that person is the Boss, unless § 3-203(c) applies.

  - "Blank" indorsement means the payor-holder is the one who voluntarily transferred 100% of all interests in the Note, including the right to enforce your Note, and without specifying a new payee. Suppose, for example, your opponent shows the contract by which it obtained possession of the Note, and that contract says the transferor transferred *all of its rights* in the Note. Such language does not prove the transferor owned 100% of the Note. If your opponent does not have proof that the transferor owned 100% of the Note, including enforcement rights, at the time of transfer to your opponent or its master, your opponent has a problem under the UCC.

§ 3-301(ii): "Nonholder, in possession, with rights of a holder"

Overview: *This person is not a holder but obtained the physical Note by legal seizure, subrogation (stepping into shoes of the predecessor via contract or statutory or equity law), or under some other law making this person the legal successor to the prior person who was Boss of the Note.* This section isn't involved unless your opponent alleges enforcement rights pursuant to it. Your opponent needs first to admit that it is not a holder pursuant to § 3-301(i) before claiming rights via § 3-301(ii), and then it has to prove how it qualifies.

- If a person previously in possession did not have the right to enforce the Note per § 3-301, the successor does not have that right. Require your opponent to provide proof of the predecessor's Boss status.

- If your opponent changes its mind as to how its authorized to enforce your Note, that indecision or change of mind is evidence of a credibility problem for your opponent that might be due to mistake or fraud.

- Remember that possession or ownership alone does not create the right to enforce the Note under the UCC.

➤ Person claiming § 3-301(ii) Boss status must prove:

- Physical possession. You must inspect the physical Note—back, front, indorsements, and all allonges (meaning they have to be affixed to the Note and not just be loose papers or temporarily paper-clipped to the Note).

- Circumstances by which the new possessor became successor to the interests of the person previously in possession of the Note, and proof that the circumstance of that possession actually gave your opponent or its master the rights owned by the previous alleged holder. Just because a person takes something from another person, for example, doesn't mean the taker had the right by law to take it.

- That the predecessor was entitled to enforce the Note at the time possession of the Note was transferred to your opponent or its master. All of the detailed tests related to Boss status per the UCC must be applied to the predecessor, and to its predecessor, and to its predecessor, etc., or your opponent or its master cannot prove Boss status.

- A person can obtain Boss status as a nonholder in possession by proving the strict requirements of § 3-203(b). So, if your opponent claims it inherited Boss status from a prior alleged Boss, your opponent must put on a lot of evidence to prove that claim. If it claims its predecessor was the Boss, make your opponent prove that. Don't assume that any company in the alleged chain of ownership and control was the Boss of your Note on any day following the day you signed the Note and delivered it to your lender.

§ 3-301(iii): "Not in possession but entitled to enforce"

Overview: *This Boss test only gets triggered if your opponent claims the right to enforce your Note when it does not have possession of the physical Note. § 3-301(iii) is the only way a person can be a Boss in a foreclosure lawsuit without the actual Note. Your opponent would have to prove Boss status via § 3-309, Enforcement of Lost, Destroyed, or Stolen Instrument.*

➤ Person claiming § 3-301(iii) Boss status must prove pursuant to § 3-309:

- That it had physical possession at the time of the loss, destruction, or theft of your Note.

- That possession was not lost as the result of any voluntary act or legal seizure.

- That it had the right to enforce the Note per § 3-301. This requires proving Boss status traceable through the entire chain of ownership and control all the way back to your lender, as if possession had not been lost, destroyed or stolen.

➤ That it cannot reasonably regain possession of the Note:

- A person who never had possession of the Note might be able to qualify for Boss status if that person acquired 100% of the rights in the Note, but no possession, from a person who qualified for Boss status per § 3-309. For example, this might come up if Company Y buys all of the rights from Company X and Company X did not have the physical Note to give to Company Y. Company Y might argue that Company X was the Boss per § 3-309, making Company Y the new Boss since it bought all of Company Y's rights. The detailed and complex proof required to satisfy this type of claim would be intense, and a lot more than just the assignment or conveyance paper Company Y would want to show. The required proof from your opponent would require extensive historical information about each predecessor and each transaction involving your Note in addition to proof that the physical Note had been lost, destroyed, or stolen when in the possession of Company X per the strict requirements of § 3-309.

Exhibit E
Example—Informal Discovery

The following is an example of a letter that could be used to identify whether the demands for payment under threat of foreclosure are actually coming from a person with the legal right to do that. The letter you send will, of course, be specific to your facts and litigation strategy, but this sample may prove helpful as you draft yours.

The company that sent you the demand notice or threat of foreclosure might call itself a trustee, bank, lender, creditor, owner, holder, beneficiary, mortgagee, loan servicer, or some other self-styled label. The notice may even come from attorneys claiming to work for one or more companies. This sample letter is drafted so that it can be used to communicate with any person involved with sending the demand or threats your way. The company answering the letter will decide which parts of the letter apply to it, so you don't have to guess about its level of involvement. And, of course, no answer means that company is admitting that it has no rights related to your Note or mortgage, at least unless it can prove otherwise someday.

If the notice or demand identifies more than one company as being involved, I think it best to send a letter to all of those companies if you have addresses for them. The important thing is to learn if any involved company actually has Boss status or represents the Boss of your Note.

The real Boss of your Note will respond with proof of its rights regarding your Note and mortgage. A person who has made a mistake will responsibly make that admission when responding to your inquiry. Silence or failure to provide genuine proof will likely be the response of a foreclosure shop that does not have the right to take your money or home.

Informal discovery via a letter is recommended in order to give those who issued the notice or threats the opportunity to prove their relationship to the Boss. If none does that, you will have good evidence for use in court that you owe nothing to them, that they have no right to enforce your Note or mortgage, and that their communications with you are driven by mistake or fraud.

This sample letter asks the recipient to respond within 15 days. That seems like a reasonable time for any company that should have already investigated Boss status and put its proof together before threatening to take a person's home. I find no requirement in the UCC regarding how much response time your opponent should have. The UCC seems only to state that, until Boss status is proven following the request for information, there has been no presentment for payment and no default or dishonor of your Note. Pick the response time that works for you, or maybe even give no requested response time at all. My guess is that the machine will respond when or if it wants to regardless of the response time you request.

Making the demand for proof of Boss status is the important objective. Sending the letter before the suit is filed makes good sense even if your opponent doesn't have much time to respond. The fact of having issued the letter is good support for the typical "upon information and belief" statements of fact. Is this a fair way to enter the lawsuit? Sure. Had the machine been concerned about fairness or justice, it would have proven its rights without you having had to ask. By applying your rights under the UCC, you're surely being a lot more straightforward and courteous than the machine's shop that is knocking on your door.

The letter makes a record of your demand for proof. The response or silence will likely establish the fact that you have not yet received proof that your attacker has Boss rights. If the day comes when you actually are satisfied your client is, in fact, the Boss or the Boss's servant, you will look more at other types of legal defenses or claims. Until that time, however, the letter and your opponent's failure to respond adequately helps protect you from a wrongful foreclosure.

....

SAMPLE LETTER—INFORMAL DISCOVERY

_____ __, 20__

_____

_____

_____

_____

RE   Home address: _____
       Loan, Mortgage, or Reference Number, per the Notice received:
       __/__/20__

Dear Sir or Madam:

Your office sent a document to me/us dated _____ and titled _____ (the "Notice"). A copy is included. I/We do not know you and do not know if you have the legal rights alleged in the Notice. I/We need to determine whether the Notice has any legal validity. I/We do not want to make payments to the wrong person or to let the wrong person take my/our Home.

Please, therefore, provide within fifteen (15) calendar days from the date of this letter the below-requested information and any additional information or documents you think establishes your right to make the demands or to carry out the threats of the Notice. Your compliance with this request will not require much time or effort if, in fact, you have such rights and you verified same before sending the Notice to me/us.

Respond only to the parts of the request that apply to you. Please let me/us know which parts you claim don't apply to you. Failure to eliminate any particular level of involvement will be viewed as your admission of claiming more than one hat regarding my/our mortgage loan and not having provided a complete and meaningful response.

If you have a document that is responsive to this request, please provide a copy of the entire document, including exhibits. A summary, abstract, or comment about a document is not acceptable, and will not be treated as genuine evidence supporting whatever position you claim regarding my/our mortgage loan and Home.

Silence or an incomplete response will be understood as your admission that the Notice was improperly issued and that your office has no right to enforce my/our mortgage loan pursuant to the Uniform

Commercial Code (the UCC) as adopted by the state where my/our Home is located and, therefore, no right to foreclose on my/our Home.

1.   If you claim to be the trustee appointed to conduct a nonjudicial foreclosure of my/our Home, you need only comply with the following:

a.   Please provide the name, address, and phone number of the company and the person(s) at that company who instructed you to commence this foreclosure process. I/we deem your receipt of this letter to be receipt by your customer, also, and I/we require responses by you and your customer accordingly.

b.   Please describe the portion or text of any document I executed regarding my mortgage loan that authorizes you to perform the foreclosure services you have agreed to perform regarding my/our Home.

c.   If you claim you received only a verbal instruction to initiate this foreclosure process, please identify the date of that instruction and the name, address, employer, and phone number of the person who gave that instruction to you.

d.   Please explain everything you did to assure yourself that the company or person who instructed you to initiate the foreclosure process was, in fact, authorized to do so by law. Further, please provide a copy of each document, digital or hardcopy, you reviewed when making that assessment.

e.   Please provide a copy of the contract or agreement, and each of them if more than one, by which you were engaged to act as trustee regarding the foreclosure of my/our Home.

f.   Please provide a copy of all communications, whether email, fax, letter, or otherwise, that you have received or sent regarding my/our Home.

g.   If you have an office manual or policy statement about how and when you engage in and prosecute foreclosures, please provide a copy.

h.   Your failure to provide the requested information will be deemed your admission that you have engaged in this foreclosure process without authority and in violation of the terms of my/our mortgage loan documents and the laws of the state in which the Home is located.

2.   If you are an attorney representing a company that is involved with the demands and foreclosure threats of the Notice, please identify your client or clients with name, address, phone number, and a description of client's relationship to my/our mortgage loan and Home. Further identify your contact person for each such identified client, including his or her name, address, employer, and phone number. I/we deem your receipt of this letter to be receipt by your client and I/we require responses by you and your client(s) accordingly.

3.   Do you claim that you are entitled to enforce my/our mortgage loan according to the Uniform Commercial Code of the state where my/our Home is located, and not in the capacity as a servant for whomever might be that person? If so, please explain and identify the circumstances by which you obtained that right and when. In addition, please provide the explanations and documents requested below:

a.   If you claim to have physical possession of the Note I/we executed, please let me/us know when you will make the Note available for inspection and copying. The place you select must be close to my/our Home, unless we all agree otherwise.

b.   Please provide a complete accounting of the amount alleged due under my/our Note from its inception to the current time, including every credit and debit. Please account for each and any insurance proceeds, claim settlement, or warranty payments made regarding my/our note and Home. If you maintain that no insurance, claim settlement, or warranty payments have been sought or received that involve, directly or indirectly, my/our mortgage loan and Home, please state so in an affidavit under oath executed by one of your officers who is also your employee.

c.   Please provide a complete history of each transfer of the physical Note and each sale, transfer, exchange or assignment of the mortgage loan, in full or part, from its creation to the current time, including but not limited to the name, address, and phone number of each transferor and each transferee in that chain. Further, for each transfer or transaction please provide, in addition to any resulting assignment or conveyance instrument, the contract(s) or agreement(s) involved with the respective transfer or transaction, as made by the parties to each respective transfer or transaction. Also, please identify the source or sources of your information regarding that chain of activity regarding my/our mortgage loan.

d.   Please provide a copy of each email, fax, letter, or other communication you sent to or received from any person or company regarding my/our mortgage loan since its inception.

4.   Do you work for a company that claims the right to enforce my/our mortgage loan pursuant to the Uniform Commercial Code of the state where my/our Home is located? If so, please identify that company with its name, address, and phone number, and identify the person or persons at that company to whom you report.

a.   If you are an agent or servant, I/we deem that your receipt of this letter constitutes receipt by the company for which you are working, and we require that company to respond as if it received this letter directly rather than through you.

b.   Please provide the contract, agreement, or document by which you were engaged to provide services for that company respecting my/our Home. If more than one contract or agreement is involved, please provide complete copies of each.

c.   Please admit that you hold no economic interest in my/our mortgage loan or Home. If you maintain otherwise, please explain and provide each and all documents that you assert create an economic interest in my/our mortgage loan or Home.

d.   Please have the company you claim hired you respecting my/our Home to provide by the hand of one of its employees, directly to me/us, its affirmation of your engagement and authority to represent it respecting my/our Home and the Notice, and all of its documents regarding my/our mortgage loan.

e.   Please provide a copy of the document or documents by which that company declared a default under my/our mortgage loan and instructed you or some other person to commence collection actions regarding same. If you claim that instruction was verbal, please identify the person who gave it to you and include the date of that instruction and that person's name, address, employer, and phone number.

You are welcome to answer that you have no such information with which to reply to any particular request. If you need more time to provide the requested information and documents, I/we would be amenable to an extension of the time subject to a reciprocal extension, day-for-day, of each deadline stated in the Notice. Additionally, during such additional time, if granted per this paragraph, your delay in providing the required answers and documentation will be nevertheless deemed your admission, pending proof to the contrary, that the Notice was issued by mistake and that neither you nor the company you claim to represent, if applicable, actually has the right by law to make the demands and threats included in the Notice.

Sincerely,

_____

Name
Address

Exhibit F
Examples—Formal Discovery

The following are examples of formal discovery requests related to the UCC-driven foreclosure fundamentals addressed by *Fighting the Foreclosure Machine*. Use them as you think helpful in light of the facts of your case and the litigation strategy you adopt.

The rules of your court may define requirements about the appearance of your formal discovery documents, such as caption, line spacing, font size or style, the use of punched or non-punched paper, etc. There may also be requirements regarding scope, limitations, and other procedural matters involving your formal discovery. As best you can, always comply with the directions of your court.

Many courts limit the number of requests for admissions or interrogatories, or the number of document production requests. Judges often have the authority to authorize additional discovery, but that requires formal procedures, and a request to have more discovery may not be granted. Issuing fewer requests than permitted initially and keeping in reserve the right to do more discovery without need of involving the judge is often good management of the arrows in your discovery quiver.

The following examples are written as if you are the plaintiff who started the lawsuit. The text would need to be modified, as you think appropriate, if the foreclosure machine starts the lawsuit. For example, the word "Complaint" would then be replaced by whatever you title your answer or counterclaim that gets filed in response to the complaint filed against you by your opponent.

[caption/heading/formatting per your court's rules]

FIRST REQUEST FOR ADMISSIONS

REQUESTING PARTY: _____
RESPONDING PARTY: _____

The Responding Party is requested to admit or deny the truth of stated facts or the genuineness of certain documents. With limited exceptions, You will not be permitted to change the answer You give. Penalties or costs may apply should Your answer be later proven by the Requesting Party to be inaccurate or false. The answers You provide, even if via Your attorney, will be deemed to be provided by You and under oath unless You clarify otherwise. You must serve Your responses on the Requesting Party in accordance with the Court's applicable rules.

Your answers to these requested admissions must be dated, verified, and signed. Whether or not You comply with such requirement, each response provided to the Requesting Party by You or Your attorney will be deemed to be provided under oath by You with an intention that the Requesting Party rely on same and deem it to be Your honest and well-reasoned response to the specific requested admission.

Definitions for Purposes of these Requests for Admissions:

"Complaint" means the _____*[use actual caption of the Complaint]*_____ filed in this lawsuit.

"Document" or "Documents" means a writing, email, or fax, whether of digital or hardcopy format, a photocopy or picture of a writing, whether handwritten, printed, or typed, and without limitation as to how the Document might be further described based on its label, title, content, size, or usage, so long as it is in Your actual or constructive possession, custody, or control.

"Letter" means the letter dated _____, a copy of which is attached as Exhibit __ to the Complaint.

"Note" means that promissory note, a copy of which as it existed when created is attached as Exhibit __ to the Complaint.

"Mortgage Loan" means the Note and Security Instrument created regarding my/our obligation under the Note and its collateralization with the Property.

"Person" means individual, corporation, government entity or agency, trust, or any other legal or business entity.

"Property" means _____*[street address]*_____ or as otherwise described in the Security Instrument. *[Caution: this text presumes you think the legal description in the Security Instrument is correct. If you doubt the accuracy of that legal description, limiting this definition to the address of the Property may be best.]*

"Security Instrument" means the Document further securing payment of the obligation under the Note. A copy of the Security Instrument is attached as Exhibit __ to the Complaint.

"You," "Your," and "Yours" mean the Responding Party.

You Are Requested to Admit that Each of the Following Facts Is True:

1. Admit that You are not an agent or servant of the Person owning all rights and interests respecting the Mortgage Loan.

   Admit _____   Deny _____

2. Admit that You never purchased or acquired an ownership interest of any kind in the Mortgage Loan.

   Admit _____   Deny _____

3. Admit that You do not know the identity of the owner of the Mortgage Loan.

   Admit _____   Deny _____

4. Admit that You did not provide all of the information requested by the Letter.

   Admit _____   Deny _____

5. Admit that You do not know the location of the physical Note.

   Admit _____   Deny _____

6. Admit that You do not know the complete history of the changes in possession and ownership of the Mortgage Loan since it was first created.

        Admit ____   Deny ____

7. Admit that You do not know if payments related to insurance proceeds, dispute settlements, or indorsement warranties have been sought or received that in any way relate to the Mortgage Loan, or any part of it.

        Admit ____   Deny ____

8. Admit that You have not reviewed each contract or agreement which involved a transfer, assignment, sale, exchange, pledge, loan servicing arrangement, or securitization of the Mortgage Loan since its creation.

        Admit ____   Deny ____

9. Admit that You do not know the identity of the Person currently entitled to enforce the Note pursuant to the version of the in use by the state where the Property is located.

        Admit ____   Deny ____

10. Admit that none of your employees is authorized by you to sign foreclosure related documents or conveyance instruments for any other company.

        Admit ____   Deny ____

Date: _____ ___, 20__

        Respectfully submitted,

        _____

        Requesting Party

....

[caption/heading/formatting per your court's rules]

FIRST SET OF INTERROGATORIES

REQUESTING PARTY: _____

RESPONDING PARTY: _____

The Responding Party is requested to answer these interrogatories within the time and by the method prescribed by the Court's applicable rules. In answering these interrogatories You are required to provide all information reasonably available to You, Your agents, representatives, employees, attorneys and investigators.

If You are unable to answer any interrogatory after exercising due diligence in attempting to do so, please answer to the extent of Your ability and indicate the reason for Your inability to answer more fully, accurately, or responsively as the case might be. The information You provide will be deemed to be all of, and the only, information you have regarding the particular interrogatory if you do not indicate otherwise as provided by this paragraph.

You are required to make a good faith effort to comply with these interrogatories, and the Court's rules of discovery require that of You.

If objections are interposed to any interrogatory, please state the complete basis of the objection to that interrogatory, including legal authority upon which You base Your objection regarding that specific interrogatory.

If You contend that any information sought is protected by attorney-client or other privilege, You are required to state the factual basis for such alleged privilege regarding the specific information requested.

If You are confused about any term or request included in these interrogatories, You are welcome to seek clarification from the Requesting Party.

If Your answer to an interrogatory requires more space than that provided below a respective interrogatory, You are welcome to use extra pages.

Unless otherwise noted, these requests are for the period commencing with the date the Note was created through the present time.

Your answers to these interrogatories must be dated, verified, and signed. Whether or not You comply with such requirement, each response provided to the Requesting Party by You or Your attorney shall be deemed to be provided under oath by You with an intention that the Requesting Party may rely on same and deem it to be Your honest and complete response to the specific interrogatory.

Definitions:

For purposes of responding to these interrogatories, the following words shall have the below ascribed meanings:

"Document" or "Documents" means a writing, email, or fax, whether of digital or hardcopy format, a photocopy or picture of a writing, whether handwritten, printed, or typed, and without limitation as to how the Document might be further described based on its label, title, content, size, or usage, so long as it is in Your actual or constructive possession, custody, or control.

"Identify" with respect to a Document means describe the type of Document (i.e., letter, memorandum, work-paper, schedule, report, contract, etc.), the title or name by which You refer to it, the date of the Document, the identity of the author(s) or the Person(s) who created the Document, how You came to have that Document, a general description of the subject matter of the Document, and whether the Document is complete as to all of its pages and exhibits. In the alternative to Identifying a Document for a particular interrogatory response, You are welcome, at Your election, to submit a complete copy of the subject Document to the Requesting Party along with Your answer to that interrogatory.

"Identify" with respect to an individual means provide that person's name, employer, business address, phone number, and the person's title at his or her place of employment.

"Letter" means the letter dated _____, a copy of which is attached as Exhibit __ to the Complaint.

"Note" means that promissory note, a copy of which as it existed when created is attached as Exhibit __ to the Complaint.

"Mortgage Loan" means the Note and Security Instrument created regarding the obligation of the Requesting Party under the Note and its collateralization with the Property.

"Person" means individual, corporation, government entity or agency, trust, or any other legal or business entity.

"Property" means _____[street address]_____ or as otherwise described in the Security Instrument. *[Caution: this text presumes you think the legal description in the Security Instrument is correct. If you doubt the accuracy of that legal description, limiting this definition to the address of the Property may be best.]*

"Security Instrument" means the Document further securing payment of the obligation under the Note. A copy of the Security Instrument is attached as Exhibit __ to the Complaint.

"You," "Your," and "Yours" mean the Responding Party.

Interrogatory No. 1:
Please Identify each and all Documents You issued to or received from the Requesting Party from the date the Note was created to the present time.

Answer:

Interrogatory No. 2:
For each requested admission You denied, or did not simply admit, please explain each such response, and Identify all of the Documents upon which You relied in making each such response.

Answer:

Interrogatory No. 3:
Please identify the Person You think has the right to enforce breaches under the Note and why You think so, including but not limited to the name, address, and phone number of such identified Person, Your relationship to such Person, and Identify the Documents, if any, upon which You base Your answer.

Answer:

Interrogatory No. 4:
If You claim an ownership interest in the Mortgage Loan, please explain Your interest, including but not limited to when You acquired that interest, whether it is a full or limited interest, whether, and in what way, Your interest has changed since You first acquired it, how much You paid for Your interest, and how much You received when Your interest was reduced or changed (if applicable), and Identify the Documents upon which You base Your answer.

Answer:

Interrogatory No. 5:
Please Identify the individual or individuals responding to these interrogatories on Your behalf, including but not limited to the answers or portions thereof provided by each such identified individual.

Answer:

Interrogatory No. 6:
If a mediation or settlement conference should occur during this litigation, please describe Your authority to negotiate a settlement of this case, including, but not limited to, whether You have unlimited authority, whether You have to obtain another Person's permission to accept or negotiate a settlement, and, if so, please identify such Person, including name, location, phone number, employer (if the Person is an individual), and relationship to You, and Identify all Documents upon which You base Your answer.

Answer:

Interrogatory No. 7:
Please describe the physical status of the Note, including, but not limited to, when You last saw it, when You first took possession of it, Identify the Documents upon which You base Your answer, and state when the Note will be available for inspection by the Requesting Party.

Answer:

Interrogatory No. 8:
Please describe the process by which You determined the identity of the Person currently holding the right to enforce the Note, including, but not limited to, when that determination was made, Identify the individual(s) who made that determination, and Identify the Documents used or investigated through that determination process, including, but not limited to, any instruction or policy papers or manual available to the people making such determination or assisting with that determination.

Answer:

Interrogatory No. 9:
If you denied, or did not simply admit, requested admission No. 10, please Identify each of your employees who is authorized to sign for other companies, the name(s) of those companies, the title(s) the respective employee uses for the other companies, and Identify the Documents upon which you base your answer.

Answer:

Date: _____ ___, 20__

Respectfully submitted,

_____
Requesting Party

....

[caption/heading/formatting per your court's rules]

FIRST REQUEST FOR PRODUCTION OF DOCUMENTS

REQUESTING PARTY: _____

RESPONDING PARTY: _____

Instructions and Guidelines:

This demand calls for Documents in Your possession or under Your control even if in the possession of Your agents, attorneys, or others.

If You object to being required to produce certain requested Documents, please set forth, with legal authority, the reasons for Your objection, along with Your statement as to whether You actually have such Documents to which Your objection relates.

You must also identify any Document responsive to the particular demand that You are withholding from production based upon a claim of privilege or other protection. As to such Document being withheld, state the particular privilege or protection being invoked and also provide for each such Document the following information to the extent known or available to You:

1. Title or subject matter of Document;

2. The date appearing on the Document;

3. Author;

4. Number of pages;

5. The identity of the individuals or entities that have received an original or copy of such Document, including, but not limited to, name, address, phone number, and, if applicable, employer, and job title;

6. The present location of the Document; and,

7. The identity of the Person which has custody, control, or possession thereof.

Unless You state otherwise, Your production of Documents will be deemed to be the totality of Your Documents, and it will be concluded that You have no other documentary evidence related to the specific request for production. Your effort to later produce or use Documents not timely produced with Your response to this First Request for Production of Documents will be denied unless circumstances for the delay or failure to timely produce same are acceptable to the Requesting Party.

You are welcome to contact the Requesting Party for further clarification as to a request made hereby.

You must serve the Requesting Party with Your produced Documents and any supplemental responses in accordance with the Court's applicable rules, or make them available for inspection and copying under an arrangement acceptable to the Requesting Party.

Unless otherwise noted, these requests are for the period commencing with the date the subject Mortgage Loan was created through the present time.

Your production of Documents must be dated, verified, and signed. Whether or not You comply with such requirement, Your production of Documents will be deemed to be all that You have in the way of Documents which are responsive to this demand unless You otherwise state in Your response that You have not provided all of the Documents requested along with an explanation of why not and You Identify each Document You have not produced.

Definitions:

The following words shall have the meanings described below:

"Document" or "Documents" means a writing, email, or fax, whether of digital or hardcopy format, a photocopy or picture of a writing, whether handwritten, printed, or typed, and without limitation as to how the Document might be further described based on its label, title, content, size, or usage, so long as it is in Your actual or constructive possession, custody or control. Production of a Document requires providing all of its pages, exhibits, and other Documents referenced therein.

"Identify" with respect to a Document means describe the type of Document (i.e., letter, memorandum, work-paper, schedule, report, contract, etc.), the title or name by which You refer to it, the date of the Document, the identity of the author(s) or the Person(s) who created the Document, how You came to have that Document, a general description of the subject matter of the Document and whether the Document is complete as to all of its pages and exhibits. *In the alternative to Identifying a Document for a particular interrogatory response, You are welcome, at Your election, to submit a complete copy of the subject Document to the Requesting Party along with Your answer to that interrogatory.*

"Identify" with respect to an individual means that person's name, employer, business address, phone number, and the person's title at his or her place of employment.

"Letter" means the letter dated _____, a copy of which is attached as Exhibit __ to the Complaint.

"Note" means that promissory note, a copy of which as it existed when created is attached as Exhibit __ to the Complaint.

"Mortgage Loan" means the Note and Security Instrument created regarding my/our obligation under the Note and its collateralization with the Property.

"Person" means individual, corporation, government entity or agency, trust, or any other legal or business entity.

"Property" means _____[street address]_____ or as otherwise described in the Security Instrument. *[Caution: this text presumes you think the legal description in the Security Instrument is correct. If you doubt the accuracy of that legal description, limiting this definition to the address of the Property may be best.]*

"Security Instrument" means the Document further securing payment of the obligation under the Note. A copy of the Security Instrument is attached as Exhibit __ to the Complaint.

"You," "Your," and "Yours" mean the Responding Party.

The Responding Party is requested to produce the following Documents:

Request for Production No. 1:
Please produce each and every Document Identified by You in Your Answer to the First Set of Interrogatories issued by the Requesting Party.

Request for Production No. 2:
Please produce all of Your Documents involving, mentioning, or about the Mortgage Loan, or any part of it, including, but not limited to, agreements or arrangements involving ownership, transfer, exchange, loan servicing, pledge, sale, purchase, or agency relationships; communications of any and every type to and from any Person that involve the Note or Security Instrument; all communications issued or received involving insurance, dispute settlement, or indorsement warranties; and all accounting and income Documents related in any way

to the Mortgage Loan, the Note or the Security Instrument.

Request for Production No. 3:
Please produce all Documents involving, mentioning, or about the already initiated or threatened foreclosure process regarding the Property, whether issued by or received by You, including, but not limited to, letters, emails, faxes, public ads or notices, contracts, agreements, notices or demands, expenditures and costs, and phone logs.

Request for Production No. 4:
Please produce all of Your Documents involving, mentioning, or about the Property, including, but not limited to, agreements or arrangements involving ownership, transfer, exchange, pledge, sale, or acquisition of any interest in the Property, whether past or to occur in the future; historical and background Documents; communications of any and every type to and from others (individuals or entities); servicing agreements related to the Property; insurance policies; insurance claims; agreements or arrangements regarding foreclosure services of any and every type involving the Property; title searches, title abstract reports, appraisals, copies of Documents recorded in public records, and all property tax Documents.

Request for Production No. 5:
Please produce all of Your Documents respecting Your arrangement or agreement mentioning, involving or about the Mortgage Loan, or any part of it, with whomever You think is entitled to enforce the obligations of the Note, including, but not limited to, all communications between You and such identified Person regarding the Note, Security Instrument, or Property, and all communications between You and others who You thought represented such identified Person regarding the Note, Security Instrument, or Property.

Date: _____ ___, 20__

Respectfully submitted,

_____
Requesting Party
Address

Table of Authorities

Cases

Words and Phrases of Interest

Other Authorities

Statutes

UCC Sections

<u>Cases</u>

Words and Phrases of Interest

Other Authorities

"A Short History Of The Subprime Mortgage Market Meltdown," by James R. Barth, Tong Li, Triphon Phumiwasana, and Glenn Yago, The Milken Institute, January 2008 ....…........endnote: 8, 19, 20, 26, 31

Affidavit testimony of William Hultman, Treasurer, Secretary and Vice President of Mortgage Electronic Registration Systems, Inc. ....… ....…..endnote: 15, 22

"Bank of America Moves to Settle Mortgage Claims," by Dan Fitzpatrick, *The Wall Street Journal,* June 29, 2011 ....endnote: 2

"Banks Hit Hurdle to Foreclosures," by Nick Timiraos, *The Wall Street Journal,* June 1, 2011 ....endnote: 50

"Big Banks Say MERS Mortgage Database Draws Probes," by Laura Marcinek, www.Bloomberg.com, March 2, 2011 ....endnote: 161

"Crisis Inquiry Panel Calls Recession Avoidable," by Adam Shell, Paul Davidson, and John Waggoner, *USA Today,* January 28, 2011 ....endnote: 28

Declaration of the Summit on Financial Markets and the World Economy, issued by the Group of 20, November 15, 2008 ....endnote: 13, 36

"Effort on Home Loans Stalls," by Nick Timiraos and Ruth Simons, *The Wall Street Journal,* September 19, 2011 ....endnote: 10

"Errors found in 84% of SF mortgages in foreclosure," by John Widermuth, *The San Francisco Chronicle,* February 16, 2012, p. A-1 ....endnote: 53

"Fewer Fall Delinquent in Paying Mortgages," by David Streitfeld, *The New York Times,* November 18, 2010 ....endnote: 34

Financial Crisis Inquiry Report ....24, 29, 31, 38 and ....endnote: 4, 12, 16, 23, 25, 27, 37

"Foreclosure Errors Cloud Homeownership With 'Blighted Title' " by Kathleen M. Howley, *Bloomberg,* October 1, 2010 ....endnote: 51

"Foreclosure, Subprime Mortgage Lending, and the Mortgage Electronic Registration System," by Christopher L. Peterson, *University of Cincinnati Law Review,* Vol. 78, No. 4, Summer 2010.....................endnote: 38, 108

"Foreclosures," by Jim Wilson, *The New York Times,* October 21, 2010 ....
....endnote: 33

"Ginnie Mae Funds Have Been Solid Performers," by John Waggoner, *USA Today,* September 7, 2010 ....endnote: 30, 41

Hawkland & Lawrence UCC Series ....endnote: 66, 81, 82, 85, 134, 135

"Home prices decline in many major metro areas," by Julie Schmidt, *USA Today,* p. 1B, December 28, 2011......................................endnote: 7

"How the Banks Put the Economy Underwater," by Yves Smith, *The New York Times,* October 30, 2010 ....endnote: 13, 51, 52, 72, 114

"In Foreclosure Controversy, Problems Run Deeper Than Flawed Paperwork," by Brady Dennis and Ariana Eunjung Cha Cha, *The Washington Post,* October 7, 2010 ....endnote: 44

Inside Job, Charles Ferguson (director), produced by Representational Pictures and Sony Picture Classics, 2010 ....endonte: 39

Lawrence's Anderson on the Uniform Commercial Code, 3d Edition ....endnote: 66, 81, 100, 103, 156

"Mired in Foreclosure," by Jessica Silver-Greenberg, *The Wall Street Journal,* September 19, 2011 ....endnote: 52

"N.M. Foreclosures Plunge in 2011," by Richard Metcalf, *Albuquerque Journal*, p. B1, January 13, 2012 ....endnote: 6

"N.M. Mortgage Delinquencies Holding Steady," by Richard Metcalf, *The Albuquerque Journal*, November 20, 2010 ....endnote: 32

"Opening the Bag of Mortgage Tricks," by Gretchen Morgenson, *The New York Times*, December 18, 2010 ....endnote: 2

Reforming America's Housing Finance Market, A Report to Congress by the Department of the Treasury and the U.S. Department of Housing and Urban Development, February 2011 ....endnote: 28, 30

Restatement of the Law Second, Agency § 1, The American Law Institute, 1958 ....endnote: 148, 151

Restatement of the Law Second, Agency § 18, The American Law Institute, 1958 ....endnote: 148

Report on Application of the UCC to Selected Issues Relating to Mortgage Notes, Permanent Editorial Board for the Uniform Commercial Code, November 14, 2011 ....165 ....and endnote: 58, 95, 100, 105, 106, 107, 120

"Say Goodbye to Fannie and Freddie," by William Poole, *The New York Times*, August 11, 2010 ....endnote: 30

"Southern Essex Registry of Deeds audit reveals that 75% of assignments of mortgages are invalid; Obrien says banks responsible for an epidemic of fraud. Once again urges Attorney's General to stop bank settlement talks," press release by Southern Essex Registry of Deeds, reported at htttp://4closurefraud.org, June 30, 2011 ....endnote: 54

Subprime Mortgage Market Turmoil: Examining the Role of Securitization—A hearing before the U.S. Senate Committee of Banking, Housing, and Urban Affairs Subcommittee on Securities, Insurance and Investment, by Christopher L. Peterson, Associate Professor of Law, University of Florida, April 17, 2007 ....endnote: 19, 20, 21

"The Case of the Missing Mortgage," by Stephen Gandel, *Time*, November 29, 2010 ....endnote: 45, 51, 160

"The Fed and Foreclosures," by Terrence Malick, *The New York Times*, November 28, 2010 ....endnote: 14

"The Stealth Stimulus: Defaulters Living for Free," by Mark Whitehouse, *The Wall Street Journal*, p. A2, November 1, 2010 ....endnote: 5

"Two Faces: Demystifying The Mortgage Electronic Registration System's Land Title Theory," by Christopher L. Peterson, *William & Mary Law Review*, Vol. 53, 2011 ....endnote: 55, 90

Underwater Home, by Brent White, 2010 ....endnote: 77

Uniform Law Commission ....57, 154 and endnote: 42

"Will Perpetrators of Financial Crimes Ever Face Justice?," by Mary Bottari, Center for Media and Democracy and www.BanksterUSA.org, *Huffington Post*, August 25, 2010 ....endnote: 49

Statutes

UCC Sections

299

Endnotes

Chapter 1

1. *Landmark National Bank v. Kesler, Millennia Mortgage Company, MERS and Sovereign Bank, et al, 216 P.3d 158* (Kansas 2009).

Chapter 2

2. Many reports have surfaced indicating litigation may become a regular part of the interaction of investor groups and members of the mortgage finance industry. Some litigation has already begun and I predict there will be lot more. The results of one such case were reported shortly before Christmas 2010. See also the following articles:

    "Opening the Bag of Mortgage Tricks," by Gretchen Morgenson, *The New York Times,* December 18, 2010, in which it was stated: "Last week, a jury in federal district court in Reno, Nev., awarded a group of 50 mortgage investors $5.1 million in punitive damages against defendants in a loan servicing case. Although the numbers in the case aren't large, its facts are fascinating. Indeed, the case exposed some of the tricks of the servicers' trade." "In short, loan servicing is a perfect setup for administrators who want to take advantage of both borrowers and lenders." As you have probably already surmised, information flowing from such legal battles may become useful to foreclosure victims as more of the workings of the mortgage finance industry are made public.

    "Bank of America Moves to Settle Mortgage Claims," by Dan Fitzpatrick, *The Wall Street Journal,* June 29, 2011: The article reports that Bank of America settled, at a price of $8.5 billion, claims of 22 investor groups which involved $424 billion of mortgage-backed securities packaged and sold by Bank of America.

3. See, e.g., the conclusions of the Financial Crisis Inquiry Commission beginning at page xv of *The Financial Crisis Inquiry Report,* issued by that Commission, January 2011. In testimony before the Commission about actual fraud that had been identified, the FBI indicated that 80% or more of fraud was caused by "industry insiders" (p. 160). Commissioners publishing their dissent to the

majority report of the Commission noted that mortgage fraud was not sufficiently present to even be quantifiable (p. 425). A copy was available at www.fcic.gov and at http://fcic.law.stanford.edu.

Chapter 3

4. *The Financial Crisis Inquiry Report,* issued by the Financial Crisis Inquiry Commission, January 2011, p. 402. A copy was available at www.fcic.gov and at http://fcic.law.stanford.edu.

5. See, e.g., "The Stealth Stimulus: Defaulters Living for Free," by Mark Whitehouse, *The Wall Street Journal,* p. A2, November 1, 2010.

6. "N.M. Foreclosures Plunge in 2011," by Richard Metcalf, *Albuquerque Journal,* p. B1, January 13, 2012, reporting the comments of RealtyTrac CEO Brandon Moore.

7. "Home prices decline in many major metro areas," by Julie Schmidt, *USA Today,* p. 1B, December 28, 2011.

8. "A Short History Of The Subprime Mortgage Market Meltdown," by James R. Barth, Tong Li, Triphon Phumiwasana, and Glenn Yago, The Milken Institute, January 2008.

9. www.RealtyTrac.com.

10. See, e.g., "Effort on Home Loans Stalls," by Nick Timiraos and Ruth Simons, *The Wall Street Journal,* September 19, 2011.

11. "Builders Hammered: 2010 2nd-Worst Year Since 1959 as Housing Starts Slump," by Martin Crutsinger, www.registerguard.com, The Associated Press, January 20, 2010.

12. *The Financial Crisis Inquiry Report,* issued by the Financial Crisis Inquiry Commission, January 2011, p. 391.

13. See, e.g., comments on Wikipedia (www.wikipedia.org) under the heading "Subprime Mortgage Crisis," that being the expression so often used in efforts to define or understand the economic downturn in the United States over recent years: "Three important catalysts of the subprime crisis were the influx of moneys from the private sector, the banks entering into the mortgage bond market and the predatory lending practices of the mortgage lenders, specifically the adjustable-rate mortgage that mortgage lenders sold directly or indirectly via mortgage brokers." Also: "During a period of strong global growth, growing capital flows, and prolonged stability earlier this decade, market participants sought higher yields without an

adequate appreciation of the risks and failed to exercise proper due diligence. At the same time, weak underwriting standards, unsound risk management practices, increasingly complex and opaque financial products, and consequent excessive leverage combined to create vulnerabilities in the system. Policy-makers, regulators and supervisors, in some advanced countries, did not adequately appreciate and address the risks building up in financial markets, keep pace with financial innovation, or take into account the systemic ramifications of domestic regulatory actions." [Citing the Group of 20's *Declaration of the Summit on Financial Markets and the World Economy*, p.15, November 2008].

Other reports have come to the same conclusions, e.g.:

"How the Banks Put the Economy Underwater," by Yves Smith, *The New York Times*, October 30, 2010: "However, the problems in the mortgage securitization market run much wider and deeper than robo-signing, and started much earlier than the foreclosure process." The article continues with a historical review of lending practices that focused on packaging and sales of mortgage loans to the exclusion of customary business practices.

New Century Mortgage Corporation v. McDonald, No. 2011-50299 (NY S.Ct. 2011): "This case epitomizes the pitfalls created by the fast and loose mortgage practices that lead to the demise of New York's once lucrative real-estate market."

14. See, e.g., "The Fed and Foreclosures," by Terrence Malick, *The New York Times*, November 28, 2010: "Yet, banks have never acted as if they bear responsibility for the mortgage mess. They have pursued foreclosures in violation of borrowers' rights to due process, as revealed by the recent robo-signing scandal. And, despite having been bailed out for their mistakes, they have pursued their self-interest, not the public interest, when it comes to modifying bad loans."

15. Affidavit testimony of William Hultman, Treasurer, Secretary and Vice President of Mortgage Electronic Registration Systems, Inc. (ShellGame-MERS), submitted in *Mortgage Electronic Registration Systems, Inc. v. Bellistri*, No. 4:09-cv-731 cas (USDCt. E.D. MO 2009): Suspiciously, the affidavit and other "evidence" filed by ShellGame-MERS was not available for viewing, having been sealed by the Court upon request of ShellGame-MERS. That case was filed May 11, 2009, and the portions of the affidavit recited by the judge in his July 1, 2010, decision evidence that the affidavit mimics the

content of the initial complaint and can therefore be reasonably understood as having provided information as of May 11, 2009.

16. Many papers and articles have been written about the causes of the economic crisis America now experiences. Consistent with my understanding of this tragedy's history is *The Financial Crisis Inquiry Report*, issued by the Financial Crisis Inquiry Commission, January 2011, available at www.fcic.gov and at http://fcic.law.stanford.edu.

17. The MERS membership directory is available online at www.mersinc.org.

18. By "private" is meant funds that were accessible to the mortgage finance industry outside of capital and financing sources available from our state and federal governments. Funds obtained from other countries are also defined as private because access to them is via Wall Street and private arrangements that did not involve our own government approval processes.

19. See, e.g., the following:

Subprime Mortgage Market Turmoil: Examining the Role of Securitization—A hearing before the U.S. Senate Committee of Banking, Housing, and Urban Affairs Subcommittee on Securities, Insurance and Investment, by Christopher L. Peterson, Associate Professor of Law, University of Florida, April 17, 2007, pp. 1-8.

"A Short History Of The Subprime Mortgage Market Meltdown," by James R. Barth, Tong Li, Triphon Phumiwasana, and Glenn Yago, The Milken Institute, January 2008.

20. For more information about the historical change of "lender" from that of the company that originated, funded, and serviced a loan into the fractionated origination, funding, and services businesses which were at their height in the 1990s and early 2000s, see, e.g.:

"A Short History Of The Subprime Mortgage Market Meltdown," by James R. Barth, Tong Li, Triphon Phumiwasana, and Glenn Yago, The Milken Institute, January 2008

Subprime Mortgage Market Turmoil: Examining the Role of Securitization—A hearing before the U.S. Senate Committee on Banking, Housing, and Urban Affairs Subcommittee on Securities, Insurance, and Investment, written testimony of Christopher L. Peterson, Associate Professor of Law, University of Florida, April 17, 2007.

21. *Subprime Mortgage Market Turmoil: Examining the Role of Securitization—A hearing before the U.S. Senate Committee of Banking, Housing, and Urban Affairs Subcommittee on Securities, Insurance and Investment,* by Christopher L. Peterson, Associate Professor of Law, University of Florida, April 17, 2007, p. 11.

22. Affidavit testimony of William Hultman, Treasurer and Secretary of Mortgage Electronic Registration Systems, Inc. (ShellGame-MERS), submitted in *Mortgage Electronic Registration Systems, Inc. v. Bellistri,* No. 4:09-cv-731 cas (USDCt. E.D. MO 2009). Suspiciously, the affidavit and other "evidence" filed by ShellGame-MERS was not available for viewing, having been sealed by the Court upon request of ShellGame-MERS. That action makes one wonder what they thought needed to be hidden from the public. That case was filed May 11, 2009, and the portions of the affidavit recited by the judge in his July 1, 2010, decision evidence that the affidavit mimics the content of the initial complaint and can therefore be reasonably understood as having provided information as of May 11, 2009, when the complaint was filed.

23. *The Financial Crisis Inquiry Report,* issued by the Financial Crisis Inquiry Commission, January 2011, p. 5.

24. Most mortgage-backed securities, at least the ones created since the late 1990s, involved home loans. Commercial properties were involved also, but data about the commercial real estate side of the problem caused by the mortgage finance industry is not as well documented. *Fighting the Foreclosure Machine* concentrates on home ownership adversely impacted by wrongful foreclosures. The foreclosure fundamentals applicable to a home foreclosure, however, should apply equally well to commercial real estate loans that have been sold and traded as investment products.

25. The 662-page *Financial Crisis Inquiry Report,* issued by the Financial Crisis Inquiry Commission, January 2011, available at www.fcic.gov and at http://fcic.law.stanford.edu, has a wealth of information and excerpts of testimony received during the investigations of that Commission. For example, page 7 notes:

"The mortgage debt of American households rose almost as much in the six years from 2001 to 2007 as it had over the course of the country's more than 200 year history"; and:

"Under the radar, the lending and the financial services industry had mutated. In the past, lenders had avoided making unsound loans because they would be stuck with them in their loan portfolios. But because of the growth of securitization, it wasn't even clear anymore who the lender was. The mortgages would be packaged, sliced, repackaged, insured, and sold as incomprehensibly complicated debt securities to an assortment of hungry investors. Now even the worst loans could find a buyer. More loan sales meant higher profits for everyone in the chain. Business boomed for Christopher Cruise, a Maryland-based corporate educator who trained loan officers for companies that were expanding mortgage originations. He crisscrossed the nation, coaching about 10,000 loan originators a year in auditoriums and classrooms. His clients included many of the largest lenders—Countrywide, Ameriquest, and Ditech among them. Most of their new hires were young, with no mortgage experience, fresh out of school and with previous jobs 'flipping burgers,' he told the FCIC. Given the right training, however, the best of them could 'easily' earn millions. 'I was a sales and marketing trainer in terms of helping people to know how to sell these products to, in some cases, frankly unsophisticated and unsuspecting borrowers,' he said. He taught them the new playbook: 'You had no incentive whatsoever to be concerned about the quality of the loan, whether it was suitable for the borrower or whether the loan performed. In fact, you were in a way encouraged not to worry about those macro issues.' He added, 'I knew that the risk was being shunted off. I knew that we could be writing crap. But in the end it was like a game of musical chairs. Volume might go down but we were not going to be hurt.'"

26. See, e.g., "A Short History Of The Subprime Mortgage Market Meltdown," by James R. Barth, Tong Li, Triphon Phumiwasana, and Glenn Yago, The Milken Institute, January 2008, p. 1.

27. *The Financial Crisis Inquiry Report*, issued by the Financial Crisis Inquiry Commission of the U.S. Congress, January 2011, p. 5.

28. See, e.g., the following:

"Crisis Inquiry Panel Calls Recession Avoidable," by Adam Shell, Paul Davidson, and John Waggoner, *USA Today,* January 28, 2011. Speaking of the causes of the terrible financial crisis, one group of reporters stated: "Trillions of dollars had been wagered on the belief that housing prices would always rise and that borrowers would seldom default on mortgages, even as their debt grew."

Reforming America's Housing Finance Market, A Report to Congress by the Department of the Treasury and the U.S. Department of Housing and Urban Development, February 2011, which recommends that Congress abolish Freddie Mac and Fannie Mae:

"But in the years leading up to the recent financial crisis, trillions of dollars worth of financial decisions were made across the U.S. economy and around the world on the faulty expectation that national house prices would only rise," p. 4.

29. See, e.g., www.censusbureau.gov.

30. Mounting evidence shows that Fannie Mae and Freddie Mac have been little more than government-supported private companies which, rather than having loyalty to the American taxpayers who made their existence possible, did what was good for the bank accounts of their officers and investors. See, e.g., the following:

"Say Goodbye to Fannie and Freddie," by William Poole, *The New York Times,* August 11, 2010: "The Federal National Mortgage Association—known as Fannie Mae—and the Federal Home Loan Mortgage Corporation—Freddie Mac—were poorly structured from the time, 40 years ago, when they were set up as so-called government-sponsored enterprises. Both of these technically private companies, designed to foster the issuance of home mortgages, enjoyed implicit federal backing in the event they got into financial trouble but only weak regulation to prevent such trouble. ... Fannie and Freddie had a license to print money. ... What a deal—borrow at the low rate, invest at a higher one, hold little capital and let the federal government bear the risks! Investors [in Freddie and Fannie] enjoyed high returns, and management enjoyed high salaries. Incidentally, politicians also got a steady flow of campaign contributions from the companies' executives."

Comments on Wikipedia (www.wikipedia.org) under the heading "Subprime Mortgage Crisis": "The federal takeover of Fannie Mae and Freddie Mac refers to the placing into conservatorship of government sponsored enterprises Fannie Mae and Freddie Mac by the U.S. Treasury in September 2008. It was one financial event among many in the ongoing subprime mortgage crisis. On September 6, 2008, the director of the Federal Housing Finance Agency (FHFA), James B. Lockhart III, announced his decision to place two Government sponsored enterprises (GSEs), Fannie Mae (Federal National Mortgage Association) and Freddie Mac (Federal Home Loan Mortgage Corporation), into conservatorship run by the FHFA. At the same press conference, United States Treasury Secretary Henry Paulson, stated that placing the two GSEs into conservatorship was a decision he fully supported, and that he advised 'that conservatorship was the only form in which I would commit taxpayer money to the GSEs.' He further said that 'I attribute the need for today's action primarily to the inherent conflict and flawed business model embedded in the GSE structure, and to the ongoing housing correction.'"

"Ginnie Mae Funds Have Been Solid Performers," by John Waggoner, *USA Today*, September 7, 2010, p. 1B: "Three years after the start of the *credit crisis sparked by mortgage-backed securities*, a top-performing investment has been ... mortgage-backed securities. But only those backed by the government or packaged by Fannie Mae or Freddie Mac." [Emphasis added.] This article mentions that mortgage-backed securities backed by the U.S. government became more attractive investments when in January 2009 the United States government committed $1.2 trillion of taxpayer dollars to guarantee the value of those investor assets.

Reforming America's Housing Finance Market, A Report to Congress by the Department of the Treasury and the U.S. Department of Housing and Urban Development, February 2011, wherein Congress is being asked to wean Freddie Mac and Fannie Mae off of taxpayer support for their private business activities: "In the past, the government's financial and tax policies encouraged housing purchases and real estate investment over other sectors of our economy, and ultimately left taxpayers responsible for much of the risk incurred by a poorly supervised housing finance market," p. 2.

31. "A Short History Of The Subprime Mortgage Market Meltdown," by James R. Barth, Tong Li, Triphon Phumiwasana, and Glenn Yago, The Milken Institute, January 2008, pp. 3-4.

32. "N.M. Mortgage Delinquencies Holding Steady," by Richard Metcalf, *The Albuquerque Journal,* November 20, 2010, p. D3, reporting comments of the President of the Mortgage Bankers Association.

33. "Foreclosures," by Jim Wilson, *The New York Times,* October 21, 2010.

34. "Fewer Fall Delinquent in Paying Mortgages," by David Streitfeld, *The New York Times,* November 18, 2010.

35. Taken from comments on Wikipedia (www.wikipedia.org) under the heading "Subprime Mortgage Crisis."

36. Excerpt from *Declaration of the Summit on Financial Markets and the World Economy,* issued by the Group of 20, November 15, 2008, reported under "Subprime Mortgage Crisis," Wikipedia (www.wikipedia.org). The full text of the Declaration is available at www.g20.org.

37. *The Financial Crisis Inquiry Report,* issued by the Financial Crisis Inquiry Commission, January 2011, p. xvii, available at www.fcic.gov and at http://fcic.law.stanford.edu.

38. "Foreclosure, Subprime Mortgage Lending, and the Mortgage Electronic Registration System," by Christopher L. Peterson, *University of Cincinnati Law Review,* Vol. 78, No. 4, Summer 2010, p. 1360, cites omitted.

39. Charles Ferguson (director), *Inside Job,* produced by Representational Pictures and Sony Picture Classics, 2010.

Chapter 4

40. See, e.g., the following court cases:

    Jackson v. Mortgage Electronic Registration Systems, Inc., No. A08-397 (MN S.Ct. 2009).

    HSBC Bank v. Thompson, 2010-Ohio-4158 (OH Ct.App. 2010).

    Deutsche Bank v. McCoy, et al., No. 2010-51664 (NY S.Ct. 2010).

    Carpenter v. Longan, 83 U.S. 271, 274 (1872): "The note and mortgage are inseparable; the former as essential, the latter as an incident. An assignment of the note carries the mortgage with it, while an assignment of the latter alone is a nullity."

41. "Ginnie Mae Funds Have Been Solid Performers," by John Waggoner, *USA Today,* September 7, 2010, p. 1B: "Three years after the start of the *credit crisis sparked by mortgage-backed securities,* a top-performing investment has been ... mortgage-backed securities. But only those backed by the government or packaged by Fannie Mae or Freddie Mac." [Emphasis added.] The article mentions that mortgage-backed securities backed by the U.S. government became more attractive investments when in January 2009 the government committed $1.2 trillion to guarantee their value.

42. For more information about the Uniform Law Commission, visit its website at www.nccusl.org.

Chapter 5

43. See, e.g., the following court cases:

    Deutsche Bank v. McCoy, et al., No. 2010-51664 (NY S.Ct. 2010).

Bank of New York v. Mulligan, No. 2010-51509 (NY S.Ct. 2010).

HSBC Bank v. Yeasmin, No. 2010-50927 (NY S.Ct. 2010)

In re Moreno (Bankr.E.D. MA 2010).

In re Rickie Walker, No. 10-21656-E-11 (Bankr. E.D. CA 2010).

US Bank v. Emmanuel, et al, No. 2010-50819 (NY S.Ct. 2010).

JP Morgan Chase Bank v. George, et al., No. 2010-50786 (NY S.Ct. 2010).

Mortgage Electronic Registration Systems, Inc. v. Graham and Martinez, 229 P.3d 420 (KS Ct.App. 2010).

Flagstar Bank v. Moore, 925 N.E.2d 203, 2010-Ohio-375 (OH Ct.App. 2010).

In re Highland, No. 08-33550 (Bankr. S.D. OH 2010).

In re Matthew J. Gilpin, No. 09-10696 (Bankr. D. VT 2009).

LaSalle Bank NA v. Richards, 2009-32305 (NY S.Ct. 2009).

In re Sheridan, Case No. 08-20381-TLM (Bankr. D. ID 2009).

In re Jacobson, 402 B.R. 359 (Bankr. W.D. WA 2009).

Bellistri v. Ocwen Loan Servicing, LLC, 284 S.W. 3d 619, 623-624 (MO Ct.App. 2009).

Saxon Mortgage Services, Inc. v. Hillery, 2008 WL 5170180 (USDCt. N.D. CA 2008).

In re Kang Jin Hwang, 396 B.R. 757 (Bankr. C.D. CA 2008), amended opinion of 393 B.R. 701.

In re Vargas, 396 B.R. 511, 517 (Bankr. C.D. CA 2008).

Mortgage Electronic Registration Systems, Inc. v. Saunders, 2010 ME 79, No. Cum-09-640 (Maine 2010).

Johnson v. Melnikoff, 2008 NY Slip Op 51832 (NY S.Ct. 2008).

In re Foreclosure Cases, 521 F.Supp. 2d 650, 653 (USDCt. S.D. OH 2007).

LaSalle Bank Nat. Ass'n v. Lamy, 824 N.Y.S.2d 769, 12 Misc3d 1191(A) (NY S.Ct. 2006).

Federal National Mortgage Assoc. v. Bradbury, etc., No. BRI-RE-09-65 (ME DCt 2010).

Mortgage Electronic Registration Systems, Inc. v. Chong, et al., No. 2:09-CV-00661-KJD-LRL (USDCt. D. NV 2009).

Delaney v. OneWest Bank, et al., Civil Case No. 10-977-KI (USDCt D. OR 2010).

US Bank v. Ibanez and Wells Fargo v. Larace, No. SJC 10694 (Massachusetts 2011).

Landmark National Bank v. Kesler, Millennia Mortgage Company, MERS and Sovereign Bank, et al., 216 P.3d 158 (Kansas 2009).

Mortgage Electronic Registration Systems, Inc. v. Southwest Homes of Arkansas, 08-1299 (Arkansas 2009).

In re Thomas, No. 10-40549-MSH (Adv. Pro. No. 10-04086) (Bankr. D. MA 2011).

Norwood v. Chase Home Finance, No. A-09-CA-940-JRN (USDCt. W.D. TX 2011).

In the Matter of the Foreclosure of a Deed of Trust Executed by Adams, No. COA09-1455 (NC Ct.App. 2010).

Anderson v. Burson, 196 Md.App. 457 (MD Ct.Spec.App. 2010): Anderson manages to postpone foreclosure for more than four years, as her measure of "win."

Deutsche Bank v. Hansen, 2011-Ohio-1223 (OH Ct.App.5th 2011).

Bank of America v. Miller, 2011-Ohio-1403 (OH Ct.App.2nd 2011).

Wells Fargo Bank v. Ford, No. A-3627-06T1 (NJ SuperiorCt. 2011).

Deutsche Bank v. Francis, No. 2011-50423 (NY S.Ct. 2011).

Aurora Loan Services v. Carlsen, No. 2010AP1909 (WI Ct.App. 2011).

Pino v. Bank of New York, No. 4D10-378 (FL Ct.App.4th 2011).

Hooker v. Northwest Trustee Services, No. 10-3111-PA (USDCt. D. OR 2011).

In re Agard, No. 810-77338-reg (Bankr. E.D. NY 2011).

44. "In Foreclosure Controversy, Problems Run Deeper Than Flawed Paperwork," by Brady Dennis and Ariana Eunjung Cha Cha, *The Washington Post*, October 7, 2010.

See also, "Mortgage Lenders Set Back in Courts," by Ruth Simon, Robin Sidel, and Nick Timaraos, *The Wall Street Journal,* November 10, 2010.

45. "The Case of the Missing Mortgage," by Stephen Gandel, *Time,* November 29, 2010: "Today it takes a bank an average of 484 days, a year and four months, to evict someone who has stopped paying his or her mortgage. That's up from 251 days in early 2008."

46. See, e.g., www.thomas.loc.gov/home/gpoxmlc111/s896_enr.xml.

47. See, e.g., the following court cases:

In re Veal, BAP Nos. AZ-10-1055 & 1056-MkKiJu (Bankr.App.Panel 9thCir. 2011).

In re Agard, No. 810-77338 (Bankr. E.D. NY 2011).

In re Rickie Walker, No. 10-21656-E-11 (Bankr. E.D. CA 2010).

In re Matthew J. Gilpin, No. 09-10696 (Bankr. D. VT 2009).

In re Kang Jin Hwang, 396 B.R. 757 (Bankr. C.D. CA 2008), amended opinion of 393 B.R. 701.

In re Kemp, No. 08-18700-JHW (Bankr. D. NJ 2010).

In re Thomas, No. 10-40549-MSH (Adv. Pro. No. 10-04086) (Bankr. D. MA 2011).

In re Doble, 10-90308-MM (Bankr. S.D. CA 2011).

In re Kennedy, 09-64432-fra7 (Bankr. D. OR 2011).

In re Koontz, 09-30024HCD (Bankr. N.D. IN 2010).

In re Box, No. 10-20086 (Bankr. W.D. MO 2010).

In re Weisbank, 427 B.R. 13 (Bankr. D. AZ 2010).

In re Wilhelm, 407 B.R. 392 (Bankr. D. ID 2009).

In re Mitchell, BK-07-16226-LBR (Bankr. D. NV 2009).

Chapter 6

No notes.

Chapter 7

48. *Securities and Exchange Commission v. Goldman Sachs & Co.,* 10-CV-3229 (Jdg. Jones)(USDCt. S.D. NY 2010). See also "SEC Charges Goldman Sachs With Fraud in Structuring and Marketing of CDO Tied to Subprime Mortgages," SEC press release, found at www.sec.gov/news/press/2010/2010-59.htm.

49. See, e.g., "Will Perpetrators of Financial Crimes Ever Face Justice?," by Mary Bottari, Center for Media and Democracy and www.BanksterUSA.org, *Huffington Post,* August 25, 2010, located at www.huffingtonpost.com/mary-bottari/will-perpetrators-of-fina_b_694691.html: "Like mushrooms popping up in a damp basement, a slew of court settlements have been registered recently involving the big banks and their role in the financial crisis. An informal review of settlements over the last two years reveals about 16 multi-million dollar payouts from the big banks amounting to some $1.6 billion in fines and restitution and $13 billion in buybacks of auction-rate securities that were represented to be as safe as cash. Sounds impressive, doesn't it? But when fines are stacked up against an elite white-collar crime spree worth trillions, it is a little less impressive." Also, "But now, two years after Wall Street's fraudulent and reckless behavior collapsed the economy, costing average Americans trillions in lost wages, savings and housing wealth and throwing eight million people out of work and some six million families out of their homes, not one Wall Street banker or predatory lender is behind bars."

50. See, e.g., "Banks Hit Hurdle to Foreclosures," by Nick Timiraos, *The Wall Street Journal,* June 1, 2011.

51. See, e.g., the following sources:

    "How the Banks Put the Economy Underwater," by Yves Smith, *The New York Times,* October 30, 2010: "One problem is well known: many lenders ceased to be concerned about the quality of the loans they were creating, since if they turned bad, someone else would suffer," not the lenders.

    "Foreclosure Errors Cloud Homeownership With 'Blighted Title'" by Kathleen M. Howley, *Bloomberg,* October 1, 2010: Commenting about clouds of title to already foreclosed homes. 'Defective documentation has created millions of blighted titles that will plague the nation for the next decade,' said Richard Kessler, an attorney in Sarasota, Florida, who conducted a study that found errors in about three-fourths of court filings related to home repossessions."

"The Case of the Missing Mortgage," by Stephen Gandel, *Time,* November 29, 2010: This article discusses how some lenders may have intentionally lost or destroyed important original loan files in order to bury the sins of their predatory lending practices, and explains that evidence was mounting that documents necessary to the enforcement of real estate notes were improperly managed, making the notes and related mortgages no longer enforceable, and in huge numbers.

Hooker v. Northwest Trustee Services, No. 10-3111-PA (USDCt. D. OR 2011): "...the MERS system greatly increased the number of investors stuck holding worthless notes. ...[I]t is apparent with the benefit of hindsight that the ability of lenders to freely and anonymously transfer notes among themselves facilitated, if not created, the financial banking crisis in which our country currently finds itself. It is not only borrowers but also other lenders who rightfully are interested in who has held a particular promissory note. For example, a lender who holds a promissory note that has become worthless may have an interest in knowing the hands through which that note passed."

For more discussion about the industry's problems regarding legal enforcement of mortgage loans, see Part Four of this book, titled *Recipe for the Foreclosure Fight.*

52. "How the Banks Put the Economy Underwater," by Yves Smith, *The New York Times,* October 30, 2010. Also see "Mired in Foreclosure," by Jessica Silver-Greenberg, *The Wall Street Journal,* September 19, 2011, which comments about foreclosure cases not being resubmitted when Florida judges request additional documentation from the foreclosure machine.

53. "Errors found in 84% of SF mortgages in foreclosure," by John Wildermuth, *The San Francisco Chronicle,* February 16, 2012, p. A-1. "More than 80 percent of the residential mortgage loans that have gone into foreclosure in San Francisco contain one or more clear violations of the law, Assessor-Recorder Phil Ting said Wednesday."

54. "Southern Essex Registry of Deeds audit reveals that 75% of assignments of mortgage are invalid; Obrien says banks responsible for an epidemic of fraud. Once again urges Attorney's General to stop bank settlement talks," press release by Southern Essex Registry of Deeds, reported at http://4closurefraud.org, June 30, 2011. "Yesterday at the Annual Conference of The International Association of Clerks, Recorders, Election Officials and Treasurers (IACREOT), Register John O'Brien revealed the results of an independent audit of

his registry. The audit, which is released as a legal affidavit was performed by McDonnell Property Analytics, examined assignments of mortgage recorded in the Essex Southern District Registry of Deeds issued to and from JPMorgan Chase Bank, Wells Fargo Bank, and Bank of America during 2010. In total, 565 assignments related to 473 unique mortgages were analyzed."

55. See, e.g., the following sources:

In re Agard, No. 810-77338 (Bankr. E.D. NY 2011): Bankruptcy court holds ShellGame-MERS has no authority to assign the mortgage or the Note, and that any company claiming rights under either the Note or the mortgage as a result of an assignment from ShellGame-MERS has nothing.

Hooker v. Northwest Trustee Services, No. 10-3111-PA (USDCt. D. OR 2011): The machine's failure to comply with Oregon recording statutes resulted in finding that an attempted nonjudicial foreclosure was invalid, and without need to even address the question of who actually had a right to enforce the Note or mortgage.

"Two Faces: Demystifying The Mortgage Electronic Registration System's Land Title Theory," by Christopher L. Peterson, *William & Mary Law Review,* Vol. 53, 2011, No. 1, 2011, available at the Social Service Review Network, www.ssrn.com/abstract=1684729, and www.wmlawreview.org/issues/53/: This article argues among other things that a mortgage may be invalid when Mortgage Electronic Registration Systems, Inc., purports to be both mortgagee and agent for the mortgagee.

56. See, e.g., the following court cases:

In re Tucker, No. 10-61004 (Bankr. W.D. MO 2010).

Chase Home Fin. v. Fequiere, 119 Conn.App. 570 (Conn.App. 2010).

57. See, e.g., the following court cases:

Renkemeyer v. Mortgage Electronic Registration Systems, Inc., No. 10-2415-JWL (USDCt. D. KS 2010).

Mortgage Electronic Registration Systems, Inc. v. Saunders, 2010 ME 79, No. Cum-09-640 (Maine 2010).

Deutsche Bank v. McCoy, et al., No. 2010-51664 (NY S.Ct. 2010).

58. See, e.g., the following sources:

Mortgage Electronic Registration Systems, Inc. v. Saunders, 2010 ME 79, No. Cum-09-640 (Maine 2010): Holding assignee of mortgage holds bare legal title as personalty, the holder of the note owns equitable title. The case doesn't address whether the owner of a Note can foreclose prior to acquiring the mortgage back from the one holding bare legal title to it.

Hawkins Tree and Landscaping, Inc. v. Paul Thomas Homes, Inc., et al., No. A10-182 (MN Ct.App. 2010): The note owner always owns security interests under the mortgage but only the mortgagee of record may conduct foreclosure. This case seems to raise factual issues, e.g., whether the party identified as mortgagee is conducting the foreclosure and also whether the identified mortgagee is actually a mortgagee per Minnesota law. Many courts, having evaluated the involvement of ShellGame-MERS, have concluded, and ShellGame-MERS has admitted, that it has no beneficial interest in the note and can therefore not be a "mortgagee."

Deutsche Bank v. Traxler, 2010-Ohio-3940 (OH Ct.App. 2010): This case suggests that if the owner of the Note or its duly appointed agent transfers the mortgage but not the Note, the mortgage is made invalid and the debt then unsecured.

In re Box, No. 10-20086 (Bankr. W.D. MO 2010): This court comments that ownership of the Note typically means ownership of the mortgage, unless the Note owner or its agent transfers the mortgage, in which case the Note could become unsecured and the mortgage invalid.

Mortgage Electronic Registration Systems, Inc. v. Graham and Martinez, 229 P.3d 420 (KS Ct.App. 2010): This case suggests that transfer of the mortgage by the Note owner or its agent can legally nullify the mortgage and make the debt unsecured.

Bellistri v. Ocwen Loan Servicing, LLC, 284 S.W. 3d 619, 623-624 (MO Ct.App. 2009): The court recognized the possibility that a mortgage can be invalidated if not owned by the owner of the Note.

Saxon Mortgage Services, Inc. v. Hillery, 2008 WL 5170180 (USDCt. N.D. CA 2008): A security instrument can't exist, much less be transferred, independent from the obligation which it secures.

In re Mitchell, Case No. BK-S-07-16226-LBR (Bankr. D. NV 2009): This case mentions the possibility that a mortgage can be made invalid if not owned by the owner of the Note.

US Bank v. Ibanez and Wells Fargo v. Larace, No. SJC 10694 (Massachusetts 2011): Massachusetts is a "title theory" state so mortgage is a conveyance of title, not a mere lien. No foreclosure can occur unless the owner of the Note also owns the security. The note owner has right in equity to first obtain the security from its owner, but until that process is completed, a foreclosure is not permitted.

In re Veal, BAP Nos. AZ-10-1055 & 1056-MkKiJu (Bankr.App.Panel 9thCir. 2011): The court concluded that the only company with the right to enforce the Note pursuant to the UCC may foreclose on a mortgage.

Report on Application of the UCC to Selected Issues Relating to Mortgage Notes, Permanent Editorial Board for the Uniform Commercial Code, November 14, 2011, pp. 15-17, a copy of which was obtained at www.ali.org/index.cfm?fuseaction=projects.proj_ip&projectid=4: The PEB argues that the UCC doesn't permit a split of the note and mortgage but indicates that a particular state's law might yield a different result.

59. See, e.g., *In re Veal,* BAP Nos. AZ-10-1055 & 1056-MkKiJu (Bankr.App.Panel 9thCir. 2011).

60. See, e.g, *Hooker v. Northwest Trustee Services,* No. 10-3111-PA (USDCt. D. OR 2011): Foreclosure could not proceed because Oregon requires each and every assignment of the mortgage to be recorded in public records, which had not happened.

61. The law of Minnesota creates a fiction that the party doing a nonjudicial foreclosure actually holds the foreclosed house or the foreclosure sales proceeds in trust for whoever had an actual right to enforce the Note. See, for example, *Jackson v. Mortgage Electronic Registration Systems, Inc.*, No. A08-397 (MN S.Ct. 2009). That fiction is ripe for abuse and fraud against citizen borrowers of that state if not closely policed. It places the foreclosed borrower at risk that the foreclosure machine, whether or not ShellGame-MERS is involved, may not actually deliver the house or proceeds of a foreclosure sale to the Boss, the only person owed money under the Note. If someone other than the Boss gets paid, the borrower is still liable under the Note. If no company or person has a legal right to enforce the Note, the Minnesota legal fiction subjects the foreclosed borrower to the risk that his or her home will have been given to someone with no legal right to take it, and I doubt the foreclosure machine will voluntarily give the foreclosed home or foreclosure sale proceeds

back to the borrower without a substantial legal battle. Assertion of the core principles discussed in *Fighting the Foreclosure Machine* should, however, help a judge put the intent of the Minnesota law and fairness to the borrower in balance.

62. *In re Rickie Walker,* No. 10-21656-E-11 (Bankr. E.D. CA 2010).

63. See, e.g., *In re Agard,* No. 810-77338 (Bankr. E.D. NY 2011).

64. See, e.g., *Aguero v. Ramirez,* 70 S.W.3d 372, 47 U.C.C. Rep. Serv. 2d 1085 (Tex. App. Corpus Christi 2002).

65. UCC § 3-118. STATUTE OF LIMITATIONS.

    (a) Except as provided in subsection (e), an action to enforce the obligation of a party to pay a note payable at a definite time must be commenced within six years after the due date or dates stated in the note or, if a due date is accelerated, within six years after the accelerated due date.

66. See, e.g., *Lawrence's Anderson on the Uniform Commercial Code,* 3d Edition [Rev], by Lary Lawrence, § 3-118:14R; and, *Hawkland & Lawrence UCC Series* § 3-118:2 (Rev.Art. 3).

67. See, e.g., *Hawkland & Lawrence UCC Series* § 3-118.1 (Rev.Art. 3); and *11 Am. Jur.2d Bills and Notes § 1059.*

68. Quiet-title type lawsuits can also be used to establish the owner of real estate when there are competing interests. For example, people who have a right to possession of a house but who are not the owner of public record might use a quiet-title action to establish that their rightful possession is superior to that of a company that has obtained title to the house via a wrongful nonjudicial foreclosure. A person with the right to be in the house could therefore, if the state law and factual circumstances are just right, become the owner of record of the house by showing that the nonjudicial foreclosure was invalid. California, for example, demands that the validity of title be raised or waived during the unlawful detainer proceeding if an eviction fight takes place after the house is sold to the party conducting the related nonjudicial foreclosure. This principle was stated in *Normile v. Green Tree,* B216836 NO3 (Calf. Ct.App.2nd 2011), which looked to *Malkoskie v. Option One Mortgage Corp., 188* Cal.App.4th 968 (Calf. Ct.App.2nd 2010) and *Vella v. Hudgins,* 20 Cal.3d 251, 255 [142 Cal.Rptr. 414, 572 P.2d 28] (California 1977). This topic about tenant or possession rights following foreclosure is beyond the scope of *Fighting the Foreclosure Machine,* but I hope to revisit this issue through www.FightingTheForeclosureMachine.com.

Chapter 8

69. Too many reported court decisions result in the foreclosure machine winning, even without being required to actually show factual proof to support its allegations. That is frequently the result when the borrower does not object and doesn't simultaneously force the opponent to actually prove its claims with facts. See, e.g., *In re Denise L. Clark,* No. 6:10-bk-09430-ABB (Bankr. M.D. FL 2010), where the judge "assumed" Deutsche Bank had rights because the borrower did not object to the bank's conclusory statements.

Some judges will exercise their *sua sponte* authority and rule against your opponent even if you don't raise an objection or if your protest is unclear or ineffective. Virtually all federal and state judges with jurisdictional authority to decide foreclosure cases have that kind of authority, but most will let you sink or swim based on what you do. Your results will be more predictable if you prepare a good fight and help your judge understand why you should win.

The following are examples of cases decided against the foreclosing party by a judge that raised his or her own challenges:

In re Box, No. 10-20086 (Bankr. W.D. MO 2010).

In re Matthew J. Gilpin, No. 09-10696 (Bankr. D. VT 2009).

Mortgage Electronic Registration Systems, Inc. v. Azize, 965 So.2d 151 (FL Ct.App. 2007).

JP Morgan v. Pocopanni, 16-2008-CA-3989 (FL Cir.Ct. 2010).

Bank of America v. Maharaj, No. 2010-51665 (NY S.Ct. 2010).

Deutsche Bank v. McCoy, et al., No. 2010-51664 (NY S.Ct. 2010).

LaSalle Bank v. Bouloute, et al., No. 2010-51513 (NY S.Ct. 2010).

IndyMac Bank v. Garcia, et al., No. 2010-51127 (NY S.Ct. 2010).

HSBC Bank v. Yeasmin, No. 2010-50927 (NY S.Ct. 2010).

US Bank v. Emmanuel, et al, No. 2010-50819 (NY S.Ct. 2010).

Wells Fargo Bank v. Hunte, et al., No. 2010-50637 (NY S.Ct. 2010).

LaSalle Bank NA v. Richards, 2009-32305 (NY S.Ct. 2009).

Mortgage Electronic Registration Systems, Inc. v. Saunders, 2010 ME 79, No. Cum-09-640 (Maine 2010).

US Bank v. Ibanez and Wells Fargo v. Larace, No. SJC 10694 (Massachusetts 2011).

Chapter 9

70. See, e.g., the following court cases:

Bank of America v. Maharaj, No. 2010-51665 (NY S.Ct. 2010): The judge noticed conflicting and inadequate evidence submissions from party wanting to foreclose against non-appearing borrower.

Deutsche Bank v. McCoy, et al., No. 2010-51664 (NY S.Ct. 2010): The judge did not believe Deutsche's evidence had merit and suspected it was contrived.

Ruscalleda v. HSBC Bank, No. 3D09-997 (FL Ct.App. 2010): HSBC and another ShellGame-MERS player filed two separate foreclosures, each suing the same borrower and each claiming the right to take the property.

HSBC Bank v. Thompson, 2010-Ohio-4158 (OH Ct.App. 2010): HSBC evidence was suspect and did not prove what it alleged, and the judge raised concerns about its veracity and a "possible incestuous relationship" between HSBC, ShellGame-MERS and others.

LPP Mortgage v. Sabine Properties, et al., No. 2010-32367 (NY S.Ct. 2010): The judge found that the ShellGame-MERS affiliate LPP Mortgage did not prove its claims that it had any right to payments under the Note or to foreclose.

US Bank v. Richards, 2010-Ohio-3981 (OH Ct.App. 2010): The judge found that US Bank, when put to the test, did not have evidence to support its claims.

Bank of New York v. Mulligan, No. 2010-51509 (NY S.Ct. 2010): Bank of New York, contrary to its claims, did not own the note and mortgage, and put forward alleged evidence that was suspicious upon close scrutiny.

IndyMac Bank v. Garcia, et al., No. 2010-51127 (NY S.Ct. 2010): The bank tried to foreclose using claims that could not be proven and evidence that lacked credibility.

In re Box, No. 10-20086 (Bankr. W.D. MO 2010): In denying BAC's request, the court stated, "With regard to the purported assignment of the loan documents to [BAC Home Loans Servicing LP f/k/a Countrywide Home Loans Servicing], the evidence in the case at bar is both scant and suspect" and that the affidavit testimony BAC tried to use was self-serving and not believable.

HSBC Bank v. Yeasmin, No. 2010-50927 (NY S.Ct. 2010): In denying HSBC's foreclosure because it had no rights under the Note and no right to foreclose, the decision even injected that HSBC's alleged facts "are so incredible, outrageous, ludicrous and disingenuous that they should have been authored by the late Rod Serling, creator of the famous science-fiction television series, *The Twilight Zone.*"

In re Rickie Walker, No. 10-21656-E-11 (Bankr. E.D. CA 2010): The court found that, contrary to their claims, neither Citibank nor BAC owned any interest in the Note or the Deed of Trust.

US Bank v. Emmanuel, et al, No. 2010-50819 (NY S.Ct. 2010): The court noted that US Bank, contrary to its claims, did not have a right to foreclose.

JP Morgan Chase Bank v. George, et al., No. 2010-50786 (NY S.Ct. 2010): Chase had no evidence to support its claim that it had a right to foreclose.

Mortgage Electronic Registration Systems, Inc. v. Graham and Martinez, 229 P.3d 420 (KS Ct.App. 2010): The judgment was reversed on appeal because ShellGame-MERS had no evidence to support its claims that it had a right to foreclose.

Flagstar Bank v. Moore, 925 N.E.2d 203, 2010-Ohio-375 (OH Ct.App. 2010): Under appellate scrutiny, claims used by the bank to win lower court judgment lacked merit and were highly questionable as to truth or accuracy.

LaSalle Bank NA v. Richards, 2009-32305 (NY S.Ct. 2009): The bank's alleged facts did not prove it had the right to foreclose.

US Bank v. Hoglund, 2009-32166 (NY S.Ct. 2009): The bank could not prove it had the right to foreclose or that the testimony it put on was true or accurate.

In re Wilhelm, 407 B.R. 392 (Bankr. D. ID 2009): Five cases were consolidated for a single ruling here. The companies trying to take the properties of the many debtors could not prove any right to enforce the obligations of the related Notes.

Mortgage Electronic Registration Systems, Inc., v. Young, 2009-TX-0608.667 (TX Ct.App. 2009): ShellGame-MERS, contrary to what it claimed in the lawsuit, could not prove that it had any right to foreclose.

Mortgage Electronic Registration Systems, Inc. v. Southwest Homes of Arkansas, 08-1299 (Arkansas 2009): The court looked at the substance of the claims of ShellGame-MERS and concluded that it had no rights to foreclose.

Landmark National Bank v. Kesler, Millennia Mortgage Company, MERS and Sovereign Bank, et al., 216 P.3d 158 (Kansas 2009): The court found that, contrary to claims by ShellGame-MERS and an affiliate, that neither had any rights in the note or mortgage.

In re Sheridan, Case No. 08-20381-TLM (Bankr. D. ID 2009): When challenged, ShellGame-MERS could put on no proof that it or any company it knew had any right to foreclose the debtor's property.

In re Jacobson, 402 B.R. 359 (Bankr. W.D. WA 2009): The company claiming the right to foreclose lost because, under close scrutiny, it could produce no genuine evidence that it had any rights against the debtor's property.

Bellistri v. Ocwen Loan Servicing, LLC, 284 S.W.3d 619, 623-624 (MO Ct.App. 2009): The company claiming rights to foreclose could produce no evidence that it had such rights or that it represented any person or company with such rights.

Saxon Mortgage Services, Inc. v. Hillery, 2008 WL 5170180 (USDCt. N.D. CA 2008): The company asserting right to foreclose argued that it got its rights from ShellGame-MERS but could not produce evidence that ShellGame-MERs ever had such rights to give or that it as assignee from ShellGame-MERS had any such rights.

In re Kang Jin Hwang, 396 B.R. 757 (Bankr. C.D. CA 2008), amended opinion of 393 B.R. 701: The court found that written testimony submitted by ShellGame-MERS, in its attempt to take the debtor's home, was incompetent and inadmissible.

In re Vargas, 396 B.R. 511, 517 (Bankr. C.D. CA 2008): The court found that ShellGame-MERS intentionally introduced false evidence.

In re Mitchell, Case No. BK-S-07-16226-LBR (Bankr. D. NV 2009): The court found that, contrary to the asserted claims, ShellGame-MERS produced no genuine evidence that it or any company claiming rights through it had any right to foreclose, and that affidavits it submitted were incompetent and inadmissible.

Mortgage Electronic Registration Systems, Inc. v. Azize, 965 So.2d 151 (FL Ct.App. 2007): Though ShellGame-MERS alleged it owned the note and mortgage with a right to foreclose, the court found that no genuine evidence to support same had been put forward by ShellGame-MERS.

LaSalle Bank Nat. Ass'n v. Lamy, 824 N.Y.S.2d 769, 12 Misc3d 1191(A) (NY S.Ct. 2006): The court stated, "The record adduced on the instant application clearly establishes that the plaintiff's claims of ownership to the mortgage for which foreclosure is herein demanded are without merit."

Federal National Mortgage Assoc. v. Bradbury, etc., No. BRI-RE-09-65 (ME DCt 2010): The court found that both the attorney and its client had filed false claims and affidavits, and that foreclosure was not proper.

Mortgage Electronic Registration Systems, Inc. v. Chong, et al., No. 2:09-CV-00661-KJD-LRL (USDCt. D. NV 2009): The court consolidated 18 similar foreclosure-driven cases and, in each, found that ShellGame-MERS had no right to make claims against the debtors or to foreclose.

JP Morgan v. Pocopanni, 16-2008-CA-3989 (FL Cir.Ct. 2010): The court found that, contrary to the claims made, JP Morgan Chase "is not, nor has ever been, the owner and holder of the Defendant's note and mortgage." The Court found JP Morgan had engaged in fraud.

In re Kemp, No. 08-18700-JHW (Bankr. D. NJ 2010): The court found Bank of New York's claims and evidence to be unbelievable.

OneWest Bank v. Drayton, 2010-20429 (NY S.Ct. 2010): The court noted OneWest Bank had no meaningful evidence upon which to assert claims against the debtor or to foreclose, and that the bank's lead affidavit contained false information.

US Bank v. Ibanez and Wells Fargo v. Larace, No. SJC 10694 (Massachusetts 2011): The court, upon looking at nonjudicial foreclosures conducted by US Bank and Wells Fargo, concluded that neither bank had any right to foreclose.

71. See, e.g., *In re Agard,* No. 810-77338 (Bankr. E.D. NY 2011).

72. "How the Banks Put the Economy Underwater," by Yves Smith, *The New York Times,* October 30, 2010. This article summarizes the industry's failures to properly address technical requirements under laws respecting real estate and the Uniform Commercial Code. "If this were a mere procedural problem, the banks could foreclose once they marshaled their evidence. But banks who are challenged in

many cases do not resume these foreclosures, indicating that their lapses go well beyond minor paperwork."

73. Theoretically, no person or company may now have the right to enforce the Note. The one company that had the legal right to receive payments under the Note may have gone out of existence years ago. The industry may have so corrupted the legal chain of rights required to establish enforcement rights under the UCC that the Note is no longer enforceable by anyone. The industry may even have chosen to intentionally not maintain a proper UCC chain of ownership in an effort to help bury predatory lending practices that it viewed as a bigger liability than the risk of foreclosure difficulty against a person who, if facing foreclosure, would then be financially strapped and not likely a very strong legal adversary.

Chapter 10

No notes.

Chapter 11

74. Boss status can also change when the Note is used as collateral to secure an obligation, for example, when the Boss of the Note borrows money and pledges that Note as collateral as added assurance that the Boss's lender will get repaid. If that Boss doesn't pay its debt on time, the Note may be lost to the Boss's lender, who then might become the new Boss per the UCC. The UCC also defines Boss status regarding a Note that may have changed hands as a result of a failed loan transaction. This successor Boss status is obtained, as you may have already guessed, only if the lender can prove that the Note it got as collateral was actually obtained from the Boss of that Note at that time.

75. A Boss, just like any other person, may appoint someone else to do things on its behalf. The person appointed could be an individual or a company, and could be referred to as a servant, agent, servicer, or representative. A body of law often referred to as the law of agency or principal and agent law has developed to address the rights and duties between the principal and the servant, and also the rights and duties of others who deal with a person that is or claims to be an agent for the principal. The section titled "The Boss's Representative or Agent" that appears in this chapter briefly addresses Boss-servant issues related to foreclosure lawsuits.

76. See, e.g., the following court cases:

Ruscalleda v. HSBC Bank, No. 3D09-997 (FL Ct.App. 2010): Two companies in separate suits against the same borrowers seek foreclosure and payment, each company alleging ownership of the same Note. Evidence shows that the two companies coordinated foreclosure efforts to win litigation advantage, even though neither may have actually been the Boss of the Note.

Union Bank v. North Carolina Furniture Express, 2010-Ohio-4176 (OH Ct.App. 2010): This case involves two lawsuits involving multiple claimants alleging rights to and through the same Note.

5-Star Management, Inc. v. Rogers, 940 F.Supp. 512 (USDCt. E.D. NY 1996): "The consequences of a separation of a mortgage from the note is amply illustrated in the case at bar wherein the pendency of two separate actions in respect of the same underlying obligation threatens [borrower] with double liability ..."

Johnson v. Melnikoff, 2008 NY Slip Op 51832 (NY S.Ct. 2008): Facts show multiple parties claiming Boss status regarding the same Note.

77. See, e.g., *Underwater Home*, by Brent White, 2010. Chapter 1, "The Moral Dimensions," is especially instructive about the unfair moral standard the industry tries to impose on borrowers targeted for foreclosure.

78. See, e.g., foreclosure cases addressing UCC requirements related to Notes (i.e., negotiable instruments per UCC § 3-104):

In re Box, No. 10-20086 (Bankr. W.D. MO 2010).

UM Capital v. Ozeran, No. B212779 (CA Ct.App. 2010).

In re Matthew J. Gilpin, No. 09-10696 (Bankr. D. VT 2009).

In re Wilhelm, 407 B.R. 392 (Bankr. D. ID 2009).

LaSalle Bank Nat. Ass'n v. Lamy, 824 N.Y.S.2d 769, 12 Misc3d 1191(A) (NY S.Ct. 2006).

In re Kemp, No. 08-18700-JHW (Bankr. D. NJ 2010).

Adams v. Madison Realty & Development, Inc., 853 F.2d 163 (3rd Cir. 1988).

Mortgage Electronic Registration Systems, Inc. v. Saunders, 2010 ME 79, No. Cum-09-640 (Maine 2010).

Chase Home Fin. v. Fequiere, 119 Conn.App. 570 (Conn.App. 2010).

Bank of New York v. Raftogianis, No. F-7356-09 (NJ SuperiorCt. 2010).

Aurora Loan Services v. Carlsen, No. 2010AP1909 (WI Ct.App. 2011).

HSBC Bank v. Thompson, 2010-Ohio-4158 (OH Ct.App. 2010).

79. See, e.g., *Bank of New York v. Raftogianis,* No. F-7356-09 (NJ SuperiorCt. 2010): "Negotiable instruments, which include negotiable notes, are governed by Article 3 of the Uniform Commercial Code (hereafter, the UCC), codified in this state as N.J.S.A. 12A:3-101, et seq. Checks, drafts and certificates of deposit are other forms of negotiable instruments which are subject to the UCC. There are specific provisions of the UCC dealing with just who may enforce an instrument. One's ability to enforce an instrument will depend on one's status, which in turn depends on what interests have been acquired and just how those were acquired."

80. See, e.g., the following court cases:

In re Kemp, No. 08-18700-JHW (Bankr. D. NJ 2010): "From the maker's standpoint, therefore, it becomes essential to establish that the person who demands payment of a negotiable note, or to whom payment is made, is the duly qualified holder. Otherwise, the obligor is exposed to the risk of double payment, or at least to the expense of litigation incurred to prevent duplicative satisfaction of the instrument."

Wells Fargo Bank v. Sessley, 2010-Ohio-2902 (OH Ct.App. 2010): The court noted "underlying concern about multiple judgments on the same debt."

In re Kang Jin Hwang, 396 B.R. 757 (Bankr. C.D. CA 2008): The court weighed whether failure to join another party to the suit might leave the borrower subject to a substantial risk of incurring multiple obligations under the same Note.

5-Star Management, Inc. v. Rogers, 940 F.Supp. 512 (USDCt. E.D. NY 1996): The court noted a policy to "protect the maker of the note, who also issues a mortgage, from being exposed to liability twice in respect of the same underlying debt."

Adams v. Madison Realty & Development, Inc., 853 F.2d 163 (3rd Cir. 1988): The court, in addressing the UCC requirement of "indorsement" when the Note is sold or transferred, mentions the importance of strict compliance with the UCC because otherwise it would be "unreasonable to impose upon the indorsee the risk that the present holder or a prior holder had negotiated the instrument to someone not in the apparent chain of title by virtue of a separate document." That is, the Court is noting that the Boss needs to be clearly identified lest there be multiple claimants to Boss status, thus meaning the borrower would also be exposed to multiple enforcement claims by more than just a true Boss of the Note.

81. See, e.g., www.law.cornell.edu/ucc, which provides a click-on link at the beginning of each article of the UCC leading to a state-by-state service showing those parts of the UCC "as enacted by a particular state and any proposed revisions."

Also see the volume titled *Local Code Variations*, of either *Lawrence's Anderson on the Uniform Commercial Code, 3d Edition* or *Hawkland & Lawrence UCC Series.*

82. See, also, *Hawkland & Lawrence UCC Series* § 3-203:9 (Rev. Art 3), which states that the intended concept is to protect a borrower from claims under a single Note by multiple claimants.

83. UCC § 3-309. ENFORCEMENT OF LOST, DESTROYED, OR STOLEN INSTRUMENT.

(a) A person not in possession of an instrument is entitled to enforce the instrument if:

(1) the person seeking to enforce the instrument

(A) was entitled to enforce the instrument when loss of possession occurred, or

(B) has directly or indirectly acquired ownership of the instrument from a person who was entitled to enforce the instrument when loss of possession occurred;

(2) the loss of possession was not the result of a transfer by the person or a lawful seizure; and

(3) the person cannot reasonably obtain possession of the instrument because the instrument was destroyed, its whereabouts cannot be determined, or it is in the wrongful possession of an unknown person or a person that cannot be found or is not amenable to service of process.

(b) A person seeking enforcement of an instrument under subsection (a) must prove the terms of the instrument and the person's right to enforce the instrument. If that proof is made, Section 3-308 applies to the case as if the person seeking enforcement had produced the instrument. The court may not enter judgment in favor of the person seeking enforcement unless it finds that the person required to pay the instrument is adequately protected against loss that might occur by reason of a claim by another person to enforce the instrument. Adequate protection may be provided by any reasonable means.

84. UCC § 3-501. PRESENTMENT.

(a) "Presentment" *means a demand made by or on behalf of a person entitled to enforce an instrument (i) to pay the instrument made to the drawee or a party obliged to pay the instrument* or, in the case of a note or accepted draft payable at a bank, to the bank, or (ii) to accept a draft made to the drawee. [Emphasis added.]

(b) The following rules are subject to Article 4, agreement of the parties, and clearing-house rules and the like:

    (1) Presentment may be made at the place of payment of the instrument and must be made at the place of payment if the instrument is payable at a bank in the United States; may be made by any commercially reasonable means, including an oral, written, or electronic communication; is effective when the demand for payment or acceptance is received by the person to whom presentment is made; and is effective if made to any one of two or more makers, acceptors, drawees, or other payors.

    (2) Upon demand of the person to whom presentment is made, the person making presentment must (i) exhibit the instrument, (ii) give reasonable identification and, if presentment is made on behalf of another person, reasonable evidence of authority to do so, and (iii) sign a receipt on the instrument for any payment made or surrender the instrument if full payment is made.

    (3) Without dishonoring the instrument, the party to whom presentment is made may (i) return the instrument for lack of a necessary indorsement, or (ii) refuse payment or acceptance for failure of the presentment to comply with the terms of the instrument, an agreement of the parties, or other applicable law or rule.

    (4) The party to whom presentment is made may treat presentment as occurring on the next business day after the

day of presentment if the party to whom presentment is made has established a cut-off hour not earlier than 2 p.m. for the receipt and processing of instruments presented for payment or acceptance and presentment is made after the cut-off hour.

85. *Hawkland & Lawrence UCC Series* § 3-501:12R.

86. "In law, standing or *locus standi* is the term for the ability of a party to demonstrate to the court sufficient connection to and harm from the law or action challenged to support that party's participation in the case." *Standing (law)*, www.wikipedia.org. In the foreclosure setting, the plaintiff filing the lawsuit must in general have a genuine economic interest in the Note and the right to assert or enforce any alleged default.

87. "In law, the real party in interest is the one who actually possesses the substantive right being asserted and has a legal right to enforce the claim under applicable substantive law. Additionally, the "real party in interest" must sue in his own name. ... The reason for the concept of the 'real party in interest' is to protect the basic principle of separation of powers, by preventing people from randomly suing on behalf of other persons or things they have no connection to." *Real Party in Interest (law)*, www.wikipedia.org.

See also, e.g., *HSBC Bank v. Thompson,* 2010-Ohio-4158 (OH Ct.App. 2010): "The purpose behind the real party in interest rule is to enable the defendant to avail himself of evidence and defenses that the defendant has against the real party in interest, and to assure him finality of the judgment, and that he will be protected against another suit brought by the real party at interest on the same matter. *Celanese Corp. of America v. John Clark Industries,* 214 F.2d 551, 556, *(5 Cir.*1954)."

88. Of importance to the borrower having to litigate his or her rights in court is the concept of compulsory or necessary joinder of parties to that lawsuit. The Federal Rules of Civil Procedure contain Rule 19, *Required Joinder of Parties,* and state courts typically have similar, if not identical, judicial guidelines for determining when another person should be joined and made a party to the lawsuit. In a foreclosure setting, if your opponent claims to be the Boss but cannot prove that in accordance with the UCC, the case should end in your favor. If, however, your opponent either initially or later in the case alleges to represent the Boss, your opponent must be able to identify the company alleged to have that status and your response should be to seek compulsory joinder of that alleged Boss.

Joinder of that alleged Boss is the only way to obtain complete and final adjudication of your rights and defenses. Without such joinder you will not be able to learn via formal discovery directed at the alleged Boss, whether the alleged Boss can actually prove its status per the UCC, rather than being limited to the information available from the middleman, that is, the alleged servant. If, of course, you can win the lawsuit without adding an additional party, that would be a victory even if your opponent is unable or unwilling to disclose the Boss during the case.

89. "Finality, in law, is the concept that certain disputes must achieve a resolution from which no further appeal may be taken, and from which no collateral proceedings may be permitted to disturb that resolution. For example, in some jurisdictions, a person convicted of a crime may not sue their defense attorney for incompetence or legal malpractice if the civil lawsuit would call into question the finality of the criminal conviction. Finality is considered to be important because, absent this there would be no certainty as to the meaning of the law, or the outcome of any legal process." *Finality (law),* www.wikipedia.org.

90. See, e.g., the following sources:

Deutsche Bank v. Sexton, 2010-Ohio-4802 (OH Ct.App. 2010): "... Every action shall be prosecuted in the name of the real party in interest"; a real party in interest is one who can "discharge the claim upon which the suit is brought... [or] is the party who, by substantive law, possesses the right to be enforced"; "In a foreclosure action, the real party in interest is the entity that is the current holder of the note and mortgage"; "The purpose behind the real party in interest rule is ... to enable the defendant to avail himself of evidence and defenses that the defendant has against the real party in interest, and to assure him finality of the judgment, and that he will be protected against another suit brought by the real party at interest on the same matter."

Landmark National Bank v. Kesler, Millennia Mortgage Company, MERS and Sovereign Bank, et al., 216 P.3d 158 (Kansas 2009): "Due process provides any interested party with the elementary and fundamental right to notice of the pendency of an action and the opportunity to present its objections in any proceeding that is to be accorded finality."

In re Kang Jin Hwang, 396 B.R. 757 (Bankr. C.D. CA 2008), amended opinion of 393 B.R. 701: The court notes that the "real party in interest requirement" of Rule 17 of the Federal Rules of Civil

Procedure must be interpreted together with Rule 19. "Joinder of a person under Rule 19 is required whenever nonjoinder would produce one of the following effects: (a) nonjoinder prevents complete relief from being accorded among those who are parties to the action; (b) the absentee claims an interest relating to the subject matter of the action and is so situated that disposing of the matter in that person's absence may (i) as a practical matter impair or impede that person's ability to protect the interest, or (ii) leave an existing party subject to a substantial risk of incurring double, multiple or otherwise inconsistent obligations because of that party's interest ... the potential risk to the debtor should it be required to pay the wrong party. ... If a person who is required to be joined if feasible cannot be joined, the court must determine whether, in equity and good conscience, the action should proceed among the existing parties or should be dismissed. The factors for the court to consider include: (1) the extent to which a judgment rendered in the person's absence might prejudice that person or the existing parties."

Wells Fargo Bank v. Sessley, 2010-Ohio-2902 (OH Ct.App. 2010): "Ensuring that the real party in interest makes absent 'the underlying concern about multiple judgments on the same debt.'"

"Two Faces: Demystifying The Mortgage Electronic Registration System's Land Title Theory," by Christopher L. Peterson, *William & Mary Law Review,* Vol. 53, 2011, No. 1, 2011, available at the Social Service Review Network,and www.wmlawreview.org/issues/53: "... [A]llowing the creation of a mortgage separate from the note will expose mortgagors to a constant threat of double liability since the holder of the promissory note and a different owner of the mortgage may both show up at different times demanding payment."

5-Star Management, Inc. v. Rogers, 940 F.Supp. 512, 520 (USDCt. E.D. NY 1996): "To allow the assignee of a security interest to enforce the security agreement would expose the obligor to a double liability, since a holder in due course of the promissory note clearly is entitled to recover from the obligor."

Bank of New York v. Raftogianis, No. F-7356-09 (NJ SuperiorCt. 2010): The jurisdiction or standing issues here involved whether plaintiff could establish its right to enforce the obligation evidenced by the note and whether it must establish that it held that right at the time the complaint was filed.

HSBC Bank v. Thompson, 2010-Ohio-4158 (OH Ct.App. 2010): The case was decided against Bank of New York for its lack of standing which depended upon "whether plaintiff could establish its right to enforce the obligation evidenced by the [N]ote. ..."

91. See, e.g., *Wells Fargo Bank v. Ford*, No. A-3627-06T1 (NJ SuperiorCt. 2011): "As a general proposition, a party seeking to foreclose a mortgage must own or control the underlying debt."

Regardless of the state law applicable in your case, the concept is uncomplicated. The mortgage is nothing more than collateral helping to ensure payment of the Note obligation to the Boss of the Note. Foreclosure of the mortgage is for the benefit of the Boss of the Note (not for anyone else). Foreclosure typically cannot be commenced without the Boss declaring a default under the Note, which triggers the right to foreclose pursuant to the mortgage. The foreclosure process is tied directly to the rights of the Boss. If your state's statute does not say that in so many words, there will be case law or legislative history that can be used, in addition to the text of the Note and mortgage, to help the judge understand that a mortgage does not stand alone and separate from the enforcement rights of the Note. Whoever is attempting to foreclose the mortgage had better be the Boss or the Boss's servant. If not, the Boss's rights and yours as the maker of the Note are both being violated. Your opponent has to prove its right to enforce the payment obligation, or else it has no right to enforce the Note and no right to foreclose the collateral for the Note.

92. *In the Matter of Foreclosure of a Deed of Trust Executed by Woodard*, 185 N.C.App. 159 (NC Ct.App. 2007): "[T]he payor of a [N]ote exposes himself or herself to double liability if he or she makes payment to someone other than the holder of the instrument, unless the other person to whom payment is made is an agent of the owner of the [N]ote."

93. UCC § 3-602. PAYMENT.

(a) Subject to subsection (b), an instrument is paid to the extent payment is made (i) by or on behalf of a party obliged to pay the instrument, and (ii) to a person entitled to enforce the instrument. To the extent of the payment, the obligation of the party obliged to pay the instrument is discharged even though payment is made with knowledge of a claim to the instrument under Section 3-306 by another person.

(b) Subject to subsection (e) a note is paid to the extent payment is made by or on behalf of a party obliged to pay the note to a person that formerly was entitled to enforce the note only if at the time of the payment the party obliged to pay has not received adequate notification that the note has been transferred and that payment is to be made to the transferee. A notification is adequate only if it is signed by the transferor or the transferee; reasonably identifies the transferred note; and provides an address at which payments subsequently can be made. Upon request, a transferee shall seasonably furnish reasonable proof that the note has been transferred. Unless the transferee complies with the request, a payment to the person that formerly was entitled to enforce the note is effective for purposes of subsection (c) even if the party obliged to pay the note has received a notification under this paragraph.

(c) Subject to subsection (e), to the extent of a payment under subsections (a) and (b), the obligation of the party obliged to pay the instrument is discharged even though payment is made with knowledge of a claim to the instrument under Section 3-306 by another person.

(d) Subject to subsection (e), a transferee, or any party that has acquired rights in the instrument directly or indirectly from a transferee, including any such party that has rights as a holder in due course, is deemed to have notice of any payment that is made under subsection (b) after the date that the note is transferred to the transferee but before the party obliged to pay the note receives adequate notification of the transfer.

(e) The obligation of a party to pay the instrument is not discharged under subsections (a) through (d) if:

(1) a claim to the instrument under Section 3-306 is enforceable against the party receiving payment and (i) payment is made with knowledge by the payor that payment is prohibited by injunction or similar process of a court of competent jurisdiction, or (ii) in the case of an instrument other than a cashier's check, teller's check, or certified check, the party making payment accepted, from the person having a claim to the instrument, indemnity against loss resulting from refusal to pay the person entitled to enforce the instrument; or

(2) the person making payment knows that the instrument is a stolen instrument and pays a person it knows is in wrongful possession of the instrument.

(f) As used in this section, "signed," with respect to a record that is not a writing, includes the attachment to or logical association with the record of an electronic symbol, sound, or process to or with the record with the present intent to adopt or accept the record.

94. *In the Matter of John T. Kemp*, No. 08-18700-JHW, Adversary No. 08-2448 (Bankr. D. N.J. 2010): "From the maker's standpoint, therefore, it becomes essential to establish that the person who demands payment of a negotiable note, or to whom payment is made, is the duly qualified holder. Otherwise, the obligor is exposed to the risk of double payment, or at least to the expense of litigation incurred to prevent duplicative satisfaction of the instrument. These risks provide makers with a recognizable interest in demanding proof of the chain of title. Consequently, plaintiffs here, as makers of the notes, may properly press defendant to establish its holder status."

95. Application of the UCC is crucial to the determination of the "person entitled to enforce" the Note. See, e.g., *Report on Application of the UCC to Selected Issues Relating to Mortgage Notes,* Permanent Editorial Board for the Uniform Commercial Code, November 14, 2011, pp. 2-4, available at www.ali.org/index.cfm?fuseaction=projects.proj_ip&projectid=4.

96. See, e.g., the following court cases:

Deutsche Bank v. Traxler, 2010-Ohio-3940 (OH Ct.App. 2010): The bank did not prove it was Boss, but the borrower lost on appeal for not having raised questions about the bank's status during the trial.

JPMorgan Chase Bank v. Brian Harp, No. Han-10-252, 2011 ME 5 (Maine 2011): The borrower loses for not having raised issues about the bank's relationship to Boss during trial, even though the evidence at trial did not show that the bank was the Boss or a representative of the Boss.

97. See, e.g., the following court cases:

In re Kang Jin Hwang, 396 B.R. 757 (Bankr. C.D. CA 2008): The initial foreclosure attacker later admitted that it did not in fact have any rights under the Note and did not know the Boss of the Note.

Diversified Mortgage, Inc, v. MERSCORP, Inc and Mortgage Electronic Registration Systems, Inc., Case No.: 8:09-cv-2497-T-33EAJ (USDCt. M.D. FL 2010): This litigation involves a disagreement regarding the identity of the Boss for 65-135 Notes.

In re Mitchell, Case No. BK-S-07-16226-LBR (Bankr. D. NV 2009): This decision consolidated and addressed about 27 different suits against various borrowers. None of the companies trying to foreclose on the properties of the borrowers were able to prove the right to enforce the related Notes.

In re Foreclosure Cases, 521 F.Supp. 2d 650, 653 (USDCt. S.D. OH 2007): Consolidation of seven cases in which none of the companies alleging to be the Boss of the respective Notes could prove Boss status.

Wells Fargo Bank v. Sessley, 2010-Ohio-2902 (OH Ct.App. 2010): The company that started the foreclosure fight was unable to prove it was the Boss as it alleged, and another company claiming that status then appeared in the case. The court noted "the underlying concern about multiple judgments on the same debt."

Mortgage Electronic Registration Systems, Inc. v. Southwest Homes of Arkansas, 08-1299 (Arkansas 2009): ShellGame-MERS was held to not be Boss of the Note, contrary to allegations filed with the court. The Boss was not identified during that case. The court looked at the substance of the claims made by ShellGame-MERS and concluded it had no rights to foreclose.

Many reported cases demonstrate false and unbelievable claims being used by the foreclosure machine. Sometimes it claims ownership of a Note or mortgage but cannot prove that when put to the test; or it uses affidavits provided under oath that are false or highly suspicious, or it changes its claims when challenged and leaves open the question of whether it is cooperating with the new party claiming foreclosure rights, especially when neither puts forward verifiable evidence of legal rights. See, e.g., the following court cases:

Bank of America v. Maharaj, No. 2010-51665 (NY S.Ct. 2010): The judge noticed conflicting and inadequate evidence submissions from party wanting to foreclose against non-appearing borrower.

Deutsche Bank v. McCoy, et al., No. 2010-51664 (NY S.Ct. 2010): The judge did not believe Deutsche's evidence had merit and suspected it was contrived.

Ruscalleda v. HSBC Bank, No. 3D09-997 (FL Ct.App. 2010): HSBC and another ShellGame-MERS player filed two separate foreclosures, each suing the same borrower and each claiming the right to take the property.

HSBC Bank v. Thompson, 2010-Ohio-4158 (OH Ct.App. 2010): HSBC evidence was suspect and did not prove what it alleged. The judge raised concerns about its veracity and a "possible incestuous relationship" between HSBC, ShellGame-MERS and others.

LPP Mortgage v. Sabine Properties, et al., No. 2010-32367 (NY S.Ct. 2010): The judge found that the ShellGame-MERS affiliate LPP Mortgage did not prove its claims that it had any right to payments under the Note or to foreclose.

US Bank v. Richards, 2010-Ohio-3981 (OH Ct.App. 2010): The judge found that US Bank, when put to the test, did not have evidence to support its claims.

Bank of New York v. Mulligan, No. 2010-51509 (NY S.Ct. 2010): Bank of New York, contrary to its claims, did not own the note and mortgage, and put forward alleged evidence that was suspicious upon close scrutiny.

IndyMac Bank v. Garcia, et al., No. 2010-51127 (NY S.Ct. 2010): The bank tried to foreclose using claims that could not be proven and evidence that lacked credibility.

In re Box, No. 10-20086 (Bankr. W.D. MO 2010): In denying BAC's request, the court stated: "With regard to the purported assignment of the loan documents to [BAC Home Loans Servicing LP f/k/a Countrywide Home Loans Servicing], the evidence in the case at bar is both scant and suspect," and said that the affidavit testimony BAC tried to use was self-serving and not believable.

HSBC Bank v. Yeasmin, No. 2010-50927 (NY S.Ct. 2010): In denying HSBC's foreclosure because it had no rights under the Note and no right to foreclose, the decision even injected that HSBC's alleged facts "are so incredible, outrageous, ludicrous and disingenuous that they should have been authored by the late Rod Serling, creator of the famous science-fiction television series, *The Twilight Zone.*"

In re Rickie Walker, No. 10-21656-E-11 (Bankr. E.D. CA 2010): The court found that, contrary to their claims, neither Citibank or BAC owned any interest in the respective Notes or Deeds of Trust.

US Bank v. Emmanuel, et al, No. 2010-50819 (NY S.Ct. 2010): The court noted that US Bank, contrary to its claims, did not have a right to foreclose.

JP Morgan Chase Bank v. George, et al., No. 2010-50786 (NY S.Ct. 2010): Chase had no evidence to support its claim that it had a right to foreclose.

Mortgage Electronic Registration Systems, Inc. v. Graham and Martinez, 229 P.3d 420 (KS Ct.App. 2010): The judgment was reversed on appeal because ShellGame-MERS had no evidence to support its claims that it had a right to foreclose.

Flagstar Bank v. Moore, 925 N.E.2d 203, 2010-Ohio-375 (OH Ct.App. 2010): Claims used by bank to win lower court judgment, under appellate scrutiny, lacked merit and were highly questionable as to truth or accuracy.

LaSalle Bank NA v. Richards, 2009-32305 (NY S.Ct. 2009): The bank's alleged facts did not prove it had the right to foreclose.

US Bank v. Hoglund, 2009-32166 (NY S.Ct. 2009): The bank could not prove it had the right to foreclose or that the testimony it put on was true or accurate.

In re Wilhelm, 407 B.R. 392 (Bankr. D. ID 2009): The companies trying to take the properties of various debtors could not present evidence of Boss rights when challenged to do so.

Mortgage Electronic Registration Systems, Inc., v. Young, 2009-TX-0608.667 (TX Ct.App. 2009): ShellGame-MERS, contrary to what it claimed in the lawsuit, could not prove that it had any right to foreclose.

Landmark National Bank v. Kesler, Millennia Mortgage Company, MERS and Sovereign Bank, et al., 216 P.3d 158 (Kansas 2009): The court found that, contrary to claims made by ShellGame-MERS and an affiliate, neither had any interests in the note or mortgage.

In re Sheridan, Case No. 08-20381-TLM (Bankr. D. ID 2009). When challenged, ShellGame-MERS could put on no proof that it or any company it knew had any right to foreclose the debtor's property.

In re Jacobson, 402 B.R. 359 (Bankr. W.D. WA 2009): The company claiming the right to foreclose lost because, under close scrutiny, it could produce no genuine evidence that it had any rights against the debtor's property.

Bellistri v. Ocwen Loan Servicing, LLC, 284 S.W. 3d 619, 623-624 (MO Ct.App. 2009): The company asserting the right to foreclose could produce no evidence that it had such rights or that it represented any person or company with such right.

Saxon Mortgage Services, Inc. v. Hillery, 2008 WL 5170180 (USDCt. N.D. CA 2008): The company asserting right to foreclose under claim that it got its rights from ShellGame-MERS could not produce evidence that ShellGame-MERs ever had such rights to transfer in the first place.

In re Vargas, 396 B.R. 511, 517 (Bankr. C.D. CA 2008): ShellGame-MERS, having first pled that it was the owner of the note and mortgage with authority to obtain the lift of stay and then to foreclose, later admitted that it was not the owner of the note, and it presented no evidence as to the identity of the Note's Boss. The court found that ShellGame-MERS intentionally introduced false evidence.

Mortgage Electronic Registration Systems, Inc. v. Azize, 965 So.2d 151 (FL Ct.App. 2007): Though ShellGame-MERS alleged it owned the note and mortgage with a right to foreclose, the court found no genuine evidence supporting those claims had been put forward by ShellGame-MERS.

LaSalle Bank Nat. Ass'n v. Lamy, 824 N.Y.S.2d 769, 12 Misc3d 1191(A) (NY S.Ct. 2006): The court stated: "The record adduced on the instant application clearly establishes that the plaintiff's claims of ownership to the mortgage for which foreclosure is herein demanded are without merit."

Federal National Mortgage Assoc. v. Bradbury, etc., No. BRI-RE-09-65 (ME DCt 2010): The court found that both the attorney and its client had filed false claims and affidavits, and that foreclosure was not proper.

Mortgage Electronic Registration Systems, Inc. v. Chong, et al., No. 2:09-CV-00661-KJD-LRL (USDCt. D. NV 2009): The court consolidated 18 similar foreclosure driven cases and, in each, found that ShellGame-MERS had no right to make claims against the debtors or to foreclose the properties.

JP Morgan v. Pocopanni, 16-2008-CA-3989 (FL Cir.Ct. 2010): Washington Mutual Bank initially alleged Boss rights and upon challenge JP Morgan stepped in, claiming it was the real Boss. It too was unable to prove Boss rights. The court found that, contrary to the claims made, JP Morgan Chase "is not, nor has ever been, the owner and holder of the Defendant's note and mortgage." The court found JP Morgan had engaged in fraud.

In re Kemp, No. 08-18700-JHW (Bankr. D. NJ 2010): The court found Bank of New York's claims and evidence to be unbelievable.

OneWest Bank v. Drayton, 2010-20429 (NY S.Ct. 2010): The court noted OneWest Bank had no meaningful evidence upon which to claim rights against the debtor or to foreclose, and that the lead affidavit contained false information.

US Bank v. Ibanez and Wells Fargo v. Larace, No. SJC 10694 (Massachusetts 2011): The court, upon looking at nonjudicial foreclosures conducted by US Bank and Wells Fargo, concluded that neither bank had any right to foreclose.

Mortgage Electronic Registration Systems, Inc. v. Disanti, No. 07-10-00267-CV (TX Ct.App. 2010): The borrower settles with ShellGame-MERS. This must have been a "win" for the borrower even though the settlement details were not disclosed in this case, in which the evidence of records put on by ShellGame-MERS did not rise to the level of UCC proof.

In re Moreno (Bankr.E.D. MA 2010): A ShellGame-MERS affiliate was unable to prove that it was a Boss or a representative of an unidentified Boss.

Mortgage Electronic Registration Systems, Inc. v. Saunders, 2010 ME 79, No. Cum-09-640 (Maine 2010): A higher court overturns a lower court decision and remands case for additional fact-finding because ShellGame-MERS did not prove it was Boss or representative of the Boss of the Note.

Deutsche Bank National Trust Company, as Trustee for GSAMP 2006-FMI v. Lippi, No. CA08-0127 (Fla. 7th Cir. Ct., St. Johns County, Feb. 11, 2010): An order was issued dismissing a foreclosure complaint with prejudice for failure to show any evidence of standing following two years of litigation and multiple dismissals with leave to amend.

Delaney v. OneWest Bank, et al., Civil Case No. 10-977-KI (USDCt D. OR 2010): This was a partial victory for a borrower. Per www.how2fightforeclosure.com, 9/30/10: "Victory in Oregon Federal Court: Judge Denies Motions to Dismiss Filed by OneWest Bank and MERS; Injunction Against Sale Granted For Duration of Borrower's Lawsuit; OneWest's Counsel Admits on the Record that MERS Cannot Transfer Promissory Notes."

HSBC Bank USA, NA as Trustee for Monura Asset Acceptance Corporation, Mortgage Pass-Through Certificates Series 2006-ARI v. Eslava, Hearing Transcript on Order to Show Cause, No. 1-2008-CA-055313, at 17-18 (Fl 11th Cir. Ct., Miami-Dade County, May 6, 2010): This ruling dismissed a foreclosure complaint with prejudice.

98. Some customized and written promises to pay real estate related debt may not be negotiable instruments. Written restrictions on

transferability and payment obligations that are contingent or dependant upon matters not calculable within the loan document can make those loans nonnegotiable. Notes used by real estate lenders for routine residential lending over the past decades, with only rare excetptions, are negotiable instruments under the Uniform Commercial Code.

99. A few courts have issued decisions that, on the surface, suggest the UCC is not relevant to nonjudicial foreclosures, but those cases should not have much precedential value, because the facts and analysis in those cases are distinguishable and should not control when the machine is faced with a proper challenge. See, e.g., *Avoid "Show Me the Note Difficulties"* in Chapter 12.

100. See, e.g., the following sources:

Lawrence's Anderson on the Uniform Commercial Code, 3d Edition [Rev], by Lary Lawrence § 3-203:24R.

Pay Center Inc. v. Milton, 632 P.2d 642, 3 U.C.C. Rep. Serv. 602 (Colo. Ct.App. 1981).

Locks v. North Towne Nat. Bank of Rockford, 115 Ill. App. 3d 729, 451 N.E.2d 19, 36 U.C.C. Rep. Serv. 1251 (2d Dist. 1983).

Perry & Greer, Inc. v. Manning, 282 Or 25, 576 P.2d 791, 24 U.C.C. Rep. Serv. 654 (Oregon 1978).

Report on Application of the UCC to Selected Issues Relating to Mortgage Notes, Permanent Editorial Board for the Uniform Commercial Code, November 14, 2011, available at www.ali.org/index.cfm?fuseaction= projects.proj_ip&projectid=4.

101. UCC § 3-308. PROOF OF SIGNATURES AND STATUS AS HOLDER IN DUE COURSE.

(a) In an action with respect to an instrument, the authenticity of, and authority to make, each signature on the instrument is admitted unless specifically denied in the pleadings. If the validity of a signature is denied in the pleadings, the burden of establishing validity is on the person claiming validity, but the signature is presumed to be authentic and authorized unless the action is to enforce the liability of the purported signer and the signer is dead or incompetent at the time of trial of the issue of validity of the signature. If an action to enforce the instrument is brought against a person as the undisclosed principal of a person who signed the instrument as a party to the instrument, the plaintiff has the burden of establishing that the defendant is liable on the instrument as a represented person under Section 3-402(a).

(b) If the validity of signatures is admitted or proved and there is compliance with subsection (a), *a plaintiff producing the instrument is entitled to payment if the plaintiff proves entitlement to enforce the instrument under Section 3-301,* unless the defendant proves a defense or claim in recoupment. If a defense or claim in recoupment is proved, the right to payment of the plaintiff is subject to the defense or claim, except to the extent the plaintiff proves that the plaintiff has rights of a holder in due course which are not subject to the defense or claim. [Emphasis added.]

102. UCC § 3-501. PRESENTMENT.

(a) *"Presentment" means a demand made by or on behalf of a person entitled to enforce an instrument* (i) to pay the instrument made to the drawee or a party obliged to pay the instrument or, in the case of a note or accepted draft payable at a bank, to the bank, or (ii) to accept a draft made to the drawee. [Emphasis added.]

(b) The following rules are subject to Article 4, agreement of the parties, and clearing-house rules and the like:

(1) Presentment may be made at the place of payment of the instrument and must be made at the place of payment if the instrument is payable at a bank in the United States; may be made by any commercially reasonable means, including an oral, written, or electronic communication; is effective when the demand for payment or acceptance is received by the person to whom presentment is made; and is effective if made to any one of two or more makers, acceptors, drawees, or other payors.

(2) *Upon demand of the person to whom presentment is made, the person making presentment must (i) exhibit the instrument, (ii) give reasonable identification and, if presentment is made on behalf of another person, reasonable evidence of authority to do so, and (iii) sign a receipt on the instrument for any payment made or surrender the instrument if full payment is made.* [Emphasis added.]

(3) Without dishonoring the instrument, the party to whom presentment is made may (i) return the instrument for lack of a necessary indorsement, or (ii) refuse payment or acceptance for failure of the presentment to comply with the

terms of the instrument, an agreement of the parties, or other applicable law or rule.

(4) The party to whom presentment is made may treat presentment as occurring on the next business day after the day of presentment if the party to whom presentment is made has established a cut-off hour not earlier than 2 p.m. for the receipt and processing of instruments presented for payment or acceptance and presentment is made after the cut-off hour.

103. *Lawrence's Anderson on the Uniform Commercial Code,* 3d Edition, [Rev], by Lary Lawrence, § 3-501:12R.

104. See, e.g., the following court cases:

In re Kemp, No. 08-18700-JHW (Bankr. D. NJ 2010).

In re Veal, BAP Nos. AZ-10-1055 & 1056-MkKiJu (Bankr.App.Panel 9thCir. 2011): The court concluded that a company claiming the right to enforce the Note must prove it in accordance with the UCC.

105. *Report on Application of the UCC to Selected Issues Relating to Mortgage Notes,* Permanent Editorial Board for the Uniform Commercial Code, November 14, 2011, p. 4. available at www.ali.org/index.cfm?fuseaction=projects.proj_ip&projectid=4.

106. *Report on Application of the UCC to Selected Issues Relating to Mortgage Notes,* Permanent Editorial Board for the Uniform Commercial Code, November 14, 2011, p. 5, available at www.ali.org/index.cfm?fuseaction=projects.proj_ip&projectid=4.

107. The UCC does not define the right to enforce the Note in terms of ownership. A "person entitled to enforce" may not be the owner of the Note. See, e.g., *Report on Application of the UCC to Selected Issues Relating to Mortgage Notes,* Permanent Editorial Board for the Uniform Commercial Code, November 14, 2011, footnote #15, available at ww.ali.org/index.cfm?fuseaction=projects.proj_ip&projectid=4.

See also *In re Wilhelm,* 407 B.R. 392 (Bankr. D. ID 2009): "Mere ownership right related to the instrument does not establish right to enforce."; and the last sentence of UCC § 3-301, i.e. "A person may be a person entitled to enforce the instrument even though the person is not the owner. ... "

108. "Foreclosure, Subprime Mortgage Lending, and the Mortgage Electronic Registration System," by Christopher L. Peterson,

University of Cincinnati Law Review, Vol. 78, No. 4, Summer 2010: "The UCC insists that the words used by the parties to a contract are not controlling. ... boiler-plate language does not control legal significance, and that includes labels used in mortgages which do not comport with substantive legal requirements."

109. See, e.g., the following court cases in which the court looked past labels, insinuation, and surface appearance in order to make its decision based upon the substance of the circumstances:

In re Agard, No. 810-77338-reg (Bankr. E.D. NY 2011).

US Bank v. Ibanez and Wells Fargo v. Larace, No. SJC 10694 (Massachusetts 2011).

HSBC Bank v. Thompson, 2010-Ohio-4158 (OH Ct.App. 2010).

Mortgage Electronic Registration Systems, Inc. v. Saunders, 2010 ME 79, No. Cum-09-640 (Maine 2010).

In re Box, No. 10-20086 (Bankr. W.D. MO 2010).

IndyMac Bank v. Garcia, et al., No. 2010-51127 (NY S.Ct. 2010).

In re Rickie Walker, No. 10-21656-E-11 (Bankr. E.D. CA 2010).

Landmark Nat'l Bank v. Kesler, Millennia Mortgage Company, MERS and Sovereign Bank, et al., 216 P.3d 158, 164 (Kansas 2009).

Bank of New York v. Raftogianis, No. F-7356-09 (NJ SuperiorCt. 2010).

110. Some courts have issued opinions involving nonjudicial foreclosures that ignore the UCC and ignore the core issue of whether or not the people having conducted the foreclosures were, or even represented, the Boss of the Note. I don't think those cases have precedential value when foreclosure fundamentals are properly before a court. Further comment about those cases is provided in Chapter 12 under the heading "Show-Me-The-Note Difficulties."

111. Uniform Commercial Code, Article 3—*Negotiable Instruments,* Part 3—*Enforcement of Instruments.* A copy can be viewed at www.law.cornell.edu/ucc/3/article3.htm. Remember that your state's statutory complement of this part of the UCC may reflect different numbering or labeling.

112. UCC § 3-104(b) defines "instrument" as "negotiable instrument" and a real estate Note is, with only rare exceptions, a negotiable instrument. Foreclosure cases routinely state or simply assume that

the subject Note is a negotiable instrument, the rights to which are defined by the UCC. See, e.g., the following court cases:

In re Box, No. 10-20086 (Bankr. W.D. MO 2010).

UM Capital v. Ozeran, No. B212779 (CA Ct.App. 2010).

In re Matthew J. Gilpin, No. 09-10696 (Bankr. D. VT 2009).

In re Wilhelm, 407 B.R. 392 (Bankr. D. ID 2009).

LaSalle Bank Nat. Ass'n v. Lamy, 824 N.Y.S.2d 769, 12 Misc3d 1191(A) (NY S.Ct. 2006).

In re Kemp, No. 08-18700-JHW (Bankr. D. NJ 2010).

Adams v. Madison Realty & Development, Inc., 853 F.2d 163 (3rd Cir. 1988).

Mortgage Electronic Registration Systems, Inc. v. Saunders, 2010 ME 79, No. Cum-09-640 (Maine 2010).

Chase Home Fin. v. Fequiere, 119 Conn.App. 570 (Conn.App. 2010).

Bank of New York v. Raftogianis, No. F-7356-09 (NJ SuperiorCt. 2010).

Aurora Loan Services v. Carlsen, No. 2010AP1909 (WI Ct.App. 2011).

HSBC Bank v. Thompson, 2010-Ohio-4158 (OH Ct.App. 2010).

113. UCC § 1-201(b)(27): "Person" means an individual, corporation, business trust, estate, trust, partnership, limited liability company, association, joint venture, government, governmental subdivision, agency, or instrumentality, public corporation, or any other legal or commercial entity."

114. See, e.g., the many cases cited in this book, and also "How the Banks Put the Economy Underwater," by Yves Smith, *The New York Times,* October 30, 2010.

115. See, e.g., *US Bank v. Ibanez and Wells Fargo v. Larace,* No. SJC 10694 (Massachusetts 2011): The brief of Amicus Curiea Marie McDonnell, CFE, filed in this case is a particularly good example of the importance of details. Her brief includes the certified fraud examination report she filed with the court after reviewing and analyzing the so-called proof put forward by the banks in their losing effort to obtain confirmation that they had not violated the borrowers' rights. A copy of her brief can be read and obtained at

http://www.scribd.com/doc/46533426/Marie-Mcdonnell-Certified-Fraud-Examiner-Amicus-Brief-regarding-the-Ibanez-U-S-Bank-case.

116. See, e.g., *In the Matter of the Foreclosure of a Deed of Trust Executed by Adams*, No. COA09-1455 (NC Ct.App. 2010): "[I]t is the fact of possession which is significant in determining whether a person is a holder, and the absence of possession defeats that status," citing *In re Foreclosure of Connolly v. Potts*, 63 N.C.App. 547, 550, 306 S.E.2d 123, 125, 1983). ..."

117. UCC § 3-204. INDORSEMENT.

(a) "Indorsement" means a *signature, other than that of a signer as maker* [i.e., other than the borrower], drawer, or acceptor, *that alone or accompanied by other words is made on an instrument* for the purpose of (i) negotiating the instrument, (ii) restricting payment of the instrument, or (iii) incurring indorser's liability on the instrument, but regardless of the intent of the signer, a signature and its accompanying words is an indorsement unless the accompanying words, terms of the instrument, place of the signature, or other circumstances unambiguously indicate that the signature was made for a purpose other than indorsement. *For the purpose of determining whether a signature is made on an instrument, a paper affixed to the instrument is a part of the instrument.* [Emphasis added for parts most basic in foreclosure litigation.]

(b) "Indorser" means a person who makes an indorsement.

(c) For the purpose of determining whether the transferee of an instrument is a holder, an indorsement that transfers a security interest in the instrument is effective as an unqualified indorsement of the instrument.

(d) If an instrument is payable to a holder under a name that is not the name of the holder, indorsement may be made by the holder in the name stated in the instrument or in the holder's name or both, but signature in both names may be required by a person paying or taking the instrument for value or collection.

118. UCC § 3-205. SPECIAL INDORSEMENT; BLANK INDORSEMENT; ANOMALOUS INDORSEMENT.

(a) If an indorsement is made by the holder of an instrument, whether payable to an identified person or payable to bearer, and the indorsement identifies a person to whom it makes the instrument payable, it is a "special indorsement." When specially indorsed, an instrument becomes payable to the identified person and may be negotiated only by the indorsement of that person. The principles stated in Section 3-110 apply to special indorsements.

(b) If an indorsement is made by the holder of an instrument and it is not a special indorsement, it is a "blank indorsement." When indorsed in blank, an instrument becomes payable to bearer and may be negotiated by transfer of possession alone until specially indorsed.

(c) The holder may convert a blank indorsement that consists only of a signature into a special indorsement by writing, above the signature of the indorser, words identifying the person to whom the instrument is made payable.

(d) "Anomalous indorsement" means an indorsement made by a person who is not the holder of the instrument. An anomalous indorsement does not affect the manner in which the instrument may be negotiated.

119. See also *HSBC Bank v. Thompson,* 2010-Ohio-4158 (OH Ct.App. 2010): When transferred, the indorsement, whether to bearer or specified party, has to be "on" the Note or else on a paper affixed to the note.

120. *Report on Application of the UCC to Selected Issues Relating to Mortgage Notes,* Permanent Editorial Board for the Uniform Commercial Code, November 14, 2011, pp. 2-7. As it discusses UCC § 3-309, it states: "If [alleged Boss] brings action on the [Note] against [borrower], [alleged Boss] must establish the terms of the [Note] and the elements of [borrower's] obligation on it. The court may not enter judgment in favor of the [alleged Boss], however, unless the court finds that [borrower] is adequately protected against loss that might occur by reason of a claim of another person (such as the finder of the [Note]) to enforce the [Note]." A copy of this report was available at www.ali.org/index.cfm?fuseaction=projects.proj_ip&projectid=4.

121. See UCC § 3-205(d).

122. UCC § 3-203(c) creates an exception by which a person who is no longer a holder of the instrument is permitted to indorse the Note. This portion of the UCC states: "Unless otherwise agreed, if an instrument is transferred for value and the transferee does not become a holder because of lack of indorsement by the transferor, the transferee has a specifically enforceable right to the unqualified indorsement of the transferor, but negotiation of the instrument does not occur until the indorsement is made." I understand this text to

permit a previous holder who has otherwise relinquished all interests in the Note to later indorse it, but only for the benefit of the person to which that previous holder had transferred the Note. This section does not authorize this previous holder to indorse the Note for some other "down the line" possessor of the Note. In this respect if, for example, your opponent tries to shore up its enforcement rights by getting an earlier holder to indorse the Note, that indorsement should fail and be of no effect unless the late indorsement is made by the person who transferred the Note to your opponent and, as with all evaluations in the chain of alleged Boss rights, that person is clearly proven to have then been the Boss of your Note.

123. UCC § 204(b) discusses "the person who makes an indorsement."

124. UCC § 3-205(a) & (b) define indorsement. Whether it be a special or blank indorsement, it has to be made by a holder as defined by the UCC. A purported indorsement by anyone who is not, at the time, of the indorsement a holder is a nullity. The only exception is per § 3-203(c), as previously discussed.

125. See UCC § 3-205(a).

126. "Payable to order" can be thought of as a short way of saying "payable to the order or demand of the person whose identity is specified by the indorsement." See also UCC § 3-109 (b).

127. UCC § 3-109. PAYABLE TO BEARER OR TO ORDER.

(a) A promise or order is payable to bearer if it:

(1) states that it is payable to bearer or to the order of bearer or otherwise indicates that the person in possession of the promise or order is entitled to payment;

(2) does not state a payee; or

(3) states that it is payable to or to the order of cash or otherwise indicates that it is not payable to an identified person.

(b) A promise or order that is not payable to bearer is payable to order if it is payable (i) to the order of an identified person or (ii) to an identified person or order. A promise or order that is payable to order is payable to the identified person.

(c) An instrument payable to bearer may become payable to an identified person if it is specially indorsed pursuant to Section 3-205(a). An instrument payable to an identified person may become payable to bearer if it is indorsed in blank pursuant to Section 3-205(b).

128. See UCC §§ 3-109(c) and 3-205(c).

129. UCC § 3-205(d).

130. UCC § 3-201. NEGOTIATION.

(a) "Negotiation" means a transfer of possession, whether voluntary or involuntary, of an instrument by a person other than the issuer to a person who thereby becomes its holder.

(b) Except for negotiation by a remitter, if an instrument is payable to an identified person, negotiation requires transfer of possession of the instrument and its indorsement by the holder. If an instrument is payable to bearer, it may be negotiated by transfer of possession alone.

131. UCC § 3-203. TRANSFER OF INSTRUMENT; RIGHTS ACQUIRED BY TRANSFER.

(a) An instrument is transferred when it is delivered by a person other than its issuer for the purpose of giving to the person receiving delivery the right to enforce the instrument.

(b) Transfer of an instrument, whether or not the transfer is a negotiation, vests in the transferee any right of the transferor to enforce the instrument, including any right as a holder in due course, but the transferee cannot acquire rights of a holder in due course by a transfer, directly or indirectly, from a holder in due course if the transferee engaged in fraud or illegality affecting the instrument.

(c) Unless otherwise agreed, if an instrument is transferred for value and the transferee does not become a holder because of lack of indorsement by the transferor, the transferee has a specifically enforceable right to the unqualified indorsement of the transferor, but negotiation of the instrument does not occur until the indorsement is made.

(d) If a transferor purports to transfer less than the entire instrument, negotiation of the instrument does not occur. The transferee obtains no rights under this Article and has only the rights of a partial assignee.

132. UCC § 3-203 (a).

133. UCC § 1-201(15). "Delivery," with respect to an instrument, document of title, or chattel paper, means voluntary transfer of possession.

134. See, e.g., *Hawkland & Lawrence UCC Series* § 3-102:3 (Rev. Art 3).

135. See, e.g., *Hawkland & Lawrence UCC Series* § 3-201:4 (Rev. Art 3).

136. See, e.g., the following court cases:

New England Savings Bank v. Bedford Realty Corp., 238 Conn. 745, 759-60, 680 A.2d 301 (Connecticut 1996): "[M]ere holder of promissory note, if not owner of the underlying debt, cannot exercise equitable power of foreclosure."

Bridgeport Harbour Place I v. Ganim, 303 Conn. 224, 232 (2011): Actual possession of what appears to be a properly indorsed Note creates a rebuttable presumption of ownership and control of the debt that can be undone with an evidentiary showing by the challenger to holder status. "The production of the note establishes his case prima facie against the makers and he may rest there. ... It [is] for the defendant to set up and prove the facts which limit or change the plaintiff's rights." This is another example that mere possession of the Note is not proof of Boss status. This guide also shows the importance of using formal discovery for the purpose of showing that your opponent's mere possession does not prove Boss status.

137. See, e.g., *Mortgage Electronic Registration Systems, Inc. v. Azize,* 965 So.2d 151 (FL Ct.App. 2007), a case in which the machine admits use of a tactic to aid its foreclosure efforts by which possession of the Note is obtained without any intent that the transferee have other than temporary and limited rights in the Note: "Here, [ShellGame-MERS's] counsel explained to the trial judge at the hearing that, in these transactions, the notes are frequently transferred to MERS for the purpose of foreclosure without MERS actually obtaining the beneficial interest in the note." Thus, ShellGame-MERS could not have been a holder because the possession it alleged to hold was less than a 100% interest in the Note, because the Note had not been transferred to ShellGame-MERS with the intent that it was in fact the full owner and Boss of that Note. UCC § 3-203 (d) establishes that any alleged transfer of less than 100% defeats the recipient's right to claim Boss rights. The borrower in that case, unfortunately, did not object to the shoddy proof introduced by the machine, so the foreclosure was approved. This case is nevertheless an example of the fact that mere possession does not prove that the person in

possession has the right to enforce the Note or to otherwise give anyone else the right to enforce the Note.

138. See, e.g., *US Bank v. Ibanez and Wells Fargo v. Larace*, No. SJC 10694 (Massachusetts 2011): The brief of Amicus Curiea Marie McDonnell, CFE, filed in this case is a particularly good example of the importance of details. Her certified fraud examination persuaded the court that the banks had violated the rights of the borrowers whose homes had been taken via foreclosure. A copy of her brief can be read and obtained at www.scribd.com/doc/46533426/Marie-Mcdonnell-Certified-Fraud-Examiner-Amicus-Brief-regarding-the-Ibanez-U-S-Bank-case.

Also see *In re Agard*, No. 810-77338-reg (Bankr. E.D. NY 2011).

139. See, e.g., *Anderson v. Burson*, 196 Md.App. 457 (MD Ct.Spec.App. 2010): "The Official Comment to the Uniform Commercial Code, concerning section 3-301 reads, in material part, as follows: 'A non-holder in possession of an instrument includes a person that acquired rights of a holder by subrogation or under section 3-203 (a). It also includes any other person who under applicable law is a successor to the holder or otherwise acquires the holder's rights.'"

140. See, e.g., *In re Wilhelm*, 407 B.R. 392 (Bankr. D. ID 2009): A non-holder in possession of the instrument who has the rights of a holder requires physical possession of an unendorsed note, and must prove the transaction(s) by which they obtained the possession, the right of the transferor to status as holder, and *the court may not assume possession constitutes entitlement to enforce*. This court further stated that a mere ownership right related to the Note does not establish the right to enforce the Note.

141. See, e.g., the following court cases:

In re Kemp, No. 08-18700-JHW (Bankr. D. NJ 2010).

US Bank v. Ibanez and Wells Fargo v. Larace, No. SJC 10694 (Massachusetts 2011).

Bank of New York v. Raftogianis, No. F-7356-09 (NJ SuperiorCt. 2010).

HSBC Bank v. Thompson, 2010-Ohio-4158 (OH Ct.App. 2010).

142. See, e.g., *Adams v. Madison Realty & Development, Inc.*, 853 F.2d 163 (3rd Cir. 1988): Right to enforce a negotiable instrument requires strict compliance with the UCC. "Financial institutions, noted for insisting on their customers' compliance with numerous

ritualistic formalities, are not sympathetic petitioners in urging relaxation of an elementary business practice. It is a tenet of commercial law that [h]oldership and the potential for becoming holders in due course should only be accorded to transferees that observe the historic protocol."

143. UCC § 3-309. ENFORCEMENT OF LOST, DESTROYED, OR STOLEN INSTRUMENT.

(a) A person not in possession of an instrument is entitled to enforce the instrument if:

(1) the person seeking to enforce the instrument

(A) was entitled to enforce the instrument when loss of possession occurred, or

(B) has directly or indirectly acquired ownership of the instrument from a person who was entitled to enforce the instrument when loss of possession occurred;

(2) the loss of possession was not the result of a transfer by the person or a lawful seizure; and

(3) the person cannot reasonably obtain possession of the instrument because the instrument was destroyed, its whereabouts cannot be determined, or it is in the wrongful possession of an unknown person or a person that cannot be found or is not amenable to service of process.

(b) A person seeking enforcement of an instrument under subsection (a) must prove the terms of the instrument and the person's right to enforce the instrument. If that proof is made, Section 3-308 applies to the case as if the person seeking enforcement had produced the instrument. The court may not enter judgment in favor of the person seeking enforcement unless it finds that the person required to pay the instrument is adequately protected against loss that might occur by reason of a claim by another person to enforce the instrument. Adequate protection may be provided by any reasonable means.

144. See, e.g., *Atlantic Nat'l Trust v. McNamee,* 984 So.2d 37 (Ala. 2007): The court concluded, without the machine having had to prove that a predecessor was in fact the Boss of the Note, that the successor obtained Boss rights upon buying the rights of the predecessor that alleged a loss of the Note during its ownership. The predecessor did not prove that it was actually a Boss at the time it lost the Note, but

the court concluded that the borrower had not challenged the Boss status of the predecessor. That is, the borrower caused his own downfall by not demanding proof of Boss status for the earlier segments of the chain of ownership and control.

145. See, e.g., *In re Kemp*, No. 08-18700-JHW (Bankr. D. NJ 2010).

146. See UCC, Article III, § 3-309(a)(2): "[T]he loss of possession was not the result of a transfer by the person or a lawful seizure."

147. See, e.g., *Weingartner v. Chase Home Finance, LLC*, No. 2:09-cv-02255-RCJ-RJJ (USDCt. D. NV 2010): The court held that an appointed trustee under a deed of trust lacks authority to appoint a substitute trustee, citing *The Restatement of the Law Second, Agency* § 18, The American Law Institute, at *3.

148. See, e.g., the following sources:

LaSalle Bank v. Bouloute, et al., No. 2010-51513 (NY S.Ct. 2010): "Recently, in *Bank of New York v. Alderazi*, 28 Misc.3d at 379-380, my learned colleague, Kings County Supreme Court Justice Wayne Saitta explained that: A party who claims to be the agent of another bears the burden of proving the agency relationship by a preponderance of the evidence (*Lippincott v. East River Mill & Lumber Co.*, 79 Misc. 559 [New York 1913]) and "[t]he declarations of an alleged agent may not be shown for the purpose of proving the fact of agency." (*Lexow & Jenkins, P.C. v. Hertz Commercial Leasing Corp.*, 122 A.D.2d 25 [2d Dept 1986].

Siegel v. Kentucky Fried Chicken of Long Is. 108 A.D.2d 218 [NY 2d Dept 1985]; *Moore v. Leaseway Transp/ Corp.*, 65 A.D.2d 697 [NY 1st Dept 1978].) "[T]he acts of a person assuming to be the representative of another are not competent to prove the agency in the absence of evidence tending to show the principal's knowledge of such acts or assent to them." (*Lexow & Jenkins, P.C. v. Hertz Commercial Leasing Corp.*, 122 A.D.2d at 26, quoting 2 NY Jur 2d, Agency and Independent Contractors § 26).

Bank of New York v. Mulligan, No. 2010-51509 (NY S.Ct. 2010): "A party who claims to be the agent of another bears the burden of proving the agency relationship by a preponderance of the evidence," and "[t]he declarations of an alleged agent may not be shown for the purpose of proving the fact of agency." "[T]he acts of a person assuming to be the representative of another are not competent to prove the agency in the absence of evidence tending to show the principal's knowledge of such acts or assent to them."

Mortgage Electronic Registration Systems, Inc. v. Graham and Martinez, 229 P.3d 420 (KS Ct.App. 2010): In ruling against the machine, which alleged that agency authority had created its right to enforce the note, the court found "... there is no evidence that MERS received permission to act as an agent for Countrywide."

Mortgage Electronic Registration Systems, Inc. v. Southwest Homes of Arkansas, 08-1299 (Arkansas 2009): The court held that ShellGame-MERS was not an agent authorized to act independently without further authorization of the lender.

Saxon Mortgage Services, Inc. v. Hillery, 2008 WL 5170180 (USDCt. N.D. CA 2008): Here there was no evidence ShellGame-MERS was ever holder of the note or given authority to assign it, so its alleged assignment and recording of the note and deed of trust was ineffective.

In re Kang Jin Hwang, 396 B.R. 757 (Bankr. C.D. CA 2008): "Thus, even if IndyMac is the loan servicer for the unidentified owner of the note here at issue (a fact that IndyMac has failed to prove), it is not the real party in interest that is required to bring the motion before the court."

In re Vargas, 396 B.R. 511, 517 (Bankr. C.D. CA 2008): In holding that the subject Deed of Trust did not give ShellGame-MERS independent authority to assign or transfer either the deed of trust or the note without identification of the true owner of the note, the court said: "It is highly unlikely that FHM has kept the promissory note: most likely, it sold the note into the market for mortgage securitization. [As] consequence, it is quite unlikely that MERS is an authorized agent of the holder of the note here at issue. By adding these unidentified movants, MERS is trying to obtain relief from the automatic stay for the current note holders without disclosing to the court their existence, identities or the source of MERS's authority to act on their behalf. This is improper. ... Thus, if FHM has transferred the note, MERS is no longer an authorized agent of the holder unless it has a separate agency contract with the new undisclosed principal. MERS presents no evidence as to who owns the note, or of any authorization to act on behalf of the present owner."

In re Mitchell, Case No. BK-S-07-16226-LBR (Bankr. D. NV 2009): In highlighting the requirement of competent evidence of an alleged agency relationship, the court stated: "The mere statement that the movant is a member of MERS does nothing but lay the groundwork for agency," and "One cannot assume that just because MERS was named as the initial nominee [i.e., agent or servant] in the deed of trust that it still retains that relationship with the holder of the note."

In re Maisel, 378 B.R. 19 (Bankr. D. MA 2007): "Claimant who is the servicer must, in addition to establishing the rights of the holder, identify itself as an authorized agent for the holder."

Mortgage Electronic Registration Systems, Inc. v. Chong, et al., No. 2:09-CV-00661-KJD-LRL (USDCt. D. NV 2009): The court in 18 consolidated cases addressed the need for proof of an alleged principal-agent relationship and stated: "An agency relationship is created when one party consents to have another act on its behalf, with the principal controlling and directing the acts of the agent."

Arcell v. Ashland Chem. Co., 152 N.J.Super. 471, 494-95 (Law Div. 1977).

Restatement of the Law Second, Agency § 1, The American Law Institute, 1958.

One West Bank v. Drayton, 2010-20429 (NY S.Ct. 2010): "MERS as 'nominee' has no independent authority and must prove its authority on behalf of the true owner of the note and mortgage."

US Bank v. Ibanez and Wells Fargo v. Larace, No. SJC 10694 (Massachusetts 2011): Neither bank proved it represented the actual owner of note and mortgage, thereby lacking authority to have initiated or conducted the wrongful foreclosures.

National Exchange Bank v. Wiley, 195 U.S. 257, 25 S.Ct. 70, 49 L.Ed. 184 (U.S. 1904): This case demonstrates that, even if a proper agency relationship exists between the Boss and a servant, once a new Boss or transferee appears, there is no automatic agency relationship between the servant and the new Boss. Regarding this, the court said: "A warrant of attorney executed by the maker of a note and authorizing, in case of nonpayment, an attorney to appear, waive process, confess judgment, waive error and right of appeal in favor of the 'holder' of the note, must be construed strictly in favor of the maker, and does not, in the absence of express terms, authorize the confession of judgment in favor of the original payee after it ceases to be the owner of the note, even though he may have the note in his possession." It further said: "The power of attorney is not negotiable, and when the legal title to the note is transferred, the power of attorney becomes invalid, and no power whatever can be exercised under it, for the benefit of the indorsee, and he holds the note as if no such power had ever been attached to it." Also: "It should not be supposed that the obligors intended, or that the payee bank ever understood them as intending, to authorize a confession of judgment in favor of one who was not entitled, or right, to demand payment from the obligors."

Weingartner v. Chase Home Finance, LLC, No. 2:09-cv-02255-RCJ-RJJ (USDCt. D. NV 2010): The court held that US Bank as an appointed trustee under a deed of trust had no independent authority to appoint a successor trustee to itself, that right being held by the principal not the servant, at *4.

149. See *In re Agard,* No. 810-77338-reg (Bankr. E.D. NY 2011): This court was responding to a legal brief submitted on behalf of ShellGame-MERS.

150. See, e.g., *National Exchange Bank v. Wiley,* 195 U.S. 257, 25 S.Ct. 70, 49 L.Ed. 184 (U.S. 1904): "A warrant of attorney executed by the maker of a note and authorizing, in case of nonpayment, an attorney to appear, waive process, confess judgment, waive error and right of appeal in favor of the 'holder' of the note, must be construed strictly in favor of the maker, and does not, in the absence of express terms, authorize the confession of judgment in favor of the original payee after it ceases to be the owner of the note, even though he may have the note in his possession"; "The power of attorney is not negotiable, and when the legal title to the note is transferred, the power of attorney becomes invalid, and no power whatever can be exercised under it, for the benefit of the indorsee, and he holds the note as if no such power had ever been attached to it"; and "It should not be supposed that the obligors intended, or that the payee bank ever understood them as intending, to authorize a confession of judgment in favor of one who was not entitled, or right, to demand payment from the obligors."

151. See, e.g., the following court cases:

Mortgage Electronic Registration Systems, Inc. v. Graham and Martinez, 229 P.3d 420 (KS Ct.App. 2010): In ruling against the machine, which alleged agency authority had created its right to enforce the note, the court found "... there is no evidence that MERS received permission to act as an agent for Countrywide."

Mortgage Electronic Registration Systems, Inc. v. Southwest Homes of Arkansas, 08-1299 (Arkansas 2009): The court held that ShellGame-MERS was not agent authorized to act independently without further authorization of the lender.

Saxon Mortgage Services, Inc. v. Hillery, 2008 WL 5170180 (USDCt. N.D. CA 2008): Here, there was no evidence ShellGame-MERS was ever holder of the note or given authority to assign it.

In re Vargas, 396 B.R. 511, 517 (Bankr. C.D. CA 2008): The court held that ShellGame-MERS was not an agent for unidentified but alleged successors to the original lender, lacking proof of an agency relationship.

In re Mitchell, Case No. BK-S-07-16226-LBR (Bankr. D. NV 2009): In highlighting the requirement of competent evidence of an alleged agency relationship, the court stated: "The mere statement that the movant is a member of MERS does nothing but lay the groundwork for agency," and "One cannot assume that just because MERS was named as the initial nominee [i.e., agent or servant] in the deed of trust that it still retains that relationship with the holder of the note."

Mortgage Electronic Registration Systems, Inc. v. Chong, et al., No. 2:09-CV-00661-KJD-LRL (USDCt. D. NV 2009): The court in 18 consolidated cases addressed the need for proof of an alleged principal-agent relationship.

Restatement of the Law Second, Agency § 1, The American Law Institute, 1958.

OneWest Bank v. Drayton, 2010-20429 (NY S.Ct. 2010): MERS as "nominee" has no independent authority and must prove its authority on behalf of the true owner of the note and mortgage.

152. See, e.g., *In re Kang Jin Hwang*, 396 B.R. 757 (Bankr. C.D. CA 2008): "The right to enforce a note on behalf of a noteholder does not convert the noteholder's agent into a real party in interest. As a general rule, a person who is an attorney-in-fact or an agent solely for the purpose of bringing suit is viewed as a nominal rather than a real party in interest and will be required to litigate in the name of his principal rather than in his own name." (6A WRIGHT § 1553.) Consequently, even if the court had found that a proper agency relationship exists between the holder of the Note and the party seeking to enforce its security, this does not excuse the agent from the requirement that an action be prosecuted in the name of the noteholder, who is the real party in interest. (FED.R.CIV.P. 17(a)(1).)

153. See, e.g., the following parts of the UCC. [Emphasis added to help direct your attention to the more salient parts]:

UCC § 3-415. OBLIGATION OF INDORSER.

(a) Subject to subsections (b), (c), and (d) and to Section 3-419(d), if an instrument is dishonored, an indorser is obliged to pay the amount due on the instrument (i) according to the terms of the instrument at the time it was indorsed, or (ii) if the indorser indorsed an incomplete instrument, according to its terms when completed, to the extent stated in Sections 3-115 and 3-407. *The obligation of the indorser is owed to a person entitled to enforce the instrument or to a subsequent indorser who paid the instrument under this section.*

(b) If an indorsement states that it is made "without recourse" or otherwise disclaims liability of the indorser, the indorser is not liable under subsection (a) to pay the instrument.

(c) If notice of dishonor of an instrument is required by Section 3-503 and notice of dishonor complying with that section is not given to an indorser, the liability of the indorser under subsection (a) is discharged.

(d) If a draft is accepted by a bank after an indorsement is made, the liability of the indorser under subsection (a) is discharged.

(e) If an indorser of a check is liable under subsection (a) and the check is not presented for payment, or given to a depositary bank for collection, within 30 days after the day the indorsement was made, the liability of the indorser under subsection (a) is discharged.

154. UCC § 3-412. OBLIGATION OF ISSUER OF NOTE OR CASHIER'S CHECK.

The issuer of a note or cashier's check or other draft drawn on the drawer is obliged to pay the instrument (i) according to its terms at the time it was issued or, if not issued, at the time it first came into possession of a holder, or (ii) if the issuer signed an incomplete instrument, according to its terms when completed, to the extent stated in Sections 3-115 and 3-407. *The obligation is owed to a person entitled to enforce the instrument or to an indorser who paid the instrument under Section 3-415.* [Emphasis added.]

155. As previously discussed, such a person might have rights to enforce the Note pursuant to UCC § 3-301(ii), depending on whether the insurer took possession of the Note upon its payment to the Boss or made an agreement permitting it to have possession should it require same.

156. This provision vests enforcement rights of a transferor upon the transferee, but with limitations if an otherwise "holder in due course" perpetrated wrongs respecting the Note. Some authorities also maintain that a holder must independently qualify as a holder in due course and cannot rise to the level of holder in due course simply because its predecessor holder may have been a holder in due course. Those authorities note that a transferor can become vested with the rights of a transferee but not the status. See, e.g., the following:

Lawrence's Anderson on the Uniform Commercial Code, 3d Edition [Rev], by Lary Lawrence, § 3-203:19R.

Estrada v. River Oaks Bank & Trust Co., 550 S.W.2d 719, 22 U.C.C. Rep. Serv. 83 (Tex. Civ. App. Houston 14th Distr. 1977, writ refused n.r.e. [Law Division 1974]).

UCC 3-305(b): If transferee meets holder in due course standards, then it can be free and clear of borrower's defenses and recoupment claims.

157. See, e.g., El Camino Resources, Ltd. v. Huntington National Bank, No. 1:07-cv-598 (USDCt. W.D. MI 2010): In noting that an alleged holder in due course bears the burden of proving that status, the court also stated the level of proof required; i.e., "… as the party with the burden of proof, the Bank has the burden of proving that the evidence is so one-sided that it must prevail as a matter of law."

Chapter 12

158. Intentionally omitted.

159. You will have no difficulty finding descriptions and examples of the standards applicable under your state's law regarding a motion to dismiss. Some relevant statements by federal courts regarding this subject are provided below:

Navarro v. Block, 250 F.3d 729, 731 (9th Cir. 2001): "A motion to dismiss pursuant to Rule 12(b)(6) of the Federal Rules of Civil Procedure tests the legal sufficiency of the claims asserted in the complaint."

Cahill v. Liberty Mutual Ins. Co., 80 F.3d 336, 337-38 (9th Cir. 1996): The court must accept all factual allegations pled in the complaint as true, and must construe them and draw all reasonable inferences from them in favor of the nonmoving party.

Bell Atl. Corp. v. Twombly, 550 U.S. 544, 570 (2007): To avoid a Rule 12(b)(6) dismissal, a complaint need not contain detailed factual allegations; rather, it must plead *"enough facts to state a claim to relief that is plausible on its face."* [Emphasis is added.]

Ashcroft v. Iqbal, ___ U.S. ___, 129 S.Ct. 1937, 1949 (2009): A claim has "facial plausibility when the plaintiff pleads factual content that allows the court to draw the reasonable inference that the defendant is liable for the misconduct alleged." However, *"a plaintiff's obligation to provide the grounds of his entitle[ment] to relief requires more than labels and conclusions, and a formulaic recitation of the elements of a cause of action will not do."* [Emphasis is added.] Also, a court need not accept "legal conclusions" as true.

Associated Gen. Contractors of Cal., Inc. v. Cal. State Council of Carpenters, 459 U.S. 519, 526 (1983): In spite of the deference the court is bound to pay to the plaintiff's allegations, it is not proper for the court to assume that "the [plaintiff] can prove facts that [he or she] has not alleged or that defendants have violated the ... laws in ways that have not been alleged."

Morgan v. Hubert, 335 F.Appx. 466, 469 (5th Cir. 2009): *"This standard simply calls for enough facts to raise a reasonable expectation that discovery will reveal evidence of the necessary claims or elements."* [Emphasis is added.]

Scanlan v. Tex. A & M Univ., 343 F.3d 533, 536 (5th Cir. 2003): In determining whether to grant a motion to dismiss, a district court may generally not "go outside the complaint."

Howard v. King, 707 F.2d 215, 220 (5th Cir. 1983): When ruling on a motion to dismiss a *pro se* complaint, however, a district court is "required to look beyond the [plaintiff's] formal complaint and to consider as amendments to the complaint those materials subsequently filed."

Clark v. Huntleigh Corp., 119 F.Appx. 666, 667 (5th Cir. 2005): Because of plaintiff's *pro se* status, "precedent compels us to examine all of his complaint, including the attachments." Also, "Pleadings must be construed so as to do justice." Fed.R.Civ.P. 8(e).

Anderson v. CitiMortgage, No. 4:10-CV-398 (USDCt. E.D. TX 2011): Furthermore, a district court may consider documents attached to a motion to dismiss if they are referred to in the plaintiff's complaint and are central to the plaintiff's claim.

Chapter 13

160. "The Case of the Missing Mortgage," by Stephen Gandel, *Time,* November 29, 2010.

161. Banks are being exposed to more investigations as a result of challenges to ShellGame-MERS that are surfacing through litigation. These probes are concerns because of the impact the investigations might have on the cash tills of the banks. Note that, unfortunately, those concerns are not directed at issues of fairness for foreclosure victims who have already lost their homes or who are being targeted for foreclosure. See, e.g., "Big Banks Say MERS Mortgage Database Draws Probes," by Laura Marcinek, www.Bloomberg.com, March 2, 2011.

162. Assumes an average $200,000 value of the homes foreclosed and taken by the industry.

www.ingramcontent.com/pod-product-compliance
Lightning Source LLC
Chambersburg PA
CBHW060820170526
45158CB00001B/36